PROC FCMP
User-Defined Functions:
An Introduction to the SAS® Function Compiler

Troy Martin Hughes

§.sas.

sas.com/books

The correct bibliographic citation for this manual is as follows: Hughes, Troy Martin. 2024. *PROC FCMP User-Defined Functions: An Introduction to the SAS® Function Compiler*. Cary, NC: SAS Institute Inc.

PROC FCMP User-Defined Functions: An Introduction to the SAS® Function Compiler

Dedication

To Art, who inspired a generation, and then another,
and Marilyn, who eternally captivated, and yet selflessly shared, her Art

Contents

About This Book xi

About the Author xv

Acknowledgments xvii

Chapter 1: Introducing Functions 1

  What Is a Function Anyway? 2

  Functions Versus Functionality 2

  The Many Facets of Software Quality and Performance 6

    Software Modularity 7

    Software Readability 9

    Software Configurability 10

    Software Reusability 11

    Software Maintainability 11

    Software Integrity 12

  Functional Components and Organization 13

    Function Specification 13

    Function Implementation 15

    Function Invocation 16

  Function Nomenclature 20

    Calling Module, Callable Module, and Called Module 20

    Functions Versus Procedures 21

    Functions Versus Subroutines 22

    Parameters Versus Arguments 23

    Return Values Versus Return Codes 24

    Built-in Functions Versus User-Defined Functions 25

  Conclusion 26

Chapter 2: Basic FCMP Syntax 27

  PROC FCMP Wrapper 28

    PROC FCMP Statement 28

    PROC FCMP OUTLIB Option 30

    Configuring the CMPLIB System Option 35

    ENCRYPT Option 36

    Terminating PROC FCMP: QUIT Versus RUN 38

Function Declaration and Signature 40
    Function Naming.. 42
    Declaring Parameters... 44
    Declaring Zero Parameters.. 48
    Specifying Parameter Call Method Using the OUTARGS Statement 50
    The VARARGS Option 56
    Declaring a Return Value.. 59
Differences between DATA Step and FCMP Syntax... 62
    Use Caution When Modifying Call-by-Value Scalar Parameters 63
    DO Loop Differences 65
    FILE LOG Statement to Direct SAS Output to SAS Log.................................. 68
    PUT Statement Differences.. 71
    Using Optional Arguments in Built-in Functions Called inside PROC FCMP 73
Concluding a Function or Subroutine 76
    The RETURN Statement 76
    ENDFUNC and ENDSUB Statements.. 79
Conclusion 79

Chapter 3: Arrays... 81
Arrays in the DATA Step 82
    DATA Step Array Declaration 82
    DATA Step Array Initialization.. 85
Passing an Array to a Function... 87
    Passing Multi-Element Arguments to a Built-in Function 88
    Passing an Array to a User-Defined Function 90
Declaring an Array inside a Function 93
    Declaring a Numeric Array to Calculate Median Word Length 93
    Declaring a Numeric Array to Make Change 97
"Returning" an Array from a Function.. 103
    Passing a One-Dimensional Array by Reference 104
    Passing a Two-Dimensional Array by Reference 105
Extending the Functionality of SORTC to a Descending Sort 109
Differences between DATA Step Arrays and FCMP Arrays 112
    The DO OVER Statement Is Not Supported by FCMP.................................... 112
    FCMP Arrays Do Not Support the IN Operator 114
    FCMP Arrays Do Not Support the OF Operator... 117
    Arrays Cannot Be Declared in Reverse within FCMP................................... 118
    Left-Handed SUBSTR Functionality Incompatible with Arrays 120
%SYSFUNC and %SYSCALL Complexities with Arrays 123
Performing Matrix Calculations Using PROC FCMP Arrays 125
    Linear Algebra Problem Set 126
    Long-Hand Solution 128
    SAS/IML Solution 129
    PROC FCMP Solution.. 130

Using READ_ARRAY to Read a Matrix from a Data Set 131
Using WRITE_ARRAY to Write a Matrix to a Data Set 133
Conclusion 134

Chapter 4: Hash Objects **135**
Data Validation 136
Validation Using the PROC FORMAT CNTLIN Option 137
Validation Using a DATA Step Hash Object 138
Validation Using an FCMP Hash Object 141
Single Variable Initialization 143
Data Initialization Using a User-Defined Format 144
Data Initialization Using a User-Defined Function Hash Object 145
Multivariable Initialization 147
A Procedural Approach to Multivariable Initialization 148
A Functional Approach to Multivariable Initialization 150
Counting Hash Keys 152
Counting Keys Using a Running Count 153
Counting Keys with a Post Hoc Hash Iterator 156
Sorting Hash Keys 158
Building Dynamic Hash Using the SAS Macro Language 162
Statically Defining a Hash Lookup Operation 163
Dynamically Defining a Hash Lookup Operation 164
Conclusion 168

Chapter 5: RUN_MACRO and RUN_SASFILE **169**
Introducing the RUN_MACRO Function 170
Implementing the DEQUOTE Function to Remove Automatic Quoting 172
Cautious Declaration of Macro Parameters When Calling Macro via RUN_MACRO 173
Generating a Return Value from a RUN_MACRO Macro 174
Reuse of Variable Names with RUN_MACRO 176
Scope Considerations for RUN_MACRO Macro Variables 179
Global Macro Variable Interaction with RUN_MACRO 182
Passing Special Characters Using RUN_MACRO 184
Running DATA Steps and SAS Procedures via RUN_MACRO 187
Executing a SAS Procedure inside a DATA Step 188
Executing a DATA Step inside a DATA Step 190
Comparison of RUN_MACRO to DOSUBL Function 191
RUN_SASFILE 195
Leveraging RUN_MACRO to Overcome FCMP Limitations 197
Conclusion 201

Chapter 6: Getters and Setters **203**
A Business Case for Evaluating Nutritional Data 204
GET_CAL Getter to Retrieve Caloric Content 206

DATA Step Setter to Initialize Caloric Content 208
FCMP Procedure Setter to Initialize Caloric Content 211
FCMP Procedure Setter to Initialize and Add Caloric Content 213
Differentiating Attributes in Getter Functions 215
Differentiating Attributes in Setter Functions 217
Differentiating Data Types in Getter Functions.. 218
Differentiating Data Types in Setter Functions 220
Conclusion 222

Chapter 7: Recursion and Memoization **223**
Introducing the FCMP STATIC Statement... 223
Using STATIC to Count Function Calls 225
Calling STATIC Functions and Subroutines Using %SYSFUNC and %SYSCALL 227
Recursion 229
Calculating a Factorial 230
Making Change Recursively 231
Making Change Recursively with STATIC.. 234
Making Change Recursively without STATIC or a Counter Variable 235
Memoization—No That's Not a Spelling Error! 239
The STATIC Statement Supporting Memoization 240
The Hash Object Supporting Memoization 243
The Dictionary Object Supporting Memoization 247
Conclusion 251

Chapter 8: Python Component Object **253**
Requirements and Setup 254
Defining a Python Function inside a Python Program File...................................... 255
Importing a Python Program File in the FCMP Procedure 256
Using the INFILE Method to Import a Python Program File................................ 257
Using the SUBMIT INTO Statement to Import a Python Program File 260
Defining a Python Function inside the FCMP Procedure 261
Creating KML Files Using PROC FCMP and Python Geocoding 263
Scenario Setup, Requirements, and Data Ingestion... 263
Creating a PROC FCMP Wrapper to Invoke Python Geocoding.......................... 265
Geocoding in Python Using the Google Maps API 266
Calculating Latitude and Longitude Coordinates in SAS 268
Creating a PROC FCMP Wrapper to Invoke Python Distance Calculations........ 270
Calculating Distance in Python Using the Google Maps API 272
Calculating Coordinates and Calculating Distances in SAS................................ 273
Introducing Memoization for Geocoding.. 275
Introducing Memoization for Distance Calculations.. 278
Creating a KML File for Las Vegas Restaurants... 282
Conclusion 287

Chapter 9: Expanding the Application of Functions **289**

User-Defined Functions Applied as Formats and Informats 290

Limitations of Functions Called by PROC FORMAT... 290

User-Defined Format Calling a User-Defined Function 291

User-Defined Function and Format Performance 295

More User-Defined Function and Format Performance 298

User-Defined Informat Calling a User-Defined Function 301

Designing a User-Defined Informat to Validate Roman Numerals 301

Designing a User-Defined Informat That Throws Exceptions............................. 304

Designing a User-Defined Informat That Evaluates Complex Business Rules 307

Applying User-Defined Functions in PROC REPORT 311

Creating a Basic HTML Report... 311

Adding Getter Functionality to Support Dynamically Color-Coded Report....................... 313

Differentiating Report Color-Coding Based on Subroutine Business Rules........................ 316

Adding More Getter Functionality to Query a Lookup Table 318

Conclusion 320

References **321**

Index **323**

About This Book

Preface

Software development represents a tremendous investment of resources; business needs must be identified and discussed, and code must be designed, written, tested, documented, deployed for use, and ultimately maintained. To maximize return on investment, software should be reused as many times as possible, by as many users as possible, for as long as possible—or at least while it continues to deliver business value.

To this end, wrapping software functionality inside modular functions is a rewarding best practice that encourages software reuse. This *software modularity* facilitates software configuration, in which varied inputs (arguments) produce dynamic output (return values). Configurable modules replace unnecessary hardcoding, and facilitate repeatable, reusable software components that can meet the needs of diverse users and diverse use cases.

The SAS language includes hundreds of built-in functions—from ABS, which calculates the absolute value of a number, to ZIPSTATE, which converts a ZIPCODE into its corresponding state abbreviation. But every programming language has its limits, and where no built-in function exists to provide some needed functionality, a user-defined function can be built to deliver that functionality and effectively *extend* the programming language.

This text introduces PROC FCMP—the SAS Function Compiler—the procedure with which SAS practitioners can create user-defined functions and subroutines. These modular, callable software components complement the diverse array of SAS built-in functions and provide a richer, more expansive development environment in which to build SAS software.

User-defined functions improve the quality of SAS software by extracting complex logic, business rules, and other operations from DATA steps. Encapsulating this functionality inside functions, yields more maintainable, readable, reusable software. User-defined functions also improve the quality of the development environment itself. The productivity of SAS practitioners surges because we are able to reuse user-defined functions rather than having to reinvent the wheel.

To those plucky practitioners, intent on advancing your SAS repertoire and resume, this book is for you! It introduces the FCMP procedure, including its use cases, syntax, best practices, and benefits. Hardcoding puts the "SAS" in disaster, but it can be averted through flexible, reusable user-defined functions!

What Does This Book Cover?

You will be introduced to the FCMP procedure and instructed how to build user-defined functions—callable, reusable, beautifully bite-sized chunks of software functionality that fundamentally change how you conceptualize, design, and develop SAS software.

But first, you will be introduced to functions themselves so that you can see how functions improve the quality of not only software but also the software development environment. And with this foundation, FCMP syntax is incrementally demonstrated through requirements-based examples. You will walk away having gained the ability to examine your own software business needs and evaluate whether, where, and how you can implement user-defined functions to overcome obstacles, provide analytic insight, and deliver business value.

Organization

PROC FCMP User-Defined Functions is intended to be read cover to cover, as concepts, syntax, and examples build incrementally from one chapter to the next. For those interested in learning about a specific FCMP statement, function, subroutine, or other syntactical element, a comprehensive index facilitates direct access to the material.

Chapter 1 introduces functions in a programming-language-agnostic sense, including both built-in and user-defined functions. SAS functions and subroutines are introduced and contrasted with SAS procedures. Function nomenclature is defined in this chapter, including software quality characteristics, which are referenced throughout the remainder of the text.

Chapter 2 introduces basic FCMP syntax, including how to build simple functions and subroutines. The majority of the chapter focuses on function communication, including how to transfer data *to* a function, and how to retrieve results *from* a function. Differences between DATA step syntax and the FCMP procedure are also explored.

Chapters 3 and 4 introduce the SAS array and hash object, respectively, which are the primary built-in data structures leveraged by user-defined functions. Later chapters rely on these data structures to deliver dynamic functionality while minimizing code complexity and maximizing efficiency.

Chapter 5 introduces the RUN_MACRO and RUN_SASFILE built-in functions, which operate only inside the FCMP procedure. They enable user-defined functions to call SAS macros or to execute SAS programs during a function call. Chapter 6 delves further into RUN_MACRO by demonstrating how it can support data lookup operations.

Chapter 7 focuses on function design, including recursion and memoization. *Recursion* describes the act of a function or subroutine calling itself, and *memoization* describes the retention of results from costly (that is, resource-intensive) function calls to improve software runtime and efficiency.

Chapter 8 demonstrates the interaction between the FCMP procedure and the Python open-source language. The Python Component Object is introduced, which facilitates interoperability by enabling SAS user-defined functions to call Python functions.

Chapter 9 introduces two powerful methods to call user-defined functions. The FORMAT procedure OTHER option is demonstrated, which enables you to design user-defined formats and informats that call user-defined functions. The REPORT procedure COMPUTE block is demonstrated, in which user-defined functions can be called to modify and add dynamic functionality to SAS reports.

Is This Book for You?

This text is intended for intermediate to advanced SAS users who have a firm grasp of the DATA step and who are looking to maximize the potential of their software. Nevertheless, because the majority of DATA step syntax can be run inside the FCMP procedure, FCMP user-defined functions can and should be incorporated early in your SAS career. For this reason, this text gradually introduces the principal built-in data structures of the FCMP procedure—the SAS array and the hash object—to ensure users of all levels can understand and confidently interact with them. Knowledge of the SAS macro language is not a prerequisite to learning the FCMP procedure; however, some examples in this text do incorporate SAS macro statements, functions, variables, and other syntax.

What Should You Know about the Examples?

This book includes tutorials for you to follow to gain hands-on experience with SAS.

Software Used to Develop the Book's Content

All examples in this text require only Base SAS; no other SAS modules are required.

Example Code and Data

You can access the example code and data for this book by linking to its author page at https://support.sas.com/en/books/authors/troy-hughes.html.

SAS OnDemand for Academics

If you are using SAS OnDemand for Academics to access data and run your programs, then please check the SAS OnDemand for Academics page to ensure that the software contains the product or products that you need to run the code: https://www.sas.com/en_us/software/on-demand-for-academics.html.

We Want to Hear from You

SAS Press books are written *by* SAS Users *for* SAS Users. We welcome your participation in their development and your feedback on SAS Press books that you are using. Please visit sas.com/books to do the following:

- Sign up to review a book
- Recommend a topic
- Request information on how to become a SAS Press author
- Provide feedback on a book

Learn more about this author by visiting his author page at https://support.sas.com/en/books/authors/troy-hughes.html. There you can download free book excerpts, access example code and data, read the latest reviews, get updates, and more.

About The Author

Troy Martin Hughes has been a SAS practitioner for more than 20 years; has managed SAS projects in support of federal, state, and local government initiatives; and is a SAS Certified Advanced Programmer, SAS Certified Base Programmer, SAS Certified Clinical Trials Programmer, and SAS Certified Professional V8. He has an MBA in information systems management and additional credentials, including: PMP, PMI-ACP, PMI-PBA, PMI-RMP, SSCP, CSSLP, CISSP, CRISC, CISM, CISA, CGEIT, Network+, Security+, CySA+, CASP+, Cloud+, CSM, CSP-SM, CSD, A-CSD, CSP-D, CSPO, CSP-PO, CSP, SAFe Government Practitioner, and ITIL Foundation. He has given more than 150 presentations, trainings, and hands-on workshops at SAS user group conferences, including SAS Global Forum, SAS Analytics Experience, SAS Explore, WUSS, MWSUG, SCSUG, SESUG, PharmaSUG, BASAS, and BASUG. He is the author of two groundbreaking books that model SAS best practices, including *SAS® Data Analytic Development: Dimensions of Software Quality* (2016), and *SAS® Data-Driven Development: From Abstract Design to Dynamic Functionality, Second Edition* (2022). Troy is a U.S. Navy veteran with two tours of duty in Afghanistan.

Learn more about this author by visiting his author page at https://support.sas.com/en/books/authors/troy-hughes.html. There you can download free book excerpts, access example code and data, read the latest reviews, get updates, and more.

Acknowledgments

So many people, through contributions to my life, as well as endurance and encouragement throughout this journey, have contributed directly and indirectly, and made this project possible.

To the family and friends grown weary of hearing "I can't—I'm writing—yes, a third book," thank you for your love, patience, understanding, and the fleeting moments of sanity that you provided.

To my English teachers who instilled a love of writing, thank you for years of red ink and encouragement: Estelle McCarthy, Lorinne McKnight, Dolores Cummings, Millie Bizzini, Patty Ely, Jo Berry, Liana Hachiya, Audrey Musson, Dana Trevethan, Cheri Rowton, Annette Simmons, and Dr. Robyn Bell.

To the mentors whose words continue to guide me, thank you for your leadership and friendship: Dr. Cathy Schuman, Dr. Barton Palmer, Dr. Kiko Gladsjo, Dr. Mina Chang, Dean Kauffman, Rich Nagy, Jim Martin, and Jeff Stillman.

To my SAS spirit guides, thank you for your continued inspiration: Art Carpenter, Frank DiIorio, Linda Jolley, Ron Cody, Mark Jordan, Lex Jansen, Dr. Gerhard Svolba, Kirk Paul Lafler, Louise Hadden, Richann Watson, Ronald Fehd, Susan Slaughter, Lora Delwiche, Paul Dorfman, Bart Jablonski, Rick Wicklin, Thomas Billings, Peter Eberhardt, Michael Raithel, and Charlie Shipp.

To SAS Institute, thank you for providing free software, without which this endeavor would have been impossible.

To Amber Elam, my SAS expediter and world-class technical support liaison who patiently guided this sometimes misguided author, thank you for the hours of support over the past three years.

To my editors, Suzanne Morgen and Catherine Connolly, thank you for four years of relentless motivation and for inarguably improving my drafts until they were ready for the masses.

To my technical reviewers, who humbled me merely by taking the time to read this content, thank you for catching my errors, and for the inquisitive questions and clarifying comments, all of which led me to revamp and revise numerous sections: Mike Whitcher, Andrew Henrick, Paul Grant, and Rick Langston.

To the SAS developers who not only birthed the FCMP procedure, but also lent their expertise through endless emails and instruction, thank you for your unending inspiration and insight: Andrew Henrick, Aaron Mays, Mike Whitcher, and Bill McNeill.

To Frank DiIorio, whose eternally comprehensive *SAS® Applications Programming: A Gentle Introduction* was the only SAS book I owned for the first five years of my career, thank you for teaching me how to SAS. My copy still bears the sticky notes where Frank introduced me to the DATA step, the SET statement, the MERGE statement, formats and informats, how to SORT, how to FREQ, how to MEANS, and so much more! And when I finally had the honor to meet Frank at SESUG in 2019, he was no less inspirational than his tome.

And finally, to Art Carpenter, whose relentless pursuit of perfection and humble brilliance has inspired millions, thank you endlessly. When Linda Jolley introduced me to SAS macros in her course in 2001, she gave us one piece of advice—buy *Carpenter's Complete Guide to the SAS® Macro Language*, still in its first edition. The dreams of some little boys do come true, and who would have imagined that years later I'd take photos as Art signed my copy, or that I'd be referenced in his third edition. So, when Art recommended in 2018 that I *really needed to look into this PROC FCMP thing*, I took him at his word, and the rest is history. Art, this one's for you!

Chapter 1: Introducing Functions

Functions deliver functionality—this much is clear. But what makes a function a function? How do functions differ from other code and software components? And most importantly, why should SAS practitioners learn to build our own (that is, *user-defined*) functions? These and other questions are explored and answered in the following chapters as functions are introduced, including their purpose, value, syntax, construction, and implementation. You will learn how to build functions using the SAS Function Compiler procedure (PROC FCMP), and how to integrate user-defined functions into SAS programs to improve software quality.

Functions are the simple syrup of software, and for those who have never bartended, allow me to explain. Simple syrup is simple—one part water, one part granulated sugar. Mix, heat, stir, dissolve, chill, and incorporate into various cocktails over several hours or days or until the carafe runs dry. Yes, the recipe is straightforward, but you wouldn't want to be caught empty-handed during a hectic happy hour—and making separate syrupy batches for each customer's drink would waste precious time! Of course, the solution is to make the syrup once, test its quality, and reuse it thereafter for effortless rounds of mojitos and daiquiris, improving the efficiency and productivity of any bartender or mixologist.

Just as various cocktails can be concocted by leveraging simple syrup, software, too, is commonly developed by combining components—including reliable, reusable functions that deliver consistent functionality each time they are used. This functionality can be predictably varied or configured through *arguments*—user-supplied input values. In this manner, functions improve software quality by promoting software configurability, reusability, and maintainability. And as the ease with which software can be developed, tested, documented, and maintained increases, developer productivity commensurately increases. Thus, functions operationalize the "working smarter not harder" mindset and improve the quality of not only software itself but also the software development *environment*—the experience of SAS practitioners writing SAS software.

This chapter introduces functions and function-related nomenclature relied upon throughout the text. Two types of callable software modules—functions and subroutines—are compared, contrasted, and disambiguated. SAS built-in functions available in Base SAS are contrasted with user-defined functions. Most importantly, specific characteristics of software quality—namely, configurability, reusability, and maintainability—are explored, including the role functions play to increase these characteristics. Thus, whereas later chapters introduce the FCMP procedure and its syntax, this chapter makes the business case for designing and implementing user-defined functions that extend the SAS language.

What Is a Function Anyway?

Some discussion of nomenclature should preface any introduction to functions to define and differentiate terminology relied upon throughout later chapters. The International Organization for Standardization (ISO) defines a *function* as a "software module that performs a specific action, is invoked by the appearance of its name in an expression, receives input values, and returns a single value" (International Organization for Standarization 2017). SAS documentation similarly defines a *function* as "a component of the SAS programming language that can accept arguments, perform a computation or other operation, and return a value" (SAS Institute Inc. 2020). In the following subsections, these definitions are further decomposed, explored, and expanded to introduce functions within the SAS language.

Every function is *callable*—that is, built as an independent software module, and *called* (executed) when its name is referenced within code. The *calling module* (or *calling program*) calls a function (the *called module*), and temporarily transfers program control to the function, after which control is returned to the calling module when the function terminates. In SAS, the DATA step typically acts as the calling module (although numerous other methods are demonstrated in this chapter), and the called module always represents a user-defined function or subroutine built and compiled using the FCMP procedure. Calling, callable, and called modules are described subsequently in more detail.

Because so many FCMP syntax elements are identical between functions and subroutines— and benefits are comparable between functions and subroutines—within this text, *function* is used generically to reference both functions and subroutines. *Subroutine* is used only in those rare instances where syntax or functionality differs. In other words, this chapter could be titled "Introducing Functions and Subroutines." When a paragraph decries how "user-defined functions increase the quality of SAS software," you should interpret this as "user-defined functions *and subroutines* increase the quality of SAS software." And they really do!

Functions Versus Functionality

Functions deliver software functionality—they perform some action to effect some result. But software often can be constructed without functions, and nevertheless provide equivalent functionality. Thus, functions differ not so much in *what* they do but in *how* they are structured. As callable software modules, functions are discrete software components (that is, bite-sized chunks of code) that can be reused over time, and typically configured through parameters to provide flexible results.

Consider the not-too-distant past when Base SAS included the UPCASE function (that converts text to uppercase) but did not have a corresponding LOWCASE function. Frank DiIorio, in his seminal book, notes in a discussion about UPCASE that "There is no analogous function [to UPCASE] to convert to lowercase" (DiIorio 1997). Fortunately, SAS did introduce the LOWCASE function. However, in a pre-LOWCASE world, SAS practitioners would have had to develop customized code to transform text to lowercase.

For example, Program 1.1 converts the Phrase variable to lowercase without calling the LOWCASE function. Instead, the DO loop uses the LENGTH function to assess the length of Phrase and iterates over each character in Phrase. The CHAR function isolates one character at a time, and RANK evaluates the ASCII numeric value of the character. The IF statement evaluates whether a character falls between the ASCII values of 65 and 90 (corresponding to uppercase A through Z in a Windows environment). If so, 32 is added to the ASCII value, and the BYTE function transforms the ASCII value back into its (lowercase) alphabetic equivalent. Finally, the SUBSTR function used on the left-hand side of the equal sign incrementally replaces each uppercase character with its lowercase equivalent.

Program 1.1: Lowercase Functionality in a Non-LOWCASE World
```
data lower;
   length phrase $100;
   phrase = 'SAS Applications Programming: A Gentle Introduction';
   do i = 1 to length(phrase);
      if 65 <= rank(char(phrase,i)) <= 90 then substr(phrase,i,1)
         = byte(rank(char(phrase,i)) + 32);
      end;
   put phrase;
run;
```

The DATA step converts the title of Frank's inimitable book to lowercase, as shown in the SAS log:

```
sas applications programming: a gentle introduction
NOTE: The data set WORK.LOWER has 1 observations and 3 variables.
```

Program 1.1 provides lowercase *functionality* but is not a *function*, as the functionality is not callable, but rather is constructed inside the DATA step. And because this functionality is not callable, the code must be re-created whenever a different variable needs to be converted to lowercase. This becomes a tedious process of copying the DO loop and lowercase functionality whenever a variable needs to be transformed; this repetition is inefficient, and risks the unnecessary introduction of errors.

Fortunately, the LOWCASE built-in function *does* exist, and Program 1.2 produces identical output with far less effort. It is in this manner that one talks about *extending* a programming language through the addition of functions—because each new function that is defined, whether built-in or user-defined, represents functionality that can be readily called rather than painstakingly re-created in subsequent programs.

Program 1.2: Functionally Equivalent Use of LOWCASE to Transform Text to Lowercase

```
data lower;
   length phrase $100;
   phrase = 'SAS Applications Programming: A Gentle Introduction';
   phrase = lowcase(phrase);
   put phrase;
run;
```

Programs 1.1 and 1.2 are said to be *functionally equivalent*—that is, their results or output are identical; however, they operate using vastly different approaches. Program 1.1 delivers functionality through a DO loop and hardcoded logic, whereas Program 1.2 relies on the LOWCASE function. Program 1.2 is more appealing and inarguably demonstrates better software design because the complexity of the LOWCASE functionality is *abstracted*—hidden from view, and concealed within unseen, proprietary SAS code.

The beauty of abstraction is that it allows the user to focus on the *functionality* that a function delivers rather than the *methods* through which that functionality is delivered. As a SAS practitioner, I do not need to understand the inner workings of LOWCASE, such as whether a DO loop is used or how the case transformation occurs. Moreover, these methods would clutter my DATA step, as demonstrated in Program 1.1, making it more difficult to understand the high-level intent and flow of the program. Thus, Program 1.2 can be said to be more *readable* than Program 1.1, which improves software quality.

The FCMP procedure empowers SAS practitioners to create our own *user-defined* functions. Although FCMP syntax is not discussed yet, Program 1.3 demonstrates the ease with which the logic from the Program 1.1 DATA step can be dropped into the FCMP procedure to create a user-defined function that converts text to lowercase. The Phrase variable has been renamed Str to improve readability, and the remainder of the DO loop is unchanged.

Program 1.3: Functionally Equivalent User-Defined TINY Function

```
* converts character variable to lowercase;
* requires single character parameter <= 100 characters;
* no exception handling for arguments that exceed 100 characters;
* tested and intended for use ONLY in a Windows environment;
proc fcmp outlib=work.funcs.char;
   function tiny(str $) $100;
      do i = 1 to length(str);
         if 65 <= rank(char(str,i)) <= 90 then substr(str,i,1)
            = byte(rank(char(str,i)) + 32);
         end;
      return(str);
      endfunc;
quit;
```

Program 1.3 defines and compiles the TINY user-defined function, whose functionality is approximately equivalent to the LOWCASE built-in function. TINY can be called in the identical fashion as LOWCASE, and Program 1.4 calls TINY and produces results identical to Programs 1.1 and 1.2. Note that the CMPLIB option (described later in greater detail) must be set, which tells SAS where to find user-defined functions.

Program 1.4: Functionally Equivalent Use of TINY to Transform Text to Lowercase
```
options cmplib = work.funcs;

data lower;
   length phrase phrase1 phrase2 $100;
   phrase = 'SAS Applications Programming: A Gentle Introduction';
   phrase1 = lowcase(phrase);
   phrase2 = tiny(phrase);
   put phrase1=;
   put phrase2=;
run;
```

The log demonstrates that LOWCASE and TINY produce identical results:

```
phrase1=sas applications programming: a gentle introduction
phrase2=sas applications programming: a gentle introduction
```

So, why the careful distinction between *identical* results yet *equivalent* functionality? Because SAS user-defined functions, as necessary as they are to building reusable functionality, inherently deliver different (and typically diminished) *performance* than their built-in function counterparts. For example, in designing TINY, no attempt was made to measure or optimize TINY's runtime or utilization of system resources. SAS user-defined functions like TINY are written in Base SAS—a fourth-generation language (4GL) that understandably lacks some of the memory and resource management capabilities that lower-level languages like C, C++, or Java provide. To be clear, this is not a deficiency in the SAS language but rather the result of the SAS application managing lower-level processes. SAS practitioners can focus instead on loftier and, arguably, more interesting pursuits such as data analysis, the production of data products, and data-driven decision-making.

Also note that TINY is said to be "approximately" equivalent to LOWCASE. This caveat acknowledges that although both functions produce identical results given *this* specific input, variability in the data or environment would cause the functions to produce different results. In other words, TINY is less robust and less reliable than LOWCASE. For example, TINY declares a return value having a length of 100, so any character variable passed to TINY that exceeds this threshold will be truncated. This could be described as a failure of *scalability*, one characteristic of software quality, because TINY as currently defined is unable to accommodate longer character values. LOWCASE, on the other hand, is scalable and overcomes these limitations.

TINY also relies on "standard" ASCII character encoding in which the uppercase letters A through Z correspond to the ASCII values 65 through 90—but this encoding is not standard across all operating environments. For example, TINY would fail on mainframe SAS running on the z/OS platform, which relies on EBCDIC encoding. This inability to provide equivalent functionality across platforms demonstrates a lack of *interoperability*, another characteristic of software quality. This is not to say that user-defined functions inherently lack quality, but rather that potential issues should be identified, and their risks evaluated to determine whether those risks should be mitigated by expanding functionality or improving performance.

For example, TINY could be modified to return longer character values, or to detect the operating system programmatically—but the decision to refactor a function should be made based on the business value those modifications produce or the risks that they mitigate. Thus, a user-defined function that will never be run on the z/OS platform because a developer runs SAS exclusively on Windows machines does not need to be engineered for that environment. To do so would waste developer resources.

Only a few pages in, and the critical importance of understanding software quality is already salient, including the use of nomenclature that describes specific characteristics of software quality. An understanding of this nomenclature benefits the discussion and documentation of software requirements and can help communicate to key stakeholders the many ways that user-defined functions provide value. Software requirements, after all, should drive the design and development of user-defined functions, communicate why a callable software module is needed, and also why a noncallable solution will not suffice. The next sections continue the discussion on software quality and provide a framework for discussing the benefits and value of user-defined functions.

The Many Facets of Software Quality and Performance

Software quality comprises a mix of both functionality and performance. If software aims to provide some algorithmic calculation but fails to generate the correct result, it can be said to lack quality because it does not produce the required functionality. But if the same software instead produces the correct result yet takes too long to compute (or hogs system resources), it also can be said to lack quality because it fails to deliver the required performance. In this vein, software requirements should convey both functional and performance requirements that specify not only what software must do but also how (or how well) it should do it.

This chapter began with the somewhat radical assertion that SAS software can produce equivalent functionality with or without the use of user-defined functions. Why then should SAS practitioners invest time in mastering the FCMP procedure and the design of user-defined functions? Because user-defined functions improve the *performance* of software, and in so doing, improve software quality.

Software performance is sometimes misconstrued as narrowly describing only processing speed or software efficiency; however, these are but two of a score of characteristics that can describe software performance. More broadly, the Institute of Electrical and Electronics Engineers (IEEE) defines *performance* as "the measurable criterion that identifies a quality attribute of a function or how well a functional requirement must be accomplished" (IEEE 2005). And "software quality attributes" comprise *external software quality* and *internal software quality*. External software quality includes software characteristics such as speed, efficiency, reliability, and robustness that can be observed (and often measured) as software executes. Internal software quality, conversely, describes performance that cannot be assessed by running software—you must pry open a program and inspect its code to determine whether it is modular, readable, or reusable.

ISO defines an *internal measure of software quality* as a "measure of the degree to which a set of static attributes of a software product satisfies stated and implied needs for the software product to be used under specified conditions" (ISO/IEC 2014). ISO further clarifies that "Static attributes include those that relate to the software architecture, structure and its components. Static attributes can be verified by review, inspection, simulation, or automated tools." Thus, user-defined functions improve software performance by increasing the internal quality of the software, as measured by static quality attributes such as modularity, maintainability, reusability, and configurability. Internal software quality is often referred to as *static performance*, and external software quality as *dynamic performance*—the distinction representing whether software must be running or not to assess a particular quality attribute.

To bring this discussion full circle, SAS user-defined functions rarely make your software run faster or more efficiently. However, user-defined functions do improve a developer's ability to maintain and modify SAS software, as well as an end user's ability to use and interact with software. In this manner, user-defined functions can improve the quality of software, the quality of the development environment (that is, the experience of SAS practitioners writing SAS software), and the quality of the end-user experience. Several static performance attributes—including modularity, readability, configurability, reusability, maintainability, and integrity—are introduced in the next sections, as user-defined functions model these quality characteristics.

No respectable book about functions could begin without the ubiquitous example that converts between temperature scales. Program 1.5 demonstrates the FAHR_TO_CEL user-defined function that converts Fahrenheit to Celsius. It is referenced and refactored in the following sections to introduce software quality.

Program 1.5: Fahrenheit Conversion (FAHR_TO_CEL) User-Defined Function
```
* converts Fahrenheit temperature to Celsius;
proc fcmp outlib=work.funcs.num;
   function fahr_to_cel(f);
      c = (f - 32) * (5 / 9);
      return(c);
      endfunc;
quit;
```

Software Modularity

Software modularity describes the cleaving of software into discrete chunks of code to achieve the goal of *module independence*—the ability of a user to alter one module without affecting or interfering with the functionality or performance of other modules. Modular software is often contrasted with *monolithic* software—*one stone*, in Greek—in which functionality is delivered through a single program file. Although modularity does tend to diminish software component size, breaking a monolithic program into bits does not, in and of itself, make it modular. Rather, truly modular software requires *loose coupling* of components, in which modules interact only where necessary, and only through prescribed communication channels.

In addition to displaying software independence, modular software is typically functionally discrete—that is, each module should have a singular focus and do *one and only one thing*. These two principal requirements for loose coupling and functional discretion are sometimes described as *low coupling with high cohesion* and contribute to module conciseness. Thus, the brevity typically demonstrated by software modules should not be considered to be a defining characteristic of software modularity, but rather a welcome consequence of functional discretion and loose coupling. It is this concise, modular design that lays the foundation for other software quality characteristics, as described in the following software quality sections.

A common method to promote software modularity is through *callable software modules*, in which a module's functionality is delivered by calling the module's name. Callable modules, which include both functions and subroutines, are introduced later in this chapter. For example, Program 1.5 demonstrates software modularity in that the FAHR_TO_CEL function does only one thing: converts Fahrenheit to Celsius. Moreover, FAHR_TO_CEL is segmented from other code—enclosed between the FUNCTION and ENDFUNC statements and encapsulated inside the FCMP procedure.

The following statement executed from a DATA step temporarily transfers program control to the FAHR_TO_CEL function when FAHR_TO_CEL is called:

```
celsius = fahr_to_cel(212)
```

However, the pinnacle of software modularity requires that callable modules not only be encapsulated but also be separated—that is, the calling module and called module should be maintained in different program files. This software design promotes software security and integrity because a user-defined function can be designed, developed, tested, and locked for read-only use prior to deployment to production. Thereafter, calling modules that use and reuse the function can be modified without risk of accidental alteration of the function itself. Moreover, reusability is promoted where functions are maintained in separate program files because multiple calling modules can call the same user-defined function.

For example, it should not be misconstrued that the prior call to FAHR_TO_CEL occurs in Program 1.5, in which FAHR_TO_CEL is defined; these represent two separate SAS program files. This distinction is made clearer in Chapter 2, in which user-defined functions are saved to a persistent SAS library rather than the ephemeral WORK library. Software modularity is discussed further in this chapter in the "Function Implementation" and "Function Invocation" sections, which explain that a function's implementation and its invocation generally should never occur in the same program file.

Software Readability

Software readability describes the ease with which software—including code, comments, and accompanying documentation—can be read and understood. Readability is especially important where software is expected to be maintained or modified by users who are not the original developers. Many aspects of code readability are not only language-dependent but also somewhat subjective. For example, indentation, line spacing, and other formatting can increase or decrease readability, as can variable-naming conventions or capitalization. But in many cases, style standardization is as important as the specific formatting or other conventions. Readability can also be improved through apt software organization and inline comments.

Notwithstanding the subjectivity that surrounds readability, some design practices do inarguably improve the ability of a developer to parse and understand code. Callable software modules (and the software modularity that they espouse) represent one such best practice. Readability of the *called module* is improved because the function is doing one and only one thing. For example, Program 1.5 converts a Fahrenheit temperature to Celsius, and nothing more, so its functionality is readily understood. The single code comment "transforms Fahrenheit temperature to Celsius" captures the high-level information that is required to call the function. *Fahrenheit* defines the input parameter, *Transforms* describes the functionality, and *Celsius* defines the return value or output.

Readability of the *calling program* is also improved through user-defined functions. Consider Program 1.6, which calls FAHR_TO_CEL to transform Temp1, and which transforms Temp2 using the equivalent hardcoded algorithm.

Program 1.6: Comparing FAHR_TO_CEL Function to Functionally Equivalent Hardcoded Transformation

```
data transformed;
   length temp_f temp_c1 temp_c2 8;
   temp_f = 212;
   temp_c1 = fahr_to_cel(temp_f);
   temp_c2 = (temp_f - 32) * (5 / 9);
run;
```

Inspecting the DATA step, it is clear that FAHR_TO_CEL is transforming the 212-degree boiling water from Fahrenheit to Celsius. Without having to recall junior high math, a developer can grasp this high-level functionality. However, the equivalent hardcoded transformation that initializes Temp_c2 is more complex both to write and to decipher. Now consider a more complex function that might perform advanced calculations comprising twenty lines of code. Despite this complexity, the function's invocation would still require only one SAS statement. But hardcode these twenty lines instead into a DATA step, and the high-level intent of the DATA step could be eclipsed by the code complexity. Thus, software design that modularizes functionality into user-defined functions enables developers to better comprehend high-level functionality without getting lost in the weeds.

Software Configurability

Software configurability describes the ease with which end users can interact with software to achieve dynamic functionality. Configurability is primarily engineered through function parameters, through which end users can alter a function's functionality by modifying one or more corresponding arguments when the function is called. Functions that are more configurable are able to meet the needs of more diverse users and more diverse use cases, and end users touting the benefits of a "highly flexibly function" are often describing a highly *configurable* function.

Program 1.5 declares a single parameter (F), which represents the temperature in Fahrenheit that is passed to the function. The resultant Celsius temperature is returned without rounding or truncation, so the following function call in which 211 is passed using the %SYSFUNC macro function returns quite a few superfluous 4s (99.4444444444444):

```
%put %sysfunc(fahr_to_cel(211));
```

The return value is accurate, although some users might prefer a rounded, more concise result. And where end-user preferences might differ, *configurability* can facilitate a single function that meets these diverse needs. The refactored FAHR_TO_CEL_RND function in Program 1.7 declares a second parameter (DEC), which defines the number of decimals of precision in the returned Celsius value.

Program 1.7: Adding a Parameter to Improve Configurability of a Function
```
* F - degrees Fahrenheit;
* DEC - decimals precision;
proc fcmp outlib=work.funcs.num;
   function fahr_to_cel_rnd(f, dec);
      c = (f - 32) * (5 / 9);
      rnd = 1 / (10**dec);
      return(round(c, rnd));
      endfunc;
quit;
```

This more configurable function, when called with two decimals of precision, now returns 99.44:

```
%put %sysfunc(fahr_to_cel_rnd(211, 2));
```

Developers and end users alike are more apt to favor configurable functions because functionality can be varied by modifying only the arguments within a function call, rather than having to modify the function's definition. In this way, configurability can facilitate more stable functions that require fewer modifications over time. Thus, rather than pursuing less sustainable *customization*, in which the needs of only one customer drive development, *configuration* instead aims to satisfy multiple, diverse customers using more flexible functions.

Software Reusability

Software reusability describes the ease with which software modules, including functions, can be reused—either in the same or future software products. Software reuse can dramatically increase the speed and efficiency with which software can be developed. For example, reuse of a user-defined function can rely on the previous design, development, testing, and documentation that has already been completed. In many cases, implementing an existing user-defined function within a new program can be drag-and-drop easy—name the location of the function using the CMPLIB system option, and call the function from the DATA step!

From a SAS practitioner's perspective, software reuse is arguably the primary rationale for mastering the FCMP procedure. We cannot maximize our productivity without embracing software reuse. And the modularity, callability, readability, and configurability discussed in the previous sections directly contribute to the likelihood that a user-defined function can and will be reused.

Modularity drives reuse because independent modules are disconnected. The requirement that modular software be loosely coupled means that a well-formed module often can be plucked from its original usage and reused elsewhere without adversity. *Callable modules*, including functions, further spur reuse because they can be invoked simply by calling the function name. Thus, productivity is radically improved when a 30-line function can be effortlessly included in your DATA step using a one-line function call.

Readability drives reuse because software modules that can be understood—especially at a high level—can be incorporated into software. In some cases, you might not understand *how* the function delivers its functionality, but as long as you understand *what* it delivers, you can still use the function. Finally, *configurability* encourages reuse because a function's functionality can be varied. Dynamic arguments produce dynamic results, and a more diverse array of users will find value in functions that can be readily configured.

Software Maintainability

Software maintainability describes the ease with which software can be maintained and modified, either by the developers who initially wrote the software or by separate developers tasked with software maintenance. Software that can be more readily modified reduces downtime and increases the speed and efficiency with which software can return to a functional state. Maintenance might be performed to correct a defect, improve performance, or extend functionality. But regardless of the driver, improved maintainability equates to higher *availability*—the "up" time that software is functioning and meeting business needs and requirements.

And software availability directly equates to dollars and cents—a language that product owners, customers, and other key stakeholders speak. The ability of user-defined functions to improve availability through increased maintainability becomes a primary talking point when demonstrating the worth of user-defined functions to decision-makers.

Maintainability is principally driven by software modularity. Because user-defined functions are functionally discrete, concise, callable modules, they can be more readily understood and modified. Consider the extension of the FAHR_TO_CEL function (Program 1.5) to the FAHR_TO_CEL_RND function (Program 1.7), in which the added DEC parameter specifies the number of decimals in the return value. FAHR_TO_CEL didn't have much junk in its trunk, so comprehension of its functionality was straightforward, and this functionality could be extended easily by adding the DEC parameter.

Software reuse also improves maintainability because *reuse* denotes a module that is relied upon across software projects or across a team or enterprise. A user-defined function might be reused a dozen or more times by a team. If its functionality needs to be extended, this maintenance can be performed once, tested once, and redeployed once to alter functionality across all dozen instances in which the function is called. Without this reuse, maintenance is impeded because developers must modify separate programs individually, rather than altering one user-defined function. And again, from a business perspective, dysfunctional software—or software that is failing to meet business needs or failing to deliver business value—equates to lost revenue.

Software Integrity

Software integrity forms one leg of the confidentiality, integrity, and availability (CIA) security triad and describes the need to protect software against malicious, unauthorized, or inadvertent access or modification. Large, monolithic program files can be riskier because inevitable maintenance exposes the entire code to the risk of alteration. The cybersecurity principle of *least privilege* specifies that as few users as possible should have access to key infrastructure (such as code) and can mitigate risks to software integrity.

One best practice that maximizes software integrity is—say it with me—modular software design! Team leads or senior SAS practitioners can be charged with maintaining a library of reusable, user-defined functions. In so doing, they alone can be granted Edit permissions to modify the critical functions that underpin multiple software projects. Less experienced SAS users can be granted Read-Only permissions to user-defined functions, and thus can leverage these functions, but with the confidence that the function definitions and functionality cannot be modified.

Other methods that facilitate software integrity include formalized change management and release management policy and processes, attention to cybersecurity best practices, and implementation of security controls that can further mitigate or eliminate risk—all of which fall outside the scope of this text. However, restricting and delegating code access through modular software design is often a first step toward greater software security.

Functional Components and Organization

At a high level, successful function design for both built-in and user-defined functions requires developers to fulfill three objectives:

1. Discuss, define, and document the function's functionality and performance that will meet some business need and requirements.
2. Write code that delivers this functionality and performance.
3. Empower users to call the function to render its functionality.

These objectives represent separate components of callable software modules. They correspond to a function's specification, implementation, and invocation, respectively. The *specification* defines the function that software developers are building and subsequently instructs end users what has been built and how to interact with it. The *implementation* comprises the code—the meat of the function. The *invocation* represents the function call through which end users run the function. The next sections describe these three function components.

Function Specification

Before any code has been written, early in the software development life cycle (SDLC), a function typically begins with a specification—the "tech specs" that define software objectives, including the required functionality and performance. ISO defines a software *specification* as a "document that fully describes a design element or its interfaces in terms of requirements (functional, performance, constraints, and design characteristics) and the qualification conditions and procedures for each requirement" (International Organization for Standarization 2017). Technical requirements are crucial because they instruct developers *what* to build, as well as *when to stop* building, thus conveying the *definition of done* for each software component or product.

For example, when SAS software developers began conceptualizing the need for the built-in LOWCASE function, they undoubtedly described the function's intended *functionality*— conversion to lowercase—in its specification. However, they also would have defined the required *performance*, such as speed (for example, characters transformed per second) or interoperability (for example, operating environments in which LOWCASE should be compatible). Thus, during the design, development, and testing phases of the SDLC, the specification guides developers and helps ensure needs and requirements are delivered. And once a function passes testing, it can be released into production for use by end users during the operations and maintenance (O&M) phase.

During the O&M phase, the specification adopts a new role and conveys to users how to interact with a function. This user-focused specification (required to *run* software) will typically be far less technical than the corresponding technical specifications (required to *build* software). Thus, the specification available to end users will typically state what the function does (its functionality), what input is required (its parameters), what output is produced (return values or return codes), as well as additional context or caveats that might assist users calling the function.

For example, as shown in Figure 1.1, the built-in LOWCASE function is masterfully described in the *SAS® 9.4 Functions and Call Routines: Reference, Fifth Edition* (SAS Institute Inc. 2020).

Figure 1.1: SAS LOWCASE Function Specification

LOWCASE Function

Converts all uppercase single-width English alphabet letters in an argument to lowercase.

Categories: Character

CAS

Restriction: This function is assigned an I18N Level 2 status, and is designed for use with SBCS, DBCS, and MBCS (UTF8). For more information, see Internationalization Compatibility.

Note: This function supports the VARCHAR type.

Table of Contents

Syntax
  Required Argument
Details
Example
See Also

Syntax

LOWCASE(*argument*)

Required Argument

argument
  specifies a character constant, variable, or expression.

Details

In a DATA step, if the LOWCASE function returns a value to a variable that has not previously been assigned a length, then that variable is given the length of the argument.

The LOWCASE function copies the character argument, converts all uppercase single-width English alphabet letters to lowercase letters, and returns the altered value as a result.

The results of the LOWCASE function depend directly on the translation table that is in effect (see TRANTAB= System Option in *SAS National Language Support (NLS): Reference Guide*) and indirectly on the ENCODING and LOCALE system options.

A specification should contain sufficient information to enable users to call a function without inspecting the function's *implementation*—its underlying code. Note that the SAS specification for LOWCASE defines a single parameter (termed *argument* in SAS parlance) that must be a "character constant, variable, or expression," and also provides details about how the function can be used. Not depicted in Figure 1.1, the SAS LOWCASE specification also demonstrates examples of how to call LOWCASE within a DATA step.

User-defined functions developed using the FCMP procedure should also be accompanied by a specification that describes their functionality and usage to end users. Because one of the primary objectives of building user-defined functions is software reusability, a function might be developed by one SAS practitioner, yet shared among teammates and users throughout an organization, and persist far beyond the employment of the original developer. In these cases, a formal specification can best convey the functionality, usage, and caveats of a user-defined function. When specifications are absent, and especially when code is poorly documented or undocumented, users unfamiliar with a particular user-defined function are more likely to abandon its use or unnecessarily re-create its functionality—because they neither understand nor trust what the function does, and because they might have neither the time nor the skill set to parse through the function's implementation.

For example, Program 1.3 contained four inline comments that introduced the TINY user-defined function. Those comments effectively comprised a brief (yet viable) specification:

```
* converts character variable to lowercase;
* requires single character parameter <= 100 characters;
* no exception handling for arguments that exceed 100 characters;
* tested and intended for use ONLY in a Windows environment;
```

The specification conveys the high-level functionality (transformation to lowercase), the single required parameter (the character variable or value being transformed), the caveat that exception handling is absent, and the caveat that the function is intended only for a Windows environment. In many cases, this type of inline specification is sufficient. However, in some environments, an inline specification is insufficient (or disallowed), and an external specification (similar to that demonstrated in Figure 1.1) should accompany all user-defined functions.

Function Implementation

A function's implementation contains its code—it *implements* the objectives stated in the function's specification to deliver functionality to the user or process calling the function. ISO broadly defines an *implementation* as a "process of translating a design into hardware components, software components, or both" (International Organization for Standarization 2017). A function's implementation is commonly referred to as the function's *definition*, as it defines the functionality that is produced.

Built-in functions typically conceal their implementations. We know *what* a SAS built-in function does from reading its specification and observing its results, but not *how* it does it because we cannot view the underlying C code. And with SAS investing billions to innovate and patent bleeding-edge technology to outpace its competitors, it is understandable why its source code remains copyrighted and concealed! User-defined functions similarly can be encrypted using the FCMP procedure ENCRYPT option, which facilitates delivering functionality without exposing proprietary methods to your user base. The ENCRYPT option is introduced and demonstrated in Chapter 2.

In general, however, SAS user-defined functions are unencrypted, and their code is exposed to the users calling them. Thus, the implementation of a user-defined function comprises the code between the FUNCTION and ENDFUNC statements, and the implementation of a user-defined subroutine comprises the code between the SUBROUTINE and ENDSUB statements. This openness facilitates a deeper understanding of functionality because SAS practitioners can inspect the code itself. It also facilitates maintainability because the function's implementation can be modified readily—either to alter or extend functionality, or to refactor the function to deliver increased performance. It is for this reason—the ease of access to the underlying code— that user-defined functions tend to be undocumented through external specifications. Many SAS practitioners instead rely on inline comments, as demonstrated in Program 1.3.

Function Invocation

The invocation is the third component of every function. It comprises the code that calls (invokes) the function. ISO defines an *invocation* as "the mapping of a parallel initiation of activities of an integral activity group that perform a distinct function and return to the initiating activity" (International Organization for Standarization 2017). More specifically, ISO defines a (function) *call* as "a transfer of control from one software module to another, usually with the implication that control will be returned to the calling module" (International Organization for Standarization 2017). In addition to transferring program control, the invocation also typically transfers arguments that are bound to parameters, as discussed later in this chapter.

SAS user-defined functions and subroutines arguably are most often called from the DATA step. When SAS encounters a function in a DATA step, in the blink of an eye, it transfers program control to the function, and when the function terminates, returns program control to the DATA step. However, numerous SAS procedures (and some SAS statements and SAS macro statements) also support calling functions. Some invocation methods limit functionality and other invocation methods expand functionality. Thus, function design will, in part, be driven by not only the function's intended functionality, but also the method(s) through which the function is intended to be invoked.

Functions, unlike subroutines, always return a value. For this reason, function calls but not subroutine calls often initialize variables through direct assignment within the DATA step. For example, as demonstrated in Program 1.4, the following statements call the LOWCASE built-in function and the TINY user-defined function, respectively. LOWCASE initializes Phrase1 to the LOWCASE return value, and TINY initializes Phrase2 to the TINY return value:

```
phrase1 = lowcase(phrase);
phrase2 = tiny(phrase);
```

Functions, unlike subroutines, can be called from the SQL procedure. For example, Program 1.8 demonstrates comparable SQL code that creates the equivalent Phrase1 and Phrase2 variables by calling LOWCASE and TINY, respectively.

Program 1.8: Calling Built-in and User-Defined Functions from PROC SQL
```
data text;
   phrase = 'SAS Applications Programming: A Gentle Introduction';
run;
proc sql noprint;
   create table lowered as
      select lowcase(phrase) as phrase1,
         tiny(phrase) as phrase2
            from text;
quit;
```

Note that user-defined functions that declare one or more array parameters (introduced in Chapter 3) cannot be called from the SQL procedure. This limitation occurs because a SAS array cannot first be declared in the SQL procedure prior to the function call as is required when these user-defined functions are called in a DATA step. Also note that user-defined *subroutines* cannot be called from the SQL procedure because the CALL statement required by subroutine invocations cannot be accommodated.

Functions, unlike subroutines, can also be called using the WHERE data set option, which can juxtapose a data set name within the DATA step or a SAS procedure. For example, in Program 1.9, the first DATA step creates two observations—the value of Phrase is title case in the first observation and lowercase in the second observation. Subsequently, the WHERE option is used in the SET statement of the DATA step and in the PRINT procedure, respectively, to select and print only the second observation.

Program 1.9: Calling User-Defined Functions Using the WHERE Data Set Option
```
data texts;
   phrase = 'SAS Applications Programming: A Gentle Introduction'; output;
   phrase = 'sas applications programming: a gentle introduction'; output;
run;

data select_lowered;
   set texts (where=(phrase=tiny(phrase)));
   put phrase=;
run;

proc print data=texts (where=(phrase=tiny(phrase)));
run;
```

In both usages, the WHERE clause evaluates that the second observation is already lowercase and selects only that observation.

As previously demonstrated, the %SYSFUNC macro function can also call a built-in or user-defined function. In the following statements, %SYSFUNC calls TINY, converts &PHRASE to lowercase, and prints the TINY return value to the log:

```
%let phrase = SAS Applications Programming: A Gentle Introduction;
%put %sysfunc(tiny(&phrase));
```

Function calls, unlike subroutine calls, can be parenthetically nested inside of other function calls or subroutine calls, with the innermost expression executing first. For example, the following DATA step statement first converts Phrase to lowercase, then converts Phrase to uppercase, after which Phrase_upper is initialized to the uppercase representation of Phrase:

```
phrase_upper = upcase(lowcase(phrase));
```

Similarly, the %SYSFUNC macro function can be parenthetically nested inside of other %SYSFUNC calls, %SYSCALL calls, or macro function calls. For example, the following statements nest the TINY function call (executed via %SYSFUNC) inside the %LENGTH macro function call:

```
%let phrase = SAS Applications Programming: A Gentle Introduction;
%put %length(%sysfunc(tiny(&phrase)));
```

TINY first lowers the case of &PHRASE, after which %LENGTH evaluates the length of the TINY return value. Note that macro functions like %LENGTH do not require the %SYSFUNC wrapper, whereas DATA step functions like LOWCASE or TINY do require %SYSFUNC when called using the SAS macro language.

For this reason, when DATA step functions are nested inside of each other and called using the SAS macro language, each function call must be wrapped in a separate instance of %SYSFUNC. For example, note the two instances of %SYSFUNC in the following %PUT statement, in which LOWCASE is first called to lower the case of &PHRASE, after which UPCASE is called to raise the case of &PHRASE:

```
%let phrase = SAS Applications Programming: A Gentle Introduction;
%put %sysfunc(upcase(%sysfunc(lowcase(&phrase))));
```

Subroutines, on the other hand, do not return a value, so subroutine calls cannot initialize a variable through direct assignment. Neither can subroutines be used in SAS expressions.

Subroutine calls, unlike function calls, also must be prefaced by the CALL statement. For this reason, subroutine calls cannot be nested inside of function calls or other subroutine calls in either DATA step statements or the SAS macro language. For example, the following DATA step statement calls the SORTC built-in subroutine to sort two variables (Var1 and Var2) horizontally:

```
call sortc(var1, var2);
```

Similarly, when called from the SAS macro language, subroutine calls must include the %SYSCALL macro statement. Note that SAS macro variables referenced in a %SYSCALL statement must be declared prior to usage. For example, the following code declares and initializes &VAR1 and &VAR2, after which %SYSCALL calls the SORTC built-in subroutine to reorder the macro variables:

```
%global var1 var2;
%let var1 = bananas;
%let var2 = apples;
%syscall sortc(var1, var2);
%put &=var1 &=var2;
```

The log demonstrates that the values of &VAR1 and &VAR2 have been switched—that is, alphabetized by SORTC:

```
VAR1=apples VAR2=bananas
```

Both functions and subroutines can be called from the COMPUTE block of the REPORT procedure, as demonstrated in Chapter 9. User-defined functions, as opposed to subroutines, can also be called from the FORMAT procedure by specifying the function name in the OTHER option, as also demonstrated in Chapter 9.

Finally, user-defined functions and subroutines can be called through, in addition to the preceding methods, an ever-increasing number of procedures, many of which leverage SAS Viya, SAS Cloud Analytic Services (CAS), and SAS LASR Analytic Server. Although not discussed in this text, the following procedures support various aspects of FCMP functionality and should be further explored:

- PROC CALIS
- PROC DS2
- PROC FORMAT
- PROC GA
- PROC GENMOD
- PROC GLIMMIX
- PROC IML
- PROC OPTMODEL
- PROC PHREG
- PROC MCMC
- PROC MODEL
- PROC MONTE
- PROC NLIN
- PROC NLMIXED
- PROC NLP
- PROC OPTMODEL
- PROC OPTLSO
- PROC QUANTREG

- SAS Risk Dimensions procedures
- PROC SEVERITY
- PROC SIMILARITY
- PROC SURVEYPHREG
- PROC SVM
- PROC TMODEL
- PROC TRANASSIGN
- PROC VARMAX

(See also, https://documentation.sas.com/doc/en/pgmsascdc/9.4_3.5/proc/n0pio2crltpr35n1ny010z rfbvc9.htm.)

Function Nomenclature

The preceding introduction to software quality and performance characteristics conveyed the importance of leveraging user-defined functions in software design, as well as how functions can improve specific aspects of software quality. But first, an introduction to quality-related nomenclature was required so that software quality characteristics could be defined and discussed. Similarly, any introduction to user-defined functions and function design is bolstered by defining programming-language-agnostic, function-related nomenclature.

The remainder of this chapter introduces function-related concepts. Calling modules, callable modules, and called modules are defined and differentiated, as are three types of SAS callable software modules—procedures, functions, and subroutines. Parameters and arguments are defined and differentiated, which aid in communicating *to* a function call, as are return values and return codes, which aid in communicating *from* a function call. Finally, built-in and user-defined functions are contrasted.

Calling Module, Callable Module, and Called Module

As defined previously, an *invocation* or *call* temporarily transfers program control—but transfers *from what*, and transfers *to what*? The *calling module* or *calling program* represents the code in which a function call occurs. For this reason, the calling module is sometimes referenced as the *parent*. For example, when the TINY function is called from the DATA step in Program 1.4, the DATA step is the calling module. And when TINY is called from the SQL procedure in Program 1.8, the SQL procedure is the calling module. The calling module transfers not only program control but also arguments (variable inputs) to the called module, and this communication is essential in enabling function flexibility.

A *callable module*, conversely, is a module executed by invoking its name. All functions and subroutines are callable modules. When a specific callable module is called, it is sometimes referenced as the *called module* to distinguish that it was, in fact, called—rather than merely having the capability to be called. SAS built-in procedures, functions, and subroutines also represent callable modules, as they are always invoked by calling their names.

To promote software modularity, a callable module nearly always should be saved as a separate program file apart from the calling module(s). Yes, during initial development, debugging, and testing of user-defined functions, it is common to both create and call a function in the same program file. However, production software typically demands that called and calling modules be separated so that they can be independently maintained. For example, once a user-defined function has been perfected and is in production, myriad programs and processes might separately use and reuse that same function, and each of those calling modules should *reference*—yet never *repeat*—that function's implementation (that is, its definition within the FCMP procedure).

Functions Versus Procedures

Procedures are commonplace within Base SAS. We use them to sort data sets (PROC SORT), analyze data (PROC MEANS), generate reports (PROC REPORT), and for myriad other actions. Procedures typically operate on entire data sets by evaluating, transforming, or representing those data. ISO defines a *procedure* as "a routine that does not return a value" (International Organization for Standardization and International Electrotechnical Commission 2012). Rather than returning a value, as a function does, a procedure typically generates output that describes a data object or modifies one or more data objects such as SAS data sets.

For example, the DATA step in Program 1.10 creates an unordered list of random numbers that ranges from 0 to 99, after which the SORT procedure orders these observations in ascending order.

Program 1.10: SORT Procedure to Order 100 Observations

```
data long (drop=i);
   length num 8;
   call streaminit(123);
   do i = 1 to 100;
      num = int(rand('uniform')*100);
      output;
      end;
run;

proc sort data=long out=long_sorted;
   by num;
run;
```

Whereas most SAS procedures operate on entire data sets, functions and subroutines typically operate on or within one observation. For example, the SORT *function* orders variables within an observation, whereas the SORT *procedure* orders observations within a data set. For this reason, the SORT function is sometimes anecdotally referred to as a *horizontal sort*, and the SORT procedure as a *vertical sort*.

Program 1.11 initializes 100 variables (Num1 to Num100) to random integers between 0 and 99, after which the SORT function subsequently reorders these values.

Program 1.11: SORT Function Orders 100 Values

```
data short (drop=rc);
   array num 8 num1 - num100;
   call streaminit(123);
   do over num;
      num = int(rand('uniform')*100);
      end;
   rc = sort(of num[*]);
run;
```

The SORT function generates a return code that reflects the completion status of the function—1 for success or 0 for failure. In this example, the RC variable is initialized but is unused, as it is unlikely that SORT will fail.

Despite the oversimplified distinction that *procedures operate on data sets,* whereas *functions operate on observations*, exceptions to this rule abound. As discussed, the OPEN built-in function opens a read-only stream to an entire data set, and CLOSE similarly closes the stream. The RUN_ MACRO and RUN_SASFILE built-in functions, both of which are supported only within the FCMP procedure, also flout this rule. RUN_MACRO, for example, enables a SAS macro, DATA step, or SAS procedure to execute from inside a user-defined function. That is, FCMP enables mind-bending acrobatics such as DATA steps that run inside other DATA steps, as showcased in Chapters 5 and 6!

Functions Versus Subroutines

Having defined *functions* (in part) as callable software modules that "return a single value," let's upend the applecart and introduce *subroutines*—another callable software component and kissing cousin of functions. Throughout SAS literature and documentation, subroutines are rather confusingly referred to as *functions*, *routines, CALL routines, call subroutines, subroutine procedures*, and *subprograms*. Within SAS documentation, subroutines are sometimes defined as a SAS component wholly apart from functions, and at other times, a subordinate construct and class of function. For example, SAS documentation defines a *subroutine* as "a special type of function where return values are optional" (SAS Institute Inc. 2020). This SAS documentation furthermore differentiates that "functions and CALL routines have the same form, except CALL routines do not return a value, and CALL routines can modify their parameters." All of this ambiguity requires a bit more precision.

To be clear, both functions and subroutines are callable software modules, and the only distinction lies in that functions always return a value and subroutines never return a value. It is because of this return value that functions can initialize a variable through direct assignment, whereas subroutines cannot. However, both functions and subroutines can modify arguments passed to them when those arguments are specified by the OUTARGS statement, as discussed in Chapter 2.

Consider two built-in callable modules—the SORT function and the SORT subroutine (sometimes referred to as *CALL SORT*). Each module provides similar functionality, although through different methods, as demonstrated in Program 1.12.

Program 1.12: Comparison of SORT Function and SORT Subroutine

```
data sorted (drop=rc);
   a = 5;
   b = 15;
   c = 10;
   call sort(a, b, c);
   put a= b= c=;
   x = 5;
   y = 15;
   z = 10;
   rc = sort(x, y, z);
   put x= y= z=;
run;
```

The log demonstrates that both the A-B-C and the X-Y-Z series have been sorted, the values of B and C have been exchanged, and the values of Y and Z have been exchanged:

```
a=5 b=10 c=15
x=5 y=10 z=15
```

The SORT *function* generates a return code whose value is initialized to RC, whereas the SORT *subroutine* must be preceded by the CALL statement and does not generate a return value or return code. The use of the CALL statement to *call* subroutines explains why subroutines are commonly referred to as *CALL routines*. However, all functions, subroutines, and procedures are *called*, which complicates this anecdotal usage.

Within this text, *functions* are consistently defined as "callable modules that return a value," and *subroutines* as "callable modules that do *not* return a value." However, although subroutines do not return a value, they are nevertheless expert communicators and capable of modifying one or more variables in the calling program. For example, as demonstrated in Program 1.12, the SORT subroutine modifies the B and C variables. Thus, subroutines can modify variables in the calling program *indirectly*—that is, through *indirect assignment*—whereas a function can modify a single variable through *direct assignment*, and multiple variables through *indirect assignment*. The OUTARGS statement enables indirect assignment in both user-defined functions and subroutines.

Parameters Versus Arguments

One of the primary jobs of function calls is to pass arguments (inputs) from the calling program to the called module. It is, after all, the variability of these inputs that spawns variability in the return value, output, or other outcome of the function. Some functions do not require input, as demonstrated in Chapter 2, although these use cases are uncommon.

Each *argument* passed to a function must first be declared inside the function as a *parameter*, which defines the data type (character versus numeric), dimensionality (scalar versus array), length, and other attributes. ISO defines an *argument* as a "constant, variable, or expression used in a call to a software module to specify data or program elements to be passed to that module" (International Organization for Standarization 2017). ISO contrasts a *parameter* as a "constant, variable, or expression that is used to pass values between software modules" (International Organization for Standarization 2017). In some literature and programming languages, parameters are referred to as *formal parameters*, and arguments are referred to as *actual parameters*.

These terms—parameter and argument—are often conflated or used interchangeably, and their usage can also differ among programming languages. Within this text, however, *parameters* denote the variables that are declared within a function, and *arguments* denote the corresponding values passed during a function call. That is, parameters exist within a function's implementation (or definition), and arguments exist within the function's invocation (or call). Stated another way, all parameters have local scope inside a function, excepting those parameters specified by the OUTARGS statement, which have global scope (and are thus accessible to the calling program). This distinction is explained in the "Declaring Parameters" section of Chapter 2.

Return Values Versus Return Codes

Whereas parameters and arguments facilitate communication *to* a callable module, including both functions and subroutines, return values and return codes communicate *from* functions (but not subroutines) to the calling program. The distinction between *return values* and *return codes* is subtle yet important, as this nomenclature can differentiate how function results are used by software. Both return values and return codes represent the results generated by functions, but return codes are conceptualized as a specific type of return value. ISO defines a *return value* as the "value assigned to a parameter by a called module for access by the calling module" (International Organization for Standarization 2017).

Within the FCMP procedure, the RETURN statement returns a value to the calling program. Built-in SAS functions operate similarly and return a single return value. For example, when the LOWCASE function lowers the case of a character variable or value, the lowercase text represents the return value.

Return codes, on the other hand, are a subset of return values that communicate completion status or other performance metrics for a called module. Thus, return values are sometimes said to convey *data* from a function, whereas return codes convey *metadata*. ISO defines a *return code* as a "code used to influence the execution of a calling module following a return from a called module" (International Organization for Standarization 2017). Because return codes can describe the success or failure of a function's execution, they are commonly used in exception handling routines that detect and handle anomalous or adverse events or states.

For example, Program 1.13 uses the OPEN function to open the File_missing data set. Because the data set does not exist, OPEN returns a *return value* of 0. However, this return value is also a *return code* because it reflects the failed state of the OPEN invocation. By convention, the variable initialized by the OPEN return code is named DSID (data set ID).

Program 1.13: Exception Handling Dynamically Routes Program Flow Based on DSID Return Code

```
data _null_;
   dsid = open('file_missing');
   if dsid > 0 then do;
      * additional code to interact with opened data set;
      sorted = attrc(dsid, 'sortedby');
      put sorted=;
      end;
   else put 'file cannot be opened';
run;
```

After DSID is initialized to the return code of 0, DSID is subsequently evaluated by the IF statement. Because the exception (that is, the missing data set) is programmatically detected, the IF block does not execute. This exception handling, facilitated by the return code of the OPEN function, ensures that subsequent actions that would require an open file (such as the ATTRC function, to retrieve the list of variables by which a data set is sorted) are not executed. Had OPEN succeeded, DSID would have been initialized to a positive integer starting with 1, and the list of sort variables (had the data set been sorted) would have been printed to the log.

In SAS literature, it is commonplace to see return codes that are generated, yet never evaluated, such as when hash methods like DEFINEKEY or DEFINEDATA initialize return codes. However, where risk exists that a function like OPEN could fail, exception handling routines are favored, and the programmatic evaluation of return codes is considered a best practice.

Built-in Functions Versus User-Defined Functions

Built-in functions are provided as part of a software application or programming language and comprise the building blocks with which developers can engineer more complex functionality. As a language matures and expands over time, the quantity and variety of built-in functions increase as new functionality is incorporated.

For example, SAS 9.4M6 introduced numerous "Git" functions such as GITFN_COMMIT, GITFN_PULL, and GITFN_PUSH for use with Git repositories like GitHub. The incorporation of these built-in functions into Base SAS *extends* the SAS programming language by increasing its out-of-the-box capabilities. The *SAS® 9.4 Functions and CALL Routines: Reference, Fifth Edition* describes hundreds of built-in functions and subroutines that span a variety of categories, including mathematical, statistical, character, date and time, file input/output (I/O), and other areas (SAS Institute Inc. 2022).

SAS built-in functions are written in C, a third-generation language (3GL) with more direct access to memory operations and other lower-level system functionality. Built-in functions are also tested rigorously to ensure they are robust to the various ways that they might be used or misused and to optimize their performance and efficiency. Finally, SAS built-in functions are documented thoroughly through SAS technical specifications that describe their syntax, usage, and caveats. Thus, when first conceptualizing whether to design a user-defined function in any language, always first exhaust language documentation to ensure that a sufficient built-in function does not already perform the needed functionality.

User-defined functions, conversely, are created by users—SAS practitioners like you and me who build SAS software. SAS user-defined functions and subroutines are defined using the FCMP procedure and can be invoked through both the SAS language and the SAS macro language. User-defined functions, like their built-in counterparts, similarly extend a programming language by defining functionality not otherwise available through built-in functions. In doing so, user-defined functions increase the quality of not only software but also the software development environment, with the objectives of reusability and maintainability making the work of SAS practitioners more productive and pleasant.

As developers shift from being function *users* to becoming function *creators*, we can build better functions by modeling the best practices evinced by built-in functions, including not only functionality but also function performance, communication, and documentation. Yes, when you're tasked to design a function that transforms Fahrenheit to Celsius, you must prioritize functionality—getting the calculation right. However, also important is how the function uses resources, and whether it does so smartly and efficiently. Communication is also key, especially how the function should alert or respond to missing, atypical, or invalid data, and where and how notes, warnings, or runtime errors should be conveyed to users. Documentation, too, should succinctly describe to end users how a user-defined function should be called, and perhaps how it should not. Each of these design objectives can be pursued by observing and mimicking built-in functions and their behavior.

Conclusion

This chapter introduced functions and subroutines within the SAS language, including both SAS built-in functions and user-defined functions built using the FCMP procedure. With functions defined, the business case was made for why user-defined functions should be incorporated into SAS software, and how user-defined functions can facilitate and improve specific characteristics of software quality, such as maintainability, modularity, reusability, readability, and integrity. Function components were defined and demonstrated, including the specification, implementation, and invocation. Various methods of calling user-defined functions and subroutines were discussed. Finally, functional nomenclature was introduced, such as the distinction among calling, callable, and called modules; among procedures, functions, and subroutines; between parameters and arguments; and between return values and return codes.

Chapter 2: Basic FCMP Syntax

Chapter 1 introduced functions, including SAS user-defined functions and subroutines—the callable, reusable software modules that are built using the FCMP procedure. As was demonstrated and described, in most cases, equivalent functionality can be achieved in the DATA step, foregoing the need to build a function—so why the added complexity of learning FCMP? Because user-defined functions can be flexibly configured and reused, which facilitates not only higher-quality software but also a higher-quality software development environment and experience.

With these objectives in mind, this chapter introduces FCMP syntax and components that facilitate building flexible, configurable, reusable functions. Simply stated, functions deliver dynamic functionality through flexible input specified at runtime. This flexibility enables functions to operate in diverse environments, for diverse purposes, and to meet the needs and requirements of diverse users more readily than equivalent hardcoded statements.

SAS user-defined functions include the following high-level components, which comprise the structure of this chapter:

- FCMP wrapper – All functions and subroutines are declared inside the FCMP procedure, which begins with the PROC FCMP statement, and concludes with the QUIT statement.
- Function declaration and signature – The function is *declared* (that is, named), and the signature declares all parameters, and includes parameter name, position, object type, data type, dimensionality, and call method. In addition, the signature specifies the data type and dimensionality of a function's return value.
- Internal functionality – DATA step statements perform the function's functionality, effectively transforming arguments passed to the function into the function's return value (or other output or outcome).
- External communication – All functions return a return value to the calling module, and both functions and subroutines can modify one or more arguments using the OUTARGS statement.

PROC FCMP Wrapper

The FCMP procedure is initiated by the PROC FCMP statement, which can include one or more options. All function and subroutine definitions occur after the PROC FCMP statement. Multiple functions and/or subroutines can be defined in a single FCMP procedure using the FUNCTION and/or SUBROUTINE statements, respectively. Like most SAS procedures, FCMP can be terminated with a RUN statement. However, if an FCMP procedure contains a compilation error, a QUIT statement will be required to terminate the aborted procedure. For this reason, and as described and demonstrated subsequently, the QUIT statement is recommended to terminate the FCMP procedure.

Where an FCMP procedure defines one or more functions, it is important to note that executing the procedure does not run these functions. Rather, executing the FCMP procedure compiles the functions so that they can be called subsequently from a calling module (like a separate DATA step). However, most DATA step statements can be executed *directly* inside the FCMP wrapper. The statements are not enclosed within a function or subroutine definition, and these statements are run when the FCMP procedure is executed. The downside of these "direct" statements, which are not enclosed in a function or subroutine, is that they are neither callable nor reusable. For this reason, although this functionality is demonstrated, nearly all examples in this text demonstrate enclosing DATA step statements inside function and subroutine definitions.

PROC FCMP Statement

Program 2.1 demonstrates a basic FCMP wrapper in which the RETURN_TODAY function is defined. The FUNCTION statement declares the user-defined function, the ENDFUNC statement terminates the function's definition, and the QUIT statement terminates the FCMP procedure. All code between and including the FUNCTION and ENDFUNC statements is considered to be the function's *implementation* or definition, as discussed in Chapter 1.

Program 2.1: RETURN_TODAY Function Successfully Compiled
```
proc fcmp;
   function return_today();
      return(today());
      endfunc;
quit;
```

When the FCMP procedure executes, it compiles the RETURN_TODAY function. However, when an attempt is made to call RETURN_TODAY, as shown in Program 2.2, the function call fails because RETURN_TODAY was not saved when it was compiled.

Program 2.2: RETURN_TODAY Function Unsuccessfully Called
```
data test;
   rc=return_today();
   put rc= mmddyy10.;
run;
```

The log states that RETURN_TODAY could not be found:

```
175   data test;
176      rc=return_today();
             ------------
             68
ERROR 68-185: The function RETURN_TODAY is unknown, or cannot be accessed.

177      put rc=;
178   run;
NOTE: The SAS System stopped processing this step because of errors.
```

At issue is the fact that RETURN_TODAY was *compiled* yet not *saved* for later reuse. One method to overcome this failure is to define and call a user-defined function in the same FCMP procedure.

For example, Program 2.3 modifies the FCMP procedure to not only define RETURN_TODAY but also call it and initialize RC to the function's return value. When both a function's definition (*implementation*) and call (*invocation*) are encapsulated inside the same FCMP procedure, the function does not need to be saved, so RETURN_TODAY is successful, and it prints the current date.

Program 2.3: RETURN_TODAY Function Compiled and Called

```
proc fcmp;
   function return_today();
      file log;
      return(today());
      endfunc;
   rc = return_today();
   put rc= mmddyy10.;
quit;
```

The function compiles and executes, but is not reusable because it is compiled, called, and removed from memory when FCMP terminates. These fly-by-night functions can be useful when initially designing, testing, and debugging user-defined functions; however, they are not the focus of this text. Rather, placing functionality inside of functions improves the quality of software through increased modularity and reuse. Notwithstanding, some FCMP functionality is viable only inside of FCMP procedures, and not the DATA step. For example, a function called from the FCMP procedure can specify the package name of the function, and a function called from the FCMP procedure can pass a dictionary component object as a parameter—neither of these capabilities are available when calling a user-defined function from the DATA step, SQL procedure, or other methods. Thus, a few examples in this text do highlight user-defined functions that must be both compiled in and called from the FCMP procedure.

PROC FCMP OUTLIB Option

The OUTLIB option instructs SAS to save all functions and subroutines defined in an instance of the FCMP procedure. That is, OUTLIB singularly facilitates function reusability.

The OUTLIB option accepts a single argument that includes a three-level name, referencing the SAS library, data set, and package in which the compiled function should be saved. Although familiar with SAS libraries and data sets, SAS practitioners might be unfamiliar with *packages*, as operationalized within Base SAS. Packages effectively apply a label to the source code data set in which compiled FCMP source code is saved. When called *only* from the FCMP procedure, a function's package can optionally be specified, which can be useful when identically named functions have been saved. Unfortunately, no other calling module (for example, the DATA step or SQL procedure) enables a function call to denote a package name, so the most recently compiled package is called by default.

Package names follow SAS variable-naming conventions and must begin with a letter or underscore symbol; subsequent characters can be letters, numbers, or underscore symbols, and package names cannot exceed 32 characters in length.

For example, Program 2.4 modifies Program 2.1 by adding the OUTLIB option to specify that the RETURN_TODAY function should be saved to the WORK library, Funcs data set, and DT package. Note that the CMPLIB system option always must point to the library and data set in which user-defined functions are saved, which enables SAS to locate user-defined functions.

Program 2.4: Specifying the OUTLIB Option to Save a Function
```
proc fcmp outlib=work.funcs.dt;
   function return_today();
       return(today());
       endfunc;
quit;

options cmplib=work.funcs;

data test;
   rc = return_today();
   put rc= mmddyy10.;
run;
```

The FCMP procedure executes and compiles the RETURN_TODAY function, saving it to the WORK. Funcs data set, and the DATA step subsequently calls RETURN_TODAY and prints today's date. Note that Programs 2.3 and 2.4 are functionally equivalent; however, Program 2.4 declares a reusable function that can be called in the future to deliver repeated, reliable functionality. It is for this reason that functions and subroutines are typically saved using the OUTLIB option, and why this text focuses exclusively on reusable functions and subroutines.

Within this text, the WORK library is consistently referenced as the location where source code for all functions and subroutines is maintained. However, real-world reliance on reusable functions requires that functions persist across SAS sessions, rather than being obliterated when the SAS application terminates, and that all users have access to the persistent library where functions are saved. Thus, in practice, only during development and testing should the developer of a user-defined function save source code in the WORK library. And once a user-defined function is in production, the OUTLIB option should reference a persistent SAS library and data set to which all end users have permissions to access. In reusing the function, these end users do not need to recompile the function by rerunning the FCMP procedure. They only need to use the CMPLIB option to reference the source code data set in which the source code is maintained.

Although it is never useful to do so, you can peel back the covers and inspect the compiled RETURN_TODAY function by opening the WORK.Funcs data set. Table 2.1 demonstrates the first few columns of this data set, which notably list the package name (DT) and function name (RETURN_TODAY) in the _Key_ variable (Model Key). Note that SAS Institute developers recommend NEVER directly modifying a data set containing FCMP function definitions, as this can corrupt the data set and the functions defined within. In other words, even if you are a fan of sausage...probably best not to visit the sausage factory to learn how the meat gets made! Just accept that it's delicious and move on with your life!

As demonstrated in Table 2.2, scrolling to the right of the WORK.Funcs data set, amid the gibberish, some functionality is decipherable, such as the function's reliance on the built-in TODAY function to retrieve the current date.

If this arcane level of detail still reveals too much information about your user-defined function, the ENCRYPT option will conceal the Value variable (XML Value), rendering the source code unreadable, as demonstrated later in this chapter.

Note that the SAS library specified in the OUTLIB option must have been previously assigned. For example, Program 2.5 fails if the MYLIB library has not been assigned or is inaccessible.

Table 2.1: Pointlessly Inspecting a Function's Source Code

	Model Key	Model Owner	Record Sequence	Record Type	Record SubType
1	DT	CMP	0	Header	Package
2	F.DT.RETURN_TODAY	CMP	0	Prototype	FCmp
3	F.DT.RETURN_TODAY	CMP	1	Header	Function
4	F.DT.RETURN_TODAY	CMP	2	Statement Source	Executable
5	F.DT.RETURN_TODAY	CMP	3	Statement Source	Executable
6	F.DT.RETURN_TODAY	CMP	4	Statement Source	Executable
7	F.DT.RETURN_TODAY	CMP	5	Symbol	

Table 2.2: Further Pointlessly Inspecting a Function's Source Code

	Record SubType	Record Name	Continue	Numeric Value	Encoded	XML Value
1	Package		0			`<L n="Header"><S n="Version"><![CDATA[1.1]]></S><N n="Datetime">.1983284344.605</N><S n="DatetimeStr"><![CDATA[05NOV22.1 n="SubType"><![CDATA[Package]]></S n="Obfuscate">0</N></L>`
2	FCmp	dt	0			`<L n="Prototype"><S n="Name"><![CDATA[return_today]]></ n="Group"><![CDATA[]]></S><N n="MaxLag">0</N><N n="Flag0">0</N><N n="Flag1">128</N><S n="ReturnType"><![CDATA[n]]></S><N n="RetSubType">1</N><N n="ReturnSize">8</N><L n="ArgList"></L></L>`
3	Function		0			`<L n="Header"><S n="Version"><![CDATA[1.1]]></S><N n="Datetime">.1983284344.621</N><S n="DatetimeStr"><![CDATA[05NOV22.1 n="SubType"><![CDATA[Function]]></S n="Obfuscate">0</N><S n="Package"><![CDATA[dt]]></S></L>`
4	Executable	FUNCTION	0	65	.	function return_today();
5	Executable	RETURN	0	1	.	return(today());
6	Executable	ENDFUNC	0	14	.	endfunc;

Program 2.5: Specifying an OUTLIB Library That Does Not Exist

```
proc fcmp outlib=mylib.funcs.dt;
   function yesterday();
      return(today()-1);
      endfunc;
quit;
```

The log demonstrates this failure:

```
ERROR: Libref MYLIB is not assigned.
ERROR: Cannot open data set mylib.funcs for Write access because it is
currently opened or already exists as a standard data set.
WARNING: The following functions will NOT be saved:
   yesterday
```

Finally, you might have noted the peculiarity that the OUTLIB option requires a three-level name comprising the library, data set, and package, whereas the CMPLIB SAS system option requires only a two-level name comprising the library and data set. Moreover, as shown in Program 2.4, when a function is called from the DATA step, there is no opportunity to specify its package (like DT). For this reason, caution must be exercised when naming a function when an identically named user-defined function already exists.

For example, Program 2.6 again defines the RETURN_TODAY function, but inside a new package, CHAR. The YYMMDDN8 format (for example, 19751021 corresponding to Oct 21, 1975) is commonly used as a file-naming convention, so this function might be used to append the current date to a filename, which would require the date to be formatted as a character value.

Program 2.6: Duplicating a Function Name within a Source Code Data Set

```
proc fcmp outlib=work.funcs.char;
   function return_today() $;
      return(put(today(),yymmddn8.));
      endfunc;
quit;
```

When the FCMP procedure executes and compiles RETURN_TODAY, it alerts that a function already exists with the same name and that the newly defined function in the CHAR package will be used by default:

```
proc fcmp outlib=work.funcs.dt_time;
   function return_today() $;
WARNING: Function 'return_today' was defined in a previous package. Function
'return_today' as defined in the current program will be used as default
when the package is not specified.
   return(put(today(),yymmddn8.));
   endfunc;
quit;
```

Viewing the WORK.Funcs source code data set (not shown) demonstrates that a second function has been added. The _Key_ variable now defines both F.DT.RETURN_TODAY within the DT package and F.CHAR.RETURN_TODAY within the CHAR package.

The new function, defined in the CHAR package, can be called using %SYSFUNC:

```
%put %sysfunc(return_today());
```

Note that because identically named functions exist within the same source code data set, although in different packages, a warning is again displayed in the SAS log that the most recently defined function (that is, the one defined in the CHAR package) will be used:

```
%put %sysfunc(return_today());
WARNING: Function 'return_today' was defined in a previous package. 'return_
today' in current package CHAR will be used as default when the package
name is not specified.
20221105
```

However, if Program 2.4 is subsequently rerun, which recompiles RETURN_TODAY in the DT package, the DT package again takes precedence over the CHAR package when RETURN_TODAY is called. Executing the %PUT statement a second time demonstrates that the default package has reverted to DT, which is observable because the DT package returns a numeric representation of the date rather than a character value:

```
%put %sysfunc(return_today());
WARNING: Function 'return_today' was defined in a previous package. 'return_
today' in current package DT will be used as default when the package name
is not specified.
22954
```

Clearly, you do not want to rely on the order of function compilation to direct which of several identically named functions (defined in the same source code data set) should be used by default! This demonstrates why identically named functions should not be declared when they are intended to be called from the DATA step.

However, function calls *from* the FCMP procedure (as well as within some elements of SAS Viya) *can* specify the package name, and this ability to differentiate functions can be beneficial. For example, Program 2.7 now calls RETURN_TODAY from the FCMP procedure. It prefaces the function name with the DT package when a numeric return value is required and the CHAR package when a character return value is required.

Program 2.7: Specifying Package During Function Call

```
proc fcmp;
   file log;
   length tomorrow 8;
   format tomorrow mmddyy8.;
   tomorrow = dt.return_today() + 1;               # calling DT package;
   filename = 'my_file_' || char.return_today();   # calling CHAR package;
   put tomorrow=;
   put filename=;
quit;
```

The log demonstrates that the two functions (DT.RETURN_TODAY and CHAR.RETURN_TODAY) were separately called:

```
138   proc fcmp;
139      file log;
140      length tomorrow 8;
141      format tomorrow mmddyy8.;
142      tomorrow = dt.return_today() + 1;
143      filename = 'my_file_' || char.return_today();
144      put tomorrow=;
145      put filename=;
146   quit;

tomorrow=08/31/23
filename=my_file_20230830
```

Despite the utility of being able to differentiate identically named functions by their respective package names, it must be restated that this functionality is limited to function calls inside the FCMP procedure and within areas of SAS Viya. For this reason, and especially when designing functions to be called from the DATA step, SQL procedure, FORMAT procedure, REPORT procedure, %SYSFUNC statement, and %SYSCALL statement, user-defined function names *should not be reused*—even when saved in separate packages.

Configuring the CMPLIB System Option

As demonstrated, it is inadvisable to define identically named functions that will be called from the DATA step. However, if requirements dictate a clear business need, a reliable method does exist, and identically named functions can be placed in separate source code data sets.

For example, consider a SAS environment in which user-defined functions under development are saved in the SAS_DEV.Funcs source code data set, and functions in production are saved in the SAS_PROD.Funcs source code data set. SAS practitioners can maintain two versions of identically named functions, and by modifying the CMPLIB system option, reliably specify which "environment" should be selected. When developing and testing user-defined functions, users can point CMPLIB to the development source code data set, and when calling user-defined functions from the production environment, users can point CMPLIB to the production source code data set.

Program 2.8 declares two more instances of the RETURN_TODAY function within both the SAS_PROD.Funcs and SAS_DEV_Funcs data sets. Two LIBNAME statements first declare these libraries, and the DLCREATEDIR system option builds the corresponding folders (c:\sas_prod\ and c:\sas_dev\) if they do not already exist.

Program 2.8: Duplicating a Function Name within Separate Source Code Data Sets
```
option dlcreatedir;
libname sas_prod "c:\sas_prod";
libname sas_dev "c:\sas_dev";

proc fcmp outlib=sas_prod.funcs.dt;
   function return_today();
      return(today());
      endfunc;
quit;

proc fcmp outlib=sas_dev.funcs.char;
   function return_today() $;
      return(put(today(),yymmddn8.));
      endfunc;
quit;
```

Yet, when the two functions are compiled, neither is selected as the default RETURN_TODAY function because the CMPLIB option continues to reference only the WORK.Funcs source code data set. Thus, despite RETURN_TODAY now being defined in both SAS_PROD.Funcs.CHAR and SAS_DEV.Funcs.DT, neither of these instances is accessible because neither is referenced by CMPLIB.

Thus, a SAS practitioner desiring to run a specific instance of RETURN_TODAY (by default) need only modify the CMPLIB option to reference its source code data set. The following code unambiguously runs the DT.RETURN_TODAY function maintained within SAS_PROD.Funcs, and generates a numeric return value:

```
options cmplib=sas_prod.funcs;
%put %sysfunc(return_today());
```

And the following code unambiguously runs the separate CHAR.RETURN_TODAY function maintained within SAS_DEV.Funcs, and generates a character return value:

```
options cmplib=sas_dev.funcs;
%put %sysfunc(return_today());
```

The log demonstrates the two function calls:

```
174   options cmplib=sas_prod.funcs;
175   %put %sysfunc(return_today());
23252
176
177   options cmplib=sas_dev.funcs;
178   %put %sysfunc(return_today());
20230830
```

Neither invocation of RETURN_TODAY now results in notes about "default packages" because each source code data set no longer contains duplicate function names. Thus, each source code data set contains only uniquely named functions and subroutines. Moreover, SAS practitioners can reliably select the correct instance of the identically named function by modifying only the CMPLIB option, and without being forced to call the function from the FCMP procedure and specify its package name. In this sense, suites of functions can be versioned during development and testing, and their functionality easily compared.

ENCRYPT Option

The FCMP statement's ENCRYPT option conceals the source code of a compiled function through encryption. Table 2.2 demonstrated subtle, but nonetheless informative, functionality that could be gleaned from inspecting the Value variable (XML Value) of a source code data set. Where the functionality of a user-defined function must be hidden from end users calling the function, ENCRYPT delivers this security and privacy.

A primary use case for ENCRYPT involves contract programming in which a consultant is contracted to deliver specific functionality but is required neither to reveal the methods that deliver the functionality nor to allow end users to modify the functionality. The use of ENCRYPT ensures that Richann (the consultant) can develop and deliver a proprietary solution to Inka (her customer) while confidentially maintaining the code that comprises the proprietary FCMP function. And because an encrypted function cannot be modified without unencrypted access to the source code, the customer must return to the consultant whenever function modifications are required. Thus, Richann is able to resell her user-defined function to Louise (a second customer) while retaining full control of the proprietary code that she (Richann) had developed. That's more money for pink heels and Corvette wheels, and all thanks to encryption!

A second use case for ENCRYPT involves environments in which functionally equivalent software solutions are being developed and compared. To ensure independent development, the development environment must guarantee that one developer or team cannot access the source code of the competing developer or team. For example, clinical trials research commonly relies on *independent double coding*, which validates that two functionally equivalent programs deliver identical functionality and results, even if using different methods. This validation is used as a software quality control check because it is unlikely that two developers or teams would err in the same way, so any discrepancy between the solutions can be investigated and remediated.

The ENCRYPT option facilitates double coding because a developer can test the functionality of the competing developer's function without exposure to the competing source code. In effect, it enables you to test whether your function delivers the correct functionality, but it prohibits you from cheating and interrogating *how* your "opponent" delivered that functionality.

Program 2.9 encrypts the RETURN_TODAY function using the ENCRYPT option.

Program 2.9: Encrypting a User-Defined Function

```
proc fcmp outlib=work.funcs.dt encrypt;
   function return_today();
      return(today());
      endfunc;
quit;
```

When the WORK.Funcs data set is viewed, the header information is identical to that shown in Table 2.1. However, Table 2.3 demonstrates the encrypted Value variable (XML Value), which now obfuscates observations 4 through 6, corresponding to the FUNCTION statement, RETURN statement, and ENDFUNC statement.

Table 2.3: Inspecting an Encrypted Source Code Data Set

	Record SubType	Record Name	Continue	Numeric Value	Encoded	XML Value
1	Package			0		`<L n="Header"><S n="Version"><![CDATA[1.1]]></S><N n="Datetime">1983295670.876</N><S n="DatetimeStr"><![CDATA[05NOV22:1 n="SubType"><![CDATA[Package]]></S n="Obfuscate">1</N></L>`
2	FCmp	DT		0		`<L n="Prototype"><S n="Name"><![CDATA[return_today]]></ n="Group"><![CDATA[]]></S><N n="MaxLag">0</N><N n="Flag0">0</N><N n="Flag1">128</N><S n="ReturnType"><![CDATA[n]]></S><N n="RetSubType">1</N><N n="ReturnSize">8</N><L n="ArgList"></L></L>`
3	Function			0		`<L n="Header"><S n="Version"><![CDATA[1.1]]></S><N n="Datetime">1983295670.876</N><S n="DatetimeStr"><![CDATA[05NOV22:1 n="SubType"><![CDATA[Function]]></S n="Obfuscate">1</N><S n="Package"><![CDATA[DT]]></S></L`
4	Executable	FUNCTION	0	65	44	àz⊥◄þaig 1.⌐Q÷İ ÊISó¨↑Üf●ùÔ6 äC¶e‡↓yg
5	Executable	RETURN	0	1	36	¿÷0┬ァ®Æ│•W4∼ OJaaۈu¦#¶e‡↓yg¿1
6	Executable	ENDFUNC	0	14	24	ÒÅ☐ⁱꟿNüↃvWY┬∼®¿ſ• ฿╂4‼

Note that the encryption of a user-defined function is a one-way journey, and once encrypted, the source code cannot be deciphered or decoded. Thus, it is critical that the unencrypted Base SAS source code (that is, the FCMP procedure in which the function is defined) is retained for all encrypted functions. By doing so, a SAS practitioner, team, or organization can privately maintain the unencrypted FCMP procedure code, and modify it when necessary, yet publicly release only the encrypted, compiled version of the function. Please ensure that you do not lose your source code, or else you will need to rewrite it from scratch!

Terminating PROC FCMP: QUIT Versus RUN

Every good thing must come to an end, and both the QUIT statement and RUN statement can be used to terminate the FCMP procedure. However, the majority of PROC FCMP technical documentation exclusively uses QUIT—so what gives? As it turns out, the QUIT statement *always* terminates the FCMP procedure, whereas the RUN statement only *sometimes* terminates it, and for this reason, the author endorses exclusive use of the QUIT statement.

Compilation errors are common in any programming language, especially when you are learning the language, as well as during development and testing. With this reality, Program 2.10 refactors Program 2.9, but the hapless SAS user has forgotten to terminate the function with the ENDFUNC statement. Note especially that the FCMP procedure is terminated with QUIT.

Program 2.10: PROC FCMP (Missing ENDFUNC Statement) Terminated with QUIT
```
proc fcmp outlib=work.funcs.dt;
   function return_today();
      return(today());
quit;
```

The log demonstrates that the FCMP procedure fails to compile, and a runtime error is written to the log:

```
6     proc fcmp outlib=work.funcs.dt;
7        function return_today();
8           return(today());
9     quit;

ERROR: Subroutine 'return_today' was not terminated with ENDSUB.
NOTE: The SAS System stopped processing this step because of errors.
```

However, had the same hapless SAS user forgotten the ENDFUNC statement, yet terminated the FCMP procedure with RUN (instead of QUIT), the procedure would linger. Program 2.11 demonstrates this use.

Program 2.11: PROC FCMP (Missing ENDFUNC Statement) Terminated with RUN

```
proc fcmp outlib=work.funcs.dt;
   function return_today();
      return(today());
run;
```

The log demonstrates that the FCMP procedure fails to compile, yet the familiar adage "The SAS System stopped processing this step because of errors" is noticeably absent:

```
10    proc fcmp outlib=work.funcs.dt;
11       function return_today();
12          return(today());
13    run;

ERROR: Subroutine 'return_today' was not terminated with ENDSUB.
NOTE: Execution canceled because of errors in program.
      Reenter the corrected program or enter "QUIT;" to exit procedure.
```

Thus, overlooking that SAS mistakenly believes you were attempting to define a "subroutine," and apropos the RUN-QUIT divide, the log explicitly directs you to execute the QUIT statement:

```
quit;
```

And only after QUIT does the log show that the FCMP procedure has terminated:

```
21    quit;

NOTE: PROCEDURE FCMP used (Total process time):
      real time            8.71 seconds
      cpu time             0.00 seconds
```

However, had the user instead attempted to run a DATA step immediately after the erroneous FCMP procedure shown in Program 2.11, which is terminated with the RUN statement, the initiation of the DATA step nevertheless would have terminated the prior FCMP procedure:

```
data _null_;
run;
```

Thus, the log (somewhat confusingly) shows both the termination of the preceding FCMP procedure (terminated with RUN), and the execution of the DATA step:

```
14    data _null_;
NOTE: PROCEDURE FCMP used (Total process time):
      real time            2:21.05
      cpu time             0.39 seconds
```

```
15    run;
NOTE: DATA statement used (Total process time):
      real time            0.03 seconds
      cpu time             0.00 seconds
```

Thus, ending the FCMP procedure with a RUN statement will not cause failures, but can generate some rather confusing SAS logs. Moreover, it becomes apparent that SAS relies on the next DATA step or procedure to terminate a preceding failed FCMP procedure when FCMP has been terminated with RUN. On the other hand, QUIT always and immediately terminates the FCMP procedure, in good times and bad, such as when compilation errors are detected. And for this reason, only QUIT is endorsed.

Function Declaration and Signature

A function declaration names the function. It also names and describes the function's parameters. SAS function declarations also specify the return value data type, whereas SAS subroutine declarations have no return value to declare. The declaration is the first statement in the function's *implementation*, which was introduced in Chapter 1. Within the FCMP procedure, user-defined functions are declared using the FUNCTION statement, and user-defined subroutines are declared using the SUBROUTINE statement. Unlike the ENDFUNC and ENDSUB statements, which are fully interchangeable aliases, FUNCTION and SUBROUTINE serve distinct purposes and cannot be swapped.

The FUNCTION and SUBROUTINE statements both "declare and describe" because they name the function or subroutine as well as its parameters. The signature represents a subset of the declaration. It only describes the inputs (parameters) and output (return value or arguments that are modified). The International Organization for Standardization (ISO) defines a *signature* (also *signature type*) as the "definition of the parameters of a given operation, including their order, data types, and passing mode; the results if any; and the possible outcomes (normal vs. exceptional) that might occur" (International Organization for Standarization 2017). The optional OUTARGS statement, described later in this chapter, declares the call method of one or more parameters. That statement is also considered to be part of both the signature and the function (or subroutine) declaration.

Program 2.12 defines the IS_PAL function and the SUB_IS_PAL subroutine. The function and subroutine both evaluate whether a character variable is a palindrome—a word or phrase that is identical when reversed—by returning a 1 for yes or a 0 for no. Note again that multiple functions and/or subroutines can be defined within a single FCMP procedure.

Program 2.12: Sample Function and Subroutine Definitions
```
proc fcmp outlib=work.funcs.char;
   function is_pal(str $);
      return(ifn(str = reverse(strip(str)), 1, 0));
      endfunc;
```

```
      subroutine sub_is_pal(str $, rc);
         outargs rc;
         rc = ifn(str = reverse(strip(str)), 1, 0);
         endsub;
quit;
```

In this example, the entire FUNCTION statement comprises the function's declaration, whereas the function's signature includes only the STR declaration—with STR naming the parameter and $ declaring its data type as character. Moreover, the lack of the optional OUTARGS statement in the function's definition indicates that the default *call-by-value* call method of passing arguments is declared for the STR parameter. Call methods are discussed later in this chapter.

Similarly, the SUBROUTINE declaration comprises both the entire SUBROUTINE statement and the optional OUTARGS statement. The subroutine's signature includes the comma-delimited enumeration of the STR and RC parameters, as well as the OUTARGS statement, which declares the *call-by-reference* method of passing an argument to the RC parameter. By omission, because OUTARGS does not specify the STR parameter, the subroutine implicitly declares the default *call-by-value* method for the STR parameter.

The IS_PAL function and SUB_IS_PAL subroutine will be incrementally modified and refactored throughout this chapter. To understand their baseline functionality, Program 2.13 iterates over a series of words—*noon*, *midday*, *dad*, and *uncle*—to evaluate whether each is a palindrome by calling IS_PAL and SUB_IS_PAL repeatedly.

Program 2.13: Calling the IS_PAL Function and SUB_IS_PAL Subroutine

```
options cmplib=work.funcs;
data temp;
   length word $100 pal sub_pal 3;
   do word = 'noon', 'midday', 'dad', 'uncle';
      pal = is_pal(word);
      call missing(sub_pal);
      call sub_is_pal(word, sub_pal);
      put @1 word @8 pal @10 sub_pal;
      end;
run;
```

The output demonstrates that both IS_PAL and SUB_IS_PAL identify that *noon* and *dad* are palindromes (shown as 1s), and that *midday* and *uncle* are not (shown as 0s):

```
noon    1 1
midday  0 0
dad     1 1
uncle   0 0
```

Of note, the MISSING built-in subroutine initializes Sub_pal to a missing value. MISSING is not required, but omission of this statement produces a note in the log that the "Variable sub_pal is uninitialized." Program 2.14 removes the MISSING subroutine to demonstrate this functionality.

Program 2.14: Omitting the MISSING Built-in Subroutine

```
options cmplib=work.funcs;
data temp;
   length word $100 pal sub_pal 3;
   do word = 'noon', 'midday', 'dad', 'uncle';
      pal = is_pal(word);
      call sub_is_pal(word, sub_pal);
      put @1 word @8 pal @10 sub_pal;
      end;
run;
```

The log demonstrates equivalent functionality (to Program 2.13), yet with the added note:

```
NOTE: Variable sub_pal is uninitialized.
noon    1 1
midday  0 0
dad     1 1
uncle   0 0
```

In some more restrictive development environments, such as clinical trials research, this type of note might be deemed unacceptable and invalidate a SAS program. For this reason, use of the MISSING built-in subroutine is considered a best practice when passing any argument that is both uninitialized and is passed by reference (via the OUTARGS statement).

Function Naming

The FUNCTION and SUBROUTINE statements declare and name functions and subroutines, respectively. A function's name should be descriptive, memorable, and concise, and this balance can be difficult to strike.

Descriptiveness gives some indication of the function's functionality—what it does. For example, IS_THIS_PHRASE_A_PALINDROME_0_1 is a valid SAS function name, describes the evaluation that it makes, and even describes the return codes—0 or 1—that are generated. But would you ever want to type this function's name when calling it? No, and for decades, Base SAS survived with built-in functions whose names were limited to eight characters. If old-school programmers could subsist on eight characters, so can you!

At the other end of the naming spectrum is concision, which is advantageous when calling functions. For example, the previous IS_PAL user-defined function could be shortened to IP, another valid function name, but this fails to describe the functionality, and is arguably not memorable. Ultimately, as you begin building a library of reusable, user-defined functions within a team or enterprise, you will want to standardize whatever naming convention is selected and avoid function names that might be confused with each other, or with SAS built-in functions.

For consistency and readability, this text adopts the PEP 8 variable- and function-naming standard espoused in the *Style Guide for Python Code*, which states that "Function names should be lowercase, with words separated by underscores as necessary to improve readability" (Guido van Rossum 2013).

SAS user-defined functions and subroutines must conform to the following naming conventions:

- The function must begin with a letter or underscore symbol.
- Subsequent characters can include letters, numbers, and the underscore symbol.
- Function names are case-insensitive.
- The length of the function name must be 59 or fewer characters, and the combined length of the package name and the function name cannot exceed 60 characters. For example, if you have taken advantage of the full 32-character maximum package name length (please don't!), your function name cannot exceed 28 characters.
- The function name cannot be an existing SAS built-in function.

Regardless of how well you believe you have named your function, some amount of documentation is important to ensure appropriate usage, especially where the users calling user-defined functions are not the original developers. Documenting a function's high-level functionality, required inputs, and expected output is considered a best practice, as is including additional context and caveats that describe the inputs or conditions that might cause a function to fail, or for which it has not been tested. For example, Program 2.15 revisits the IS_PAL function defined in Program 2.12 and adds header comments containing this information.

Program 2.15: Adding Header Comments to the IS_PAL Function

```
/*
The IS_PAL function determines whether a word or phrase is a palindrome.
The single parameter is case sensitive, and limited to alphanumeric characters.
Spaces that occur in the parameter are also counted as characters.
IS_PAL returns the following return codes:
- 1 - the word is a palindrome
- 0 - the word is not a palindrome
*/
proc fcmp outlib=work.funcs.char;
   function is_pal(str $);
       return(ifn(str = reverse(strip(str)), 1, 0));
       endfunc;
quit;
```

Only after understanding both a function's functionality and caveats can SAS practitioners determine whether a user-defined function meets their needs. It goes without saying that as a function's functionality is modified or extended throughout the function's lifespan, the accompanying documentation must be commensurately updated to reflect these changes. The only thing worse than *no* documentation is *outdated* or otherwise *incorrect* documentation!

Declaring Parameters

Parameters facilitate *variable* input—that is, input that varies—and deliver dynamic and diverse functionality. In this sense, parameters poke pinholes in the otherwise static black box that surrounds a function's implementation and transfer data during a function call from the *calling* program to the *called* module. The ISO defines a *parameter* as a "constant, variable, or expression that is used to pass values between software modules" (International Organization for Standarization 2017). A parameter declaration names the parameter and describes its position, object type, data type, dimensionality, and call method, all of which are incrementally introduced.

When a function is called and parameters have been declared within its implementation, data can be passed to the function via *arguments*, which are constants, variables, or literal values that correspond to each parameter within the calling program. ISO defines an *argument* as a "constant, variable, or expression used in a call to a software module to specify data or program elements to be passed to that module" (International Organization for Standarization 2017). When a function is called, its arguments *bind* to the corresponding parameters (within the function's implementation), which ISO defines as "to assign a value to an identifier" such as "to assign a value to a parameter" (International Organization for Standarization 2017). This binding gives the function access to the argument values. *Call by value* binds a copy of the argument. *Call by reference* binds the actual argument (or its memory location).

Given this clear differentiation between *parameters* and *arguments*, this text adopts the ISO convention that parameters are declared and used solely within a function's implementation, whereas arguments exist solely in the calling program. Thus, a function has no access to variables or values that exist in a calling program unless they are passed as arguments to the function. Similarly, parameters within a function maintain local scope; they cannot be accessed by the calling program unless a parameter is returned in a return value, or the parameter is declared using OUTARGS, as discussed later in this chapter. As with function names, this text similarly adopts the PEP 8 Python standard in representing parameters and variables in lowercase, with underscores added to improve readability.

SAS user-defined functions and subroutines can declare zero or more parameters. When declared, parameters must conform to the following SAS variable-naming conventions:

- The parameter name must begin with a letter or underscore symbol.
- Subsequent characters can include letters, numbers, and the underscore symbol.
- Parameter names are case insensitive.
- Parameter length cannot exceed 32 characters.

Parameters are declared parenthetically within the FUNCTION or SUBROUTINE statements. When multiple parameters are declared in a single function, they are delimited with commas. Parameters are a special type of variable that can reference scalar variables, arrays, and even hash objects, and dictionary objects. The parameter dimensionality (scalar versus array) and object type (value versus hash versus dictionary) determine how a function can be called, as introduced in Chapter 1. For example, functions that declare an array parameter cannot be called using %SYSFUNC or the SQL procedure, and functions that declare a hash or dictionary parameter can be called only from the FCMP procedure.

Table 2.4 demonstrates which call methods support specific parameter types. Scalar variables, including character and numeric data types, arguably represent the most common type of parameter, in which a single value is passed to a parameter. All function call techniques support functions that declare scalar parameters. The single exception occurs when a user-defined function is called using the FORMAT procedure OTHER option, in which case no more than one scalar parameter can be declared in the referenced function.

Character parameters are declared using a trailing $, and numeric parameters have no $. The following FUNCTION statement declares a character parameter (CHAR) and a numeric parameter (NUM):

```
function two_vars(char $, num);
```

SAS arrays are introduced in Chapter 3 and are contrasted with scalar variables that contain a single value. An array represents a named collection that references a series of same-type variables, either character or numeric. Functions that declare an array parameter can be called only from the DATA step or FCMP procedure. This limitation exists because a corresponding array must be declared in the calling program prior to passing an array

Table 2.4: Function Parameter Types Supported by Various Call Methods

	Character or Numeric Scalar Variable	Character or Numeric Array	Hash Object	Dictionary Object
DATA step	Yes	Yes	No	No
WHERE statement	Yes	No	No	No
PROC REPORT COMPUTE block	Yes	No	No	No
%SYSFUNC macro function	Yes	No	No	No
%SYSCALL macro statement	Yes	No	No	No
PROC SQL	Yes	No	No	No
PROC FORMAT OTHER option	Yes (limited to only one parameter)	No	No	No
PROC FCMP	Yes	Yes	Yes	Yes

argument to a user-defined function. Arrays are declared using the ARRAY statement in the DATA step or the FCMP procedure, or the VARARGS option in the FCMP procedure.

Array parameters are denoted by a trailing asterisk in square brackets, and character arrays also include a trailing $. The following FUNCTION statement declares a character array parameter (ARR_CHAR) and a numeric array parameter (ARR_NUM):

```
function two_arrays(arr_char[*] $, arr_num[*]);
```

Two additional parameter types supported by the FCMP procedure are the hash object and dictionary object, which represent complex data objects introduced in Chapters 4 and 7, respectively. Dictionary objects are supported by the FCMP procedure but are not recognized within the DATA step. Hash objects are supported by the DATA step, but they cannot be passed (as arguments) to user-defined functions—even to a function declaring a hash object parameter. In other words, as demonstrated in Table 2.4, functions that declare either a hash object parameter or a dictionary object parameter can be called only from the FCMP procedure.

Hash object parameters are denoted with a trailing "hash" keyword. Dictionary object parameters are denoted with a trailing "dnary" keyword. The following FUNCTION statement declares the my_hash hash object parameter and the my_dict dictionary object parameter:

```
function my_function(my_hash hash, my_dict dnary);
```

Note that the MY_FUNCTION function cannot be called from either the DATA step or the %SYSFUNC statement due to these complex parameters. One final distinction is that although hash arguments are passed by value (by default), dictionary objects are passed by reference to maximize performance. Although both hash objects and dictionary objects are demonstrated within the FCMP procedure in this text, neither hash parameters nor dictionary parameters are demonstrated.

Program 2.16 modifies Program 2.12 to add a numeric parameter (CASE) that describes whether the palindrome evaluation should be case sensitive or case insensitive. A 0 denotes case *insensitivity*, and 1 (or, more precisely, any number except for 0) denotes case *sensitivity*.

Program 2.16: Sample Function and Subroutine Definitions

```
/*
STR is the character variable, value, or expression tested for palindrome evaluation
CASE defines case sensitivity:
- 0 - case insensitive
- 1 - case sensitive
*/
proc fcmp outlib=work.funcs.char;
   function is_pal(str $, case);
      if case = 0 then new_str = lowcase(str);
      else new_str = str;
      return(ifn(new_str = reverse(strip(new_str)), 1, 0));
      endfunc;
   subroutine sub_is_pal(str $, case, rc);
```

```
        outargs rc;
        if case = 0 then new_str = lowcase(str);
        else new_str=str;
        rc = ifn(new_str = reverse(strip(new_str)), 1, 0);
        endsub;
quit;
```

Note the comma-delimited declaration of the STR and CASE parameters in both the FUNCTION and SUBROUTINE statements. Also note the importance of parameter order. Arguments must be passed to SAS functions in the exact order that the corresponding parameters are declared. Thus, in the SUBROUTINE statement, the CASE parameter is inserted between the existent STR and RC parameters to ensure that the first and second parameters remain identical in the function and the subroutine.

Program 2.17 modifies Program 2.13 to reference the CASE parameter in the function and subroutine calls. Each of the four test words also now includes uppercase characters that will cause a case-sensitive evaluation to fail.

Program 2.17: Calling Case-Insensitive Function and Case-Sensitive Subroutine
```
data _null_;
    length word $100 pal sub_pal 3;
    do word = 'Noon', 'MIDday', 'Dad', 'UNCle';
        pal = is_pal(word, 0);
        call missing(sub_pal);
        call sub_is_pal(word, 1, sub_pal);
        put @1 word @8 pal @10 sub_pal;
        end;
run;
```

The output demonstrates that the case-insensitive call to IS_PAL identifies the two palindromes—*noon* and *dad*—whereas the case-sensitive call to SUB_IS_PAL does not identify them:

```
Noon    1 0
MIDday  0 0
Dad     1 0
UNCle   0 0
```

As user-defined functions are positionally declared, each of the arguments in the DATA step must be passed in the corresponding order in which the parameters are declared within the FCMP procedure. The data types of all arguments must match the data types declared in the corresponding parameters. If a character value is passed as an argument to the CASE numeric parameter, SAS would attempt to convert the character value to a number while generating the infamous "Character values have been converted to numeric values" note in the log.

One major difference between SAS built-in and user-defined functions is that the former support optional parameters whereas the latter do not. Thus, any parameter declared within a user-defined

Figure 2.1: ROUND Function Syntax

Syntax

ROUND(*argument* <, *rounding-unit*>)

Required Argument

argument
    is a numeric constant, variable, or expression to be rounded.

Optional Argument

rounding-unit
    is a positive, numeric constant, variable, or expression that specifies the rounding unit.

function or subroutine always must have a corresponding argument that is passed during invocation. In some instances, this can limit the versatility of FCMP functions and subroutines. It also contrasts with SAS user-defined macros, in which optional parameters can be declared.

For example, the built-in ROUND function (whose specification is shown in Figure 2.1) declares two parameters—a required parameter, the number being rounded, and an optional parameter, the "rounding unit" that specifies the degree of rounding to perform. However, when the optional parameter is omitted, ROUND nevertheless rounds the number, and by default, rounds to the nearest integer. In other words, when the second argument is omitted during a call to ROUND, "1" is substituted by default and effectively bound to the optional parameter. Similar functionality cannot be engineered within the FCMP procedure.

Declaring Zero Parameters

Not every function or subroutine declares a parameter. Even some built-in SAS functions lack parameters, such as DATE, DATETIME, TIME, and TODAY. The commonality among these functions is their ability to derive dynamic input not from users but from the system or environment. For example, TODAY does not require an argument because the SAS application reaches out to the operating system—not the user—to ascertain today's date. Although uncommon, user-defined functions and subroutines similarly can be defined without declaring any parameters.

For example, the TOMORROW function in Program 2.18 returns tomorrow's date. And because TOMORROW can rely on the TODAY built-in function to retrieve today's date, it requires no arguments to be passed. Note that empty (trailing) parentheses are still required by the FUNCTION statement despite the lack of parameters.

Program 2.18: Generate Tomorrow's Date without a Parameter Declaration
```
proc fcmp outlib=work.funcs.dt;
    function tomorrow();
        return(today() + 1);
        endfunc;
quit;
```

Similarly, when TOMORROW is called, empty (trailing) parentheses must follow the function's name:

```
%put %sysfunc(tomorrow());
%put %sysfunc(tomorrow(), mmddyy10.);
```

The log demonstrates both the unformatted and formatted date for tomorrow. In this example, you're calling the TOMORROW function on December 24, 2021, as you anxiously await the launch of the James Webb Space Telescope (JWST) the following day:

```
23639
12/25/2021
```

Thus, parentheses are required for all function calls—including for built-in and user-defined function calls as well as calls that declare parameters and those that do not. The parentheses—even when empty—convey to the SAS application that the named element should be interpreted as a function name.

Parameter-less functions are sometimes constructed where all input can be derived from SAS automatic macro variables. A list of all automatic macro variables available in your SAS session can be printed to the log using the following %PUT statement:

```
%put _automatic_;
```

For example, consider an organization that is simultaneously operating several instances of SAS software across its enterprise and is running multiple SAS versions or maintenance releases. For example, the Marketing Department is running SAS 9.4M7, and the Sales Department is running SAS 9.4M2. Thus, evaluating the &SYSVER, &SYSVLONG, or &SYSVLONG4 automatic macro variables might be required to determine whether a program that relies on newly released SAS syntax can run in a legacy SAS environment:

```
%put &sysver;
9.4

%put &sysvlong;
9.04.01M7P080520

%put &sysvlong4;
9.04.01M7P08052020
```

Program 2.19 demonstrates the RELEASE function, which extracts the release number (M7) from the &SYSVLONG automatic macro variable. The RELEASE function could be used to evaluate programmatically whether a sufficiently new release of SAS is in use. Environments that maintain multiple SAS versions (for example, SAS 9.3 and 9.4) would need to evaluate the version number in addition to the release number.

Program 2.19: Extracting the SAS Release Number Using a Parameter-Less Function

```
proc fcmp outlib=work.funcs.admin;
    function release() $;
        pos = index("&sysvlong", "M");
        return(substr("&sysvlong" ,pos, 2));
        endfunc;
quit;


%put %sysfunc(release());
```

The log demonstrates the release number:

```
M7
```

In general, nearly all user-defined functions and subroutines require the declaration of one or more parameters. However, it is important to understand that not all callable modules declare parameters.

Specifying Parameter Call Method Using the OUTARGS Statement

The *call method* of a callable module defines how arguments are *bound*—transferred from the calling program to the called module during invocation. Within Base SAS, two call methods are available when designing user-defined functions and subroutines. The first is *call by value* (also *pass by value*), the default call method for passing scalar variables and arrays. The second is *call by reference* (also *pass by reference*), which is denoted by the OUTARGS statement. Call methods for hash object parameters and dictionary object parameters do not use the OUTARGS statement and are discussed in Chapters 4 and 7, respectively.

Call methods must be understood because they influence the functionality, performance (including efficiency and speed), and security of a function. For example, a function can be made more efficient by directly accessing (rather than copying) large volumes of data passed to it, but it can also be rendered less secure when arguments (rather than copies thereof) are modified directly by the called module.

In general, call by value is more commonly associated with functions. Call by reference is more commonly associated with subroutines. Some legacy SAS documentation and other references incorrectly differentiate that "functions do not use OUTARGS, and subroutines can use OUTARGS."

However, to be clear, both user-defined functions and user-defined subroutines can use OUTARGS optionally to denote scalar and array parameters passed by reference. Moreover, some parameters can be passed by value and other parameters by reference within the same function or subroutine. Thus, only the presence or absence of the OUTARGS statement—and not the distinction of being a function or subroutine—distinguishes call method for scalar and array parameters.

By default, the OUTARGS statement is omitted, and SAS user-defined functions and subroutines pass scalar arguments and array arguments by value. In this situation, *a copy* is made of an argument when it is bound to its corresponding parameter during invocation. The copied value is referenced by the parameter name within the called module and has local scope; that is, changes to a variable within a function will not affect the original argument value within the calling program. In other words, if you pass a variable *by value* from a DATA step to a user-defined function, there is zero chance of that function accidentally modifying the variable in the DATA step—because only a copy of the variable is passed.

For example, Program 2.20 passes the State variable *by value* from the calling program (the DATA step) to the CHECK_STATE function, in which State is bound to the ST parameter, which is referenced by the ST variable. The ST variable is a copy of State and maintains only local scope inside the function. The actual State variable remains unmodified in the DATA step. Thus, because CHECK_STATE uses only a copy of State, SAS practitioners can confidently call the function without concern that it will modify any arguments that are passed, such as the State variable.

Program 2.20: Passing Argument by Value to a Function
```
proc fcmp outlib=work.funcs.test;
   function check_state(st $) $;
      if st in ('California', 'Kalifornia', 'Cali')
         then abbr = 'CA';
      return(abbr);
      endfunc;
quit;

data _null_;
   length state $20 abbreviation $2;
   state = 'Kalifornia';
   abbreviation = check_state(state);
   put @1 state @20 abbreviation;
run;
```

The output demonstrates that CHECK_STATE located the incorrectly spelled "Kalifornia" in the list of lookup values and returned the correct CA abbreviation to the DATA step. Afterward, this return value is initialized to the Abbreviation variable:

```
Kalifornia          CA
```

But what if a SAS practitioner wanted to return not only the state abbreviation but also the cleaned state name, which requires returning two values? By definition, a function *returns* one and only one value. However, a function or subroutine can *modify* additional values (in the calling program) that are passed by reference. One way to fulfill this new requirement is to declare one or more parameters as call by reference using OUTARGS, which enables CHECK_STATE to modify these arguments in the DATA step.

Program 2.21 modifies Program 2.20 so that the ST parameter is declared as call by reference (within the CHECK_STATE_REF function) rather than call by value (as in CHECK_STATE). Changes to the ST variable inside the function are now reflected in the State variable in the calling program. Note that the MISSING subroutine does not need to be called on the State variable in the DATA step because the State variable is initialized to "Kalifornia" prior to being passed to the function, despite the argument being passed by reference.

Program 2.21: Passing Argument by Reference to a Function

```
proc fcmp outlib=work.funcs.test;
   function check_state_ref(st $) $;
      outargs st;
      if st in ('California', 'Kalifornia', 'Cali') then do;
         st = 'California';
         abbr = 'CA';
         end;
      return(abbr);
      endfunc;
quit;

data _null_;
   length state $20 abbreviation $2;
   state = 'Kalifornia';
   abbreviation = check_state_ref(state);
   put @1 state @20 abbreviation;
run;
```

When the DATA step executes, the log demonstrates that calling the CHECK_STATE_REF function not only returns the state abbreviation, which is initialized to the Abbreviation variable, but also corrects the spelling of the State variable, the argument passed *by reference* to CHECK_STATE_REF:

```
California          CA
```

The risk of this usage, of course, is the inability to compare or otherwise use the original State value once it has been modified by the CHECK_STATE_REF function. Thus, after CHECK_STATE_REF is executed, the DATA step no longer has access to the original—that is, misspelled—version of State, previously recorded as "Kalifornia." For this reason, although it is possible to validate or clean data using call-by-reference functions, it is far more common to rely on call-by-value functions that enable subsequent comparisons between the raw and transformed versions of the argument.

An arguably more common (and apt) usage of a user-defined function that relies on call by reference generates a return code rather than a return value, with the return code representing the function completion status. For example, Program 2.22 modifies the CHECK_STATE_REF function in Program 2.21 to generate a return code that denotes whether the ST value is located, and whether the ST value has been modified.

Program 2.22: Passing Arguments by Reference to a Function (with a Return Code)
```
/*
CHECK_STATE_REF_2 determines whether a valid state name is evaluated,
and generates the state abbreviation for valid and invalid state names.
Return codes include the following:
- 0 - state name not known, no abbreviation returned
- 1 - state name is valid and recognized, abbreviation returned
- 2 - state name is invalid but recognized, abbreviation returned
The state name is corrected for all invalid but recognized results.
*/
proc fcmp outlib=work.funcs.test;
   function check_state_ref_2(st $, st_abbr $);
      outargs st, st_abbr;
      length st_new $20 rc 8;
      if st in ('California', 'Kalifornia', 'Cali') then do;
         st_new = 'California';
         st_abbr = 'CA';
         end;
      * remaining state transformations go here;
      if st = st_new then rc = 1;
      else if ^missing(st_abbr) then do;
         rc = 2;
         st = st_new;
         end;
      else do;
         rc = 0;
         st_abbr = '';
         end;
      return(rc);
      endfunc;
quit;
```

CHECK_STATE_REF_2 demonstrates the transformation of only California-specific spelling variations, although other state names presumably would be checked and transformed. In reality, rather than a 50-step IF-THEN-ELSE logic block, this data validation and cleaning would be handled by more advanced methods, such as a hash object lookup, or natural language processing. Thus, California cleansing is shown only for demonstration purposes to contrast parameter call methods. Hash-based lookup operations are demonstrated throughout Chapter 4.

Program 2.23 demonstrates two DATA steps, the first of which creates a sample data set, and the second of which transforms the data by calling CHECK_STATE_REF_2. Note that the second DATA step now requires the MISSING subroutine to be called on the Abbreviation variable if you want to eliminate the "uninitialized" note. This contrasts with Program 2.21, which did not require the MISSING subroutine, because Abbreviation is otherwise uninitialized when it is passed to CHECK_STATE_REF_2.

Program 2.23: Calling the CHECK_STATE_REF_2 Function
```
data states;
   length state $20;
   state = 'Kalifornia'; output;
   state = 'California'; output;
   state = 'Calif'; output;
run;

data _null_;
   set states;
   length abbreviation $2;
   call missing(abbreviation);
   return_code = check_state_ref_2(state, abbreviation);
   put @1 state @20 abbreviation @24 return_code;
run;
```

When the second DATA step executes, it evaluates that "Kalifornia" represents a recognized misspelling that is corrected and "California" represents the correct spelling. "Calif" is invalid, and thus it cannot be transformed into a valid state name and abbreviation:

```
California        CA   2
California        CA   1
Calif                  0
```

Thus, the CHECK_STATE_REF_2 return code alerts the user whenever State is misspelled (2) or when State is unrecognized (0) and cannot be transformed. To transform "Calif," this value would need to be added to the comma-delimited list of spelling variations in Program 2.22. The benefit of this methodology, as opposed to that demonstrated in Program 2.21, is that both raw and refined values are retained, and thus can be used for reporting, quality control metrics, or other operations.

Functionally equivalent user-defined subroutines can be designed that similarly standardize state names and resolve their state abbreviations. However, because subroutines cannot generate a return value, all variables that need to be modified or initialized within the calling program—including the raw state name, state abbreviation, and return code—must be passed *by reference* when the subroutine is invoked.

For example, Program 2.24 demonstrates a comparable subroutine that evaluates the state name, transforms it to a correctly spelled name (if it is misspelled), generates the state abbreviation, and generates a return code that describes whether the state name is correct, misspelled, or unrecognized.

Program 2.24: Subroutine to Clean and Transform State Name

```
proc fcmp outlib=work.funcs.test;
   subroutine sub_check_state_ref(st $, st_abbr $, rc);
      outargs st, st_abbr, rc;
      length st_new $20 rc 8;
      if st in ('California', 'Kalifornia', 'Cali') then do;
         st_new = 'California';
         st_abbr = 'CA';
         end;
      * remaining state transformations go here;
      if st = st_new then rc = 1;
      else if ^missing(st_abbr) then do;
         rc = 2;
         st = st_new;
         end;
      else do;
         rc = 0;
         st_abbr = '';
         end;
      endsub;
quit;
```

Note that three parameters (ST, ST_ABBR, and RC) now must be declared in the SUBROUTINE statement, and that the subroutine call must pass three arguments. This contrasts with the functionally equivalent function (CHECK_STATE_REF_2) that declares only two parameters. Within the subroutine, the OUTARGS statement must declare that all three parameters are passed by reference to provide access to their values to the calling program.

When Program 2.25 calls the SUB_CHECK_STATE_REF subroutine, it generates identical output to that produced by the DATA step that calls the CHECK_STATE_REF_2 function (in Program 2.23). Similarly, the MISSING subroutine is relied upon to remove the "uninitialized" note from the log and now must pass two variables—Abbreviation and Return_code—because neither are initialized prior to being passed to the SUB_CHECK_STATE_REF subroutine.

Program 2.25: Calling the SUB_CHECK_STATE_REF Subroutine

```
data _null_;
   set states;
   length abbreviation $2 return_code 8;
   call missing(abbreviation, return_code);
   call sub_check_state_ref(state, abbreviation, return_code);
   put @1 state @20 abbreviation @24 return_code;
run;
```

Note the two differences between the DATA step in Program 2.25 and the DATA step in Program 2.23: the Return_code variable now must be declared by the LENGTH statement, and the empty Return_code variable must be passed as an argument in the SUB_CHECK_STATE_REF invocation.

Within function and subroutine definitions, the OUTARGS statement is considered to be part of the signature because it (or its absence) denotes the call method of scalar and array parameters. Thus, the parameter call method is so central to a function's functionality that users calling a function cannot interact with it without knowing each parameter's respective call method—by value or by reference. For this reason, placing the OUTARGS statement immediately after the FUNCTION or SUBROUTINE statement is considered to be a best practice. It groups signature statements together and conveys to developers how each argument must be passed.

The VARARGS Option

The VARARGS option is specified in a FUNCTION or SUBROUTINE statement and denotes that the last parameter being declared is an array that can accept multiple arguments. To use VARARGS, the last parameter must have a bracketed asterisk [*] that declares it as an array. VARARGS is compatible with both character and numeric arrays, and it supports passing an array name or a series of same-type variables and/or same-type literal values.

Thus, as previously demonstrated, when an array parameter is declared *without* the VARARGS option, only an array name can be passed to the function:

```
function avg(var[*]);
```

However, VARARGS expands the ways in which a series of same-type data can be passed to a parameter array. It enables a series of arguments not yet aggregated into an array to be passed to a function. VARARGS only supports this extended functionality, however, when a function is called from the FCMP procedure. Thus, the following use of VARARGS supports passing a series of numeric variables or numeric literals to the AVG function—but only when AVG is called from the FCMP procedure:

```
function avg(var[*]) varargs;
```

The FUNCTION statement in Program 2.26 denotes the VARARGS option, which is applied to the VAR parameter in defining the AVG function. Subsequently, AVG is called inline within the FCMP procedure after its definition. That is, AVG is declared, immediately called, and discarded all within the same FCMP procedure. Also note the lack of an OUTLIB statement, which indicates AVG is not saved for reuse.

Program 2.26: VARARGS Option Supports Passing a Series of Variables and/or Literals
```
proc fcmp;
   function avg(var[*]) varargs;
      file log;
      total = 0;
      do i = 1 to dim(var);
         total + var[i];
         end;
```

```
      return(total / dim(var));
      endfunc;
   mean = avg(3, 5, 7, 9);
   put mean=;
quit;
```

The log shows the calculated mean:

```
mean=6
```

Array parameters and the DIM function are discussed in Chapter 3. For now, it is only important to understand that the bracketed asterisk denotes that the VAR parameter can expand to receive multiple values and that the DIM function evaluates the number of values that are provided at runtime. Thus, the DO loop iterates over the Var array, which represents a named collection that references multiple values.

VARARGS is unnecessary, however, when declaring reusable functions and subroutines that are called from the DATA step—the focus of this text—because they require array arguments to be explicitly declared as an array in the calling program prior to invocation. For example, Program 2.27 demonstrates a functionally equivalent *reusable* AVG_REUSE function (that does not require VARARGS), now saved to the WORK.Funcs source code data set.

Program 2.27: VARARGS Option Unnecessary in Reusable Function (Called from DATA Step)

```
proc fcmp outlib=work.funcs.stats;
   function avg_reuse(var[*]);
      total = 0;
      do i = 1 to dim(var);
         total + var[i];
         end;
      return(total / dim(var));
      endfunc;
quit;
```

With AVG_REUSE now saved, the function can be called from a DATA step rather than from the FCMP procedure itself. However, in contrast to the prior AVG function that could accept constants, variables, and numeric literals, passing a multi-element array to a reusable function requires the array to have already been declared using the ARRAY statement. Thus, Program 2.28 requires the four numeric literals—3, 5, 7, and 9—to be containerized in the Arr_values array, after which the array is passed to AVG_REUSE to generate identical results as the AVG function.

Program 2.28: Calculate Mean of Four Numeric Literals

```
data _null_;
   array arr_values[4] 8 (3, 5, 7, 9);
   mean = avg_reuse(arr_values);
   put mean=;
run;
```

So, if the output of Programs 2.26 and 2.28 is identical, and if the VARARGS option is unnecessary when declaring an array parameter for a function called from the DATA step, can VARARGS be cast aside and forgotten? I once thought this, but no. Especially when you want to build flexible functions that can be called from both the DATA step and the FCMP procedure, VARARGS does have value.

For example, now that AVG_REUSE has been built and saved, you might want to reuse it within the FCMP procedure, such as to replace the static calculation of Mean in Program 2.26. The FCMP procedure in Program 2.29 refactors Program 2.26, and now instead calls AVG_REUSE to calculate Mean.

Program 2.29: Attempting to Pass Multiple Values in PROC FCMP
```
proc fcmp;
   file log;
   mean = avg_reuse(3, 5, 7, 6);
   put mean=;
quit;
```

The log demonstrates the failure that occurs because AVG_REUSE expects *only* an array to be passed, as opposed to a series of variables and/or literal values:

```
560  proc fcmp;
561     file log;
562     mean = avg_reuse(3, 5, 7, 6);
ERROR: The function avg_reuse takes a maximum of 1 arguments. There are too many
arguments for the function avg_reuse.
563     put mean=;
564  quit;
```

To overcome this limitation and expand the flexibility of AVG_REUSE, the AVG_VARARGS function is defined in Program 2.30, in which only the VARARGS option is added to the FUNCTION statement—as it appeared in the original AVG function (in Program 2.26), which was not saved.

Program 2.30: VARARGS Option Necessary When Calling Function from PROC FCMP
```
proc fcmp outlib=work.funcs.stats;
   function avg_varargs(var[*]) varargs;
      total = 0;
      do i = 1 to dim(var);
         total + var[i];
         end;
      return(total / dim(var));
      endfunc;
quit;
```

When the AVG_VARARGS function is called in Program 2.31 from the FCMP procedure, numeric literals can now be passed without causing the previous runtime error, and the resultant mean is again calculated to be 6.

Program 2.31: Successfully Passing Multiple Elements in PROC FCMP Using VARARGS
```
proc fcmp;
    file log;
    mean = avg_varargs(3, 5, 7, 9);
    put mean=;
quit;
```

Only VARARGS enables users to build a single function that can accept arrays when called from the DATA step, and a series of variables and/or values when called from the FCMP procedure. This flexibility can be paramount when a user-defined function is anticipated to be called from various calling modules, especially to include both the DATA step and the FCMP procedure.

Declaring a Return Value

The final component of a function's signature (and, thus, its declaration) is the return value—the output that is generated when a function terminates, and which is returned to the calling program. As differentiated in Chapter 1, return codes represent a subset of return values that describe the completion status or other metadata for a function's execution. Subroutines do not return a value, so no return value can be declared in the SUBROUTINE statement.

The FUNCTION statement declares a numeric return value by default, which is indicated by the lack of a trailing $ after the parenthetical declaration of parameters. For example, Program 2.32 defines the PASS_NUM function, which inputs a number and spits it right back out. Within PASS_NUM, the RETURN statement can return only a numeric value because of the implicit numeric return value declaration in the FUNCTION statement.

Program 2.32: Declaring a Numeric Return Value by Default
```
proc fcmp outlib=work.funcs.test;
    function pass_num(num);
        return(num);
        endfunc;
quit;
```

More commonly, the return value is calculated inside the function, in which case a LENGTH (or ATTRIB) statement declares the return value data type. For example, Program 2.33 defines the PASS_NUM_PLUS_ONE function and denotes that the RETURN statement is returning the Num_plus variable. Because the function must return a numeric value, Num_plus is declared by the LENGTH statement as having a numeric data type.

Program 2.33: Declaring a Numeric Return Value by Default
```
proc fcmp outlib=work.funcs.test;
    function pass_num_plus_one(num);
        length num_plus 8;
        num_plus = num+1;
        return(num_plus);
        endfunc;
quit;
```

Conversely, a character return value is declared using a trailing $ after the parenthetical declaration of parameters. The default character length returned by a function is 33 characters. For example, Program 2.34 declares the PASS_CHAR function, and the trailing $ denotes that the return value will be truncated (by default) at 33 characters.

Program 2.34: Declaring a 33-Character Default Length Return Value
```
proc fcmp outlib=work.funcs.test;
   function pass_char(char $) $;
      return(char);
      endfunc;
quit;

data _null_;
   length char_1 char_2 $40;
   char_1 = repeat('x', 39);
   char_2 = pass_char(char_1);
   put char_1=;
   put char_2=;
run;
```

The DATA step demonstrates the 40-character value *before* the function call and the 33-character value returned *from* the function call:

```
char_1=xxxxxxxxxxxxxxxxxxxxxxxxxxxxxxxxxxxxxxxxx
char_2=xxxxxxxxxxxxxxxxxxxxxxxxxxxxxxxxx
```

To be clear, the entire Char_1 value can be accessed inside the function via the CHAR parameter, so it is not the case that data passed *to* the function are being truncated, but rather that data passed *from* the function are being truncated.

To modify the default length of a character return value, specify the character length as a value after the trailing $. For example, the following declaration statement further truncates the return value and generates a 10-character return value:

```
function pass_char(char $) $10;
```

The following declaration statement generates a 50-character return value that now can hold the entire 40-character length of the argument passed to the CHAR parameter:

```
function pass_char(char $) $50;
```

You can also specify the length of a character return value using the LENGTH statement, but this is valid only for character lengths that are 33 characters or longer. For example, the following declaration similarly allows PASS_CHAR to return a value up to 50 characters long:

```
function pass_char(char $) $;
   length char $50;
```

However, LENGTH has no effect when attempting to declare the length of a character return value that has fewer than 33 characters. Thus, the following declaration still returns the 33-character default length:

```
function pass_char(char $) $;
   length char $10;
```

In each of the previous examples, the parameter being declared is simultaneously also the return value being declared. A more likely scenario occurs when a new variable is declared and initialized inside the FCMP procedure, and subsequently passed as a return value. Program 2.35 demonstrates initializing the New_char variable to the value passed to the CHAR parameter. However, because no LENGTH or ATTRIB statement explicitly declares New_char, including its data type and length, the initialization statement also represents an *implicit* declaration.

Program 2.35: Initializing a Return Value without an Explicit Declaration
```
proc fcmp outlib=work.funcs.test;
   function pass_char(char $) $;
      file log;
      new_char = char;
      len_char = length(char);
      len_new_char = length(new_char);
      put len_char= len_new_char=;
      return(new_char);
      endfunc;
quit;

data _null_;
   length char_1 char_2 $40;
   char_1 = repeat('x', 39);
   char_2 = pass_char(char_1);
   put char_1=;
   put char_2=;
run;
```

It turns out that if a character variable is not explicitly declared within the FCMP procedure, it is implicitly declared as having a length of 33. Thus, although the CHAR parameter receives a value that is 40 characters in length (demonstrated by the Len_char value of 40), when New_char is initialized, only the first 33 characters are saved, as demonstrated by the Len_new_char value of 33:

```
len_char=40 len_new_char=33
char_1=xxxxxxxxxxxxxxxxxxxxxxxxxxxxxxxxxxxxxxxxx
char_2=xxxxxxxxxxxxxxxxxxxxxxxxxxxxxxxxxxx
```

Thus, a SAS practitioner might see these results and believe that the remedy is to add an explicit character length declaration to the FUNCTION statement. For example, changing the $ to $50 ensures the return value can pass 50 characters back to the calling function:

```
proc fcmp outlib=work.funcs.test;
   function pass_char(char $) $50;
```

However, when this code is executed (not shown), the results are identical, and New_char remains truncated despite the explicit declaration of the return value to a length of 50 characters. The problem is that any character variable that is initialized within the FCMP procedure must have an explicit declaration of length—using either the LENGTH or ATTRIB statement—or it must be initialized to a character literal value that has the maximum length.

For example, the following code now explicitly declares the length of New_char using LENGTH, so despite the return value length not being explicitly declared in the FUNCTION statement, the RETURN statement successfully returns the full 40-character value:

```
proc fcmp outlib=work.funcs.test;
   function pass_char(char $) $;
      length new_char $50;
```

The second method to pass a longer return value (without explicitly declaring its length) is to initialize the return value to a character literal. For example, the following code implicitly declares New_char when it is initialized to 40 Xs (using the REPEAT function), and the resulting 40-character return value will be returned to the calling program:

```
proc fcmp outlib=work.funcs.test;
   function pass_char(char $) $;
      new_char = repeat('x', 39);
```

Despite the complexity in declaring character return values, and the somewhat arbitrary 33-character limit that emerges when the return value length is not explicitly declared, two simple rules ensure that any character return value can be successfully created and passed: 1) always return a variable that is not a parameter, and 2) always explicitly declare the return value (including its length) using either the LENGTH or ATTRIB statement.

Differences between DATA Step and FCMP Syntax

Thus far, this chapter has primarily focused on function communication—that is, how to transfer data *into* a user-defined function and how to pass data *from* a user-defined function. With communication modalities in place, all that remains is a function's functionality—what it does. The majority of DATA step statements and syntax can be copied from a DATA step and effortlessly dropped into the FCMP procedure without modification. This interoperability is demonstrated in Programs 1.1 and 1.3, in which a DO loop and other logic required no changes before being moved from a DATA step to a user-defined function.

However, every rule has an exception. Some notable differences do exist between DATA step and FCMP statements and functionality. In some cases, equivalent functionality can be achieved within the FCMP procedure by subtly modifying syntax. In other cases, no workaround exists, and specific functionality is compromised or vacated in the FCMP procedure. And finally, some aspects of the FCMP procedure provide greater functionality than can be achieved through the DATA step.

The following five sections demonstrate some of these differences. Several additional sections in Chapter 3 illustrate differences in array functionality between the DATA step and the FCMP procedure. Finally, the SAS technical documentation "PROC FCMP and DATA Step Differences" should be consulted for other syntax differences not described in this text (SAS Institute Inc. 2023).

Use Caution When Modifying Call-by-Value Scalar Parameters

By default, scalar (and array) parameters are declared as call by value, as previously described. As such, changes to an argument bound to a call-by-value parameter are not communicated back to the calling program. Stated another way, the values associated with call-by-value parameters maintain only local scope within the function and are deleted at function termination.

Given this functionality, it would seem appropriate to modify a call-by-value parameter within a function, so long as the modifications are not intended to be communicated back to the calling program. For example, Program 2.36 modifies the CHAR_VAR parameter by applying the STRIP and UPCASE functions.

Program 2.36: Modifying a Call-by-Value Parameter
```
proc fcmp outlib=work.funcs.test;
   function pass_char(char_var $) $;
      file log;
      char_var = strip(upcase(char_var));
      put 'INSIDE ' char_var=;
      return(char_var);
      endfunc;
quit;
```

However, when the FCMP procedure is compiled, a warning appears in the log. It states that a "read-only argument" should never be modified:

```
9     proc fcmp outlib=work.funcs.test;
10       function pass_char(char_var $) $;
11          char_var = strip(upcase(char_var));
WARNING:  The variable 'char_var' should not be the result of the '='
operation because it is a read-only argument to 'pass_char'. Any changes
to this argument will not be returned from 'pass_char'. Use the OUTARGS
statement to allow return values.
12          put 'INSIDE ' char_var=;
13          return(char_var);
14          endfunc;
15    quit;

NOTE: Function pass_char saved to work.funcs.test.
```

Despite the warning, however, the function is compiled and saved. The DATA step in Program 2.37 calls the PASS_CHAR function and converts the lowercase "hello" to an uppercase "HELLO."

Program 2.37: Calling the PASS_CHAR Function
```
data _null_;
   char = 'hello';
   new_char=pass_char(char);
   put 'OUTSIDE ' char= new_char=;
run;
```

The output demonstrates the initial lowercase and subsequent uppercase values:

```
INSIDE   char_var=HELLO
OUTSIDE char=hello new_char=HELLO
```

Unfortunately, this warning is far more pernicious than it might appear. Despite the function's success in *this instance*, the reinitialization of a call-by-value parameter can cause unwanted results and even failure of the SAS application.

Consider a revised function, demonstrated in Program 2.38, that instead attempts to append "SAS User" to the CHAR_VAR parameter. The identical DATA step follows and calls the PASS_CHAR function.

Program 2.38: Modifying a Call-by-Value Parameter
```
proc fcmp outlib=work.funcs.test;
   function pass_char(char_var $) $;
      file log;
      char_var = char_var || ' SAS User';
      put 'INSIDE ' char_var=;
      return(char_var);
      endfunc;
quit;

data _null_;
   char = 'hello';
   new_char = pass_char(char);
   put 'OUTSIDE ' char= new_char=;
run;
```

The output demonstrates that despite the attempt to concatenate "SAS User," the initial "hello" value is unchanged by the function:

```
INSIDE   char_var=hello
OUTSIDE char=hello new_char=hello
```

At issue here is the fact that when the five-character Char variable is passed to PASS_CHAR, the function allocates a maximum of five characters for the parameter. The STRIP and UPCASE functions (demonstrated in Program 2.36) do not cause the character value to be lengthened, so they succeed. However, a concatenation operation does attempt to lengthen CHAR_VAR, and in doing so, fails. Moreover, because CHAR_VAR is declared as a parameter, its length cannot be modified within the function using the LENGTH statement. Finally, even adding a LENGTH statement to the DATA step prior to the function call fails to remedy this issue.

But the critical failure (not shown) occurs when you attempt to call a function that reinitializes a call-by-value parameter from the FORMAT procedure OTHER option. This method of calling user-defined functions is demonstrated in Chapter 9. If FORMAT encounters a function that reinitializes a parameter, your entire SAS application will crash without a note, warning, or runtime error. For all these reasons, it is far safer never to modify call-by-value parameters. That is, as a best practice, a parameter should never be reinitialized unless the parameter is specified by the OUTARGS statement.

Thus, the preferred method is to declare a new variable using the LENGTH statement, initialize that variable to the value of the parameter, and modify only that new variable. Program 2.39 demonstrates this more secure and reliable initialization and modification.

Program 2.39: Safely Not Modifying a Call-by-Value Parameter

```
proc fcmp outlib=work.funcs.test;
   function pass_char(char_var $) $;
      file log;
      length new_char_var $50;
      new_char_var = char_var || ' SAS User';
      put 'INSIDE ' new_char_var=;
      return(new_char_var);
      endfunc;
quit;
```

When the identical DATA step is executed a third time, the log demonstrates that New_char_var is successfully initialized to the correct value, which is subsequently returned to the DATA step:

```
INSIDE  new_char_var=hello SAS User
OUTSIDE char=hello new_char=hello SAS User
```

Also note that the modified PASS_CHAR function no longer results in that pesky warning message. Problem solved!

DO Loop Differences

Although uncommonly observed within the SAS language, it is possible to iterate lists of numeric literals or character literals in a DO loop. The iteration of literals is uncommon because the iteration of variables provides far greater flexibility. However, in some cases in which a data structure is never modified (such as the numeric enumeration of the days of the month or the character enumeration of the days of the week), the iteration of literals is appropriate. And in these cases, within the DATA step, an ephemeral, linear data structure is effectively iterated and deleted.

For example, the DATA step in Program 2.40 iterates over Dates, which represents an abbreviated list of dates in some specific month, and over Days, which represents an abbreviated list of days of the week.

Program 2.40: Iterating Numeric Literals and Character Literals
```
data _null_;
   do dates = 1, 2, 3;
      put dates;
      end;
   do days = 'Mon', 'Tue', 'Wed';
      put days;
      end;
run;
```

The log demonstrates that Dates and Days are iteratively assigned to each of the values in their respective literal lists:

```
1
2
3
Mon
Tue
Wed
```

However, if the same two DO loops are placed inside the FCMP procedure, only the Dates list of numeric literals will succeed; the list of character literals will fail. For example, Program 2.41 copies these DO loops verbatim into the DO_NOTHING function.

Program 2.41: Failure of Attempt to Iterate List of Character Literals
```
proc fcmp outlib=work.funcs.test;
   function do_nothing();
      file log;
      do dates = 1, 2, 3;
         put dates;
         end;
 ✹ do days = 'Mon', 'Tue', 'Wed';
         put days;
         end;
      return(.);
      endfunc;
quit;
```

The log demonstrates this failure:

```
309  proc fcmp outlib=work.funcs.test;
310     function do_nothing();
311        do dates=1, 2, 3;
312           put dates;
313           end;
314        do days='Mon', 'Tue', 'Wed';
ERROR: The value for the DO statement must be numeric. The character DO
statement value is invalid at line 314 column 7.
315           put days;
316           end;
317        return(.);
318        endfunc;
319  quit;


NOTE: The SAS System stopped processing this step because of errors.
```

To overcome this subtle limitation, SAS numeric and character arrays can be initialized with constant values when they are declared by the ARRAY statement. In doing so, an array of constants can function equivalently to a list of literals, and thereby protect against accidental modification. Constant arrays are declared when initialized values are enumerated without enclosing parentheses. For example, the following statements declare the Dates numeric array of constants and the Days character array of constants:

```
array dates[3] 1 2 3;
array days[3] $10 'Mon' 'Tue' 'Wed';
```

No values within these arrays can be modified in the remainder of the FCMP procedure. Any attempt to do so will result in a runtime error:

```
ERROR: Attempt to assign to a constant ARRAY element in statement number X
at line Y column Z.
```

By contrast, enclosing initializing values in parentheses declares variables—not constants—that can be modified inside the FCMP procedure:

```
array dates[3] (1 2 3);
array days[3] $10 ('Mon' 'Tue' 'Wed');
```

Taking this into account, the DO_NOTHING function in Program 2.41 is modified in Program 2.42 to leverage constant arrays rather than lists of literals.

Program 2.42: Replacing Numeric and Character Literals with Arrays of Constants

```
proc fcmp outlib=work.funcs.test;
   function do_nothing();
      file log;
      array dates[3] (1 2 3);
      do cnt_dates = 1 to dim(dates);
         put dates[cnt_dates];
         end;
      array days[3] $10 ('Mon' 'Tue' 'Wed');
      do cnt_days = 1 to dim(days);
         put days[cnt_days];
         end;
      return(.);
      endfunc;
quit;
```

The DATA step in Program 2.43 calls the DO_NOTHING function and generates output identical to the DATA step in Program 2.40.

Program 2.43: Calling the DO_NOTHING Function from a DATA Step

```
data _null_;
   rc = do_nothing();
run;
```

And, more importantly, if any attempt is made to change any element in either the Dates array or the Days array, a runtime error prevents this modification, thus securing the contents of the arrays.

FILE LOG Statement to Direct SAS Output to SAS Log

Within user-defined functions, the PUT statement is primarily used during development, testing, and debugging as a means to capture variable values during a function call. The default output location for PUT differs, however, between the DATA step and the FCMP procedure, with the DATA step defaulting to the SAS log and the FCMP procedure defaulting to the Output window. Thus, throughout this text, the FILE statement is required to specify the LOG option whenever the PUT statement occurs inside of an FCMP procedure.

For example, Program 2.44 defines the TEST_FUNC function that transforms a character value passed as an argument by prepending "Returned:" to the value. The PUT statement inside the FCMP procedure simulates printing Var to the log during testing or debugging of the function. Thus, because Var has only local scope, a developer might need to know its value prior to the subsequent transformation to New_var. PUT provides this functionality.

Program 2.44: Using the PUT Statement without the FILE LOG Statement

```
proc fcmp outlib=work.funcs.logging;
   function test_func(var $) $;
      length new_var $50;
      put var=;
```

```
      new_var = 'Returned: ' || var;
      return(new_var);
      endfunc;
quit;

data _null_;
   x = test_func('Hi there!');
   put x=;
run;
```

The DATA step, by default, prints the contents of PUT statements to the SAS log, so when TEST_ FUNC is called inside the DATA step in Program 2.44, the FCMP procedure first prints VAR to the log, after which the DATA step prints X to the log:

```
var=Hi there!
x=returned: Hi there!
```

However, and somewhat surprisingly, the default output location for the FCMP procedure is not the SAS log, but rather the Output window. To demonstrate, the following statement calls TEST_ FUNC again, now using the %SYSFUNC macro statement:

```
%put %sysfunc(test_func(Hi there!));
```

However, the SAS log now only shows the value of X, and the PUT statement inside the FCMP procedure seemingly has no effect:

```
35   %put %sysfunc(test_func(Hi there!));
returned: Hi there!
```

However, run the %PUT statement a second time and watch what happens. With "Bye there!" passed, the two function calls can be contrasted:

```
%put %sysfunc(test_func(Bye there!));
```

Once again, the SAS log only shows the results of the PUT statement inside the DATA step, and not the PUT statement inside the FCMP procedure:

```
36   %put %sysfunc(test_func(Hi there!));
returned: Hi there!
```

However, the SAS application has also opened the Output window, where the following output from the FCMP PUT statement has been printed:

```
var=Hi there!
```

Thus, SAS delayed printing the FCMP PUT statement from the first function call until the second function call, and no output from the second function call has been printed.

However, when the following DATA step is subsequently executed after the two %SYSFUNC calls, the FCMP PUT statement from the second call is finally revealed:

```
data _null_;
run;
```

When the DATA step executes, the output from the second PUT statement is printed to the Output window:

```
var=Bye there!
```

Thus, by default, SAS delays PUT statements inside the FCMP procedure when user-defined functions are called using %SYSFUNC, or user-defined subroutines are called using %SYSCALL. Moreover, the output from FCMP PUT statements is surprisingly sent to the Output window, rather than the SAS log.

To remedy this issue, and as demonstrated throughout this text, all user-defined functions that use a PUT statement also should include the FILE LOG statement to direct that the output from PUT statements will be sent to the log immediately.

Program 2.45 refactors the TEST_FUNC function in Program 2.44 into the TEST_FUNC_LOG function, which uses the FILE LOG statement to direct output from the PUT statement to the log.

Program 2.45: Using the PUT Statement with the FILE LOG Statement

```
proc fcmp outlib=work.funcs.logging;
   function test_func_log(var $) $;
      file log;
      length new_var $50;
      put var=;
      new_var = 'Returned: ' || var;
      return(new_var);
      endfunc;
quit;

data _null_;
   x = test_func_log('Hi there!');
   put x=;
run;
```

When the DATA step executes, the results of both PUT statements are printed to the log—identical to the functionality of Program 2.44:

```
var=Hi there!
x=returned: Hi there!
```

However, the real magic occurs when %SYSFUNC again invokes TEST_FUNC_LOG:

```
%put %sysfunc(test_func_log(Hi there!));
```

Because the FILE LOG statement directs output to the SAS log, %SYSFUNC now displays identical functionality to the preceding DATA step, and prints both variables to the log:

```
var=Hi there!
x=returned: Hi there!
```

The lesson here is that whenever a PUT statement is used inside of the FCMP procedure, it should be preceded by the FILE LOG statement to direct all output from the PUT statement to the SAS log. The full functionality of the FILE statement lies outside the scope of this text, but note that where a SAS log must be saved to a file—to include output generated inside the FCMP procedure—the FILE statement can alternatively specify a file to which log contents are saved.

PUT Statement Differences

Several differences exist in how the PUT statement operates in the FCMP procedure, including both what can be printed and where it is printed. For example, Programs 2.44 and 2.45 in the preceding section demonstrate that the default location for output printed by PUT differs between the DATA step and the FCMP procedure.

PUT statement functionality also differs inside the FCMP procedure where arrays are being printed. Within both the FCMP procedure and the DATA step, methods exist to print entire arrays or individual array elements. Similarly, the equal sign (=) is used by PUT to preface a value with its corresponding variable name. For example, the DO_ARRAYS function in Program 2.46 demonstrates eight successive uses of PUT. The first four PUT statements print the entire array, and the last four print the first element of the array.

Program 2.46: Declaring, Initializing, and Printing Arrays within PROC FCMP

```
proc fcmp outlib=work.funcs.test;
   function do_arrays();
      file log;
      array nums[5] (1 2 3 4 5);
      * print entire array;
      put nums; /* is equivalent to PUT nums[*]  */
      put nums=; /* is equivalent to PUT nums[*] */
      put nums[*];
      put nums[*]=;
      * print first element of array;
```

```
        put nums[1];
        put nums[1]=;
        put nums1;
        put nums1=;
        return(.);
        endfunc;
quit;


%put %sysfunc(do_arrays());
```

The log demonstrates the variations that are produced when %SYSFUNC calls the DO_ARRAYS function:

```
1 2 3 4 5
nums[1]=1 nums[2]=2 nums[3]=3 nums[4]=4 nums[5]=5
1 2 3 4 5
nums[1]=1 nums[2]=2 nums[3]=3 nums[4]=4 nums[5]=5
1
nums[1]=1
1
nums1=1
```

However, when equivalent code is run inside the DATA step, demonstrated in Program 2.47, the first two PUT statements generate errors.

Program 2.47: Declaring, Initializing, and Printing Arrays within the DATA Step
```
data _null_;
    array nums[5] (1 2 3 4 5);
    * put nums; /* generates ERROR: Illegal reference to the array nums */
    * put nums=; /* generates ERROR: Illegal reference to the array nums */
    put nums[*];
    put nums[*]=;
    put nums[1];
    put nums[1]=;
    put nums1;
    put nums1=;
run;
```

This limitation of the DATA step is negligible, however, as the functionally equivalent third and fourth PUT statements print the same results to the log as the PUT statements that cause runtime errors.

A final difference in the PUT statement extends its functionality within the FCMP procedure beyond the DATA step, by supporting the ability to print not only values but also expressions. For example, by enclosing an expression inside parentheses, it can be printed by the FCMP procedure:

```
put 'IN ' (length(str)/countw(str));
```

This functionality is demonstrated in Program 2.48, in which the PUT statement prints the average word length:

Program 2.48: Printing Expressions Using the PUT Statement
```
proc fcmp outlib=work.funcs.test;
   function calc_word_len(str $);
      file log;
      length avg 8;
      avg = length(str) / countw(str);
      put 'IN ' (length(str) / countw(str));
      return(avg);
      endfunc;
quit;

%put OUT %sysfunc(calc_word_len(one two three four five six));
```

The log demonstrates that both %PUT and PUT print the average word length, with IN being printed from the FCMP procedure, and OUT being printed as the resolved value of the %SYSFUNC call of the CALC_WORD_LEN function:

```
OUT 4.5
IN  4.5
```

Conversely, when used inside the DATA step, the PUT statement cannot print expressions.

Using Optional Arguments in Built-in Functions Called inside PROC FCMP

Built-in SAS functions, unlike the user-defined functions designed within the FCMP procedure, can support optional arguments. This flexibility is quite useful. For example, the COMPRESS function declares three parameters, the last two of which are optional. The first (required) parameter specifies the variable or text that is being compressed. The second (optional) parameter specifies a list of characters that are to be removed (unless the third parameter specifies a "K"), and the third (optional) parameter specifies modifiers.

For example, Program 2.49 calls the COMPRESS function from the DATA step five times to remove all spaces through various methods. A blank space in the second argument denotes that spaces should be removed, and an "S" in the third argument also denotes that spaces should be removed.

Program 2.49: Calling COMPRESS from the DATA Step
```
data _null_;
   length phrase w1-w6 $40;
   phrase = 'Once upon a midnight dreary';
   w1 = compress(phrase);
   w2 = compress(phrase,'');
```

```
      w3 = compress(phrase,' .');
      w4 = compress(phrase,,'s');
      w5 = compress(phrase, ,'s');
      w6 = compress(phrase,'','s');
      put w1=;
      put w2=;
      put w3=;
      put w4=;
      put w5=;
      put w6=;
run;
```

The log demonstrates identical functionality for each call to COMPRESS:

```
w1=Onceuponamidnightdreary
w2=Onceuponamidnightdreary
w3=Onceuponamidnightdreary
w4=Onceuponamidnightdreary
w5=Onceuponamidnightdreary
w6=Onceuponamidnightdreary
```

However, when these statements are copied into the FCMP procedure, not all calls to COMPRESS are successful. The TEST_COMPRESS function in Program 2.50 reattempts these six COMPRESS calls.

Program 2.50: Calling COMPRESS from the FCMP Procedure
```
proc fcmp outlib=work.funcs.test;
    function test_compress();
        file log;
        length phrase $40 w1-w6 $40;
        phrase = 'Once upon a midnight dreary';
        w1 = compress(phrase);
        w2 = compress(phrase,'');
        w3 = compress(phrase,' ');
        w4 = compress(phrase,,'s');
        w5 = compress(phrase, ,'s');
        w6 = compress(phrase,'','s');
        put w1=;
        put w2=;
        put w3=;
        put w4=;
        put w5=;
        put w6=;
        return(.);
        endfunc;
quit;

%put %sysfunc(test_compress());
```

The log demonstrates the failure of the second call to COMPRESS, in which it fails to remove spaces, as it did in the DATA step:

```
w1=Onceuponamidnightdreary
w2=Once upon a midnight dreary
w3=Onceuponamidnightdreary
w4=Onceuponamidnightdreary
w5=Onceuponamidnightdreary
w6=Onceuponamidnightdreary
```

A second example removes spaces using a different methodology. The second argument is omitted, and the third argument specifies "KA"—this corresponds to "keep all alphabetic characters." The DATA step in Program 2.51 removes spaces from the first call to COMPRESS but not the second.

Program 2.51: Calling COMPRESS from the DATA Step

```
data _null_;
   length phrase $40 w1-w2 $40;
   phrase = 'Once upon a midnight dreary';
   w1 = compress(phrase,,'ka');
   w2 = compress(phrase,'','ka');
   put w1=;
   put w2=;
run;
```

The log demonstrates that the second call to COMPRESS does not remove the spaces:

```
w1=Onceuponamidnightdreary
w2=Once upon a midnight dreary
```

The TEST_COMPRESS function in Program 2.52 repeats the two calls to COMPRESS.

Program 2.52: Calling COMPRESS from the FCMP Procedure

```
proc fcmp outlib=work.funcs.test;
   function test_compress();
      file log;
      length phrase $40 w1-w2 $40;
      phrase='Once upon a midnight dreary';
      w1 = compress(phrase,,'ka');
      w2 = compress(phrase,'','ka');
      put w1=;
      put w2=;
      return(.);
      endfunc;
quit;

%put %sysfunc(test_compress());
```

However, the log demonstrates that the results are frighteningly reversed!

```
2143   proc fcmp outlib=work.funcs.test;
2144      function test_compress();
2145         file log;
2146         length phrase $40 w1-w2 $40;
2147         phrase = 'Once upon a midnight dreary';
2148         w1 = compress(phrase,,'ka');
NOTE: Numeric value converted to character for argument 2 of 'COMPRESS'
      operation.
2149         w2=compress(phrase,'','ka');
2150         put w1=;
2151         put w2=;
2152         return(.);
2153      endfunc;
2154   quit;

2155
2156   %put %sysfunc(test_compress());
.
w1=Once upon a midnight dreary
w2=Onceuponamidnightdreary
```

This failure pattern of the FCMP procedure unfortunately occurs with all built-in functions for which an optional parameter is skipped when the function is called. For this reason, use extreme caution when calling built-in functions such as COMPRESS or SCAN that pass missing values via optional arguments. In many cases, when attempting to achieve equivalent functionality in the FCMP procedure, you will need to explicitly include a set of single or double quotation marks that denote omitted optional character arguments.

Concluding a Function or Subroutine

Prior to function termination, the final component of all functions and many subroutines is communication back to the calling program. Functions always communicate via the mandatory return value, and both functions and subroutines can optionally communicate via one or more parameters specified by the OUTARGS statement. The OUTARGS statement is discussed previously in this chapter. The RETURN statement facilitates returning a return value from a user-defined function. Finally, the definition of each function or subroutine concludes with the ENDFUNC or ENDSUB statement, respectively.

The RETURN Statement

The RETURN statement returns a scalar value from a called function to its calling program. RETURN is only supported within user-defined functions, not subroutines. RETURN also transfers program control from a user-defined function back to its calling program, so once RETURN has been called, no other statements within the function will execute. For this reason, although a function can have multiple RETURN statements, only one RETURN statement will ever execute during a given function call.

Note that RETURN removes all formatting from the return value. Program 2.53 demonstrates this functionality, with the Tom variable declared as having the MMDDYY10 format inside the function.

Program 2.53: Demonstrating the RETURN Statement Removing a Date Format
```
proc fcmp outlib=work.funcs.dt;
   function tomorrow();
      file log;
      length tom 8;
      format tom mmddyy10.;
      tom = today()+1;
      put tom=;
      return(tom);
      endfunc;
quit;

%put %sysfunc(tomorrow());
```

However, despite the Tom variable being displayed in MMDDYY10 format inside the function, the RETURN statement strips the format when returning the value, so the %PUT statement instead displays the date as an unformatted SAS date. Thus, when executing this code on Christmas Eve 2021 while anxiously awaiting the launch of the JWST, the %PUT statement first prints 23639, after which the PUT statement prints the formatted date:

```
23639
tom=12/25/2021
```

Because RETURN strips all formats from return values, it is often unnecessary to format variables inside a function because the ultimate return value will be unformatted. However, formatting a variable inside a function can provide value during software testing and debugging. For example, the PUT statement inside the TOMORROW function could be used to validate that the internal Tom variable does represent a date.

One common practice within user-defined functions adds one or more quality control checks that validate the input received through arguments. For example, the NEXT_DAY function, demonstrated in Program 2.54, adds a day to a parameterized date (DT), rather than to the current date. In providing more flexibility, it might be beneficial to restrict the input to some range of dates (for example, to dates in the 21st Century). This conditional logic first evaluates whether the DT parameter falls within the current century. If it does not, the first RETURN statement immediately returns a missing value and terminates the function.

Program 2.54: Demonstrating Multiple RETURN Statements in a User-Defined Function

```
proc fcmp outlib=work.funcs.dt;
   function next_day(dt);
      if dt < '01jan2001'd or dt > '31dec2100'd then return(.);
      length tom 8;
      tom = dt + 1;
      return(tom);
      endfunc;
quit;


%put %sysfunc(next_day(' 24dec2021'd), mmddyy10.);
```

Because the argument passed (December 24, 2021) falls within the *acceptable* range of dates, program flow bypasses the first RETURN statement and executes the remaining statements, including the second RETURN statement that returns the Tom variable (representing the next day). The log demonstrates the successful return of tomorrow's date:

```
343  %put %sysfunc(next_day('24dec2021'd), mmddyy10.);
12/25/2021
```

Thus, as described, a user-defined function can have multiple RETURN statements; however, only one RETURN will execute during a given function call. To execute the first RETURN statement, an invalid date (occurring in 3022 in the next century) can be passed:

```
%put %sysfunc(next_day('01nov3022'd), mmddyy10.);
```

The log now demonstrates that the first RETURN statement returned only the period representing a missing numeric value:

```
346  %put %sysfunc(next_day('01nov3022'd), mmddyy10.);
.
```

Finally, it is worth noting the versatility of the RETURN statement. It can comprise a combination of variables, values, and expressions, and this design often can produce a more concise solution that requires initializing fewer (or no) intermediate variables.

For example, Program 2.55 refactors Program 2.54 and reduces the function's syntax to a one-line RETURN statement.

Program 2.55: Compressing Functionality into the RETURN Statement

```
proc fcmp outlib=work.funcs.dt;
   function next_day(dt);
      return(ifn('01jan2001'd <= dt <= '31dec2100'd, dt+1, .));
      endfunc;
quit;
```

Thus, in lieu of the IF statement, the IFN function now evaluates whether the DT parameter falls within the acceptable range. If it does, IFN evaluates to the DT date plus one. If it does not, IFN evaluates to a missing value. This reduction of code arguably does not diminish readability. However, it does eliminate the need to declare and initialize the Tom variable, and it takes far fewer lines of code to produce identical output.

ENDFUNC and ENDSUB Statements

ENDFUNC and ENDSUB are the statements that terminate both user-defined function and subroutine definitions, respectively. These statements are aliases, however, and are fully interchangeable. That is, a function can be terminated by ENDSUB, and a subroutine can be terminated by ENDFUNC. Some users prefer to differentiate usage for readability, as is done throughout this text, whereas many organizations singly adopt either ENDFUNC or ENDSUB to terminate all functions and subroutines. Whatever methodology is selected, it should be applied consistently to promote readability.

As demonstrated in Program 2.16, a single FCMP procedure can define multiple functions and/ or subroutines. In these cases, multiple ENDFUNC and/or ENDSUB statements are required. Note that each individual function or subroutine requires only one ENDFUNC or ENDSUB statement.

Conclusion

This chapter provided an overview of FCMP syntax and focused primarily on communication between the calling program (typically a DATA step) and the called module (the user-defined function or subroutine). Parameters declared inside a user-defined function facilitate the receipt of dynamic input from the calling program, which yields dynamic functionality and results. The signature of a function defines its parameters, including its name, position, object type, data type, dimensionality, and call method. The OUTARGS statement was discussed, which specifies that one or more scalar or array parameters should be passed by reference, in which changes made to parameters inside a function are reflected in the calling program after the function terminates. Finally, although the majority of SAS syntax is interoperable between the DATA step and the FCMP procedure, several sections demonstrated differences in syntax or functionality between the DATA step and FCMP procedure.

Chapter 3: Arrays

Within Base SAS, arrays are conceptualized as temporary labels that reference a group of variables—they are not data structures. Arrays can reference linear or multidimensional elements, and they are contrasted with *scalar* variables that contain a single value. Developers familiar with other programming languages are likely accustomed to arrays that function as actual data types or data structures; however, SAS documentation makes clear the distinction of SAS arrays:

> Arrays in the SAS language are different from arrays in many other languages. A SAS array is simply a convenient way of temporarily identifying a group of variables. It is not a data structure, and *array-name* is not a variable. (SAS Institute Inc. 2021)

Despite the major differences between SAS arrays and arrays in other languages, many high-level concepts and benefits of arrays are identical. Integral to arrays is the ability to containerize distinct data elements into a cohesive collection. Thereafter, the collection can be iterated to perform some action repeatedly on each element, or in some cases, an action or operation can be performed universally across the collection. Both methods reduce code volume and complexity and produce cleaner software that is more readable and maintainable.

This chapter introduces SAS arrays and demonstrates some of their capabilities within the DATA step, after which arrays are contrasted in the FCMP procedure. Arrays provide the only method to pass multi-element arguments to and from user-defined functions and the DATA step. In other cases, arrays are declared and initialized inside a function, used for some operation, and deleted (rather than returned) when the function terminates. Finally, the READ_ARRAY built-in function ingests numeric data from a data set into a user-defined function, and the WRITE_ARRAY built-in function writes numeric data to a data set from a user-defined function.

Although much array functionality is identical between the DATA step and the FCMP procedure, some aspects of array syntax and functionality do differ. In some cases, array functionality is enhanced within FCMP, such as the DYNAMIC_ARRAY built-in subroutine, which dynamically resizes an array to minimize memory consumption. In other cases, FCMP arrays are more limited, such as the inability to use the OF operator with FCMP arrays. Several sections demonstrate these differences and suggest workarounds for some FCMP array limitations. Also demonstrated is how array usage differs for functions called by the %SYSFUNC macro function and subroutines called by the %SYSCALL macro statement. The chapter concludes with a demonstration of how two-dimensional arrays leveraged inside the FCMP procedure can replicate SAS/IML functionality to solve linear algebra equations.

Arrays in the DATA Step

SAS arrays are commonly used to reduce redundancy and simplify code. They improve the readability and maintainability of DATA step syntax by facilitating *scalability*—the ability of software to flexibly accommodate additional variables (or values) with ease. In other cases, SAS arrays can additionally improve software speed and efficiency, such as when an array is leveraged to provide hashing functionality or to operationalize a sparse matrix. These latter usages of arrays, however, are not detailed within this text, and the vast publications of experts such as Paul Dorfman, Don Henderson, Richard DeVenezia, and Bart Jablonski should instead be consulted. Thus, the array functionality that is demonstrated improves *internal*—not *external*—measures of software quality, as contrasted in Chapter 1.

However, within the realm of the FCMP procedure, arrays are absolutely essential and do impart functionality that cannot otherwise be achieved. For example, arrays provide the only method to communicate multi-element arguments from a DATA step to a user-defined function or to retrieve multi-element arguments from a function. Other data structures, including the hash object and dictionary object, can be instantiated and used inside a function, but only the array can communicate between a user-defined function and the DATA step. In the following sections, arrays are first demonstrated within the DATA step, after which later sections build upon this foundation to demonstrate arrays in the FCMP procedure.

DATA Step Array Declaration

SAS arrays are declared using the ARRAY statement, which names the array, specifies its data type as character or numeric, and specifies the dimensions—the number of elements the array contains. The ARRAY statement optionally can initialize the array elements with values. Arrays are not data structures themselves, but rather resemble a label describing a list of SAS variables. Thus, array elements can have a data type of either character or numeric, but no array can contain both character and numeric variables or values.

Like SAS variables, SAS arrays are declared as numeric data type by default. A $ is required to declare a character array. Within the DATA step, the ARRAY statement can declare arrays explicitly or implicitly. *Explicit* arrays declare an index and require an index to access individual elements of the array, whereas *implicit* arrays declare only the array name, yet require a list of variables to be mapped into the array; these can be new or existing variables. Both explicit and implicit arrays can be declared within a DATA step and passed to a function through an array parameter.

Implicit arrays are sometimes referred to as *implicitly indexed arrays* or *unindexed arrays*. To be clear, all SAS arrays are indexed, and even implicit arrays can be referenced after their initialization by their index number. Conversely, explicit arrays are sometimes referred to as *explicitly indexed arrays* or *indexed arrays*; once again, all SAS arrays are indexed. Rather, the distinction lies in that an explicit array always must be referenced by its subscripted (bracketed) index number, whereas an implicit array can be referenced either by the array name or subscripted index notation.

Program 3.1 declares the explicit array (Prices_explicit) and implicit array (Prices_implicit). Array names follow standard SAS variable-naming conventions. Note that explicit array declarations always require trailing brackets that identify the array dimensions, whereas implicit array declarations do not.

Program 3.1: Declaring Explicit and Implicit Default Numeric Arrays

```
data test;
    array prices_explicit[3];
    array prices_implicit this_price that_price other_price;
run;
```

When the DATA step executes, the first ARRAY statement automatically creates three numeric variables—Prices_explicit1, Prices_explicit2, and Prices_explicit3—based on the array dimensions (3). The second ARRAY statement similarly creates three numeric variables, but it relies on the variable names that are provided—This_price, That_price, and Other_price—rather than explicit dimensions. Thus, implicit array declarations must count the number of variables listed in the ARRAY statement to generate the array index, whereas explicit array declarations generate the array index from the bracketed dimensions.

Character arrays are similarly declared using the ARRAY statement and require a trailing $ after the array name. Program 3.2 declares the Names_explicit and Names_implicit character arrays, with all six variables created using the default character variable length of eight characters.

Program 3.2: Declaring Explicit and Implicit Character Arrays

```
data test;
    array names_explicit[3] $;
    array names_implicit $ this_name that_name other_name;
run;
```

More commonly, you will want to declare character arrays that have a specific length, which is accomplished by adding a length value after the $. Program 3.3 declares the Names_explicit array as having a length of 10, and the Names_implicit array as having a length of 20.

Program 3.3: Declaring Explicit and Implicit Character Arrays with Lengths

```
data test;
   array names_explicit[3] $10;
   array names_implicit $20 this_name that_name other_name;
run;
```

Explicit arrays can optionally enumerate specific variables to be containerized, and this method of array declaration is demonstrated in Program 3.4, in which Names_explicit is declared.

Program 3.4: Declaring Explicit and Implicit Character Arrays with Explicit Variables

```
data test;
   array names_explicit[3] $10 my_name his_name her_name;
   array names_implicit $20 this_name that_name other_name;
run;
```

Now, rather than the Names_explicit array containing the Names_explicit1, Names_explicit2, and Names_explicit3 variables, it instead contains the My_name, His_name, and Her_name variables. However, if SAS can automatically create multiple variables during an explicit array declaration, why would anyone inefficiently choose to name the variables manually?

This is commonly required when an array is declared not to create *new* variables, but rather to associate *existing* variables within an array. For example, Program 3.5 first declares the variables My_name, His_name, and Her_name using a LENGTH statement, after which the ARRAY statement declares the Names_explicit array as containing these three variables, with each variable retaining its original character length. Although a character array must contain only character variables, those variables can have different lengths.

Program 3.5: Declaring an Explicit Character Array with Existent Variables

```
data test;
   length my_name $5 his_name $10 her_name $20;
   array names_explicit[3] $ my_name his_name her_name;
run;
```

Another tool available for explicit array declaration enables array dimensions to be evaluated automatically by specifying an asterisk [*] rather than a dimension value. Where [*] is specified, the associated variable names also must be enumerated, as shown in Program 3.6. Now, H: specifies that all variables beginning with "H" should be assigned to the Names_explicit array when it is declared.

Program 3.6: Declaring an Explicit Character Array with Existent Variables and Dynamic Dimensions

```
data test;
   length my_name $5 his_name $10 her_name $20;
   array names_explicit[*] $ h:;
   put names_explicit[*]=;
run;
```

The log demonstrates that Names_explicit contains two variables—His_name and Her_name:

```
NOTE: Variable my_name is uninitialized.
his_name=  her_name=
NOTE: The data set WORK.TEST has 1 observations and 3 variables.
```

Note that My_name is declared by LENGTH but never referenced; thus, the "uninitialized" note is printed. Also note that both His_name and Her_name are empty, as these variables have not been initialized.

In summary, the ARRAY statement declares an array of new or existing variables and supports both explicit and implicit indexing. Although the ARRAY statement can optionally initialize array variables, array variables can also be initialized either before or after the ARRAY statement, as demonstrated in the next section.

DATA Step Array Initialization

Array variables can be initialized—that is, filled with data—during the array declaration via the ARRAY statement, or initialization can occur either before or after array declaration. In the case of an array declaration that associates several existent variables to a new array, these variables might already have values—and those values are retained after the array declaration. In other cases, the ARRAY statement not only declares the array but also creates the variables therein, in which case the array is empty, and must be initialized after the array declaration. Finally, array variables can be initialized during the ARRAY statement by listing literal values to be containerized. All three methods of array initialization are demonstrated in this section, and all three methods are supported by the DATA step and the FCMP procedure.

Program 3.7 declares four numeric variables (Price1 through Price4) using the LENGTH statement and initializes these four variables using separate assignment statements. The ARRAY statement subsequently declares the Prices array that contains the four variables.

Program 3.7: Initializing Numeric Variables before Array Declaration

```
data test;
   length price1-price4 8;
   price1=55000;
   price2=59000;
   price3=57000;
   price4=53000;
   array prices [*] price1 price2 price3 price4;
   put prices[*];
   put prices[*]=;
run;
```

The first PUT statement prints the values of Prices1 through Prices4 to the log, whereas the second PUT statement includes each array element variable and its corresponding value:

```
55000 59000 57000 53000
price1=55000 price2=59000 price3=57000 price4=53000
```

A functionally equivalent, more compact ARRAY statement could reference the range of variables from Price1 to Price4:

```
array prices [*] price1-price4;
```

An even more compact array assignment instead references all variables beginning with "Price" by using a trailing colon—and does so in the order in which they were declared in the program data vector (PDV):

```
array prices [*] price:;
```

Program 3.8 similarly declares four character variables, then it initializes the variables with fruit names and declares the Names array to reference the four variables.

Program 3.8: Initializing Character Variables before Array Declaration
```
data test;
    length name1-name4 $20;
    name1='Orange';
    name2='Banana';
    name3='Persimmon';
    name4='Mango';
    array names[*] $ name1-name4;
run;
```

In other cases, the ARRAY statement both declares and initializes an array, in which case the array is populated with literal values. Program 3.9 demonstrates declaring and initializing a numeric array in which array elements are separated by spaces.

Program 3.9: Initializing Numeric Variables inside an Array Declaration
```
data test;
    array prices[4] (55000 59000 57000 53000);
run;
```

A functionally equivalent solution separates the array elements with commas in lieu of spaces:

```
array prices[4] (55000,59000,57000,53000);
```

Similarly, the ARRAY statement in Program 3.10 declares a character array and initializes its variables to character literals. Note that the character length must be declared in the ARRAY statement or else the default variable length of 8 characters will be used, in which case "Persimmon" would be truncated.

Program 3.10: Initializing Character Variables inside Array Declaration
```
data test;
   array names[4] $20 ('Orange' 'Banana' 'Persimmon' 'Mango');
run;
```

Like the initialization of numeric arrays, character elements can optionally be separated by commas. Thus, the following ARRAY statement is functionally equivalent:

```
array names[4] $20 ('Orange','Banana','Persimmon','Mango');
```

Finally, in some cases, the array is declared first, and thereafter is initialized during the DATA step, often in a loop that iterates over array elements. The DIM function retrieves the dimensions of an array and is commonly used to loop over an array. In a unidimensional array, DIM accepts a single argument—the array name. Program 3.11 demonstrates this iteration, in which the Cnt variable is incremented to iterate the array.

Program 3.11: Initializing Numeric Array after Array Declaration
```
data test (drop=cnt);
   array prices[4];
   do cnt=1 to dim(prices);
      if cnt=1 then prices[cnt]=55000;
      else if cnt=2 then prices[cnt]=59000;
      else if cnt=3 then prices[cnt]=57000;
      else if cnt=4 then prices[cnt]=53000;
      end;
run;
```

For example, in the first iteration of the DO loop, Cnt resolves to 1, so the IF statement initializes the first element of the array (Prices[1]) to 55000. Note that in Base SAS, array dimensions and elements begin with 1, as opposed to 0, as in many programming languages.

In reality, far more complex business rules could be used to initialize array elements, but these examples demonstrate the basics of array initialization. With this introduction to array declaration and initialization within the DATA step, the next sections dive into array usage in user-defined functions.

Passing an Array to a Function

Many built-in functions and subroutines accept a variable number of arguments. For example, the built-in MEAN function computes the average (mean) of a series of numbers, and it acts identically whether one or 100 values are supplied. Similar user-defined functions that accept a variable number of arguments but return a single value can be designed by passing an array to a user-defined function.

Passing Multi-Element Arguments to a Built-in Function

The MEAN function accepts a variable number of arguments, which can comprise numeric constants, numeric variables, or numeric literals. Another way to express this is that the MEAN function accepts a *non-scalar argument*—that is, a *multi-element argument*, or an argument that represents a collection of elements. For example, in Program 3.12, four variables (Price1 to Price4) are passed to MEAN and bound to a single parameter.

In this series of examples, only numeric variables are demonstrated. Program 3.12 calls MEAN and passes a comma-delimited list of variables to the function.

Program 3.12: Passing a Multi-Element Argument to a Function
```
data test;
   length price1-price4 avg_price 8;
   price1=55000;
   price2=59000;
   price3=57000;
   price4=53000;
   avg_price=mean(price1, price2, price3, price4);
   put avg_price=;
run;
```

The DATA step executes and demonstrates the mean of the four variables:

```
avg_price=56000
```

However, as demonstrated in the previous section, a functionally equivalent solution could instead use the OF operator to pass all variables (alphabetically) between Price1 and Price4:

```
avg_price=mean(of price1-price4);
```

A functionally equivalent solution uses OF (and a colon) to pass all variables that begin with "Price":

```
avg_price=mean(of price:);
```

Unfortunately, these three methods are viable for passing multi-element arguments only to *built-in* functions; they are incompatible with *user-defined* functions. Thus, in passing multi-element arguments to a user-defined function, SAS practitioners must first declare an array and pass that array to the function.

Program 3.13 declares four numeric variables (Price1 to Price4) using the LENGTH statement, after which the ARRAY statement declares the Prices array that references these variables. Thereafter, as the Prices variables are initialized, they are simultaneously initialized within the array, overwriting the default missing values that the ARRAY statement had populated. Finally, the MEAN function leverages the OF operator to pass the Prices array.

Program 3.13: Passing a Multi-Element Array to a Function
```
data test;
   length price1-price4 avg_price 8;
   array prices[*] price:;
   price1=55000;
   price2=59000;
   price3=57000;
   price4=53000;
   avg_price=mean(of prices[*]);
   put avg_price=;
run;
```

The Prices subscript [*] denotes that all elements in the Prices array (that is, Price1 through Price4) are passed to MEAN. If only an alphabetic subset of an array should be passed to a function, the series can be denoted by a hyphen between the starting and ending variable names, as demonstrated previously.

Passing an array in lieu of an equivalent list of variables does require the extra step of declaring the array. Thus, Program 3.13 requires the ARRAY statement, whereas Program 3.12 does not. Arrays can more readily be passed to built-in functions because arrays can scale to accommodate endless variables without cluttering code.

For example, consider the requirement to compute not only the mean but also the median, standard deviation, and variance for the same series of variables. Program 3.14 adds this functionality, as well as the realism of more diverse variables, such as This_price and That_price, that cannot be grouped alphabetically.

Program 3.14: Passing a Multi-Element Argument to Several Functions
```
data test;
   length this_price that_price my_price your_price 8;
   this_price=55000;
   that_price=59000;
   my_price=57000;
   your_price=53000;
   avg_price=mean(this_price, that_price, my_price, your_price);
   med_price=median(this_price, that_price, my_price, your_price);
   std_price=std(this_price, that_price, my_price, your_price);
   var_price=var(this_price, that_price, my_price, your_price);
   put avg_price= med_price= std_price= var_price=;
run;
```

The DATA step is functional, but note the redundancy that a long list of variables is repeatedly passed to different functions. Moreover, any addition, deletion, or modification of a variable name will require changing multiple statements. SAS arrays improve maintainability by declaring the array contents only once, and thereafter referencing and passing only the array name—not its individual elements. Thus, Program 3.15 repeatedly passes the Prices array (as Prices[*]) to the various built-in functions.

Program 3.15: Passing a Multi-Element Array to Several Functions
```
data test;
   length this_price that_price my_price your_price 8;
   array prices[*] this_price that_price my_price your_price;
   this_price=55000;
   that_price=59000;
   my_price=57000;
   your_price=53000;
   avg_price=mean(of prices[*]);
   med_price=median(of prices[*]);
   std_price=std(of prices[*]);
   var_price=var(of prices[*]);
   put avg_price= med_price= std_price= var_price=;
run;
```

When the list of variables in the array inevitably needs to be modified, this change can occur solely in the ARRAY statement, rather than having to introduce the new variable into each successive function call, as was demonstrated in Program 3.14.

Passing an Array to a User-Defined Function

As previously mentioned, when a multi-element argument must be passed to a user-defined function, separate arrays must be declared in both the calling program and the called function. The previous example demonstrated how to declare an array inside of the DATA step and how to leverage the OF operator to pass an array to a built-in function. An equivalent array construct must be declared inside the user-defined function to which the multi-element argument is passed.

Consider the need to compute the mean of a series of variables. As demonstrated previously, the built-in MEAN function delivers this functionality. However, by reverse engineering MEAN functionality, a functionally equivalent user-defined function can be designed using the FCMP procedure. Program 3.16 defines the AVG function, which computes the mean for a series of variables maintained in an array.

Program 3.16: Defining the AVG User-Defined Function
```
proc fcmp outlib=work.funcs.stats;
   function avg(num[*]);
      total = 0;
      do cnt = 1 to dim(num);
         total + num[cnt];
         end;
      return(total / (cnt-1));
      endfunc;
quit;
```

The AVG function declares a single numeric parameter (NUM), and the trailing bracketed asterisk [*] specifies that NUM is a numeric array that can hold a multi-element argument. No ARRAY statement is required inside the function. As previously demonstrated, the DIM function evaluates the size of the array, and the DO loop iterates over the array to sum its elements. Finally, the RETURN statement returns the quotient (of Total and Cnt, the number of elements) to produce the average.

If large volumes of data are anticipated to be passed to a user-defined function, whether in array or non-array form, the call-by-reference call method is preferred because it does not require creating a copy of the data elements that are passed. Especially where an array is passed but a single value is returned (as in the case of many statistical functions), call by reference is preferred.

To convert the NUM parameter from call by value to call by reference, the OUTARGS statement must be added and specify the NUM array, as demonstrated in Program 3.17.

Program 3.17: Passing the Num Array by Reference

```
proc fcmp outlib=work.funcs.stats;
   function avg(num[*]);
      outargs num;
      total = 0;
      do i = 1 to dim(num);
         total + num[i];
         end;
      return(total / (i-1));
      endfunc;
quit;
```

Program 3.18 declares and initializes the Prices array and subsequently calls AVG and passes the Prices array. Note that the OF operator is not required (as was the case when calling MEAN), and that the array name (Prices) is passed rather than (Prices[*]). Whenever arrays are passed to user-defined functions, it is necessary to pass only the array name—no bracketed asterisk is required.

Program 3.18: Calling the AVG User-Defined Function

```
options cmplib=work.funcs;
data test;
   array prices[4] (55000 59000 57000 53000);
   avg_price=avg(prices);
   put avg_price=;
run;
```

When the DATA step executes, AVG computes the mean of the four numeric variables, and the result (56,000) is identical to the that of the MEAN function. It must be noted that although MEAN and AVG are functionally equivalent, the performance of the built-in MEAN function will far surpass that of the user-defined AVG function because MEAN is constructed in a lower-level language. Thus, although reverse engineering built-in functions provides excellent practice for how one would design equivalent functionality using the FCMP procedure, you would never use AVG because MEAN will have greater speed, efficiency, and reliability as a built-in function.

However, consider the requirement to *extend* the functionality of the AVG function so that it not only computes averages but also counts values and sums values. These native capabilities exist in Base SAS, operationalized through the COUNT and SUM functions, respectively. Thus, a function could be conceptualized in which the user first specifies the statistic that is being calculated (average, count, or sum) and next specifies an array holding the values to be calculated.

Program 3.19 defines the STATS function, which declares two parameters: STAT, a character parameter that denotes the name of the statistic to calculate, and NUM, the familiar numeric array that contains the data to be analyzed.

Program 3.19: Defining the STATS User-Defined Function

```
proc fcmp outlib=work.funcs.stats;
   function stats(stat $, num[*]);
      if lowcase(stat)='count' then return(dim(num));
      total = 0;
      do i = 1 to dim(num);
         total + num[i];
         end;
      if lowcase(stat)='sum' then return(total);
      else if lowcase(stat)='mean' then return(total / (i-1));
      else return(.);
      endfunc;
quit;
```

STATS first evaluates whether the Stat variable is "count" and, if so, immediately returns the count of elements that was passed to the Num array. Otherwise, the sum of all elements in the Num array is computed, and either the sum or mean is returned. If the value passed to the STAT parameter does not match any of the three statistical terms, STATS returns a missing numeric value, denoted by a period.

Program 3.20 declares and initializes the Prices array, after which the STATS function is called four times.

Program 3.20: Calling the STATS User-Defined Function

```
data test;
   array prices[4] (55000 59000 57000 53000);
   avg_price=stats('mean',prices);
   sum_price=stats('sum',prices);
   cnt_price=stats('count',prices);
   err_price=stats('wrong',prices);
   put avg_price= sum_price= cnt_price= err_price=;
run;
```

The log demonstrates that the mean, sum, and count are successfully calculated, after which the "wrong" value returns a missing value to the calling program:

```
avg_price=56000 sum_price=224000 cnt_price=4 err_price=.
```

In general, arrays passed to user-defined functions provide software scalability. This scalability, in turn, makes the code both more readable and maintainable. That is, the Prices array is initialized to (and enumerates) its four values only once, and all subsequent references to these values only require referencing Prices. The DATA step code is simplified, and Prices values can be modified (if necessary) by altering a single statement rather than many statements.

Declaring an Array inside a Function

In some cases, an array is neither passed to nor returned from a function—yet, behind the scenes, arrays are used inside the function to iterate over or operate on linear or matrixed data. When complex data transformation or analysis methods can be concealed inside a user-defined function, SAS practitioners reap the rewards of array utilization while simultaneously avoiding the complexity of directly declaring arrays in the DATA step. This improves software readability where multiple statements can be distilled into a single function call. The next two sections demonstrate how arrays can be declared and used inside the FCMP procedure.

Declaring a Numeric Array to Calculate Median Word Length

In the mathematical analysis of language, various "readability" scores attempt to quantify the ease with which text (for example, a book, research paper, or technical documentation) can be read and understood. These methods commonly define metrics such as average word length, average number of syllables per word, and average number of words per sentence. These metrics are subsequently compared among various texts to evaluate their respective readability. Readability metrics can be calculated using SAS. President Lincoln's indefatigable Gettysburg Address represents excellent subject matter, and it is ingested in Program 3.21.

Program 3.21: The Gettysburg Address

```
data gettys;
   length text $10000;
   text="Four score and seven years ago our fathers brought forth on
this continent, a new nation, conceived in Liberty, and dedicated to the
proposition that all men are created equal. Now we are engaged in a great
civil war, testing whether that nation, or any nation so conceived and so
dedicated, can long endure. We are met on a great battle-field of that war.
We have come to dedicate a portion of that field, as a final resting place for
those who here gave their lives that that nation might live. It is altogether
fitting and proper that we should do this. But, in a larger sense, we can
not dedicate — we can not consecrate — we can not hallow — this ground. The
brave men, living and dead, who struggled here, have consecrated it, far
above our poor power to add or detract. The world will little note, nor long
remember what we say here, but it can never forget what they did here. It is
for us the living, rather, to be dedicated here to the unfinished work which
they who fought here have thus far so nobly advanced. It is rather for us to
be here dedicated to the great task remaining before us — that from these
```

```
honored dead we take increased devotion to that cause for which they gave the
last full measure of devotion — that we here highly resolve that these dead
shall not have died in vain — that this nation, under God, shall have a new
birth of freedom — and that government of the people, by the people, for the
people, shall not perish from the earth.";
run;
```

Program 3.22 computes mean word length by dividing the total number of alphabetic characters by the number of words contained in the Text variable. The COUNTW function first counts the number of words, after which COMPRESS deletes all non-alphabetic characters so that the total length of characters (with spaces removed) can be calculated.

Program 3.22: Calculate Mean Word Length in DATA Step
```
data get_mean;
   set gettys;
   num_words=countw(compress(text,,'KAS'));
   len_chars=length(compress(text,,'KA'));
   chars_per_word=len_chars / num_words;
   put chars_per_word=;
run;
```

The log demonstrates that the average word length is 4.24 characters:

```
chars_per_word=4.2398523985
```

This functionality can be replicated inside a user-defined function, which removes the calculation complexity from the DATA step and enables the functionality to be reused in the future. Program 2.23 defines the MEAN_WORD_LEN function, which declares a single character parameter and returns the mean word length for the phrase that is passed.

Program 3.23: Calculate Mean Word Length in User-Defined Function
```
proc fcmp outlib=work.funcs.stats;
   function mean_word_len(phrase $);
      return(length(compress(phrase,'','KA')) / countw(compress(phrase,'', 'KAS')));
      endfunc;
quit;

data _null_;
   set gettys;
   mean=mean_word_len(text);
   put mean=;
run;
```

As discussed in Chapter 2, note that built-in functions that declare optional parameters must be called differently within the FCMP procedure than within the DATA step. Thus, when the

COMPRESS function is called inside the FCMP procedure, the missing second argument must be replaced by empty single quotation marks. However, within the DATA step, this same argument is simply omitted.

The DATA step calls the MEAN_WORD_LEN function, initializes the variable Mean to the return value, and prints the mean word length (4.24 characters) to the log:

```
mean=4.2398523985
NOTE: There were 1 observations read from the data set WORK.GETTYS.
```

The calculation of mean word length is straightforward—sum the length of words, sum the number of words, and divide the former by the latter. Thus, calculation of a mean does not require reordering of the words being analyzed. Calculation of the *median*, however, requires sorting the text by word length, and subsequently selecting the central word length value. Whenever an operation requires element-level interaction with a data structure, such as rearranging or reordering its elements, an array can facilitate and simplify this action.

The DATA step in Program 3.24 calculates the median word length. It exemplifies far greater complexity than the prior calculation of the mean. The text of the Gettysburg Address is first compressed to remove punctuation, after which the individual word lengths are initialized into the Word_len numeric array. Word_len is declared as having 800 elements to ensure the entire text will fit. After Word_len has been sorted, any missing values will occur first, followed by the word lengths. Finally, the IF-ELSE block initializes the Med variable to the median. The block must evaluate whether the array contains an even or odd number of words. The median of an odd number of elements is the middle value, whereas the median of an even number of elements is the mean of the two central values.

Program 3.24: Compute Median Word Length in the DATA Step

```
data get_median;
   set gettys;
   length new_phrase $10000;
   new_phrase=compress(text,,'KAS');
   num_words=countw(new_phrase);
   array word_len[800];
   do i=1 to num_words;
      word_len[i]=length(strip(scan(new_phrase,i,,'S')));
      end;
   call sortn(of word_len[*]);
   if mod(num_words,2)^=0 then med=word_len[((num_words + 1)/2) + (800 - num_words)];
   else med=(word_len[(num_words/2) + (800 - num_words)] + word_len[(num_words/2) +
      (1 + 800 - num_words)])/2;
   put med=;
run;
```

The DATA step executes and demonstrates that the median word length for the Gettysburg Address is four characters, just below its mean word length of 4.24 characters:

```
med=4
NOTE: There were 1 observations read from the data set WORK.GETTYS.
NOTE: The data set WORK.GET_MEDIAN has 1 observations and 805 variables.
```

This median functionality can be transplanted into a user-defined function, as demonstrated in Program 3.25. By encapsulating median functionality inside the FCMP procedure, the median can be calculated in the DATA step using a single function call. Thus, the MEDIAN_WORD_LEN function calculates the median length of words passed to the PHRASE parameter and returns the median value (Med) to the calling program. Note again that although an array is declared inside the function to facilitate iteration and reordering of individual words, no arrays are passed to or from the function.

Program 3.25: User-Defined Function to Calculate Median Word Length
```
proc fcmp outlib=work.funcs.stats;
   function median_word_len(phrase $);
      length new_phrase $10000;
      new_phrase=compress(phrase,'','KAS');
      num_words=countw(new_phrase);
      array word_len[800];
      do i=1 to num_words;
         word_len[i]=length(strip(scan(new_phrase,i,'','S')));
         end;
      call sortn(of word_len[*]);
      if mod(num_words,2)^=0 then med=word_len[((num_words + 1)/2) + (800 - num_words)];
      else med=(word_len[(num_words/2) + (800 - num_words)] + word_len[(num_words/2)
         + (1 + 800 - num_words)])/2;
      return(med);
      endfunc;
quit;

data _null_;
   set gettys;
   median=median_word_len(text);
   put median=;
run;
```

As is typical, nearly all of the DATA step syntax can be moved to the FCMP procedure without modification. The single exception, as mentioned previously, is the requirement that the COMPRESS and SCAN functions in Program 3.25 include empty quotation marks denoting missing optional arguments, whereas these quotation marks are omitted in Program 3.24.

The DATA step is now far more readable than Program 3.24 because MEDIAN_WORD_LEN is calculated using one statement rather than nine, and the complexity of array declaration, initialization, and iteration is hidden from view.

Declaring a Numeric Array to Make Change

Consider the need to make change; that is, given some purchase price, and given some currency tendered to buy an item, what are the specific bills and/or coins that should be returned to the buyer? Because this sounds like generalizable functionality that could be applied to various purchases of various amounts by various customers, it should be constructed inside a reusable user-defined function.

This chapter began with DATA step statements that declared and initialized arrays with numeric or character variables or values. Inside the FCMP procedure, however, character and numeric arrays can also be initialized with *constants*—immutable, literal values that cannot be modified once initialized. Thus, only within the FCMP procedure (but not the DATA step), an array of constants is initialized by enumerating literal values without commas or parentheses.

For example, within the FCMP procedure, the following ARRAY statement initializes the Days array to the seven days of the week:

```
array days[*] $10 'Sunday' 'Monday' 'Tuesday' 'Wednesday' 'Thursday' 'Friday'
'Saturday';
```

Because the days of the week are static and should never be modified, it is appropriate to protect the Days array by declaring it as a constant array. Once declared and initialized, any attempt to modify the constant array (or its constituent elements) will yield a runtime error.

Similarly, the following ARRAY statement initializes common United States bill and coin denominations into the Amt constant array, with the uncommon $500 greenback and 50-cent piece omitted:

```
array amt[*] 100 50 20 10 5 1 .25 .1 .05 .01;
```

Consider Program 3.26, which declares the Days array, and subsequently attempts to reinitialize Days[1] (Sunday) to its Spanish equivalent (Domingo).

Program 3.26: Attempting to Modify a Constant Array Yields a Runtime Error
```
proc fcmp outlib=work.funcs.constants;
   function print_constants();
      array days[*] $10 'Sunday' 'Monday' 'Tuesday' 'Wednesday' 'Thursday' 'Friday'
         'Saturday';
      put days[*];
      days[1]='Domingo';
```

```
      return(.);
      endfunc;
quit;

data _null_;
   rc=print_constants();
run;
```

Because the Days array contains constants, the attempt to reinitialize Days[1] produces a runtime error:

```
data _null_;
   rc=print_constants();
run;


ERROR: Attempt to assign to a constant ARRAY element in statement number 3 at line 7
column 8.
      The statement was:
   0     (7:8)      days[1] = "Domingo"
NOTE: The SAS System stopped processing this step because of errors.
```

Continuing the change-making scenario, the Amt constant array is used to calculate change to be returned to a customer. The MAKE_CHANGE function, shown in Program 3.27, uses a DO loop to iterate the array, and repeatedly evaluates whether the change required should include each denomination. For example, the DO loop first evaluates whether one or more $100 bills should be returned, and then whether one or more $50 bills should be returned, and so on, until the loop concludes by returning between zero and four pennies to the customer.

The PRICE parameter declares the item price, and the PAID parameter declares the money that was tendered. The Change_left variable is initialized to the difference between PRICE and PAID, and it will be 0 if the customer pays the exact amount. Otherwise, Change_left is modified each time a denomination is selected for return to the customer, so as bills and coins are incrementally evaluated, their values are subtracted from the remaining amount to be returned.

Program 3.27: Defining the MAKE_CHANGE Function

```
proc fcmp outlib=work.funcs.money;
   function make_change(price, paid) $;
      array amt[*] 100 50 20 10 5 1 .25 .1 .05 .01;
      length text $20 text_tot $100 change_left num 8;
      change_left = paid - price;
      do i=1 to dim(amt);
         if change_left >= amt[i] then do;
            num = int(change_left / amt[i]);
            change_left = mod(change_left, amt[i]);
            text = put(amt[i], dollar8.2) || ': ' || strip(put(num, 8.0));
            text_tot = catx(', ',text_tot, text);
```

```
            end;
         end;
      return(text_tot);
      endfunc;
quit;
```

The FUNCTION statement declares a character return value using the trailing $, and the RETURN statement denotes that Text_tot is being returned to the calling program. Thus, the LENGTH statement is required to declare the character length of Text_tot to $100. The Text_tot variable is modified each time a denomination is selected for return to the customer, and both the denomination value and the number of bills or coins are concatenated to the Text_tot value.

For example, the first DATA step in Program 3.28 initializes sample purchase data, and the second DATA step calls MAKE_CHANGE to calculate the denominations to be returned for each purchase.

Program 3.28: Calling MAKE_CHANGE on Sample Purchase and Payment Data
```
data transactions;
   length item_price item_paid 8;
   item_price=7.54; item_paid=10; output;
   item_price=4.35; item_paid=20; output;
   item_price=.78; item_paid=1.03; output;
   item_price=3.12; item_paid=5; output;
run;

data change;
   set transactions;
   length change_text $100;
   change_text=make_change(item_price, item_paid);
   put change_text=;
run;
```

When the second DATA step executes, the change to be returned is shown in the log:

```
change_text=$1.00: 2, $0.25: 1, $0.10: 2, $0.01: 1
change_text=$10.00: 1, $5.00: 1, $0.25: 2, $0.10: 1, $0.05: 1
change_text=$0.25: 1
change_text=$1.00: 1, $0.25: 3, $0.10: 1, $0.01: 3
```

Note that although an array is generated internally by the function call, the Amt array is not available to the DATA step in which MAKE_CHANGE is called. Thus, only the return value (Text_tot) has global scope and is returned to the calling program.

The function is straightforward to call because it declares only two parameters (inputs) and only one return value (output), despite the complexities of iterating Amt and the calculations required to evaluate the quantity of each denomination to return. Hiding this complexity inside the function's implementation (rather than exposing the DATA step to this madness) improves the readability and maintainability of the DATA step that calls MAKE_CHANGE. Moreover, MAKE_

CHANGE is more likely to be reused in the future because its functionality is encapsulated within a single function call.

But what if you wanted the function to return not only a textual rendering of currency denominations, but also the *total amount* of the returned change as a numeric value? This requires returning one character value and one numeric value to the calling program. Functions, by definition, return only a single value.

The solution is to pass these two variables *by reference*—not by value—so that changes to their values inside the function will be available in the calling program. The OUTARGS statement declares the call method of one or more variables as call by reference. Although it can be implemented within both user-defined functions and subroutines, it is more commonly associated with subroutines.

Program 3.29 modifies the MAKE_CHANGE function into the SUB_MAKE_CHANGE subroutine, in which four parameters are now declared. The PRICE and PAID parameters are identical to those in MAKE_CHANGE. However, the CHANGE parameter is declared as numeric, the TEXT_TOT parameter is declared as character, and OUTARGS denotes that both parameters are passed by reference.

Program 3.29: Defining the SUB_MAKE_CHANGE Subroutine

```
proc fcmp outlib=work.funcs.money;
    subroutine sub_make_change(price, paid, change, text_tot $);
        outargs change, text_tot;
        array amt[*] 100 50 20 10 5 1 .25 .1 .05 .01;
        length text $20 text_tot $100 change change_left num 8;
        change = paid - price;
        change_left = change;
        do i=1 to dim(amt);
            if change_left >= amt[i] then do;
                num = int(change_left / amt[i]);
                change_left = mod(change_left, amt[i]);
                text = put(amt[i], dollar8.2) || ': ' || strip(put(num, 8.0));
                text_tot = catx(', ',text_tot, text);
                end;
            end;
        endsub;
quit;
```

Note that because subroutines do not return a value, the trailing dollar sign has been removed from the SUBROUTINE statement, and the RETURN statement has also been eliminated. For consistency and cosmetic reasons only, the ENDFUNC statement has been replaced with the ENDSUB statement. These statements are aliases and can be used interchangeably in both functions and subroutines.

The subroutine must retain the value of total change to be returned to the customer, so an additional variable (Change) is created:

```
change = paid - price;
```

The DATA step in Program 3.30 calls the SUB_MAKE_CHANGE subroutine, which calculates the total change to be returned to the customer and creates a textual description of specific currency denominations. Note that the Item_price and Item_paid variables pass actual values to the subroutine and are bound to the PRICE and PAID parameters, respectively. However, the My_change and Change_text variables pass only missing values to the subroutine. They are bound to the CHANGE and TEXT_TOT parameters, respectively. Thus, the LENGTH statement declares My_change and Change_text, the MISSING subroutine initializes these variables to missing values, and the SUB_MAKE_CHANGE subroutine call reinitializes these variables to their calculated values.

Program 3.30: Calling the SUB_MAKE_CHANGE Subroutine
```
data change;
   set transactions;
   length my_change 8 change_text $100;
   format my_change dollar8.2 change_text $100.;
   call missing(my_change, change_text);
   call sub_make_change(item_price, item_paid, my_change, change_text);
   put my_change= change_text=;
run;
```

Note that the CALL statement is required to call both built-in and user-defined subroutines, including MISSING and SUB_MAKE_CHANGE, respectively. Arguments passed to a subroutine must be listed in the same order in which they are declared as parameters in the SUBROUTINE statement.

When the DATA step executes, the values of My_change and Change_text are printed to the log:

```
my_change=$2.46 change_text=$1.00: 2, $0.25: 1, $0.10: 2, $0.01: 1
my_change=$15.65 change_text=$10.00: 1, $5.00: 1, $0.25: 2, $0.10:
1, $0.05: 1
my_change=$0.25 change_text=$0.25: 1
my_change=$1.88 change_text=$1.00: 1, $0.25: 3, $0.10: 1, $0.01: 3
NOTE: There were 4 observations read from the data set WORK.TRANSACTIONS.
NOTE: The data set WORK.CHANGE has 4 observations and 4 variables.
```

Consider yet another requirements shift for the MAKE_CHANGE function demonstrated in Program 3.27. What if a user instead wanted to return a numeric array itself, with each array element representing the quantity returned for a specific denomination? This array might provide more value than the textual representation of these denominations because the numeric array could be subsequently used in calculations within the calling program.

Program 3.31 *attempts* this feat, and it defines the MAKE_CHANGE_ARR function. Now, not only the Amt array of constant denomination values but also the Arr_change array are declared. The Arr_change array holds the quantity of each denomination to be returned. Note that this initial version of the function returns the literal 1 rather than the Arr_change array—this is explained subsequently.

Program 3.31: Defining the MAKE_CHANGE_ARR Function

```
proc fcmp outlib=work.funcs.money;
   function make_change_arr(price, paid);
      array amt[*] 100 50 20 10 5 1 .25 .1 .05 .01;
      array arr_change[1] / nosymbols;
      call dynamic_array(arr_change, dim(amt));
      change_left = paid - price;
      do i=1 to dim(amt);
         if change_left >= amt[i] then do;
            arr_change[i] = int(change_left / amt[i]);
            change_left = mod(change_left, amt[i]);
            end;
         end;
      put arr_change[*]=;
      return(1);
      endfunc;
quit;

data change;
   set transactions (obs=1);
   rc=make_change_arr(item_price, item_paid);
run;
```

The Arr_change array is declared as a *dynamic array* (having a dimension of 1) using the NOSYMBOLS option:

```
array arr_change[1] / nosymbols;
```

The NOSYMBOLS option specifies that Arr_change is declared without the accompanying variable names. That is, NOSYMBOLS requires that an array be referenced by subscripted (that is, *index*) values because variables are not created (for example, Arr_change1 or Arr_change2). The NOSYMBOLS option saves memory because these additional variables are not created, and its functionality is similar to the _TEMPORARY_ option for DATA step arrays. Note that NOSYMBOLS can be applied only to numeric arrays, not to character arrays.

The NOSYMBOLS option also denotes that an array can be resized—that is, have its dimensions increased or decreased based on the number of nonmissing values that it contains. Resizing arrays improves efficiency because oversized arrays are not created that needlessly hold missing values. For this reason, the Arr_change array is initially declared with a dimension of 1 because it will be immediately resized.

The DYNAMIC_ARRAY built-in subroutine resizes arrays and only supports arrays declared using the NOSYMBOLS option. Thus, DYNAMIC_ARRAY cannot be called on arrays passed to a user-defined function. The first argument for DYNAMIC_ARRAY specifies the array to be resized, and the second argument specifies the new dimensions:

```
call dynamic_array(arr_change, dim(amt));
```

Thus, the CALL statement resizes Arr_change to match the dimensions of the Amt array. For example, if the 50-cent piece is added to the Amt array so that 50-cent pieces can be returned as change, the combination of the NOSYMBOLS option and the DYNAMIC_ARRAY subroutine resizes the Arr_change array automatically to accommodate this modification.

When the DATA step executes, MAKE_CHANGE_ARR is successful in making change, as demonstrated in the following log. The change returned to the customer for a $7.54 purchase with a $10 bill includes two dollar bills, one quarter, two dimes, no nickels, and one penny:

```
arr_change[1]=. arr_change[2]=. arr_change[3]=. arr_change[4]=. arr_change[5]=.
arr_change[6]=2 arr_change[7]=1 arr_change[8]=2 arr_change[9]=. arr_change[10]=1
```

However, although MAKE_CHANGE_ARR successfully *initializes* the Arr_change array with the correct values, the function fails to *return* the array to the DATA step—and any attempt to do so will fail. Thus, modification of the RETURN statement to attempt to return the array (rather than 1) fails:

```
return(arr_change);
```

The updated MAKE_CHANGE_ARR subroutine no longer compiles and fails with a runtime error:

```
ERROR: The array 'arr_change' cannot be assigned to a non-array symbol.
```

As it turns out, the failure occurs because you cannot create an array in a function and subsequently return that array from the function because the RETURN statement returns only scalar variables, not arrays. However, when an array is specified in the OUTARGS statement, which also requires that the array is passed as a parameter to the function, then that array has global scope. It can be modified by the function and is subsequently available to the calling program after the function terminates. The following section demonstrates this methodology.

"Returning" an Array from a Function

When a user-defined function or subroutine needs to return an array to the calling program, a three-step process is required. First, an array must be declared in the calling program and passed as an argument to the function. Second, the array must be declared as a parameter within the function. And third, the OUTARGS statement must further declare that the array is passed by reference—meaning the array itself, and not a copy thereof, is made available inside the FCMP procedure. Collectively, these steps overcome the limitations shown in Program 3.31 that prevent the MAKE_CHANGE_ARR function from "returning" the Arr_change array from the function to the DATA step.

Note that despite any anecdotal mention of a SAS function "returning" an array, in truth, arrays cannot be returned from user-defined functions or subroutines. More precisely, OUTARGS denotes that an array passed to a function has global scope. Therefore, changes made to the array inside the function will persist in the DATA step after the function has terminated. Although the array is not truly *returned* from the function, it nevertheless is made available to the calling program, which understandably spurs the anecdotal use of *return* in speaking of *returned arrays*. Thus, as stated previously, the RETURN statement returns only scalar variables or values, and the only true return values are those returned by RETURN.

Passing a One-Dimensional Array by Reference

The SUB_MAKE_CHANGE_ARR subroutine is demonstrated in Program 3.32. It now declares the ARR_CHANGE parameter as a numeric array and leverages the OUTARGS statement to declare that Arr_change should be passed by reference.

Program 3.32: Passing an Array by Reference
```
proc fcmp outlib=work.funcs.money;
   subroutine sub_make_change_arr(price, paid, arr_change[*]);
      outargs arr_change;
      call zeromatrix(arr_change);
      array amt[*] 100 50 20 10 5 1 .25 .1 .05 .01;
      change_left = paid - price;
      do i=1 to dim(amt);
         if change_left >= amt[i] then do;
            arr_change[i] = int(change_left / amt[i]);
            change_left = mod(change_left, amt[i]);
            end;
         end;
      endsub;
quit;
```

Note that the ZEROMATRIX built-in subroutine initializes the entire Arr_change array to 0 values. Any values passed inside Arr_change to the function will be overwritten by 0s:

```
call zeromatrix(arr_change);
```

This statement ensures that array elements that lack a value (for example, when a denomination like a $50 bill does not need to be returned to a customer) will contain a 0 rather than be empty.

The subsequent DATA step in Program 3.33 calls SUB_MAKE_CHANGE_ARR and must declare the My_change array before it can be passed by reference to the subroutine. Thus, whenever the position, data type, or call method of parameters is modified inside a function, calls to that function typically need to be modified to ensure they conform to the function's new signature. Most notably, now that the Arr_change array is declared as a parameter in the SUBROUTINE statement, the associated array argument must be passed (*bound*) to this parameter, which requires the ARRAY statement in Program 3.33 to first declare the array. Finally, note that although the My_change array in the DATA step and the Arr_change array in the subroutine have different names, they are in fact the same array; that is, they reference the same variables in memory.

Program 3.33: Passing an Array by Reference
```
data change;
   set transactions (obs=1);
   array my_change[10];
   call sub_make_change_arr(item_price, item_paid, my_change);
   put my_change[*]=;
run;
```

When the DATA step executes, the PUT statement prints the modified array for the first observation, as specified by the OBS=1 option in the SET statement:

```
my_change1=0 my_change2=0 my_change3=0 my_change4=0 my_change5=0 my_
change6=2 my_change7=1 my_change8=2 my_change9=0 my_change10=1
```

The log is identical to the array printed in Program 3.31 and represents the quantity of each bill or coin to be returned as change. However, whereas the Arr_change array in Program 3.31 had local scope and was only available inside the function, the My_change array in Program 3.33 has global scope, and thus is available to the calling program.

In creating an array of currency denominations, subsequent calculations (not shown) could be performed on the My_change array in the DATA step. However, a potential criticism of the solution is the difficulty in parsing what specific currency value is represented by each array element. For example, without viewing the definition of the SUB_MAKE_CHANGE_ARR subroutine, a user would not know that My_change1 corresponds to $100 bills. One method to clarify the solution defines a two-dimensional array that includes not only the quantity of each denomination, but also the denomination value itself, to ensure that results are unambiguously interpreted. Multidimensional arrays are introduced in the next section.

Passing a Two-Dimensional Array by Reference

As demonstrated in the previous section, a one-dimensional array can return the quantities of bill and coin denominations to be given to a customer in change, but it cannot convey both the denomination and the quantity. For example, the log from Program 3.33 reflects that one penny is returned in change. However, this certainty that the tenth element in the array corresponds to a one-cent piece requires review of the Amt array in the SUB_MAKE_CHANGE_ARR subroutine, which is defined in Program 3.32.

Moreover, any changes to the value of denominations that are available (that is, changes to the initialized constant values within the Amt array) will fundamentally alter the position of specific denominations in the Arr_change array. For example, if a fifty-cent piece is added to the Amt array in the SUB_MAKE_CHANGE_ARR subroutine, it must be added to the seventh position, which shifts the quarter, dime, nickel, and penny one position each to the right. This change would also lengthen the array dimensions from 10 to 11. Multidimensional arrays can facilitate a more stable, reliable, and flexible method to represent both currency denominations and the quantities thereof to be provided in change.

Although multidimensional arrays declared within the DATA step can have a limitless number of dimensions, arrays declared within the FCMP procedure can have only six dimensions. Only a two-dimensional array is demonstrated in this section, which defines the row in the first dimension, and the column in the second dimension. For example, if a double espresso costs $3.12, and you tender $5.00 to the barista, you can expect to receive $1.88 in change, which can be demonstrated in a one-dimensional array:

```
0 0 0 0 0 1 3 1 0 3
```

This linear array represents that your change should include a one-dollar bill, three quarters, one dime, no nickels, and three pennies. A more descriptive two-dimensional matrix, however, can explicitly state the denomination values of each array position to ensure that change values are unambiguously interpreted:

```
100 50 20 10 5 1 0.25 0.10 0.05 0.01
0   0  0  0  0 1 3    1    0    3
```

With denominations occupying the first row and quantities occupying the second row, it is now clearer that the sixth array element represents a one-dollar bill. That single one-dollar bill should be returned in change from the barista.

The DATA step in Program 3.34 calls the SUB_MAKE_CHANGE subroutine shown in Program 3.35, which leverages a two-dimensional array. Note that a 2 by 12 array is declared, which facilitates more flexibility in the subroutine. For example, the 500-dollar bill and fifty-cent piece can now be added within the subroutine, and the larger array size will accommodate these additional denominations.

Program 3.34: Declaring a Two-Dimensional Matrix to Hold Change Denominations and Quantities
```
data change;
   set transactions (obs=1);
   array my_change[2, 12];
   call sub_make_change(item_price, item_paid, my_change);
   put my_change[*]=;
run;
```

The array dimensions must first be declared within the DATA step so that they can be passed to SUB_MAKE_CHANGE. Note that values are not required to initialize the array—only to declare its name, data type, and dimensions using the ARRAY statement. The SUB_MAKE_CHANGE subroutine defined in Program 3.35 is next called, and the My_change array is passed as the third argument.

Program 3.35: Passing, Resizing, and Transforming Multidimensional Arrays

```
proc fcmp outlib=work.funcs.money;
   subroutine sub_make_change(price, paid, arr_change[*, *]);
      outargs arr_change;
      array arr_amt[10] /nosymbols (100 50 20 10 5 1 .25 .1 .05 .01);
      call dynamic_array(arr_amt, dim1(arr_change), dim2(arr_change));
      do i=1 to dim1(arr_amt);
         do j=1 to dim2(arr_amt);
            if missing(arr_amt[i, j]) then arr_amt[i, j]=0;
            end;
         end;
      call zeromatrix(arr_change);
      call addmatrix(arr_amt, arr_change, arr_change);
      change_left = paid - price;
      do j=1 to dim2(arr_change);
         if arr_change[1, j] > 0 and change_left >= arr_change[1, j] then do;
            arr_change[2, j] = int(change_left / arr_change[1, j]);
            change_left = mod(change_left, arr_change[1, j]);
            end;
         end;
      endsub;
quit;
```

The SUB_MAKE_CHANGE subroutine declares three parameters. PRICE and PAID are numeric parameters passed by value, and they represent the item price and the amount tendered, respectively. The ARR_CHANGE parameter is declared as a two-dimensional numeric array parameter, as indicated by the two comma-delimited asterisks in the SUBROUTINE statement:

```
arr_change[*, *]
```

The OUTARGS statement declares that the Arr_change array will be passed by reference, so any changes made to array values inside the subroutine are available to the DATA step calling the subroutine:

```
outargs arr_change;
```

The Arr_amount array is declared as a one-dimensional numeric array having 10 elements, and the NOSYMBOLS option prescribes that this array can be resized. NOSYMBOLS also requires that the array be declared with numeric literals rather than constants, so the denomination amounts are now enclosed in parentheses:

```
array arr_amt[10] /nosymbols (100 50 20 10 5 1 .25 .1 .05 .01);
```

The DYNAMIC_ARRAY subroutine subsequently resizes the one-dimensional Arr_amt array ([1, 10]) to match the two-dimensional Arr_change array ([2, 12]), so the ten values in the first ten elements of Arr_amt remain in place, with two additional elements added, plus one additional row:

```
call dynamic_array(arr_amt, dim1(arr_change), dim2(arr_change));
```

When DYNAMIC_ARRAY expands the Arr_amt array to a two-dimensional array, the extra elements are initialized as missing values, so a DO loop is required to convert these missing values to 0s:

```
do i=1 to dim1(arr_amt);
   do j=1 to dim2(arr_amt);
      if missing(arr_amt[i, j]) then arr_amt[i, j]=0;
      end;
   end;
```

Similarly, all values in the Arr_change array that are passed from the calling program must be converted from missing values to 0s. Because the entire array is being "zeroed out," the ZEROMATRIX subroutine can be used in lieu of a DO loop:

```
call zeromatrix(arr_change);
```

At this point, the Arr_amt array has been resized to match the dimensions of Arr_change, and any missing values in both arrays have been converted to 0s. This enables the arrays to be added, and because the Arr_change contains only 0s at this point, the ADDMATRIX subroutine effectively copies the contents of the Arr_amt array (bill and coin denominations) into the first row of the Arr_change array:

```
call addmatrix(arr_amt, arr_change, arr_change);
```

Finally, the remainder of the subroutine iteratively calculates which bills and coins should be returned to the customer, using logic from prior examples:

```
change_left = paid - price;
do j=1 to dim2(arr_change);
   if arr_change[1, j] > 0 and change_left >= arr_change[1, j] then do;
      arr_change[2, j] = int(change_left / arr_change[1, j]);
      change_left = mod(change_left, arr_change[1, j]);
      end;
   end;
```

When the subroutine terminates, the first row of the Arr_change array has been initialized to the denomination values. The second row of the array has been initialized to the quantity of the corresponding bills or coins to be returned. For example, executing the DATA step in Program 3.34 produces the following output, with only the results of the fourth observation demonstrated for clarity:

```
my_change1=100 my_change2=50 my_change3=20 my_change4=10 my_change5=5 my_
change6=1 my_change7=0.25 my_change8=0.1 my_change9=0.05 my_change10=0.01
my_change11=0 my_change12=0
my_change13=0 my_change14=0 my_change15=0 my_change16=0 my_change17=0
my_change18=1 my_change19=3 my_change20=1 my_change21=0 my_change22=3 my_
change23=0 my_change24=0
```

Thus, values for My_change1 through My_change12 comprise the first row of the array and represent the denomination values. Note that My_change11 and My_change12 contain 0s, as only ten denominations are defined within the SUB_MAKE_CHANGE subroutine.

The values for My_change13 through My_change24 comprise the second row of the array and represent the quantities of each denomination that should be returned to the customer. In this way, the two-dimensional array provides clarity because both the denomination values and the respective quantities are maintained within the same data structure. Moreover, the SUB_MAKE_CHANGE subroutine could be modified to include different denominations—perhaps for a different country's currency—and the only line of code that would need to be modified would be the initial declaration of the Arr_amt array, which contains the currency values.

Extending the Functionality of SORTC to a Descending Sort

The SAS built-in functions SORTC and SORTN sort a series of values—character and numeric, respectively—in ascending order. These functions are sometimes referred to as performing a *horizontal sort* because values or variables *within* an observation are being sorted, rather than one or more variables *across* all observations. For example, Program 3.36 sorts five variables. The values within each of those variables are rearranged in ascending alphabetical order.

Program 3.36: Sorting Variables Using the SORTC Subroutine

```
data _null_;
   length var1-var5 $20;
   var1 = 'banana';
   var2 = 'papaya';
   var3 = 'avocado';
   var4 = 'mango';
   var5 = 'blackberry';
   put var1-var5;
   call sortc(of var1-var5);
   put var1-var5;
run;
```

Note that the OF operator is used within the SORTC subroutine to specify the range of variables that should be sorted. This subroutine call is equivalent to the following code:

```
call sortc(var1, var2, var3, var4, var5);
```

The DATA step performs a horizontal sort on Var1 through Var5 and produces the following output:

```
banana papaya avocado mango blackberry
avocado banana blackberry mango papaya
```

For example, the value of Var1 is changed from "banana" to "avocado."

The most common method to reference a series of same-type variables is to declare an array. Program 3.37 produces identical functionality as Program 3.36, but instead declares and initializes the Arr array. Afterward, Arr—rather than its constituent variables or their values—is passed to the SORTC subroutine.

Program 3.37: Sorting an Array with the SORTC Subroutine
```
data _null_;
   array arr[5] $20 ('banana' 'papaya' 'avocado' 'mango' 'blackberry');
   put arr[*];
   call sortc(of arr[*]);
   put arr[*];
run;
```

Thus, the first element of the Arr array—the Arr1 variable—is initialized as "bananas" but is changed to "apples" by the SORTC subroutine. Arr2, similarly, is initialized as "apples" but is change to "bananas" by SORTC.

Neither SORTC nor SORTN is able to sort variables in descending order. However, by reversing the order of the variable series in Program 3.36 within the SORTC subroutine, SORTC performs a descending sort:

```
call sortc(of var5-var1);
```

With this single line changed in Program 3.37, the DATA step sorts the variables in descending order:

```
banana papaya avocado mango blackberry
papaya mango blackberry banana avocado
```

When attempting to transplant this reverse sorting functionality into a user-defined subroutine, you will encounter numerous obstacles. As described later in this chapter, this reversal trick produces a runtime error if attempted inside the FCMP procedure. Moreover, the OF operator is also unfortunately incompatible with dynamic arrays, which include arrays passed to functions as well as arrays declared using the NOSYMBOLS option. This limitation dramatically reduces the functionality and value of dynamic arrays inside user-defined functions because OF is the primary operator through which users pass arrays to SAS built-in functions.

As an ugly workaround, a second array (Temp) must be declared and initialized. Because Temp is not dynamic (its dimensions are defined to be 800), the SORTC subroutine can pass the Temp array as an argument. After Temp has been sorted, a DO loop iterates the original Values array and reinitializes each of its variables—in reverse order—to the sorted values in Temp. Of note, Temp is declared as an 800-element array because this is the maximum number of elements that the SORTC and SORTN built-in subroutines can pass when called inside the FCMP procedure—a limitation of the OF operator discussed later in this chapter.

Program 3.38: Defining the REV Subroutine for Reverse Character Sort

```
proc fcmp outlib=work.funcs.sorts;
   subroutine rev(values[*] $);
      outargs values;
      num_val=dim(values);
      array temp[800] $20;
      do i=1 to num_val;
         temp[i]=values[i];
         end;
      call sortc(of temp[*]);
      do i=1 to num_val;
         values[i]=temp[800-i+1];
         end;
      endsub;
quit;
```

The subroutine is neither graceful nor efficient, but it is at least functional. The DATA step in Program 3.39 declares and initializes the Fruit array as comprising the variables My_fruit, Your_fruit, His_fruit, Her_fruit, and Our_fruit. It subsequently reorders Fruit in reverse by calling the user-defined REV subroutine.

Program 3.39: Calling the REV Subroutine to Perform Reverse Horizontal Sort

```
data _null_;
   length my_fruit your_fruit his_fruit her_fruit our_fruit $20;
   my_fruit = 'banana';
   your_fruit = 'papaya';
   his_fruit = 'avocado';
   her_fruit = 'mango';
   our_fruit = 'blackberry';
   array fruit[*] $20 my_fruit your_fruit his_fruit her_fruit our_fruit;
   put fruit[*]=;
   call rev(fruit);
   put fruit[*]=;
run;
```

The second line of the log demonstrates that the fruits have been sorted in reverse order. The first declared variable of the array (My_fruit) contains the last value alphabetically, which is "papaya":

```
my_fruit=banana your_fruit=papaya his_fruit=avocado her_fruit=mango our_
fruit=blackberry
my_fruit=papaya your_fruit=mango his_fruit=blackberry her_fruit=banana our_
fruit=avocado
```

Thus, despite the inability to leverage the OF operator within user-defined functions when interacting with dynamic arrays, workarounds can be contrived. Moreover, this demonstrates the benefit of maintaining data within a containerized data structure such as an array because they can be readily manipulated.

Differences between DATA Step Arrays and FCMP Arrays

Several differences exist between array functionality in the DATA step and in the FCMP procedure. As demonstrated previously, the DYNAMIC_ARRAY built-in subroutine enables arrays to be resized only in the FCMP procedure. However, in many cases, the FCMP procedure limits array functionality. For example, some aspects of implicit arrays, such as the DO OVER statement, are not supported by the FCMP procedure. The IN operator is used in the DATA step to evaluate membership of some value in an array, but it is not supported by the FCMP procedure. Similarly, the FCMP procedure fails to support the OF operator when used to reference dynamic arrays.

The DO OVER Statement Is Not Supported by FCMP

The DATA step in Program 3.40 declares the Nums_explicit subscripted array and the Nums_ implicit implicit array. The subscripted array is iterated by initializing a counter (Cnt) that increments array position to print each array element. And the implicit array is iterated using the DO OVER loop, which iterates the array itself—not a counter representing the array element.

Program 3.40: Iterating an Explicit Array and an Implicit Array in the DATA Step
```
data _null_;
   array nums_explicit[*] exp1-exp5;
   array nums_implicit imp1-imp5;
   do cnt=1 to dim(nums_explicit);
      nums_explicit[cnt]=cnt;
      end;
   do over nums_implicit;
      nums_implicit=_i_;
      end;
   put nums_explicit[*]=;
   put nums_implicit[*]=;
run;
```

Although DO OVER does not use a counter to iterate the implicit array, a counter is required to evaluate the position in the loop, and the automatic variable _I_ performs this function. Thus, when the DO OVER loop initiates, _I_ is automatically initialized to 1. Irrespective of the differences between subscripted and implicit arrays, and how they are iterated, both arrays are initialized to identical values, as shown in the log:

```
imp1=1 imp2=2 imp3=3 imp4=4 imp5=5
exp1=1 exp2=2 exp3=3 exp4=4 exp5=5
```

However, when the statements are transplanted to the FCMP procedure, as shown in Program 3.41, the DO OVER statement is shown to be incompatible with the FCMP procedure.

Program 3.41: Attempting to Iterate an Implicit Array within PROC FCMP

```
proc fcmp outlib=work.funcs.test;
   function test_unindexed();
      file log;
      array nums_explicit[*] exp1-exp5;
      array nums_implicit imp1-imp5;
      do cnt=1 to dim(nums_explicit);
         nums_explicit[cnt]=cnt;
         end;
      do over nums_implicit;
         nums_implicit=_i_;
         end;
      put nums_explicit[*]=;
      put nums_implicit[*]=;
      return(.);
      endfunc;
quit;
```

The log demonstrates a failure in the DO OVER statement because DO OVER is not supported within the FCMP procedure:

```
435  proc fcmp outlib=work.funcs.test;
436     function test_implicit();
437        file log;
438        array nums_explicit[*] exp1-exp5;
439        array nums_implicit imp1-imp5;
440        do cnt=1 to dim(nums_explicit);
441           nums_explicit[cnt]=cnt;
442           end;
443        do over nums_implicit;
                    ------------
                    73
ERROR 73-322: Expecting an =.
444           nums_implicit=_i_;
445           end;
446        put nums_explicit[*]=;
447        put nums_implicit[*]=;
448        return(.);
449        endfunc;
450  quit;

NOTE: The SAS System stopped processing this step because of errors.
```

To remedy this failure, the implicit array (Nums_implicit) must be referenced explicitly using subscripted notation. Program 3.42 updates these changes and overcomes the failure that occurs in Program 3.41.

Program 3.42: Declaring and Iterating an Implicit Array within PROC FCMP

```
proc fcmp outlib=work.funcs.test;
   function test_implicit();
      file log;
      array nums_explicit[*] exp1-exp5;
      array nums_implicit imp1-imp5;
      do cnt=1 to dim(nums_explicit);
         nums_explicit[cnt]=cnt;
         end;
      do cnt=1 to dim(nums_implicit);
         nums_implicit[cnt]=cnt;
         end;
      put nums_explicit[*]=;
      put nums_implicit[*]=;
      return(.);
      endfunc;
quit;


%put %sysfunc(test_implicit());
```

The log demonstrates the successful declaration, iteration, and initialization of both arrays to identical values:

```
nums_explicit[1]=1 nums_explicit[2]=2 nums_explicit[3]=3 nums_explicit[4]=4
nums_explicit[5]=5
nums_implicit[1]=1 nums_implicit[2]=2 nums_implicit[3]=3 nums_implicit[4]=4
nums_implicit[5]=5
```

This example also serves as final proof that even implicit arrays are indexed, and that there is no such thing as an *unindexed SAS array*, as some charlatans would have you believe!

FCMP Arrays Do Not Support the IN Operator

The IN operator evaluates membership of a variable or value within a series of variables or values, and it is a powerful lookup operation within the DATA step. The IN operator's flexibility is further expanded when the lookup is directed not at a comma-delimited series, but rather at a SAS array that references a series of variables. This design also improves software readability because a comma-delimited series of data can be replaced with a single array name.

Program 3.43 demonstrates the successful use of IN to evaluate the Nums numeric array within the DATA step. The numbers 1 through 10 are evaluated for array membership, and because the array contains only the numbers 1 through 5, the first five values are evaluated to exist in the array and printed to the log.

Program 3.43: Using the IN Operator to Evaluate Array Membership in the DATA Step

```
data _null_;
    array nums[5] (1 2 3 4 5);
    do cnt=1 to 10;
        if cnt in nums then put cnt=;
        end;
run;
```

The log demonstrates the elements in the Nums array:

```
cnt=1
cnt=2
cnt=3
cnt=4
cnt=5
```

However, when the same DO loop is attempted inside the FCMP procedure, as shown in Program 3.44, the incompatibility of IN is demonstrated.

Program 3.44: Failure of the IN Operator inside the FCMP Procedure

```
proc fcmp outlib=work.funcs.test;
    function test_in();
        file log;
        array nums[5] (1 2 3 4 5);
        do cnt=1 to 10;
            if cnt in nums then put cnt=;
            end;
        return(.);
        endfunc;
quit;
```

The log demonstrates that the FCMP procedure does not support the IN operator when referencing an array:

```
54    proc fcmp outlib=work.funcs.test;
55       function test_in();
56          file log;
57          array nums[5] (1 2 3 4 5);
58          do cnt=1 to 10;
59             if cnt in nums then put cnt=;
                         ----              -
                         79                22
                                           200
ERROR 79-322: Expecting a (.
ERROR 22-322: Syntax error, expecting one of the following: a name, a quoted string,
              a numeric constant, a datetime constant, a missing value, ), ',', -, :,
```

```
_ALL_,_CHARACTER_, _CHAR_, _NUMERIC_.
ERROR 200-322: The symbol is not recognized and will be ignored.
60              end;
61          return(.);
62          endfunc;
63    quit;


NOTE: The SAS System stopped processing this step because of errors.
```

This failure of IN occurs for all arrays, including those passed by reference from a DATA step.

A workaround exists for the minority of cases in which the variables referenced by the array are incrementally named (for example, Nums1, Nums2, Nums3) and the array is declared in the FCMP procedure. Rather than parenthetically referencing the array name (Nums) using the IN operator, the set of all variables beginning with "Nums" can be referenced, as demonstrated in Program 3.45.

Program 3.45: Overcoming IN Failure in the FCMP Procedure

```
proc fcmp outlib=work.funcs.test;
    function test_in();
        file log;
        array nums[5] (1 2 3 4 5);
        do cnt=1 to 10;
            if cnt in (nums:) then put cnt=;
            end;
        return(.);
        endfunc;
quit;

%put %sysfunc(test_in());
```

The log shows the successful output, demonstrating the IN operator functioned as expected:

```
cnt=1
cnt=2
cnt=3
cnt=4
cnt=5
```

However, this is a small victory, considering that the workaround fails for all dynamic arrays, including both those declared with the NOSYMBOLS option and those passed to a function from a DATA step. Program 3.46 demonstrates this latter failure.

Program 3.46: Failure of IN Operator with Dynamic Array

```
proc fcmp outlib=work.funcs.test;
    function test_in(nums[*]);
        file log;
        do cnt=1 to 10;
```

```
        if cnt in (nums:) then put cnt=;
        end;
    return(.);
    endfunc;
quit;
```

The log shows the failure:

```
557  proc fcmp outlib=work.funcs.test;
558     function test_in(nums[*]);
559        file log;
560        do cnt=1 to 10;
561           if cnt in (nums:) then put cnt=;
ERROR: The array 'nums' cannot be an argument of the 'IN' operation.
562           end;
563        return(.);
564        endfunc;
565  quit;

NOTE: The SAS System stopped processing this step because of errors.
```

Unfortunately, no array-based workaround exists for this failure. However, more advanced lookup operations can be operationalized through the hash object, as demonstrated in Chapter 4.

FCMP Arrays Do Not Support the OF Operator

Within the DATA step, the OF operator enables arrays to be passed to numerous character and numeric built-in functions and subroutines, such as SUM, MIN, MEAN, SORTC, and CATX. When OF references an array, all elements of the array are passed to the function. In doing so, code is simplified because only the array name—not its constituent variables—must be specified in the function call.

Program 3.47 instantiates the Nums array and initializes its five elements. Thereafter, the array is passed to the SUM function to add these values.

Program 3.47: Using the OF Operator with an Array
```
data _null_;
   array nums[5] (1 2 3 4 5);
   tot=sum(of nums[*]);
   put tot=;
run;
```

The DATA step is successful and prints the total (15) to the log. However, when equivalent code is attempted within the FCMP procedure, shown in Program 3.48, it fails because the OF operator does not support dynamic arrays.

Program 3.48: Failure of the OF Operator in the FCMP Procedure

```
proc fcmp outlib=work.funcs.test;
   function test_of(nums[*]);
      file log;
      tot=sum(of nums[*]);
      put tot=;
      endfunc;
quit;
```

Thus, the TEST_OF function fails to compile:

```
573  proc fcmp outlib=work.funcs.test;
574     function test_of(nums[*]);
575        file log;
576        tot=sum(of nums[*]);
ERROR: The OF operator isn't allowed on an ARRAY with a dynamic size.
577        put tot=;
578        endfunc;
579  quit;

NOTE: The SAS System stopped processing this step because of errors.
```

Unfortunately, this limitation indicates that no arrays can be passed from the DATA step to a built-in function called inside the FCMP procedure. No workarounds exist for this issue.

Arrays Cannot Be Declared in Reverse within FCMP

Software sometimes requires that an array be reordered by its values, and either an ascending or descending sort might be warranted. The SORTN and SORTC subroutines reorder numeric and character arrays, respectively, and leverage the OF operator—discussed in the previous section— to pass the array to the subroutine.

An ascending sort is straightforward and is the default behavior of both SORTN and SORTC. A descending sort, on the other hand, can be effected by leveraging the OF operator with a reversed variable range. For example, the DATA step in Program 3.49 first performs an ascending sort on the Nums array by leveraging the OF operator within the SORTN subroutine. Thereafter, the OF operator is used to perform a descending sort—not on the Nums array, but rather on the reverse range of variables referenced by the Nums array, from Nums5 to Nums1.

Program 3.49: Successful Ascending and Descending Sorts in the DATA Step

```
data _null_;
   array nums[5] (6 5 3 9 2);
   put nums[*];
   * sort ascending;
   call sortn(of nums[*]);
   put nums[*];
```

```
   * sort descending;
   call sortn(of nums5-nums1);
   put nums[*];
run;
```

The log demonstrates the initial (unsorted) order, ascending order, and descending order, respectively:

```
6 5 3 9 2
2 3 5 6 9
9 6 5 3 2
```

This parlor trick is successful in the DATA step, but unfortunately fails when transplanted to the FCMP procedure. The TEST_ARRAY_DESCENDING function, defined in Program 3.50, fails to compile due to the attempted descending sort.

Program 3.50: Failure of the OF Operator to Support Reverse Variable Ranges in the FCMP Procedure
```
proc fcmp outlib=work.funcs.test;
   function test_array_descending();
      file log;
      array nums[5] (6 5 3 9 2);
      put nums[*];
      * sort ascending;
      call sortn(of nums[*]);
      put nums[*];
      * sort descending;
      call sortn(of nums5-nums1);
      put nums[*];
      return(.);
      endfunc;
quit;
```

Unfortunately, despite being syntactically correct, the function fails compilation with the following runtime error:

```
580   proc fcmp outlib=work.funcs.test;
581      function test_array_descending();
582         file log;
583         array nums[5] (6 5 3 9 2);
584         put nums[*];
585         * sort ascending;
586         call sortn(of nums[*]);
587         put nums[*];
588         * sort descending;
589         call sortn(of nums5-nums1);
ERROR: The numeric suffix for first variable is greater than that of the
second for the
```

```
         variable list nums1.
590          put nums[*];
591          return(.);
592          endfunc;
593   quit;


NOTE: The SAS System stopped processing this step because of errors.
```

A workaround for this limitation is demonstrated in Chapter 4 and leverages the hash object to reorder values within the FCMP procedure.

Left-Handed SUBSTR Functionality Incompatible with Arrays

The SUBSTR built-in function has two invocation patterns, each of which provides distinct functionality. When placed on the *right* side of the equal sign, SUBSTR subsets a character variable or value. For example, the following call to SUBSTR subsets my name, starting in the second position:

```
name=substr('troy martin hughes',2);
```

This usage yields my grandfather, Roy Martin Hughes, an oilfield worker and numismatist. An optional third argument can also specify the number of characters to retain in the subset. For example, the following call to SUBSTR subsets my name, starting in the sixth position, for a total length of 13 characters:

```
name=substr('troy martin hughes',6,13);
```

This usage yields my great-great-great grandfather, Martin Hughes, who farmed Indiana in the 1830s.

When placed on the *left* side of the equal sign, SUBSTR replaces—rather than subsets—text. For example, the following call to SUBSTR replaces the first four characters of my name:

```
name='troy martin hughes';
substr(name,1,4)='john';
```

This usage reinitializes Name to my great grandfather, John Martin Hughes, a brothel and saloon owner in Bakersfield, California. Unfortunately, this left-handed usage of SUBSTR is not supported by the FCMP procedure.

Consider the need to generate random "words"—that is, randomly generated alphabetic text—for use in software testing. The DATA step in Program 3.51 declares the Word array, which is populated with random characters.

Program 3.51: Generate Five Random Eight-Character "Words"

```
data _null_;
   array word[5] $10;
   call streaminit(123);
   do cnt=1 to 5;
      do let=1 to 8;
         substr(word[cnt],let,1)=byte(rand('uniform',65,91));
         end;
      end;
   put word[*];
run;
```

The log demonstrates the five random words:

```
PACKIJIE BCYFMZTW IVALXCCD STYTNYLX LZQHPYXQ
```

This functionality could be useful inside a reusable function, especially if the word length could be parameterized, and an array could be filled with these randomized words. The SUB_MAKE_WORDS subroutine, defined in Program 3.52, attempts to deliver this functionality. The Words parameter is a character array that the OUTARGS statement declares as being passed by reference. Thus, an empty array can be passed to SUB_MAKE_WORDS, and the subroutine will fill each element with a random word of the length specified by the LETTERS parameter.

Program 3.52: Attempting to Define the SUB_MAKE_WORDS Subroutine to Create Random "Words"

```
proc fcmp outlib=work.funcs.test;
   subroutine sub_make_words(words[*] $, letters);
      outargs words;
      call streaminit(123);
      do word_cnt=1 to dim(words);
         do let_cnt=1 to letters;
            substr(word[word_cnt],let_cnt,1)=byte(rand('uniform',65,91));
            end;
         end;
      endsub;
quit;
```

However, although the left-handed usage of SUBSTR is supported by the DATA step, it is not supported within the FCMP procedure for array initialization, and the subroutine fails to compile:

```
543  proc fcmp outlib=work.funcs.test;
544     subroutine sub_make_words(words[*] $, letters);
545        outargs words;
546        call streaminit(123);
547        do word_cnt=1 to dim(words);
```

```
548              do let_cnt=1 to letters;
549                  substr(word[word_cnt],let_cnt,1)=byte(rand('uniform',65,91));
                              -
                             78
                             76
ERROR 78-322: Expecting a ','.
ERROR 76-322: Syntax error, statement will be ignored.
550                  end;
551              end;
552          endsub;
553   quit;


NOTE: The SAS System stopped processing this step because of errors.
```

To overcome this limitation, rather than directly initializing an array within the SUBSTR call, a temporary variable can be initialized and incrementally built, after which the array variable can be initialized to the final value of the temporary variable. The redefined SUB_MAKE_WORDS subroutine, shown in Program 3.53, now defines the Temp_word variable that—because it is not an array—can be initialized using the left-handed SUBSTR.

Program 3.53: Redefining the GET_RANDO Subroutine to Create an Array of Random "Words"

```
proc fcmp outlib=work.funcs.test;
   subroutine sub_make_words(words[*] $, letters);
      outargs words;
      length temp_word $100;
      call streaminit(123);
      do word_cnt=1 to dim(words);
         temp_word='';
         do let_cnt=1 to letters;
            substr(temp_word,let_cnt,1)=byte(rand('uniform',65,91));
            end;
         words[word_cnt]=temp_word;
         end;
      endsub;
quit;
```

The DATA step in Program 3.54 is functionally equivalent to the DATA step in Program 3.51 and calls the SUB_MAKE_WORDS subroutine to initialize the Words array by filling its five elements with random eight-letter "words." Note the simplicity that Program 3.54 no longer requires DO loops, the STREAMINIT subroutine, or the RAND function—all functionality is encapsulated within the subroutine implementation.

Program 3.54: Calling the SUB_MAKE_WORDS Subroutine to Fill an Array with Random "Words"
```
data _null_;
   array word[5] $10;
   call sub_make_words(word, 8);
   put word[*];
run;
```

The log demonstrates that Program 3.54 produces output identical to that of Program 3.51:

```
PACKIJIE BCYFMZTW IVALXCCD STYTNYLX LZQHPYXQ
```

Moreover, the increased flexibility and configurability of the SUB_MAKE_WORDS subroutine increases the likelihood that it will be reused. For example, any character array, having any array name, any number of elements, and any length of character values can be passed to the SUB_MAKE_WORDS subroutine and populated with randomized data.

The past several sections examined differences in array functionality and syntax between the DATA step and the FCMP procedure, including several limitations of array functionality inside the FCMP procedure. Some additional array differences exist in between the DATA step and the FCMP procedure and are discussed in SAS documentation (SAS Institute Inc. 2023).

%SYSFUNC and %SYSCALL Complexities with Arrays

Thus far, this chapter has demonstrated how to declare, initialize, iterate, and use arrays within both the DATA step and the FCMP procedure. A final footnote must discuss a critical limitation in *calling* user-defined functions, which is that a user-defined function that declares an array parameter cannot be called via %SYSFUNC, nor can a subroutine that declares an array parameter be called via %SYSCALL. As Table 2.4 demonstrates, user-defined functions that declare an array parameter can be called only from the DATA step or the FCMP procedure. This limitation occurs because arrays can be declared only within the DATA step and the FCMP procedure, whereas the SAS macro language has no array construct that it can pass to a user-defined function or subroutine.

For example, consider the requirement to calculate the sum of 5, 10, and 15 to produce the value 30. Calling the SUM built-in function yields this result when called from the DATA step or the %SYSFUNC macro function. Program 3.51 demonstrates these functionally equivalent methods of calling SUM.

Program 3.55: Summation Using Built-in SUM Function
```
data _null_;
   tot = sum(5, 10, 15);
   put tot;
run;

%put %sysfunc(sum(5, 10, 15));
```

Both solutions print 30 to the log, and no array needs to be declared because built-in functions can accommodate multi-element arguments (including a mix of constants, variables, and numeric literals) without an explicit array declaration.

Conversely, user-defined functions and subroutines require an explicit array declaration in the DATA step whenever a multi-element argument needs to be passed. To demonstrate this difference, SUM functionality is approximated in the SUMMATION user-defined function that returns the sum of one or more values passed to it, as demonstrated in Program 3.56.

Program 3.56: Defining the SUMMATION Function to Sum Variables
```
proc fcmp outlib=work.funcs.math;
   function summation(var[*]);
      total = 0;
      do j = 1 to dim(var);
         total = total + var[j];
         end;
      return(total);
      endfunc;
quit;
```

When SUMMATION is called from the DATA step in Program 3.57, the ARRAY statement must first declare the Arr array prior to passing the array to SUMMATION. Again, note the additional limitations that neither numeric variables nor numeric literals can be passed to SUMMATION— only a previously declared array can be passed because SUMMATION is a user-defined function.

Program 3.57: Calling the SUMMATION Function from the DATA Step
```
data _null_;
   array arr[3] (5 10 15);
   tot = summation(arr);
   put tot;
run;
```

The DATA step prints the same result (30) to the log.

However, any attempt to call SUMMATION using the %SYSFUNC function fails with a runtime error. For example, the following call attempts to pass three numeric literals to summation:

```
%put %sysfunc(summation(5, 10, 15));
```

The log denotes that SUMMATION failed due to "too many arguments." This failure represents the inability of %SYSFUNC (and the SAS macro facility) to interpret the three numbers as a multi-element argument:

```
ERROR: The function SUMMATION referenced by the %SYSFUNC or %QSYSFUNC macro
function has too many arguments.
```

Because arrays cannot be declared in the SAS macro language, there is no way to pass a multi-element argument like an array to a function called by %SYSFUNC or to a subroutine called by %SYSCALL. For this reason, it is important for SAS practitioners relying on user-defined functions to understand each function's signature—including whether one or more parameters are declared as an array. And for those functions and subroutines that do declare one or more array parameters, SAS practitioners must understand that these modules cannot be called through SAS macro language invocations like %SYSFUNC or %SYSCALL.

Performing Matrix Calculations Using PROC FCMP Arrays

The remainder of this chapter demonstrates how SAS arrays, leveraged by user-defined functions, can perform linear and matrix algebra. The FCMP procedure supports a suite of built-in functions and subroutines that manipulate matrices operationalized as two-dimensional arrays. For example, the ADDMATRIX built-in subroutine already demonstrated in Program 3.35 shows how two arrays can be summed. The ZEROMATRIX built-in subroutine was used in Programs 3.32 and 3.35 to initialize arrays with all zero values.

SAS/IML (Interactive Matrix Language) is a powerful SAS tool that supports matrix programming, in which matrices (rather than data sets) are manipulated using the IML procedure. SAS/IML is standard in some SAS environments, such as SAS Viya and SAS OnDemand for Academics (SODA), and it is the preferred method for matrix calculations. For example, matrices can be added, subtracted, multiplied, or inverted—to name just a few operations. However, the SAS/IML module is not included in Base SAS, and for this reason is absent from many SAS environments.

When SAS/IML is unavailable, the FCMP procedure can support several matrix calculations by effectively simulating the matrix data structure using SAS arrays. Although the matrix data structure is not supported by the FCMP procedure or the DATA step, a two-dimensional array can be manipulated through built-in FCMP subroutines to simulate a matrix and its operations.

The following sections introduce a problem set that can be solved through linear algebra and demonstrate equivalent manual calculations, SAS/IML calculations, and FCMP calculations.[1] Although matrix and linear algebra lie far outside the scope of this text, some introduction is necessary to demonstrate FCMP functionality in this mathematical arena.

The following built-in subroutines are supported by the FCMP procedure and are demonstrated in this chapter (SAS Institute Inc. 2023):

- ADDMATRIX subroutine – Performs an elementwise addition of two matrices or a matrix and a scalar.
- INV subroutine – Calculates a matrix that is the inverse of the provided input matrix that should be a square, non-singular matrix.

[1] Special thanks to Rick Wicklin for his incomparable book "Statistical Programming with SAS/IML Software" and his numerous blogs, without which this section would have been impossible to write.

- MULT subroutine – Calculates the multiplicative product of two input matrices.
- ZEROMATRIX subroutine – Replaces all of the element values of the numeric input matrix with 0.

The following built-in subroutines are not demonstrated due to the complexity of the mathematical operations that they perform (SAS Institute Inc. 2023):

- CHOL subroutine – Calculates the Cholesky decomposition for a given symmetric matrix.
- DET subroutine – Calculates the determinant of a specified matrix that should be square.
- ELEMMULT subroutine – Performs an elementwise multiplication of two matrices.
- EXPMATRIX subroutine – Returns a matrix e^{tA} given the input matrix A and a multiplier t.
- FILLMATRIX subroutine – Replaces all of the element values of the input matrix with the specified value.
- IDENTITY subroutine – Converts the input matrix to an identity matrix.
- POWER subroutine – Raises a square matrix to a given scalar value.
- SUBTRACTMATRIX subroutine – Performs an element-wide subtraction of two matrices or a matrix and a scalar.
- TRANSPOSE subroutine – Returns the transpose of a matrix.

Finally, the READ_ARRAY and WRITE_ARRAY built-in FCMP functions are demonstrated. READ_ ARRAY reads SAS data sets into FCMP arrays. WRITE_ARRAY writes SAS arrays to SAS data sets. These built-in functions enable matrices to be maintained and manipulated within SAS data sets, as opposed to forcing a matrix to be passed to a user-defined function using an array parameter.

Linear Algebra Problem Set

Consider two unparalleled SAS editors, Suzanne and Catherine, and their task of shaping this book into something both readable and relatable. Impossible task, eh? Also, consider that their respective rates of editing (let's say pages per hour) are dependent on the number of cups of coffee each has consumed (denoted by X):

$$f(x_{Suzanne}) = 3x + 2$$

$$f(x_{Catherine}) = 8x - 3$$

These linear equations represent only approximations. They fail to limit that negative cups of coffee cannot be consumed, that negative velocities would be invalid, and that at some point, excess coffee would no doubt yield decreased performance due to shakiness or heart palpitations!

Suppose you needed to calculate the number of cups of coffee that each editor would need to drink to achieve the same editing speed. In other words, what is the value of X when $f(x_{Suzanne})$ is equal to $f(x_{Catherine})$?

Various methods can be used to perform this calculation, such as variable substitution, graphing the equations, long-hand matrix algebra, or matrix algebra performed in SAS/IML or an FCMP user-defined function. For example, setting the equations equal to each other yields the following:

```
3x +2 = 8x - 3

5x = 5

x = 1
```

Thus, when Suzanne and Catherine each consume one cup of coffee, their productivity is identical, and they each can edit five pages per hour. This can also be demonstrated by graphing the two equations, which intersect at (X=1, Y=5), which demonstrates both the coffee consumed (X=1) and the editing velocity (Y=5). Figure 3.1 demonstrates this intersection.

The following sections demonstrate the matrix algebra to arrive at this solution, including the long-hand calculations, SAS/IML code, and FCMP code.

Figure 3.1: Intersection of Suzanne's Velocity and Catherine's Velocity at (X=1, Y=5)

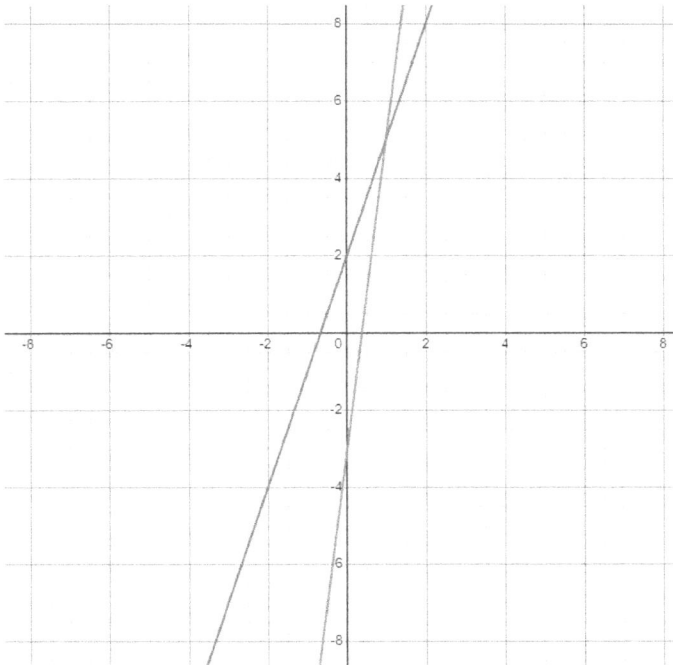

Long-Hand Solution

Although you would never rely on matrix algebra for so simple a problem, far more complex equations can be solved using the equivalent approach. Because the solution requires $f(x_{Suzanne})$ to equal $f(x_{Catherine})$, both functions can be rewritten using Y:

y = 3x + 2

y = 8x − 3

Placing all constants on the right-hand side yields equivalent equations:

3x − y = -2

8x − y = 3

These equations can be represented by setting a coefficient matrix and variable matrix (both left-hand side) equal to the constant matrix (right-hand side):

$$\begin{bmatrix} 3 & -1 \\ 8 & -1 \end{bmatrix} \begin{bmatrix} x \\ y \end{bmatrix} = \begin{bmatrix} -2 \\ 3 \end{bmatrix}$$

First, the inverse of the coefficient matrix is calculated:

$$\frac{1}{(3)(-1) - (8)(-1)} \begin{bmatrix} -1 & 1 \\ -8 & 3 \end{bmatrix}$$

$$\frac{1}{5} \begin{bmatrix} -1 & 1 \\ -8 & 3 \end{bmatrix}$$

$$\begin{bmatrix} -\frac{1}{5} & \frac{1}{5} \\ -\frac{8}{5} & \frac{3}{5} \end{bmatrix}$$

Next, the inverse matrix is multiplied by both sides of the equation. First, the inverse matrix is multiplied by the coefficient matrix to yield the identity matrix, which demonstrates that the inverse was calculated correctly:

$$\begin{bmatrix} -\frac{1}{5} & \frac{1}{5} \\ -\frac{8}{5} & \frac{3}{5} \end{bmatrix} \begin{bmatrix} 3 & -1 \\ 8 & -1 \end{bmatrix} \begin{bmatrix} x \\ y \end{bmatrix}$$

$$\begin{bmatrix} \left(-\frac{1}{5}\right)(3) + \left(\frac{1}{5}\right)(8) & \left(-\frac{1}{5}\right)(-1) + \left(\frac{1}{5}\right)(-1) \\ \left(-\frac{8}{5}\right)(3) + \left(\frac{3}{3}\right)(8) & \left(-\frac{8}{5}\right)(-1) + \left(\frac{3}{5}\right)(-1) \end{bmatrix} \begin{bmatrix} x \\ y \end{bmatrix}$$

$$\begin{bmatrix} 1 & 0 \\ 0 & 1 \end{bmatrix} \begin{bmatrix} x \\ y \end{bmatrix}$$

With the identity matrix calculated, the solution is next calculated by multiplying the inverse coefficient matrix by the constant matrix:

$$\begin{bmatrix} -\dfrac{1}{5} & \dfrac{1}{5} \\ -\dfrac{8}{5} & \dfrac{3}{5} \end{bmatrix} \begin{bmatrix} -2 \\ 3 \end{bmatrix}$$

$$\begin{bmatrix} \left(-\dfrac{1}{5}\right)(-2) & \left(\dfrac{1}{5}\right)(3) \\ \left(-\dfrac{8}{5}\right)(-2) & \left(\dfrac{3}{5}\right)(3) \end{bmatrix} = \begin{bmatrix} 1 \\ 5 \end{bmatrix}$$

This solution is demonstrated by setting the identity matrix equal to the solution:

$$\begin{bmatrix} x \\ y \end{bmatrix} = \begin{bmatrix} 1 \\ 5 \end{bmatrix}$$

The solution demonstrates that (X=1, Y=5) satisfies both original functions. That is, when either Catherine or Suzanne has consumed one cup of coffee, their editing velocities are each five pages per hour. Given the complexity of the matrix calculations, SAS/IML enables SAS practitioners to perform these steps with ease.

SAS/IML Solution

The functionality and syntax of SAS/IML and the IML procedure lie outside the scope of this text. However, a single example demonstrates how to calculate the previous solution using the IML procedure. Program 3.58 declares the Mat matrix, which represents the coefficient matrix, and the Mat_const matrix, which represents the constant matrix.

Program 3.58: Calculating the Inverse, Identity, and Multiplicative Matrices in SAS/ IML

```
proc iml;
   mat        = {  3 -1,
                   8 -1};
   mat_const = {-2,
                 3};
   mat_inv = inv(mat);
   mat_iden = mat_inv * mat;
   mat_mult = mat_inv * mat_const;
   print mat_inv;
   print mat_iden;
   print mat_mult;
run;
```

The resultant inverse coefficient matrix, identity matrix, and multiplicative matrix (that is, the solution) are shown in the SAS output window, as demonstrated in Figure 3.2.

Figure 3.2: PROC IML Output Demonstrating Inverse Matrix, Identity Matrix, and Multiplicative Matrices

mat_inv	
-0.2	0.2
-1.6	0.6

mat_iden	
1	0
0	1

mat_mult
1
5

Note the simplicity of using SAS/IML and the built-in matrix data structure to perform matrix calculations. Although the built-in matrix data structure is neither recognized by the DATA step nor the FCMP procedure, user-defined functions can simulate many matrix calculations by relying on built-in FCMP functions and subroutines.

PROC FCMP Solution

As many SAS practitioners have no access to the SAS/IML module, a workaround relies on FCMP built-in functions and subroutines to effectively replicate SAS/IML functionality. Program 3.59 leverages the FCMP procedure to calculate the inverse coefficient matrix, identity matrix, and multiplicative matrix (solution). Note that all "matrices" must first be declared as an array, including array dimensions. For example, the Mat array is declared as a two-dimensional array that includes two elements per dimension. Thus, Mat corresponds to a two-by-two matrix, in which the first row of the matrix is listed in the first and second array positions, after which the second row of the matrix is listed in the third and fourth array positions.

Program 3.59: Calculating the Inverse, Identity, and Multiplicative Matrices in PROC FCMP

```
proc fcmp;
   file log;
   array mat[2, 2] (3, -1, 8, -1);
   put mat=;
   array mat_inv[2, 2];
   call inv(mat, mat_inv);
   array mat_iden[2, 2];
```

```
      call mult(mat_inv, mat, mat_iden);
      array mat_mult[2, 1];
      array mat_const[2, 1] (-2, 3);
      call mult(mat_inv, mat_const, mat_mult);
      put mat_inv=;
      put mat_iden=;
      put mat_mult=;
quit;
```

The first line of the log demonstrates how the Mat coefficient matrix is stored in the Mat array:

```
mat[1, 1]=3 mat[1, 2]=-1 mat[2, 1]=8 mat[2, 2]=-1
```

Thus, Mat[1,1] corresponds to the upper-left element of the matrix, Mat[1,2] corresponds to the upper-right element of the matrix, Mat[2,1] corresponds to the lower-left element of the matrix, and Mat[2,2] corresponds to the lower-right element of the matrix.

The second line of the log demonstrates the inverse coefficient matrix (Mat_inv) that is calculated using the INV built-in subroutine, which calculates the inverse of a matrix:

```
mat_inv[1, 1]=-0.2 mat_inv[1, 2]=0.2 mat_inv[2, 1]=-1.6 mat_inv[2, 2]=0.6
```

The third line of the log demonstrates the identity matrix (Mat_iden) that is calculated using the MULT built-in subroutine, which multiplies two matrices:

```
mat_iden[1, 1]=1 mat_iden[1, 2]=0 mat_iden[2, 1]=0 mat_iden[2, 2]=1
```

Finally, the multiplicative matrix is calculated by multiplying the inverse matrix (Mat_inv) by the constant matrix (Mat_const) using the MULT built-in subroutine:

```
mat_mult[1, 1]=1 mat_mult[2, 1]=5
```

The Mat_mult array demonstrates the identical solution: when Catherine and Suzanne have each had one cup of coffee, their performance will be identical, and they each will be able to edit five pages of a manuscript per hour. This section has only scratched the surface of the matrix operations possible using the FCMP procedure. Consult *Base SAS® 9.4 Procedures Guide, Seventh Edition* to gain an understanding of all built-in matrix functions and subroutines.

Using READ_ARRAY to Read a Matrix from a Data Set

The READ_ARRAY built-in function operates only in the FCMP procedure and reads a data set into a SAS array. For example, in Program 3.59, the Mat array (the coefficient matrix) and Mat_const array (the constant matrix) are declared and initialized within the FCMP procedure:

```
array mat[2, 2] (3, -1, 8, -1);
array mat_const[2, 1] (-2, 3);
```

A more flexible approach might instead maintain these matrices in SAS data sets and read the data sets to declare and initialize the arrays. For example, Program 3.60 creates the Matrix data set, which can be used to define both the coefficient and constant matrices.

Program 3.60: Creating a Data Set to Hold the Coefficient and Constant Matrices
```
data matrix;
    infile datalines dsd;
    length editor $20 x y const 8;
    input editor $ x y const;
    datalines;
Suzanne, 3, -1, -2
Catherine, 8, -1, 3
```

Next, Program 3.61 refactors Program 3.59 to read the Matrix data set to create both the coefficient matrix and constant matrix. Thus, rather than explicitly initializing values for Mat, the READ_ARRAY function instead leverages READ_ARRAY to populate the two-dimensional Mat array.

Program 3.61: Refactoring PROC FCMP to Read the Matrix Data Set
```
proc fcmp;
    file log;
    array mat[2, 2] / nosymbols;
    rc=read_array('matrix', mat, 'x', 'y');
    put mat=;
    array mat_inv[2, 2];
    call inv(mat, mat_inv);
    array mat_iden[2, 2];
    call mult(mat_inv, mat, mat_iden);
    array mat_mult[2, 1];
    array mat_const[2, 1] / nosymbols;
    rc=read_array('matrix', mat_const, 'const');
    call mult(mat_inv, mat_const, mat_mult);
    put mat_inv=;
    put mat_iden=;
    put mat_mult=;
quit;
```

The READ_ARRAY function initializes a return code to 0 to demonstrate success, which is captured in the RC variable in Program 3.61. The first READ_ARRAY argument must be a character literal or variable that denotes the data set name being ingested. The second READ_ARRAY argument denotes the array being initialized and must correspond to a local array declared using the NOSYMBOLS option. Subsequently, optional READ_ARRAY arguments specify the variables in the data set to be ingested into the array. Thus, although the Matrix data set contains the Editor character variable, which denotes the editor's name, these character data are not ingested into the Mat array. This would result in failure, as arrays must contain only same-type data. Omitting these optional arguments in a READ_ARRAY function call, by default, ingests all variables in the specified data set.

Program 3.61 produces identical output to that of Program 3.59:

```
mat[1, 1]=3 mat[1, 2]=-1 mat[2, 1]=8 mat[2, 2]=-1
mat_inv[1, 1]=-0.2 mat_inv[1, 2]=0.2 mat_inv[2, 1]=-1.6 mat_inv[2, 2]=0.6
mat_iden[1, 1]=1 mat_iden[1, 2]=0 mat_iden[2, 1]=0 mat_iden[2, 2]=1
mat_mult[1, 1]=1 mat_mult[2, 1]=5
```

Note that the NOSYMBOLS option must be specified for any array that is later initialized using the READ_ARRAY function. However, because READ_ARRAY dynamically resizes the array as it is ingested, the array's dimensions or size do not need to be specified in the array statement. Thus, by convention, the ARRAY statement commonly declares a dimension of [1] whenever the NOSYMBOLS option specifies that a dynamic array is being declared.

For example, the following two ARRAY statements are functionally equivalent to those in Program 3.61, as the NOSYMBOLS option specifies that each array will be automatically resized:

```
array mat[1] / nosymbols;
array mat_const[1] / nosymbols;
```

The advantage of leveraging READ_ARRAY to ingest matrices into SAS arrays is that FCMP can derive all input from data sets, as opposed to statically defined arrays. This flexibility facilitates more reusable matrix operations and functionality.

Using WRITE_ARRAY to Write a Matrix to a Data Set

Program 3.61 demonstrates how to read the Matrix data set using the READ_ARRAY built-in function to create both the coefficient and constant matrices. Similarly, the results of some matrix operations might need to be saved to a data set, and the built-in WRITE_ARRAY function facilitates this objective. Program 3.62 refactors Program 3.61 to write the solution matrix to the Matrix_solution data set.

Program 3.62: Reading Data Sets into Arrays and Writing Arrays to SAS Data Sets
```
proc fcmp;
   file log;
   array mat[1] / nosymbols;
   rc=read_array('matrix', mat, 'x', 'y');
   array mat_inv[2, 2];
   call inv(mat, mat_inv);
   array mat_iden[2, 2];
   call mult(mat_inv, mat, mat_iden);
   array mat_mult[2, 1];
   array mat_const[1] / nosymbols;
```

```
    rc=read_array('matrix', mat_const, 'const');
    call mult(mat_inv, mat_const, mat_mult);
    rc=write_array('matrix_solution', mat_mult);
quit;
```

The WRITE_ARRAY built-in function similarly initializes a return code to 0 to demonstrate success, which is captured in the RC variable in Program 3.62. The first WRITE_ARRAY argument must be a character literal or variable that denotes the name of the data set being created. For example, Program 3.62 specifies the Matrix_solution data set (in the WORK library). The second WRITE_ARRAY argument specifies the dynamic array being written to the data set. Subsequently, optional WRITE_ARRAY arguments specify the variables to write to the data set. In Program 3.62, because the Mat_mult array does not contain extraneous variables, these optional arguments are omitted in the WRITE_ARRAY call.

Rather than generating output to the log, Program 3.62 instead creates the Matrix_solution data set in which the matrix solution is saved. Presumably, although not shown, this resultant data set would be used to drive subsequent mathematical operations or analyses. Thus, the combination of READ_ARRAY and WRITE_ARRAY can enable SAS practitioners to simulate the built-in matrix data structure (available only in SAS/IML) by saving matrices as data sets and by manipulating these data sets as two-dimensional arrays. The possibilities are endless!

Conclusion

SAS arrays are arguably the most important built-in data structure in function and subroutine design because they alone enable multi-element collections of arguments to be passed to and from user-defined functions and subroutines. This chapter introduced the declaration and initialization of arrays within the DATA step, after which FCMP procedure array syntax and usage was demonstrated. The OUTARGS statement, which specifies the call method of an array as call by reference, was demonstrated as facilitating the "return" of arrays from a user-defined function. In other cases, an array having local scope can be declared within a function to simplify some calculation or operation, after which the array is deleted when the function terminates. In all cases that were demonstrated, the introduction of arrays is not intended to improve the speed or efficiency with which software executes, but rather to make software more maintainable, readable, and reusable. Arrays also improve software scalability because they enable a limitless number of variables to be referenced by an array that is subsequently iterated or evaluated as a collection. Finally, this chapter briefly introduced built-in FCMP functions and subroutines that can be leveraged to manipulate matrices within two-dimensional SAS arrays and demonstrated how the READ_ARRAY and WRITE_ARRAY built-in functions can further extend matrix algebra operations.

Chapter 4: Hash Objects

The SAS data set lies at the heart of the SAS ecosystem. It represents the primary built-in data structure that is leveraged by SAS procedures, functions, and subroutines to evaluate and transform data. However, SAS data sets, with the exception of those loaded into RAM by the SASFILE statement, or those maintained within in-memory environments such as SAS Visual Analytics, are exclusively stored on disk. That is, operations that interact with a data set invariably incur input/output (I/O) costs. The hash object, a second SAS built-in data structure, is instead maintained in memory and can be queried with minimal I/O overhead. Hash objects are prized because in-memory operations can provide substantial performance benefits over equivalent disk-based operations. User-defined functions can incorporate hash objects and benefit from their performance while hiding the complexity of hash operations inside a function's implementation.

Hash objects are indexed by *keys*, which provide immediate access to associated data *values*. These *key-value pairs* comprise the input and output of hash lookup operations. Unique keys ensure that only one observation is returned per hash lookup, and although the MULTIDATA argument supports duplicate keys within SAS hash objects, it is not discussed in this text. *Simple keys* comprise a single key variable, whereas *composite keys* comprise multiple variables in which each combination of keys must be unique.

In their most basic functionality, hash objects perform membership validation—evaluating whether some value appears as a key inside a hash object. In more complex operations, hash objects can return one or more values that correspond to a key. In this sense, a hash lookup effectively performs a table join, and it can replace comparable DATA step MERGE statements or SQL procedure JOIN clauses. More complex uses for hash objects include sorting values, counting the frequencies of discrete values, or determining the mode (the most commonly occurring value) among a series of values.

Despite the unmistakable power of hash, its adoption has been arguably slowed by its perceived complexity. In an otherwise procedural language like Base SAS, hash-oriented *methods* might seem other-worldly to some SAS practitioners. Moreover, each hash object must be instantiated, initialized, queried, possibly updated, and closed, and all of these statements can obscure software readability. However, by instantiating a hash object *inside* a user-defined function, the FCMP procedure facilitates the abstraction of hash functionality—that is, complex hash syntax can be encapsulated within a user-defined function, and concealed from view. This chapter first introduces the hash object within the DATA step, after which various hash methods and hash-based solutions are demonstrated within the FCMP procedure.

Data Validation

The simplest hash lookup performs data validation and determines whether a value is a member of some data structure—that is, whether a *key* occurs in some *hash object*. Hash lookups effectively return a Boolean value (True or False) that represents hash membership, and this return value can drive subsequent operations. For example, given a hash object holding a list of state abbreviations, a hash lookup could evaluate whether a given abbreviation is valid or not, and where invalid, could initialize the invalid value to missing or to another representative value.

Hash objects used in validation operations typically represent *master tables*—data sets known to be true and accurate that can be used to validate or overwrite data that are less trusted. For example, Program 4.1 defines a master table that includes abbreviations for all 50 states and the District of Columbia. This State_list data set can also be used to validate state abbreviations maintained in other data sets.

Program 4.1: Master Table Containing 51 State Abbreviations
```
data state_list;
   infile datalines dsd delimiter=',';
   input state_abbr $ @@;
   datalines;
AK, AL, AR, AZ, CA, CO, CT, DC, DE, FL, GA, HI, IA, ID, IL, IN, KS, KY, LA,
MA, MD, ME, MI, MN, MO, MS, MT, NC, ND, NE, NH, NJ, NM, NV, NY, OH, OK, OR,
PA, RI, SC, SD, TN, TX, UT, VA, VT, WA, WI, WV, WY
;
```

For example, a transactional data set might be received at recurring intervals that references state abbreviation, and which occasionally contains erroneous (for example, misspelled) or otherwise invalid abbreviations. Program 4.2 demonstrates the Cities transactional data set, which includes the U.S. territory Puerto Rico (PR).

Program 4.2: Less Trusted Data Set Containing State Abbreviations
```
data cities;
   length st_abbr $2 city $20;
   st_abbr = 'CA'; city = 'Gustine'; output;
   st_abbr = 'CA'; city = 'Los Banos'; output;
   st_abbr = 'OH'; city = 'Columbus'; output;
   st_abbr = 'PR'; city = 'San Juan'; output;
run;
```

The next several sections demonstrate various methods to validate the Cities transactional data set using the State_list master table, including format- and hash-based solutions,

DATA step solutions, and FCMP solutions. In comparing these various methods, the clear advantages of encapsulating validation functionality inside user-defined functions is demonstrated.

Validation Using the PROC FORMAT CNTLIN Option

SAS formats, like hash objects, also comprise key-value pairs. User-defined formats can similarly represent master tables that are used to validate data. The CNTLIN option of the FORMAT procedure builds a user-defined format or informat based on a specified data set, as opposed to hardcoded values maintained in a SAS program file. CNTLIN requires a specially structured data set, in which the Start variable represents the *key* and the Label variable represents the *value* (for the key-value pairs). The Fmtname variable names the format or informat being created, and the Type variable (C) denotes that a character format is being defined.

The DATA step in Program 4.3 transforms the State_list data set into the structure required by CNTLIN, after which the FORMAT procedure specifies the transformed data set in the CNTLIN option.

Program 4.3: Defining the ST_LIST User-Defined Character Format

```
data st_fmt;
   set state_list (rename=(state_abbr=start)) end=eof;
   label = start;
   retain fmtname 'st_list' type 'c' hlo 'u';
   output;
   if eof then do;
      start = '';
      label = '';
      hlo = 'o';
      output;
      end;
run;

proc format cntlin=st_fmt;
run;
```

The DATA step also includes an optional IF block, in which invalid values are mapped to a missing value via the HLO variable. Thus, when the format is applied, any values not listed in the State_list data set (like PR) are transformed into a missing value, as specified by the initialization of Start and Label to missing values within the IF block. This functionality enables the ST_LIST format to validate state abbreviations maintained in transactional data sets or other data sets. For example, the DATA step in Program 4.4 initializes the new variable ST_valid to the validated state abbreviation by applying the ST_LIST format to the ST_abbr variable.

Program 4.4: Validating State Abbreviations Using the ST_LIST Format

```
data validate_states;
   set cities;
   st_valid = put(st_abbr, $st_list.);
   put st_abbr= st_valid=;
run;
```

The log demonstrates that Puerto Rico is reset to missing because PR does not appear in the State_list master table, created in Program 4.1:

```
st_abbr=CA st_valid=CA
st_abbr=CA st_valid=CA
st_abbr=OH st_valid=OH
st_abbr=PR st_valid=
```

One benefit of a data-driven solution like the CNTLIN option is that only the referenced control table (State_list) needs to be modified—and the user-defined format re-created—to update the user-defined format. For example, State_list could be updated to include Puerto Rico (PR) and the ST_LIST format recompiled, after which the DATA step in Program 4.4 would recognize the PR abbreviation as being valid. A data-driven solution also enables the underlying State_list master table to be used to drive other functionality, such as the hash objects demonstrated in the next two sections.

Validation Using a DATA Step Hash Object

Hash object validation can rely on the same underlying master tables that are used by the CNTLIN option to initialize user-defined formats within the FORMAT procedure. For example, the State_list data set created in Program 4.1 can be used to populate a hash object. An immediate benefit is that hash objects can directly rely on master tables, as opposed to the CNTLIN option, which requires an intermediate data transformation that creates the Start, Label, Fmtname, Type, and HLO variables (shown in Program 4.3).

Program 4.5 demonstrates an equivalent hash object that validates the Cities data set, defined in Program 4.2, which similarly evaluates that Puerto Rico does not appear in the State_list master table.

Program 4.5: Validating State Abbreviations Using a DATA Step Hash Object

```
data validate_states (drop = rc);
   set cities;
   length state_abbr $2;
   if _n_ = 1 then do;
      declare hash h(dataset: 'state_list');
      rc = h.defineKey('state_abbr');
      rc = h.defineDone();
      call missing(state_abbr);
      end;
```

```
   rc = h.check(key: st_abbr);
   put st_abbr= rc=;
run;
```

The invalid value (PR) is identified in the output because the return code (RC) of the CHECK method is initialized to a value other than zero (160038):

```
st_abbr=CA rc=0
st_abbr=CA rc=0
st_abbr=OH rc=0
st_abbr=PR rc=160038
```

Stepping through the code in Program 4.5, the hash declaration should occur only once, and the IF block ensures it executes only when the first observation is read:

```
if _n_ = 1 then do;
```

The DECLARE HASH statement instantiates the hash object (H), and the DATASET option specifies the data set that should be loaded into the hash object—that is, into memory:

```
declare hash h(dataset: 'state_list');
```

The hash object remains in memory only for the duration of the DATA step. Upon DATA step termination, the hash object is deleted from memory. For this reason, and especially when large data sets are loaded into hash objects, it can be more efficient to perform all hash operations in a single DATA step so that the hash object does not need to be reloaded multiple times across multiple DATA steps.

The DEFINEKEY method declares the State_abbr variable as the hash object key and requires that State_abbr exist in the State_list data set:

```
rc = h.defineKey('state_abbr');
```

The DEFINEKEY method generates a return code, and by convention, the RC variable is initialized. Composite keys, which contain two or more variables, are declared by enumerating a list of comma-delimited variables. Also note that because State_abbr is the only variable in the State_list data set, the following functionally equivalent ALL argument could have been used:

```
rc = h.defineKey(all: 'yes');
```

The DEFINEDONE method terminates the definition of all keys and data values. Had a data value been defined, the DEFINEDATA method would have preceded the DEFINEDONE method:

```
rc = h.defineDone();
```

The MISSING built-in subroutine is optional. It assigns missing values to the State_abbr variable, which eliminates the "uninitialized" note in the SAS log:

```
call missing(state_abbr);
```

Because State_abbr is a key value in the hash object, and because State_abbr does not appear in the Cities data set, it must first be declared within the DATA step using the LENGTH statement. And because the State_abbr value is not populated when the hash object is instantiated, the hash object declaration yields the following pesky note if the MISSING subroutine is omitted:

```
NOTE: Variable state_abbr is uninitialized.
```

Although a hash object is declared only once per DATA step, subsequent hash operations should typically run across observations, so these statements should appear after (and outside of) the initial hash declaration block. Thus, the hash CHECK method assesses whether the value of some variable appearing in the Cities data set is found in the key variable (defined using the DEFINEKEY method) of the hash object. And because the ST_abbr variable is found in the Cities data set, yet the State_abbr variable is the hash object key, the optional KEY argument must specify the ST_abbr variable within the CHECK method:

```
rc = h.check(key: st_abbr);
```

The CHECK method returns a 0 when the key is found, and a nonzero value when the key is not found. Thus, the Program 4.5 log, demonstrated previously, denotes that the PR abbreviation is invalid.

With this understanding of the CHECK method, Program 4.5 can be refactored so that it produces results identical to the previous user-defined format validation, shown in Program 4.4. Program 4.6 now leverages the IFC function to return the original state abbreviation when it appears in the hash object (that is, when the state is valid) and a missing value when the state abbreviation is not found in the hash object.

Program 4.6: Updated DATA Step Hash Object Validation of State Abbreviation
```
data validate_states (drop = state_abbr rc);
   set cities;
   length state_abbr $2 st_valid $2;
   if _n_ = 1 then do;
      declare hash h(dataset: 'state_list');
      rc = h.defineKey('state_abbr');
      rc = h.defineDone();
      call missing(state_abbr);
      end;
   st_valid = ifc(h.check(key: st_abbr)=0,st_abbr,'');
   put st_abbr= st_valid=;
run;
```

The log demonstrates that Program 4.6 is functionally equivalent to Program 4.4, with both methods relying on the underlying State_list master table to validate state abbreviations:

```
st_abbr=CA st_valid=CA
st_abbr=CA st_valid=CA
st_abbr=OH st_valid=OH
st_abbr=PR st_valid=
```

However, note the simplicity of building a user-defined format in Program 4.4 and being able to apply it in a single statement. Program 4.6, on the other hand, requires several lines of hash statements that inarguably clutter the functional intent. After all, seven lines of code are required to determine whether the hash object contains a specific state abbreviation!

This complexity of hash, in part, explains why its adoption by some SAS practitioners has been stymied, if not altogether withheld. However, by encapsulating hash objects and operations inside of user-defined functions, as demonstrated in the next section, hidden hash can render your software both powerful and pretty!

Validation Using an FCMP Hash Object

Hash objects can be instantiated not only in the DATA step but also in user-defined functions and subroutines created with the FCMP procedure. In doing so, the complexities of hash operations are abstracted and encapsulated, and the DATA steps (that call these functions and subroutines) are rendered more concise and readable.

To be clear, not all hash functionality is available within the FCMP procedure. Table 4.1 enumerates the differences between DATA step hash functionality and FCMP hash functionality. Only half (15 of 30) of the hash methods and attributes are supported within FCMP, so experienced hashers might immediately reach for—and be unable to find—core hash functionality within FCMP. Even the DECLARE statement itself, which instantiates hash objects, is limited within FCMP. For example, data set options such as password encryption, FIRSTOBS, and OBS that are available within the DATA step are absent from the FCMP procedure.

Despite the caveat of substantially decreased hash functionality within the FCMP procedure, the functionality that remains will inarguably strengthen the performance of your SAS lookup operations. Moreover, with just a few lines of code, a savvy SAS practitioner can readily re-create some built-in hash functionality that is omitted from the FCMP procedure. For example, the later section "Counting Hash Keys" demonstrates how to re-create SUM method functionality within user-defined functions.

The DATA step hash functionality demonstrated in Program 4.6 is refactored in Program 4.7 to demonstrate the equivalent FCMP procedure instantiation of a hash object. The ST_VALIDATE function is declared, and returns either a validated state abbreviation or a missing value.

Table 4.1: Comparison of Hash Methods and Attributes between DATA Step and PROC FCMP

Hash Method (or Attribute)	Available in DATA Step	Available in PROC FCMP
DECLARE (statement)	Yes	Yes (with limitations)
ADD	Yes	Yes
CHECK	Yes	Yes
CLEAR	Yes	Yes
DEFINEDATA	Yes	Yes
DEFINEDONE	Yes	Yes
DEFINEKEY	Yes	Yes
DELETE	Yes	Yes
DO_OVER	Yes	
EQUALS	Yes	
FIND	Yes	Yes
FIND_NEXT	Yes	
FIND_PREV	Yes	
FIRST	Yes	Yes
HAS_NEXT	Yes	
HAS_PREV	Yes	
ITEM_SIZE (attribute)	Yes	
LAST	Yes	Yes
NEXT	Yes	Yes
NUM_ITEMS (attribute)	Yes	Yes
OUTPUT	Yes	
PREV	Yes	Yes
REF	Yes	
REMOVE	Yes	Yes
REMOVE_DUP	Yes	
REPLACE	Yes	Yes
REPLACE_DUP	Yes	
RESET_DUP	Yes	
SETCUR	Yes	
SUM	Yes	
SUM_DUP	Yes	

Program 4.7: Hash Lookup Validation inside a User-Defined Function

```
proc fcmp outlib=work.funcs.lookup;
   function st_validate(state_abbr $) $;
      declare hash h(dataset: 'state_list');
      rc = h.defineKey('state_abbr');
      rc = h.defineDone();
      return(ifc(h.check()=0, state_abbr, ''));
      endfunc;
quit;
```

The hash operations in ST_VALIDATE are nearly identical to those in Program 4.6. Within a user-defined function, however, the hash object is instantiated only the first time the function is called within a specific DATA step, so hash operations no longer require an IF block. Similarly, the MISSING subroutine no longer needs to be called for hash objects declared within user-defined functions. Note that keys passed as parameters do not need to be declared with the LENGTH statement, so the LENGTH statement is also omitted.

Because the STATE_ABBR parameter is identically named to the State_abbr variable in the ST_list data set, the hash CHECK method no longer needs to include the KEY argument. Thus, when KEY is omitted, the CHECK method by default evaluates the key(s) declared by the DEFINEKEY method.

When the ST_VALIDATE function is called from a DATA step, if the value passed to the STATE_ ABBR parameter is located in the hash object, the RETURN statement returns this same value. If the value is not found, the RETURN statement returns a missing value, which is used to indicate an invalid abbreviation. For example, the DATA step in Program 4.8 calls the ST_VALIDATE function, initializes the ST_valid variable to its return value, and prints the results to the log, which are identical to the results of Programs 4.4 and 4.6.

Program 4.8: Validating State Abbreviations Using an FCMP Hash Object

```
options cmplib=work.funcs;

data validate_states;
   set cities;
   length st_valid $8;
   st_valid = st_validate(st_abbr);
   put st_abbr= st_valid=;
run;
```

Note that the hash operation complexity that overwhelmed the functionally equivalent DATA step in Program 4.7 is now encapsulated within the user-defined function, so the DATA step now combines the performance of hash and the readability of a single-line function call. And from here, hash only gets better.

Single Variable Initialization

The previous section demonstrated the use of hash objects to validate whether some value appears in a list of keys—that is, either the value is found, or it is not, as demonstrated in

Program 4.6. However, more complex business rules can be embedded within validation functions, and the refactored function in Program 4.8 instead returns either the original value (representing a valid value) or a missing value (representing an invalid value).

An arguably more common usage of hash objects (and lookup tables in general) is declaring key-value pairs and when a key is found, returning one or more associated values that are initialized to one or more variables in the calling program. Similar to validation functionality, this initialization functionality can be operationalized through numerous methods, including DATA step MERGE statements, SQL procedure JOIN clauses, user-defined formats, and hash object lookups.

The DATA step in Program 4.9 creates the Some_states master table. The master table is subsequently used by various lookup methods in the next sections and includes an abbreviated list of state names, abbreviations, and associated Federal Information Processing Standard (FIPS) codes. FIPS codes standardize critical data at the federal level and uniquely identify each state and US territory.

Program 4.9: Abbreviated State Lookup Table

```
data some_states;
    length abbr $2 state $20 fips $2;
    abbr = 'CA'; fips = '06'; state = 'California'; output;
    abbr = 'OH'; fips = '39'; state = 'Ohio'; output;
    abbr = 'PA'; fips = '42'; state = 'Pennsylvania'; output;
    abbr = 'MD'; fips = '24'; state = 'Maryland'; output;
    abbr = 'VA'; fips = '51'; state = 'Virginia'; output;
run;
```

For example, consider the requirement to append the state FIPS codes and state names to the Cities data set—that is, to *initialize* new variables based on the state abbreviation. This initialization can also be characterized as a lookup or join operation, as it effectively represents a left join of the transactional data set (Cities) to the lookup data set (Some_states). A benefit of data-driven design is demonstrated in the next several sections where the Some_states master table is used for various initialization methods, including both the FORMAT procedure CNTLIN option and the hash object.

Data Initialization Using a User-Defined Format

Given the Some_states data set, which was created in Program 4.9, and the need to append either the FIPS code or state name to a separate transactional data set, a user-defined format is an efficient data-driven method to perform this lookup and initialize the new variable. For example, Program 4.10 defines the ST_TO_FIPS user-defined format that leverages the CNTLIN option in the FORMAT procedure.

Program 4.10: Defining the ST_FIPS User-Defined Character Format

```
data st_fmt (drop=abbr);
    set some_states (rename=(fips=label)) end=eof;
    length start $8;
```

```
      start = abbr;
      retain fmtname 'st_to_fips' type 'c' hlo 'u';
      output;
      if eof then do;
         start = '';
         label = '';
         hlo = 'o';
         output;
         end;
run;

proc format cntlin=st_fmt;
run;
```

The DATA step in Program 4.11 applies the ST_TO_FIPS user-defined format to the ST_abbr variable to initialize the FIPS_state variable. Note that as previously demonstrated, a state abbreviation that cannot be found in the format will result in a missing value.

Program 4.11: Initialize Variable Using a User-Defined Format
```
data init_states;
   set cities;
   length fips_state $2;
   fips_state=put(st_abbr,$st_to_fips.);
   put st_abbr= fips_state=;
run;
```

The DATA step executes and generates the following log in which the FIPS_state variable has been initialized based on each valid state abbreviation:

```
st_abbr=CA fips_state=06
st_abbr=CA fips_state=06
st_abbr=OH fips_state=39
st_abbr=PR fips_state=
```

User-defined formats such as ST_TO_FIPS represent an efficient, data-driven solution that enables simple data mappings to initialize new variables. However, note that the Some_states data set, created in Program 4.9, maps the state abbreviation to not only the state FIPS code but also the full state name. Because a SAS format can only map one value to another, it is impossible to use a SAS format to look up a state abbreviation and to return both its FIPS code and state name. This is where the functionality of hash objects begins to outshine simpler lookup methods such as user-defined formats because hash objects *can* perform lookup operations that initialize multiple variables!

Data Initialization Using a User-Defined Function Hash Object

As demonstrated previously, one of the benefits of defining a hash-based function as opposed to a comparable user-defined format is its simplicity. No intermediate data set is required by hash, as opposed to the very finicky FORMAT procedure CNTLIN option, which requires four (or five) precisely named variables. Program 4.12, which defines the ST_TO_FIPS function, returns the FIPS state code when provided a valid state abbreviation.

Program 4.12: Hash Lookup Validation inside a User-Defined Function
```
proc fcmp outlib=work.funcs.lookup;
   function st_to_fips(abbr $) $;
      length fips $2;
      declare hash h(dataset: 'some_states');
      rc = h.defineKey('abbr');
      rc = h.defineData('fips');
      rc = h.defineDone();
      return(ifc(h.find()=0, fips, ''));
      endfunc;
quit;
```

As mentioned previously, keys passed as parameters do not need to be declared. However, the FIPS variable must be declared using the LENGTH statement because it appears in the DEFINEDATA method:

```
length fips $2;
```

The DECLARE HASH statement uploads the Some_states data set into the hash object (H) without any cumbersome transformations, which were required to build the functionally equivalent user-defined format:

```
declare hash h(dataset: 'some_states');
```

The DEFINEKEY method directs that the Abbr variable should be used as the unique key:

```
rc = h.defineKey('abbr');
```

ST_TO_FIPS differs primarily from the previously defined ST_VALIDATE function in Program 4.7 in that the hash FIND method returns data values for all matching key-value pairs, whereas the hash CHECK method only validates whether a key is found in the hash object. Thus, the FIND method requires that at least one data value be defined using the DEFINEDATA method:

```
rc = h.defineData('fips');
```

The FIND method returns a 0 when a key is found. In addition, it initializes all variables (corresponding to variables listed in the DEFINEDATA method) to the corresponding values in the lookup table. Thus, because DEFINEDATA specifies the FIPS variable, when a key value is matched, the FIPS variable (within the ST_TO_FIPS function) is initialized to the value of FIPS in the hash object corresponding to the matched key. In other words, when the FIND method matches a key, the corresponding variable(s) whose names are specified by the DEFINEDATA method are initialized within the user-defined function.

The RETURN statement returns the FIPS value to the calling program when a state abbreviation is found as a key in the hash object. When a state abbreviation is not found, FIND returns a nonzero value, and the IFC function causes RETURN to return a missing value to the calling program:

```
return(ifc(h.find()=0, fips, ''));
```

The DATA step in Program 4.13 initializes the FIPS_state variable to the return value of the ST_TO_FIPS function. If the ST_abbr variable is not found in the hash object, ST_TO_FIPS returns a missing value to the DATA step.

Program 4.13: Initialize Variable Using User-Defined Function
```
data init_states;
   set cities;
   length fips_state $2;
   fips_state=st_to_fips(st_abbr);
   put st_abbr= fips_state=;
run;
```

The log is identical to that of Program 4.11, which initialized the FIPS_state variable using a user-defined format:

```
st_abbr=CA fips_state=06
st_abbr=CA fips_state=06
st_abbr=OH fips_state=39
st_abbr=PR fips_state=
```

Note that variables declared by the DEFINEDATA method within a function maintain local scope—that is, they are available only inside the function and cannot be used by the calling program unless passed by the RETURN statement or specified in the OUTARGS statement. Thus, although the FIND method does initialize the FIPS variable inside the ST_TO_FIPS function to the corresponding FIPS value found in the hash object, this initialization in no way alters the FIPS_state variable in the calling program (shown in Program 4.13). For this reason, the RETURN statement must explicitly reference the FIPS variable to return the FIPS value to the DATA step, where the FIPS_state variable is initialized to the function's return value.

Although this initial user-defined function returns a single value (that is, the validated state abbreviation) to the calling program, its functionality can be expanded to return multiple values—including any key or non-key value maintained in the master table (that is, the Some_states data set). In the next section, various methods to return multiple values are demonstrated, which culminate in user-defined subroutines that can modify multiple values in their calling modules.

Multivariable Initialization

For many use cases, returning a *single* value from a lookup operation is inefficient, if not altogether useless, because multiple associated variables might need to be joined or returned.

User-defined formats fail here because they map only two variables—one key to one corresponding value, or many key values to one corresponding value. For this reason, many SAS practitioners instinctually reach for the tried-and-true DATA step MERGE or SQL procedure JOIN to perform a multivariable lookup.

For example, consider the Some_states data set, expanded from Program 4.14, which now represents a lookup table containing state abbreviations, state FIPS codes, state names, and U.S. Census 2021 population estimates.

Program 4.14: Abbreviated State Lookup Table
```
data some_states;
   length abbr $2 state $20 fips $2 pop 8;
   abbr = 'CA'; fips = '06'; state = 'California';   pop = 39237836; output;
   abbr = 'OH'; fips = '39'; state = 'Ohio';         pop = 11780017; output;
   abbr = 'PA'; fips = '42'; state = 'Pennsylvania'; pop = 12964056; output;
   abbr = 'MD'; fips = '24'; state = 'Maryland';     pop = 6165129; output;
   abbr = 'VA'; fips = '51'; state = 'Virginia';     pop = 8642274; output;
run;
```

Also consider the Cities data set, reprised in Program 4.15, which represents a transactional data set to which not only state FIPS code but also state name and state population need to be appended.

Program 4.15: Less Trusted Transactional Data Set Containing State Abbreviations
```
data cities;
   length st_abbr $2 city $20;
   st_abbr = 'CA'; city = 'Gustine'; output;
   st_abbr = 'CA'; city = 'Los Banos'; output;
   st_abbr = 'OH'; city = 'Columbus'; output;
   st_abbr = 'PR'; city = 'San Juan'; output;
run;
```

Given these data sets and the requirement to initialize three new variables, both procedural and functional lookup solutions exist—with the former requiring either a merge or join, and the latter requiring only a single function call. These respective solutions are compared in the following sections, and the advantages of the functional approach are demonstrated.

A Procedural Approach to Multivariable Initialization

Yes, this is a fancy way of saying: *Hey, I need to add some variables to my data set from this other data set*. Stated granularly, the requirement is to create a new data set called Init_states that retains all observations in the Cities data set, merges the ST_abbr variable in the Cities data set with the Abbr variable in the Some_states data set, and initializes three new variables (FIPS, State, and Pop) to the associated values in the Some_states data set. But as convoluted as this sounds, a seasoned SAS practitioner can write the corresponding DATA step or SQL procedure in less time than this scenario took to explain.

The syntax overhead exists because the MERGE statement requires the data sets to either be sorted by or indexed on the variable(s) listed in the BY statement. Thus, as Program 4.16 demonstrates, both the Cities and Some_states data sets must be sorted before the DATA step can perform the merge to initialize the three new variables.

Program 4.16: SORT Procedures and DATA Step Merge to Add Three Variables
```
proc sort data=some_states out=some_states_sorted;
   by abbr;
run;

proc sort data=cities out=cities_sorted;
   by st_abbr;
run;

data init_states;
   merge cities_sorted (in=a) some_states_sorted (in=b rename=(abbr=st_abbr));
   by st_abbr;
   if a;
run;
```

Notwithstanding the three steps required to initialize these variables, the DATA step yields the correct results, and the FIPS, State, and Pop variables are appended to the Init_states data set, as shown in Table 4.2. Note that as the PR key was not located in the lookup table, no associated data could be retrieved for Puerto Rico, and its State, FIPS, and Pop variables remain missing.

A second functionally equivalent procedural method foregoes the separate SORT procedures and instead relies on the SQL procedure's ability to join even unruly, unsorted data sets. Program 4.17 produces the identical Init_states data set, demonstrated in Table 4.2, but does so in far less code than Program 4.16. Note that the alias "D" represents the "data set," and the alias "H" represents the "hash object"—that is, the lookup table.

Program 4.17: SQL Procedure to Join Three Variables
```
proc sql noprint;
   create table init_states as
      select d.*, h.state, h.fips, h.pop
         from cities as d
            left join some_states as h
               on d.st_abbr = h.abbr;
quit;
```

Table 4.2: The Init_states Data Set

st_abbr	city	state	fips	pop
CA	Gustine	California	06	39237836
CA	Los Banos	California	06	39237836
OH	Columbus	Ohio	39	11780017
PR	San Juan			

Although many SAS practitioners select DATA step merges or equivalent SQL joins based on the process that delivers the highest performance or efficiency, in many cases, data sets are not large enough to demonstrate appreciable benefits of one method over the other. In other cases, SAS practitioners might be more familiar or comfortable with one method than the other. This is all to say that in many cases, the decision to select the DATA step over the SQL procedure—or vice versa—is as much one of personal preference as one that evaluates functionally equivalent alternatives based on performance.

With personal preference in mind, it is only fair that SAS practitioners be equitably armed with the functionally equivalent *functional* method of performing a lookup operation that initializes multiple variables. This *even more* concise functionality is demonstrated in the next section.

A Functional Approach to Multivariable Initialization

Program 4.12 defined the ST_TO_FIPS user-defined function that inputs a state abbreviation and returns the corresponding FIPS state code. However, because a function returns only a single value, it cannot fulfill the updated requirement to initialize not only the FIPS code but also the state name and population. By passing multiple parameters *by reference*, however, user-defined functions and subroutines can initialize multiple variables at once. Although the call-by-reference call method is most often associated with subroutines, and as discussed in Chapters 1 and 2, both functions and subroutines that invoke the OUTARGS statement can pass values by reference.

The SUB_STATE_TO_NAME_FIPS_POP subroutine, defined in Program 4.18, declares four parameters (ABBR, STATE, FIPS, and POP), the last three of which are passed by reference to make these variables available in the calling program.

Program 4.18: SUB_ST_TO_NAME_FIPS_POP Subroutine

```
proc fcmp outlib=work.funcs.lookup;
   subroutine sub_st_to_name_fips_pop(abbr $, state $, fips $, pop);
      outargs state, fips, pop;
      declare hash h(dataset: 'some_states');
      rc = h.defineKey('abbr');
      rc = h.defineData('state', 'fips', 'pop');
      rc = h.defineDone();
      rc = h.find();
      endsub;
quit;
```

The SUBROUTINE statement declares the subroutine name, three character parameters (ABBR, STATE, and FIPS), and one numeric parameter (POP). Thereafter, the OUTARGS statement declares the call method for the STATE, FIPS, and POP parameters as *call by reference*. ABBR is not listed, so it is declared as *call by value* (by default):

```
subroutine sub_st_to_name_fips_pop(abbr $, state $, fips $, pop);
   outargs state, fips, pop;
```

Note that no LENGTH statement is required because all variables are either key variables (namely, Abbr, later specified by the DEFINEKEY method) or call-by-reference parameters that are specified by the OUTARGS statement. There is no need to specify the length of Abbr because the variable is not returned to the calling program, and there is no need to specify the length of the remaining variables because their lengths are inherited implicitly from the calling program, which occurs for all parameters specified by the OUTARGS statement.

The hash object (H) is instantiated, and the DATASET option loads the Some_states data set into the hash object:

```
declare hash h(dataset: 'some_states');
```

The DEFINEKEY method specifies that the Abbr variable is the unique key:

```
rc = h.defineKey('abbr');
```

The DEFINEDATA method specifies that the State, FIPS, and Pop variables each should be uploaded into the hash object:

```
rc = h.defineData('state', 'fips', 'pop');
```

With the hash key and data values defined, the DEFINEDONE method terminates the hash object declaration:

```
rc = h.defineDone();
```

Finally, the hash FIND method not only validates that a value passed as an argument to the ABBR parameter is in the hash object, but also returns all associated data values when a key is located. Thus, when FIND returns a 0 (indicating success), the variables State, FIPS, and Pop are simultaneously initialized to the associated values maintained in the hash object:

```
rc = h.find();
```

The DATA step in Program 4.19 calls the SUB_ST_TO_NAME_FIPS_POP subroutine and initializes the State_name, FIPS_state, and Pop_state variables, which correspond to and are passed by reference to the STATE, FIPS, and POP parameters, respectively. Note that the LENGTH statement must declare State_name, FIPS_state, and Pop_state prior to the subroutine call because arguments passed by reference must be explicitly declared prior to the invocation of a function or subroutine to which they are passed.

Program 4.19: Calling the SUB_ST_TO_NAME_FIPS_POP Subroutine

```
data init_states;
   set cities;
   length state_name $20 fips_state $2 pop_state 8;
   call missing(state_name, fips_state, pop_state);
   call sub_st_to_name_fips_pop(st_abbr, state_name, fips_state, pop_state);
   put @1 city= @18 st_abbr= @30 state_name= @53 fips_state= @71 pop_state=;
run;
```

The Init_states data set is identical to that produced by the DATA step MERGE and SQL procedure JOIN, demonstrated in Programs 4.16 and 4.17, respectively. The following output is generated in the log:

```
city=Gustine        st_abbr=CA  state_name=California    fips_state=06
pop_state=39237836
city=Los Banos      st_abbr=CA  state_name=California    fips_state=06
pop_state=39237836
city=Columbus       st_abbr=OH  state_name=Ohio          fips_state=39
pop_state=11780017
city=San Juan       st_abbr=PR  state_name=              fips_state=
pop_state=.
```

Note the simplicity of the *functional* approach to multivariable initialization. A single, unassuming line of code delivers equivalent functionality to two SORT procedures and a DATA step, or to a SQL procedure having several lines of code! Thus, the exceptional speed of in-memory hash lookups has been encapsulated within the subroutine implementation, which yields a more concise, readable DATA step.

Counting Hash Keys

In previous examples, the role of a hash object has been to confirm that a key exists inside a hash object, or to return associated values when a key exists. Hash objects can also be used, however, to count keys. By incrementing a specific key's count each time it is encountered (that is, passed as an argument to the function instantiating the hash object), a hash object can operationalize a frequency table.

DATA step hash functionality provides the built-in hash SUM method and the associated DECLARE statement SUMINC argument, which in combination can be used to build frequency table hash objects. Unfortunately, neither the SUM method nor the SUMINC argument are supported by FCMP hash functionality. Fortunately, equivalent functionality can be engineered within the FCMP procedure from more basic hash building blocks.

For example, consider the requirement to evaluate word frequency in the Gettysburg Address, and more specifically, to find the *modal* word—the most frequently occurring word in the speech. Program 4.20 creates the Gettys data set in which the Text variable holds the text of the Gettysburg Address.

Program 4.20: Gettysburg Address

```
data gettys;
   length text $10000;
   text="Four score and seven years ago our fathers brought forth on this
continent, a new nation, conceived in Liberty, and dedicated to the proposition
that all men are created equal. Now we are engaged in a great civil war,
testing whether that nation, or any nation so conceived and so dedicated, can
long endure. We are met on a great battle-field of that war. We have come to
dedicate a portion of that field, as a final resting place for those who here
gave their lives that that nation might live. It is altogether fitting and
proper that we should do this. But, in a larger sense, we can not dedicate — we
can not consecrate — we can not hallow — this ground. The brave men, living and
dead, who struggled here, have consecrated it, far above our poor power to add
or detract. The world will little note, nor long remember what we say here, but
it can never forget what they did here. It is for us the living, rather, to be
dedicated here to the unfinished work which they who fought here have thus far
so nobly advanced. It is rather for us to be here dedicated to the great task
remaining before us — that from these honored dead we take increased devotion
to that cause for which they gave the last full measure of devotion — that we
here highly resolve that these dead shall not have died in vain — that this
nation, under God, shall have a new birth of freedom — and that government of
the people, by the people, for the people, shall not perish from the earth.";
run;
```

If each word instead represented a separate observation within a SAS data set, the FREQ procedure could yield the mode. However, FREQ is not helpful when assessing the frequency of values within a single observation. Instead, a hash object can organize and count words as they are incrementally parsed.

Counting Keys Using a Running Count

The SUB_MODAL_WORD subroutine, defined in Program 4.21, evaluates a character variable and returns the modal word with character case and punctuation ignored. The subroutine creates a key entry (Word) in the hash object for each unique word in the PHRASE parameter and a corresponding value entry (Tot) that represents the number of times the word has been encountered.

Program 4.21: Calculate Modal Word within a Phrase

```
proc fcmp outlib=work.funcs.stats;
   subroutine sub_modal_word(phrase $, mode_word $, mode_tot);
      outargs mode_word, mode_tot;
      length new_phrase $10000 word $30 cnt tot 8;
      * instantiate the hash object;
      declare hash h();
      rc = h.defineKey('word');
      rc = h.defineData('tot');
      rc = h.defineDone();
      * clean text and initialize arguments;
      new_phrase = lowcase(compress(phrase, ' ', 'KAS'));
```

```
         mode_word = '';
         mode_tot = 0;
         * iterate all words in the phrase;
         do cnt=1 to countw(new_phrase);
            word = strip(scan(new_phrase, cnt, '', 'S'));
            select;
               * increment a key that has been seen;
               when(h.find()=0)
                  tot + 1;
                  rc = h.replace();
               * initialize first occurrence of key;
               otherwise
                  tot = 1;
                  rc = h.add();
               end;
            * update mode values if tot > previous max;
            if tot > mode_tot then do;
               mode_word = word;
               mode_tot = tot;
               end;
            end;
         endsub;
quit;
```

The SUB_MODAL_WORD subroutine declares three parameters:

- PHRASE is a character parameter passed by value, which denotes the phrase to be analyzed.
- MODE_WORD is a character parameter passed by reference, as denoted in the OUT-ARGS statement, and returns the modal word.
- MODE_TOT is a numeric parameter, also passed by reference, and returns the frequency of the modal word.

```
proc fcmp outlib=work.funcs.stats;
   subroutine sub_modal_word(phrase $, mode_word $, mode_tot);
      outargs mode_word, mode_tot;
```

The hash object (H) is instantiated using the DECLARE HASH statement. One key (Word) is defined, as well as one value (Tot), which correspond to each word and its frequency, respectively:

```
declare hash h();
rc = h.defineKey('word');
rc = h.defineData('tot');
rc = h.defineDone();
```

The New_phrase variable standardizes the PHRASE parameter by removing all non-alphabetic characters using the COMPRESS function, and by lowering the case using LOWCASE:

```
new_phrase = lowcase(compress(phrase, '', 'KAS'));
```

The Mode_word variable is initialized to a missing value, and the Mode_tot variable is initialized to 0:

```
mode_word = '';
mode_tot = 0;
```

A DO loop iterates over the words in New_phrase, in which the FIND method evaluates whether Word is a key inside the hash object. When a key already exists (that is, FIND evaluates to 0), the FIND method also resets the Tot variable to the value of Tot inside the hash object (corresponding to the key). Thereafter, the Tot variable is incremented by 1, after which the REPLACE method updates the Tot value in the hash object. Thus, within the SELECT block, the WHEN block increments the counter for each word that already exists in the hash object:

```
do cnt=1 to countw(new_phrase);
   word = strip(scan(new_phrase, cnt, '', 'S'));
   select;
      * increment a key that has been seen;
      when(h.find()=0)
         tot + 1;
         rc = h.replace();
```

The FIND method evaluates to a nonzero value when a new word is encountered in New_phrase that does not exist in the hash object. When this occurs, the OTHERWISE block executes and adds Word and Tot to the hash object using the ADD method:

```
otherwise
   tot = 1;
   rc = h.add();
end;
```

The final block within the DO loop evaluates the current value of Tot against Mode_tot. If Tot is greater, then Mode_word and Mode_tot are reinitialized:

```
if tot > mode_tot then do;
   mode_word = word;
   mode_tot = tot;
   end;
end;
```

Thus, when the DO loop terminates, this final block will have set Mode_word to the modal word found in the hash object and Mode_tot to the number of times the modal word appeared in New_phrase. As Mode_word and Mode_tot are declared as call-by-reference parameters, these variables are updated in the calling program.

The DATA step in Program 4.22 calls the SUB_MODAL_WORD subroutine to parse the Gettysburg Address and evaluate the modal word. Note that the Fav_word and Word_tot variables must be declared using the LENGTH statement prior to the subroutine call; this is required whenever arguments are passed by reference.

Program 4.22: Calling the SUB_MODAL_WORD Subroutine
```
data get_mode;
   set gettys;
   length fav_word $30 word_tot 8;
   call missing(fav_word, word_tot);
   call sub_modal_word(text, fav_word, word_tot);
   put fav_word= word_tot=;
run;
```

The log demonstrates that "that" is the most commonly occurring word in the Gettysburg Address, with 13 occurrences:

```
fav_word=that word_tot=13
NOTE: There were 1 observations read from the data set WORK.GETTYS.
NOTE: The data set WORK.GET_MODE has 1 observations and 3 variables.
```

Note that if two or more words are tied for maximum occurrences, only the first word that achieves the maximum count is resolved to be the modal word. A second, functionally equivalent method to evaluate modal word is demonstrated in the next section, in which the hash object is first instantiated and filled, after which it is manually iterated to evaluate modal word.

Counting Keys with a Post Hoc Hash Iterator

The SUB_MODAL_WORD subroutine, defined in Program 4.21, evaluates the modal word in a character variable by generating a running count of the maximum word occurrence. A second, functionally equivalent solution is demonstrated in Program 4.23. In that solution, the subroutine uploads all words and their respective frequencies to the hash object, after which the object is iterated to retrieve the modal word and value.

The DECLARE statement in the FCMP procedure declares and instantiates the hash object, but it can also be used to declare and instantiate an optional hash object *iterator* using the DECLARE HITER statement. A hash object iterator must reference a specific hash object and facilitate manual traversal of that hash object. Declaration of an iterator enables the following four hash methods to be called within the FCMP procedure:

- FIRST returns the first record in the associated hash object.
- LAST returns the last record in the associated hash object.
- NEXT returns the next record in the associated hash object or, if no current record is specified, returns the first record.
- PREV returns the previous record in the associated hash object or, if no current record is specified, returns the last record.

Program 4.23 demonstrates the functionally equivalent subroutine that evaluates the modal word in a character variable. As this version of the SUB_MODAL_WORD subroutine does not maintain a running modal word and modal word count, the HITER object is required to iterate the hash object's records after the entire hash has been loaded.

Program 4.23: Calculate Modal Word within Phrase

```
proc fcmp outlib=work.funcs.stats;
   subroutine sub_modal_word(phrase $, mode_word $, mode_tot);
      outargs mode_word, mode_tot;
      length new_phrase $10000 word $30 cnt tot 8;
      * instantiate the hash object;
      declare hash h();
      declare hiter iter('h');
      rc = h.defineKey('word');
      rc = h.defineData('word', 'tot');
      rc = h.defineDone();
      * clean text;
      new_phrase = lowcase(compress(phrase, '', 'KAS'));
      * iterate all words in the phrase;
      do cnt = 1 to countw(new_phrase);
         word = strip(scan(new_phrase, cnt, '', 'S'));
         if h.find() = 0 then tot + 1;
         else tot = 1;
         rc = h.replace();
         end;
      * iteratively find modal word and frequency;
      mode_word = '';
      mode_tot = 0;
      do while(iter.next()=0);
         if tot > mode_tot then do;
            mode_word = word;
            mode_tot = tot;
            end;
         end;
      endsub;
quit;
```

Program 4.23 is functionally equivalent to Program 4.21 and is similar in many respects. However, immediately after the hash object declaration, the hash object iterator (Iter) is declared and references the hash object (H):

```
declare hash h();
declare hiter iter('h');
```

Note that the DO loop has been greatly simplified, in part because the modal value is no longer calculated as the hash object is filled. The SELECT-WHEN-OTHERWISE components have also been replaced with a single IF statement. Finally, because the default functionality of the REPLACE method is to add a key when that key is not found in the hash object, the ADD method and its accompanying code block can be removed:

```
do cnt = 1 to countw(new_phrase);
   word = strip(scan(new_phrase, cnt, '', 'S'));
   if h.find() = 0 then tot + 1;
   else tot = 1;
```

```
    rc = h.replace();
    end;
```

When the entire phrase has been uploaded into the hash object, the DO loop terminates, and the NEXT method iterates through the hash object to retrieve its values one by one. NEXT returns a 0 when an additional record in the hash object exists and a nonzero value when the entire hash object has been parsed:

```
mode_word = '';
mode_tot = 0;
do while(iter.next()=0);
    if tot > mode_tot then do;
        mode_word = word;
        mode_tot = tot;
        end;
    end;
```

Thus, rather than performing the Tot versus Mode_tot comparison when each value is uploaded into the hash object (as occurred in Program 4.21), this comparison now occurs within the DO loop after the hash object has been filled. Iterator methods are important tools, as some hash evaluations or calculations cannot occur until after the entire hash object has been populated.

Note that the hash objects in both Programs 4.21 and 4.23 are filled in the order in which the words in New_phrase are encountered; that is, the ADD method effectively appends a record to the end of the hash object, creating an unsorted hash object. Sorted hash options are explored in the next section.

Sorting Hash Keys

The ORDERED option in the DECLARE statement instantiates a hash object that is sorted by its key(s). For example, the following declaration statements instantiate the hash object (H) and the hash iterator object (Iter) and sort the hash object by Var:

```
declare hash h(ordered: 'ascending');
declare hiter iter('h');
rc = h.defineKey('var');
```

The ASCENDING keyword specifies an ascending sort, and the DESCENDING keyword specifies a descending sort. A hash object sorted in ascending order maintains its lowest key value(s) in the first record; thus, the FIRST hash method yields the lowest key value, and the LAST hash method yields the highest. This enables an ordered hash object to be exported to an array, after which the array will contain a sorted list of values. This functionality can be used to mimic the built-in SORTC and SORTN subroutines.

The SORTC subroutine performs a horizontal sort or character variables or values, and can reorder an array of character variables. One limitation when calling SORTC or SORTN from a user-defined function does exist: the array size is limited to 800 elements, as demonstrated in Chapter 3. However, a more scalable solution can be built using an FCMP procedure that leverages an ordered hash object.

The SORT_CHAR subroutine, defined in Program 4.24, is functionally equivalent to, albeit slower than, the SORTC built-in subroutine. However, it expands the number of variables that can be sorted beyond 800.

Program 4.24: Extending the Scalability of the SORTC Subroutine

```
proc fcmp outlib=work.funcs.sorts;
   subroutine sort_char(vars[*] $);
      outargs vars;
      length var $30 tot cnt cnt_dup 8;
      declare hash h(ordered: 'ascending');
      declare hiter iter('h');
      rc = h.defineKey('var');
      rc = h.defineData('var', 'tot');
      rc = h.defineDone();
      * build hash object;
      do cnt = 1 to dim(vars);
         var = vars[cnt];
         if h.find() = 0 then tot + 1;
         else tot = 1;
         rc = h.replace();
         end;
      * build ordered array;
      cnt = 1;
      do while(iter.next()=0);
         do cnt_dup = 1 to tot;
            if ^missing(var) then do;
               vars[cnt] = var;
               cnt + 1;
               end;
            end;
         end;
      endsub;
quit;
```

The SORT_CHAR subroutine is called by the DATA step in Program 4.25 after the COMPRESS function removes all non-alphabetic characters from the Gettys data set created in Program 4.20 and the LOWCASE function lowers the case of the words. Note that whenever an array is declared as a parameter within a function or subroutine, an array must first be declared in the calling program and passed to the function.

Program 4.25: Calling the SORT_CHAR Subroutine to Sort Words in Array

```
data sort_characters;
   set gettys;
   array words[1000] $30;
   cleaned_text = lowcase(compress(text, '', 'KAS'));
```

```
   do cnt = 1 to countw(text);
      words[cnt] = scan(cleaned_text, cnt, '', 'S');
      end;
   call sort_char(words);
   put words[*];
run;
```

The log demonstrates the contents of the Words array after it has been sorted:

```
a a a a a a above add advanced ago all altogether and and and and and and
any are are are as battlefield be be before birth brave brought but but by can
can can can can cause civil come conceived conceived consecrate consecrated
continent created dead dead dead dedicate dedicate dedicated dedicated
dedicated dedicated detract devotion devotion did died do earth endure
engaged equal far far fathers field final fitting for for for for for forget
forth fought four freedom from from full gave gave god government great great
great ground hallow have have have have have here here here here here here
here here highly honored in in in in increased is is is it it it it it larger
last liberty little live lives living living long long measure men men met
might nation nation nation nation nation never new new nobly nor not not not
not not note now of of of of of on on or or our our people people people
perish place poor portion power proper proposition rather
rather remaining remember resolve resting say score sense seven shall shall
shall should so so so struggled take task testing that that that that that
that that that that that that that that the the the the the the the the the
the the their these these they they they this this this this those thus to to
to to to to to to to under unfinished us us us vain war war we we we we we we we
we we we what what whether which which who who who will work world years
```

Note the repeated words, which are salient after the text has been reordered. Hash objects, by definition, must contain unique keys, so how then are both the key values and their associated quantities maintained? The trick is to compile a hash object of key frequency counts, similar to the counts generated in Programs 4.21 and 4.23. Thus, the 13 instances of "that" are recorded in the Tot variable within the hash object, so "that" is subsequently initialized into 13 consecutive array elements when the array is created.

The SUBROUTINE statement declares the SORT_CHAR subroutine as having a single array parameter (VARS), which the OUTARGS statement declares as being passed by reference:

```
proc fcmp outlib=work.funcs.sorts;
   subroutine sort_char(vars[*] $);
      outargs vars;
```

The DECLARE HASH and DECLARE HITER statements declare and instantiate the hash object and hash iterator object, respectively. Note that the ORDERED argument specifies an ascending sort, and the hash iterator object will enable the hash object to be parsed manually:

```
      length var $30 tot cnt cnt_dup 8;
      declare hash h(ordered: 'ascending');
```

```
declare hiter iter('h');
rc = h.defineKey('var');
rc = h.defineData('var', 'tot');
rc = h.defineDone();
```

Also note that whereas the Var variable is declared as the hash object key, both the Var and Tot variables are specified as data values. Var is required to be both a key and a value to enable Var to be returned from the hash object when a lookup operation is performed. Thus, if Var were declared only as a key and not also as a data value, the hash object could be iterated by the key, but the key could not be subsequently written to an array for return to the calling program.

The DO loop iterates over the array, relying on the DIM function to evaluate the dimensions (length) of the single-dimensional array. The DO loop is equivalent to the DO loops in both Programs 4.21 and 4.23, in which the FIND method first evaluates whether a value exists as a key in the hash object and subsequently increments the frequency counter (Cnt):

```
do cnt = 1 to dim(vars);
   var = vars[cnt];
   if h.find() = 0 then tot + 1;
   else tot = 1;
   rc = h.replace();
   end;
```

Finally, an outer DO loop leverages the NEXT hash method to iterate the hash object, and an inner DO loop counts to the number of instances of the word being evaluated. For example, when examining the modal word "that," the inner loop would iterate from one to 13 to add 13 instances of "that" to 13 consecutive array elements. Each time the outer loop iterates, the NEXT method resets both the Word and Tot variables to the values pulled from the hash object, and the Vars array is iteratively overwritten with the Word values:

```
cnt = 1;
do while(iter.next()=0);
   do cnt_dup = 1 to tot;
      if ^missing(var) then do;
         vars[cnt] = var;
         cnt + 1;
         end;
      end;
   end;
```

Because the OUTARGS statement declares the VARS parameter as an array that is passed by reference, when the subroutine terminates, the calling program has access to the array that has been reordered. So, although the SORTC and SORTN built-in subroutines are likely adequate for many use cases, in those cases where more than 800 variables might need to be reordered (within the FCMP procedure), the combination of a hash- and array-based solution can neatly pack this tremendous functionality inside a user-defined subroutine.

Building Dynamic Hash Using the SAS Macro Language

Throughout the numerous hash object examples in this chapter, one limitation may have become apparent—the many hash statements that require character literals, which reduce flexibility in declaring and instantiating hash objects within the FCMP procedure (but not the DATA step). For example, the DATASET option in the *FCMP* DECLARE HASH statement requires a character literal enclosed in quotation marks, so the data set name must be static and known at the time of function compilation. (SAS Institute Inc. 2023) However, the DATASET option in the *DATA step* DECLARE HASH statement accepts not only a character literal but also a character variable, making it vastly more flexible. (SAS Institute Inc. 2023) This rigidity of FCMP hash reduces the flexibility of the user-defined functions that leverage it, although the SAS macro language can overcome this limitation.

Program 4.26 creates the Planets data set, which includes planetary metrics from NASA. (NASA 2022) And, yes, Pluto is a planet. Please do not ruin my childhood. Note that the Planets data set represents only a miniscule number of the metrics that could be attributed to these planets.

Program 4.26: Creating the Planets Data Set
```
/*
diameter = km
sun_distance = 10^6 km (or in million km)
average_temp = Celsius
gravity = m/2^2
*/
data planets;
   infile datalines dsd delimiter=',';
   length name $10 type $20 diameter sun_distance average_temp gravity 8;
   input name $ type $ diameter sun_distance average_temp gravity;
   format diameter sun_distance comma8.0;
   datalines;
mercury,terrestrial,4879,57.9,167,3.7
venus,terrestrial,12104,108.2,464,8.9
earth,terrestrial,12756,149.6,15,9.8
mars,terrestrial,6792,228,-65,3.7
jupiter,gas giant,142984,778.5,-110,23.1
saturn,gas giant,120536,1432,-140,9
uranus,gas giant,51118,2867,-195,8.7
neptune,gas giant,49528,4515,-200,11
pluto,dwarf,2376,5906.4,-225,0.7
;
```

A user-defined function might be envisioned that could return a specific metric from the table when passed the planet name (the key) and the metric name (the value to be returned). However, the flexibility of that operation would be limited by the preceding requirements that hash statements remain stable—that is, attributes such as the name, number, and type of data to be returned by the function could not be varied.

A static solution to this scenario is first presented in the next section. Thereafter, a subsequent solution leverages the SAS macro language to overcome these and other limitations by dynamically generating character literals and other statements within the FCMP procedure.

Statically Defining a Hash Lookup Operation

Although a function can generate only one return value, lookup operations can return zero, one, or many values from a hash object, which can be subsequently passed by reference to a calling program. Placing a lookup operation within a function or subroutine, and subsequently using the OUTARGS statement to update one or more variables, can facilitate a flexible solution.

It is fairly straightforward to design a function that returns a single value from a lookup operation. The GET_PLANET_DIAMETER function, demonstrated in Program 4.27, returns the diameter (in kilometers) of the specified planet.

Program 4.27: Returning a Single Metric from a Lookup Table
```
proc fcmp outlib=work.funcs.planets;
   function get_planet_diameter(planet $);
      length name $10 diameter 8;
      name = lowcase(planet);
      declare hash h(dataset: 'planets');
      rc = h.defineKey('name');
      rc = h.defineData('diameter');
      rc = h.defineDone();
      rc = h.find();
      return(diameter);
      endfunc;
quit;

%put %sysfunc(get_planet_diameter(pluto),comma8.0);
```

The log demonstrates that the diameter of the planet Pluto is 2,376 kilometers:

```
2,376
```

However, because the DEFINEDATA hash method requires a literal character value and cannot accommodate a variable, a different function would need to be defined to return each metric. This is where getters and setters are beneficial, as demonstrated throughout Chapter 6. For example, a GET_SPACE_METRIC function could be defined (not shown), that accepts two arguments—the planet name and the metric name—and returns the planet's specified metric. But what if you want to update multiple values in the calling program? Here, the SAS macro language can assist, as demonstrated in the next section.

Dynamically Defining a Hash Lookup Operation

Program 4.28 defines the CREATE_DYNAMIC_SUBROUTINE macro, which dynamically creates a subroutine that performs a dynamic lookup operation. The macro is fully deconstructed and described subsequently.

Program 4.28: Dynamically Building a Subroutine

```
%macro create_dynamic_subroutine(
   sub_name /* subroutine name to create */,
   dsn /* data set name for hash object */,
   keys /* space-delim key(s) */,
   values /* space-delim var(s) */);
%local i var type params outargs length varlen definekey definedata;
%let dsid=%sysfunc(open(&dsn));
* create list of parameters;
%do i=1 %to %sysfunc(countw(&keys &values));
   %let var=%scan(&keys &values,&i,,S);
   %let type=%sysfunc(vartype(&dsid,%sysfunc(varnum(&dsid,&var))));
   %if %eval(&i>1) %then %let params=&params,;
   %let params=&params &var;
   %if &type=C %then %let params=&params $;
   %end;
* create OUTARGS statement;
%do i=1 %to %sysfunc(countw(&values));
   %let var=%scan(&values,&i,,S);
   %if %eval(&i>1) %then %let outargs=&outargs,;
   %let outargs=&outargs &var;
   %end;
* create LENGTH statement for value(s);
%do i=1 %to %sysfunc(countw(&values));
   %let var=%scan(&values,&i,,S);
   %let type=%sysfunc(vartype(&dsid,%sysfunc(varnum(&dsid,&var))));
   %if &type=C %then %let
   varlen=%sysfunc(varlen(&dsid,%sysfunc(varnum(&dsid,&var))));
   %let length=&length &var;
   %if &type=C %then %let length=&length $&varlen;
   %else %let length=&length 8;
   %end;
* create DefineKey argument(s);
%do i=1 %to %sysfunc(countw(&keys));
   %let var=%scan(&keys,&i,,S);
   %if %eval(&i>1) %then %let definekey=&definekey,;
   %let definekey=&definekey "&var";
   %end;
* create DefineData argument(s);
%do i=1 %to %sysfunc(countw(&values));
   %let var=%scan(&values,&i,,S);
   %if %eval(&i>1) %then %let definedata=&definedata,;
   %let definedata=&definedata "&var";
   %end;
```

```
* dynamically build subroutine;
proc fcmp outlib=work.funcs.dynamic;
   subroutine &sub_name(&params);
      outargs &outargs;
      length &length;
      declare hash h(dataset: "&dsn");
      rc = h.defineKey(&definekey);
      rc = h.defineData(&definedata);
      rc = h.defineDone();
      rc = h.find();
      endsub;
quit;
%mend;
```

The following code executes the CREATE_DYNAMIC_SUBROUTINE macro and compiles the dynamically built subroutine inside it:

```
%create_dynamic_subroutine(get_values_from_dsn,
   planets, name, type diameter sun_distance average_temp gravity);
```

The CREATE_DYNAMIC_SUBROUTINE macro declares and requires four parameters:

- SUB_NAME is the name of the user-defined subroutine to be created.
- DSN represents the data set that is being imported into the hash object.
- KEYS is a space-delimited list of the one or more keys that is used to query the hash object.
- VALUES is a space-delimited list of the one or more values that is returned from the hash object. Because these values will be passed by reference, they will be made available to the calling program.

To begin to understand the macro functionality, the following %PUT statements can be added to Program 4.28 (immediately prior to the %MEND statement) to print the macro variables that generate the dynamic functionality:

```
%put &=sub_name;
%put &=params;
%put &=outargs;
%put &=length;
%put &=dsn;
%put &=definekey;
%put &=definedata;
```

The log displays the macro variables, each of which is used in the FCMP procedure (inside the macro definition) to configure the function:

```
SUB_NAME=get_values_from_dsn
```

```
PARAMS=name $, type $, diameter, sun_distance, average_temp, gravity
OUTARGS=type, diameter, sun_distance, average_temp, gravity
LENGTH=type $20 diameter 8 sun_distance 8 average_temp 8 gravity 8
DSN=planets
DEFINEKEY="name"
DEFINEDATA="type", "diameter", "sun_distance", "average_temp", "gravity"
```

Thus, given the previous call to CREATE_DYNAMIC_SUBROUTINE, the FCMP procedure demonstrated in Program 4.29 is dynamically created and compiled inside the macro.

Program 4.29: GET_VALUES_FROM_DSN Subroutine That Is Dynamically Created

```
proc fcmp outlib=work.funcs.dynamic;
   subroutine get_values_from_dsn(name $, type $, diameter, sun_distance,
         average_temp, gravity);
      outargs type, diameter, sun_distance, average_temp, gravity;
      length type $20 diameter 8 sun_distance 8 average_temp 8 gravity 8;
      declare hash h(dataset: "planets");
      rc = h.defineKey("name");
      rc = h.defineData("type", "diameter", "sun_distance", "average_temp", "gravity");
      rc = h.defineDone();
      rc = h.find();
      endsub;
quit;
```

For example, the DATA step in Program 4.30 calls the GET_VALUES_FROM_DSN subroutine, which is statically defined nowhere within the program because it is generated by the CREATE_ DYNAMIC_SUBROUTINE macro and the specific arguments passed to that macro. Note that when the GET_VALUES_FROM_DSN subroutine is called, the order of arguments passed must correspond in parameter name, order, and data type to the parameters that were effectively defined in the macro call to CREATE_DYNAMIC_SUBROUTINE.

Program 4.30: Calling the Dynamically Created GET_VALUES_FROM_DSN Subroutine

```
data _null_;
   length type $20 diameter sun_distance average_temp gravity 8;
   call missing(type, diameter, sun_distance, average_temp, gravity);
   call get_values_from_dsn('pluto', type, diameter, sun_distance, average_temp,
      gravity);
   put _all_;
run;
```

The DATA step executes, calls the GET_VALUES_FROM_DSN subroutine, and prints the values that are returned to the log:

```
type=dwarf diameter=2376 sun_distance=5906.4 average_temp=-225 gravity=0.7
```

Within the CREATE_DYNAMIC_SUBROUTINE macro, the first DO loop creates the &PARAMS macro variable, which dynamically declares all parameters—including both hash keys and values—in the SUBROUTINE statement:

```
* create list of parameters;
%do i=1 %to %sysfunc(countw(&keys &values));
   %let var=%scan(&keys &values,&i,,S);
   %let type=%sysfunc(vartype(&dsid,%sysfunc(varnum(&dsid,&var))));
   %if %eval(&i>1) %then %let params=&params,;
   %let params=&params &var;
   %if &type=C %then %let params=&params $;
   %end;
```

The next DO loop dynamically creates a list of the parameters that will be specified by the OUTARGS statement. Hash key values are passed by value, so they do not need to be specified here:

```
* create OUTARGS statement;
%do i=1 %to %sysfunc(countw(&values));
   %let var=%scan(&values,&i,,S);
   %if %eval(&i>1) %then %let outargs=&outargs,;
   %let outargs=&outargs &var;
   %end;
```

The third DO loop dynamically generates the LENGTH statement that similarly must enumerate all values that are being returned from the hash object:

```
* create LENGTH statement for value(s);
%do i=1 %to %sysfunc(countw(&values));
   %let var=%scan(&values,&i,,S);
   %let type=%sysfunc(vartype(&dsid,%sysfunc(varnum(&dsid,&var))));
   %if &type=C %then %let varlen=%sysfunc(varlen(&dsid,%sysfunc(varnum(&dsid,&var))));
   %let length=&length &var;
   %if &type=C %then %let length=&length $&varlen;
   %else %let length=&length 8;
   %end;
```

The final two DO loops build the literal character values that are called by the DEFINEKEY and DEFINEDATA methods, respectively:

```
* create DefineKey argument(s);
%do i=1 %to %sysfunc(countw(&keys));
   %let var=%scan(&keys,&i,,S);
   %if %eval(&i>1) %then %let definekey=&definekey,;
   %let definekey=&definekey "&var";
   %end;
* create DefineData argument(s);
%do i=1 %to %sysfunc(countw(&values));
```

```
%let var=%scan(&values,&i,,S);
%if %eval(&i>1) %then %let definedata=&definedata,;
%let definedata=&definedata "&var";
%end;
```

Although the DEFINEKEY and DEFINEDATA hash methods require character literals and cannot accommodate variables or other sources of variability such as expressions, the SAS macro language can be used to construct quotes-enclosed character literals. The FCMP procedure is none the wiser when it compiles and executes this elegantly dynamic subroutine.

Conclusion

This chapter introduced the hash object, the primary in-memory, built-in data structure in the SAS language. Hash objects are both powerful and efficient, and where their underlying complexity can be hidden inside a user-defined function, SAS practitioners benefit from hash while avoiding its complexity. This chapter demonstrated hash operations that validate data, transform data (effectively performing a join or merge), sort data, and evaluate the frequency of categorical data. The hash iterator was also introduced, which enables hash objects to be manually traversed to evaluate or modify their contents. Finally, although the FCMP procedure offers only half of the hash methods and attributes that are available in DATA step programming, in some cases, functionally equivalent operations can be engineered within user-defined functions.

Chapter 5: RUN_MACRO and RUN_SASFILE

The FCMP procedure supports several built-in SAS functions not otherwise available in Base SAS. RUN_MACRO and RUN_SASFILE are two of the most powerful functions, with the former calling a SAS macro and the latter calling a SAS program file from inside a user-defined function or subroutine. RUN_MACRO and RUN_SASFILE enable SAS macros, which can enclose Base SAS statements, DATA steps, and procedures, to be executed inside of functions. This versatility facilitates some pretty unimaginable software design, not otherwise possible in the SAS language.

In a general, programming-language-agnostic sense, functions communicate with a calling module by returning a value—the *return value*—as discussed throughout Chapter 1. FCMP functions and subroutines can further communicate with a calling module by updating arguments passed *by reference*—that is, parameters specified in the optional OUTARGS statement. This limited communication between the calling program and the called module is intentional, as it minimizes software dependencies that would otherwise limit a function's modularity and reusability. In other words, by limiting the scope and functionality of a function, its utility can be increased because it can safely and reliably do one and only one thing, and it can communicate only through a single return value or through one or multiple variables passed by reference.

Enter the RUN_MACRO and RUN_SASFILE functions, which upend decades of function design. They not only upset the applecart, they dismantle it, set it ablaze, and dance circles 'round its fiery demise. For example, if you have ever wanted to run a DATA step inside another DATA step or a SAS procedure inside a DATA step, both RUN_MACRO and RUN_SASFILE can perform these seemingly magical feats. However, this functionality can increase not only software flexibility and functionality but also software complexity and dependency, so caution should be exercised. Caveats aside, RUN_MACRO and RUN_SASFILE are powerful, peerless tools, and this chapter introduces their syntax and usage.

I first learned of RUN_MACRO while attending an insightful, inspirational talk by Art Carpenter at the Western Users of SAS Software (WUSS) conference. I found his description of RUN_MACRO to be *incredible*—as in *literally unbelievable*! What was this black magic? And who was this sorcerer claiming he could run a DATA step inside another DATA step?! Yet, RUN_MACRO and RUN_SASFILE are truly as remarkable as Art's claims, as demonstrated throughout this chapter.

Introducing the RUN_MACRO Function

The RUN_MACRO function calls a macro during FCMP function execution and runs the macro in a side session of SAS. The first argument of RUN_MACRO corresponds to the macro name, and subsequent optional arguments pass variables to and from the macro. For example, the following RUN_MACRO call invokes the TEST_MACRO macro:

```
rc=run_macro('test_macro', char, num);
```

Note that the macro name must appear either as a quoted character literal (as above) or as a variable (as below):

```
macro_name='test_macro';
rc=run_macro(macro_name, char, num);
```

In both examples, RUN_MACRO passes the values of Char and Num to the TEST_MACRO macro, in which corresponding macro variables &CHAR and &NUM are automatically initialized.

Program 5.1 demonstrates the TEST_MACRO macro, which is called by the TEST function. TEST declares a character parameter (CHAR) and numeric parameter (NUM), both of which are passed via RUN_MACRO to the TEST_MACRO macro. Within TEST_MACRO, the &CHAR and &NUM macro variables are automatically initialized. When the macro terminates, the values of &CHAR and &NUM overwrite the prior values of the Char and Num variables, respectively, inside the FCMP procedure.

Program 5.1: Building a RUN_MACRO Function

```
%macro test_macro();
%put 1. INSIDE MACRO;
%put &=char &=num;
%let char=!&char!;
%let num=%eval(&num+1);
%put &=char &=num;
%mend;

proc fcmp outlib=work.funcs.test;
    function test(char $, num);
        put '2. INSIDE FCMP';
        put char= num=;
        rc = run_macro('test_macro', char, num);
        put '3. INSIDE FCMP';
        put rc=;
        put char= num=;
```

```
        return(1);
      endfunc;
quit;
```

Note that the DATA step in Program 5.2 calls the TEST function, passing "hello" to CHAR and 5 to NUM.

Program 5.2: Calling the RUN_MACRO Function

```
options cmplib=work.funcs;

data _null_;
   x = test('hello', 5);
run;
```

The output demonstrates the order in which the statements are executed. Thus, the text generated inside TEST_MACRO is printed to the log before text generated inside the TEST function:

```
1. INSIDE MACRO
CHAR='hello' NUM=5
CHAR=!'hello'! NUM=6
2. INSIDE FCMP
char=hello num=5
ERROR: Return value "char" truncated to 5 characters.
3. INSIDE FCMP
rc=0
char=!'hel num=6
```

Also note that character variables passed via RUN_MACRO are initialized with both leading and trailing single quotation marks within the macro. Thus, when "hello" (without quotation marks) is passed from the TEST function to TEST_MACRO, the value of &CHAR is initialized to 'hello' (with single quotation marks). For this reason, whenever RUN_MACRO passes a character variable, the DEQUOTE function is typically called via %SYSFUNC to remove the quotation marks. And although TEST_MACRO attempts to append both leading and trailing exclamation points to &CHAR, it succeeds at the former but fails at the latter because the length of &CHAR is limited to the five characters initially passed in the Char variable—hello.

Thus, note the runtime error in the log, in which the Char variable inside the FCMP procedure is unable to accept the updated value ("!hello!"). This failure can be remedied either by initializing a new variable within the TEST function, rather than attempting to modify Char, or by passing a variable with a greater length to the function.

For example, Program 5.3 again calls the TEST function, but now passes a variable with a length of 10 rather than the character literal "hello". In doing so, SAS now relies on this explicit declaration of variable length, as opposed to implicitly setting the length to five, as occurred when the character literal "hello" was passed in Program 5.2.

Program 5.3: Lengthening the Argument Passed to a Function

```
data _null_;
   length var $10;
   var = 'hello';
   x = test(var, 5);
run;
```

The output demonstrates that RUN_MACRO again encloses the argument in quotation marks. However, note that the initial value of &CHAR is padded with spaces after "hello" and before the trailing single quotation mark. When &CHAR is returned to the TEST function, however, the trailing exclamation point, trailing quotation mark, and trailing spaces are all removed:

```
1. INSIDE MACRO
CHAR='hello      ' NUM=5
CHAR=!'hello      '! NUM=6
2. INSIDE FCMP
char=hello num=5
ERROR: Return value "char" truncated to 10 characters.
3. INSIDE FCMP
rc=0
char=!'hello num=6
```

Again, the final instance of Char is missing its trailing exclamation point because TEST_MACRO attempted to add the exclamation point after the series of unnecessary spaces and trailing single quotation mark. In the next section, the DEQUOTE built-in function overcomes this failure.

Implementing the DEQUOTE Function to Remove Automatic Quoting

The solution to eliminating the automatic quoting of character arguments is the DEQUOTE built-in function, which can be invoked by %SYSFUNC to remove quotation marks from macro variables. For example, adding the following statement to the TEST_MACRO macro removes the single quotation marks from &CHAR and enables "!hello!" to be returned from TEST_MACRO to the TEST function:

```
%let char=%sysfunc(dequote(&char));
```

Thus, Program 5.4 demonstrates an updated TEST_MACRO definition that incorporates DEQUOTE to remove the single quotation marks added to &CHAR. The DEQUOTE function is unnecessary when passing numeric variables because RUN_MACRO only quotes character variables.

Program 5.4: Removing Automatic Quotes with the DEQUOTE Function

```
%macro test_macro();
%let char=%sysfunc(dequote(&char));
%put 1. INSIDE MACRO;
%put &=char &=num;
%let char=!&char!;
%let num=%eval(&num+1);
%put &=char &=num;
%mend;
```

When the unrevised DATA step (shown in Program 5.3) executes, the anticipated output is printed to the log, as the &CHAR macro variable is no longer truncated by RUN_MACRO:

```
INSIDE MACRO
CHAR=hello NUM=5
CHAR=!hello! NUM=6
2. INSIDE FCMP
char=hello num=5
3. INSIDE FCMP
rc=0
char=!hello! num=6
```

In general, DEQUOTE should always be implemented inside macros that receive character arguments via RUN_MACRO.

Cautious Declaration of Macro Parameters When Calling Macro via RUN_MACRO

Finally, those familiar with the SAS macro language will note the discrepancy that the TEST_MACRO macro is defined in Programs 5.1 and 5.4 without explicit parameter declarations for either of the &CHAR or &NUM macro variables. This design is acceptable when building macros that are only intended to be called via RUN_MACRO. However, as some macros might need to be both directly invoked from a SAS statement and indirectly invoked from the RUN_MACRO function inside a user-defined function, it is important to understand how macro parameter declarations affect RUN_MACRO.

For example, the following %MACRO statement is typically observed when declaring two parameters, &CHAR and &NUM, in which positional parameters are comma delimited and parenthetically enclosed:

```
%macro test_macro(char, num);
```

The revised TEST_MACRO macro, shown in Program 5.5, now explicitly declares the &CHAR and &NUM macro variables as parameters.

Program 5.5: Declaring Macro Variable Parameters in RUN_MACRO Macros

```
%macro test_macro(char, num);
%put 1. INSIDE MACRO;
%put &=char &=num;
%let char=!&char!;
%let num=%eval(&num+1);
%put &=char &=num;
%mend;
```

When the DATA step shown in Program 5.3 is executed again, the log demonstrates that neither &CHAR nor &NUM were successfully initialized within TEST_MACRO:

```
INSIDE MACRO
CHAR= NUM=
CHAR=!! NUM=1
2. INSIDE FCMP
char=hello num=5
3. INSIDE FCMP
rc=0
char=hello num=5
```

Note that &CHAR and &NUM are initialized to Null values within TEST_MACRO, rather than the character and numeric variables (Char and Num) that are passed from the TEST function. Next, although &CHAR is initialized to !! and &NUM is initialized to 1, neither of these values are returned to the TEST function. In the end, the final values of Char and Num are "hello" and 5, as if RUN_MACRO had never executed. This failure demonstrates that where identically named macro parameters are declared within a macro, macro variables of the same name cannot be passed via the RUN_MACRO function.

Generating a Return Value from a RUN_MACRO Macro

All functions return a value, and this return value is commonly used by the calling module after the function terminates. RUN_MACRO macros similarly can be used for this purpose. For example, consider the need to add two values and to return the total. This calculation can be performed inside a RUN_MACRO macro, as demonstrated in Program 5.6, in which &A and &B are added to resolve to &C.

Program 5.6: Generating a Numeric RUN_MACRO Return Value

```
%macro return_sum();
%let c=%eval(&a+&b);
%mend;

proc fcmp outlib=work.funcs.test;
   function sum_it(a, b);
      rc = run_macro('return_sum', a, b, c);
```

```
        return(c);
        endfunc;
quit;
```

The following call to SUM_IT adds 3 and 6. Within RETURN_SUM, &C is computed to be the sum of &A (3) and &B (6), and &C (9) is returned to SUM_IT:

```
%put SUM: %sysfunc(sum_it(3,6));
```

The log demonstrates that the sum is calculated to be 9:

```
SUM: 9
```

However, when a character return value is generated using the same methodology, issues arise. Consider the updated RETURN_CONCAT macro and CONCAT_IT function, demonstrated in Program 5.7.

Program 5.7: Attempting to Generate a Character RUN_MACRO Return Value

```
%macro return_concat();
%let c=A: &a B: &b;
%let d=A: &a B: &b;
%put &=c;
%put &=d;
%mend;

proc fcmp outlib=work.funcs.test;
   function concat_it(a, b);
       rc = run_macro('return_concat', a, b, c);
       return(c);
       endfunc;
quit;
```

Because C is passed as a RUN_MACRO argument, yet never explicitly declared within the function, SAS implicitly declares C as a numeric data type in the function. Thus, within the RETURN_CONCAT macro called by RUN_MACRO, the corresponding &C macro variable is prohibited from being initialized to a character value. The following call to CONCAT_IT fails to return the expected character value:

```
%put CONCAT: %sysfunc(concat_it(3, 6));
```

Thus, &C cannot be initialized to a character value and is set to a period to denote a missing numeric value. However, &D is successfully initialized, as its data type has not been restricted by RUN_MACRO:

```
C=.
D=A: 3 B: 6
CONCAT: .
```

To rectify the issue, C must be declared as a character variable within the CONCAT_IT function prior to the RUN_MACRO call. The CONCAT_IT function is updated in Program 5.8 to first declare C as a character variable using the LENGTH statement.

Program 5.8: Generating a Character RUN_MACRO Return Value

```
%macro return_concat();
%put &=c;
%let c=A: &a B: &b;
%mend;

proc fcmp outlib=work.funcs.test;
    function concat_it(a, b) $;
        length c $20;
        rc = run_macro('return_concat', a, b, c);
        return(c);
        endfunc;
quit;
```

CONCAT_IT is again called:

```
%put CONCAT: %sysfunc(concat_it(3, 6));
```

The log demonstrates that &C is initialized by default as a series of blanks enclosed in single quotation marks, after which it is reinitialized to the correct result and passed back to the CONCAT_IT function:

```
C='                    '
CONCAT: A: 3 B: 6
```

Here, it is not necessary to call DEQUOTE to remove the leading quotation mark, spaces, and trailing quotation mark from the &C macro variable because the entire variable is overwritten by the %LET statement. In other words, the C argument is only a placeholder in the RUN_MACRO call. Although C is initialized by the RUN_MACRO call, only missing data are transmitted to the RETURN_CONCAT macro when it is invoked via RUN_MACRO. In all other cases, however, use DEQUOTE to remove the automatic quotation marks and trailing spaces whenever RUN_MACRO passes character variables that do need to be analyzed or modified.

Reuse of Variable Names with RUN_MACRO

Issues can arise when variable names are reused in association with RUN_MACRO. Consider a first example in which two independent functions, FUNC_NUM and FUNC_CHAR, first declare the Result variable as numeric and subsequently declare it as character. Program 5.9 defines the functions and subsequently calls FUNC_NUM and FUNC_CHAR.

Program 5.9: Reuse of Variable Name without RUN_MACRO Execution

```
proc fcmp outlib=work.funcs.test;
   function func_num();
      length result 8;
      result = 55;
      put result=;
      return(result);
      endfunc;
   function func_char() $;
      length result $10;
      result = 'some words';
      put result=;
      return(result);
      endfunc;
quit;

data _null_;
   length num 8 char $10;
   num = func_num();
   char = func_char();
   put num= char=;
run;
```

No issues occur, and Num and Char are successfully initialized and printed to the log:

```
result=55
result=some words
num=55 char=some words
```

However, when RUN_MACRO is added to the preceding FUNC_NUM and FUNC_CHAR functions, the macro fails. Consider Program 5.10, which defines the NOTHING_NUM and NOTHING_CHAR macros that are called by the FUNC_NUM and FUNC_CHAR functions, respectively.

Program 5.10: Failure Caused by Reuse of Variable Name with RUN_MACRO

```
%macro do_nothing_num();
%put INSIDE NUM &=result;
%mend;
%macro do_nothing_char();
%put INSIDE CHAR &=result;
%mend;

proc fcmp outlib=work.funcs.test;
   function func_num();
      length result 8;
      result = 55;
      put result=;
      rc = run_macro('do_nothing_num', result);
      return(result);
      endfunc;
```

```
    function func_char() $;
        length result $10;
        result = 'some words';
        put result=;
        rc = run_macro('do_nothing_char', result);
        return(result);
        endfunc;
quit;

data _null_;
    length num 8 char $10;
    num = func_num();
    char = func_char();
    put num= char=;
run;
```

Note that FUNC_NUM declares Result as a numeric variable, whereas FUNC_CHAR subsequently declares Result as a character variable. These two functions should be independent—but because of undefined FCMP functionality, they are not. What results is the inability of FUNC_CHAR to initialize &RESULT to a character value because the previous numeric declaration erroneously persists:

```
INSIDE NUM RESULT=55
result=55
INSIDE CHAR RESULT=.
result=some words
num=55 char=.
```

For this reason, Result cannot be initialized to "some words" within the FUNC_CHAR function, and &RESULT is instead initialized to a period (denoting a missing numeric variable) inside the macro. Moreover, when the macro terminates, &RESULT is returned to the FUNC_CHAR function as a period, and that period is subsequently returned to the calling DATA step and initialized to the Char variable.

The defect does not occur when functions are called using %SYSFUNC, so the following statement is successfully executed:

```
%put %sysfunc(func_num()) %sysfunc(func_char());
```

The log demonstrates the successful execution when relying on %SYSFUNC:

```
INSIDE NUM RESULT=55
INSIDE CHAR RESULT='some words'
55 some words
```

The reliable method to remedy this issue is to ensure that variable names are not reused across functions that call RUN_MACRO. This is especially important where generic variable names are commonly used to represent return values and return codes, such as RC or RV (that is, return code or return value).

Scope Considerations for RUN_MACRO Macro Variables

Variable scope defines the extent to which a variable is accessible to software. For example, within callable modules such as functions, subroutines, and macros, *local scope* denotes that a variable is accessible only during the call to the module, and only by code in the module. That is, when the module terminates and returns control to the calling program, local variables are deleted and are unavailable to the calling module. It is for this reason that a function explicitly returns a value.

Global scope is contrasted in that a global variable is accessible anywhere—not just in the confines of a callable module or other software component. Within the SAS macro language, a global symbol table maintains all global macro variables. Separate local symbol tables can be created by macros that are called. Because RUN_MACRO and RUN_SASFILE inherently create side sessions of SAS, global and local symbol tables perform differently than otherwise observed in the SAS macro language.

Thus far, within this chapter, RUN_MACRO has passed variables to macros, and those macros have initialized or modified the corresponding variables using macro statements (for example, using the %LET statement). However, within the DATA step, the SYMPUT and SYMPUTX subroutines similarly can initialize macro variables, and their usage can differ when called via the RUN_MACRO function.

Consider the SUM_IT function, which calls the RETURN_SUM macro via the RUN_MACRO function, both of which are demonstrated in Program 5.11. The SYMPUT subroutine, by default, declares the &C macro variable as a global macro variable, which enables it to be returned to the SUM_IT function. The _USER_ automatic list generates a list of all user-defined macro variables, including both global and local variables, which confirms that &C is declared as a global macro variable.

Program 5.11: Generating a RUN_MACRO Return Value Using SYMPUT
```
%macro return_sum();
data _null_;
   c = &a + &b;
   call symput('c', put(c, 8.));
run;
%put INSIDE;
%put _user_;
%mend;

proc fcmp outlib=work.funcs.test;
   function sum_it(a, b);
```

```
      rc = run_macro('return_sum', a, b, c);
      return(c);
      endfunc;
quit;
```

The following code calls SUM_IT, after which the _USER_ automatic list of variables is again printed:

```
%put SUM: %sysfunc(sum_it(3, 6));
%put OUTSIDE;
%put _user_;
```

The log demonstrates that although &A, &B, and &C are all considered to be global macro variables inside the RETURN_SUM macro, once the macro has terminated, the variables are removed from the global symbol table:

```
1040   %put SUM: %sysfunc(sum_it(3, 6));
INSIDE
GLOBAL A 3
GLOBAL B 6
GLOBAL C 9
SUM: 9
1041   %put OUTSIDE;
OUTSIDE
1042   %put _user_;
```

The log results are not truncated—there are simply no global macro variables that persist after SUM_IT terminates! What occurs is that although &A, &B, and &C are considered to be global macro variables while the RETURN_SUM macro is executing. Because the macro is running only in a side session of SAS, when the macro terminates and returns program control to the SUM_IT function, neither the function nor the main SAS session can access these so-called global macro variables. That is, the "global" scope of &A, &B, and &C is limited to the side session of SAS in which only RETURN_SUM is executing.

The SYMPUTX subroutine has multiple advantages over the legacy SYMPUT subroutine. Some of the advantages include the automatic removal of leading and trailing spaces in the value being initialized, as well as the ability to initialize a macro variable to a number without having to convert it to a character value first, which the PUT function accomplished in Program 5.11. Because of these and other advantages, SYMPUTX is more commonly used to declare and initialize macro variables than SYMPUT.

One final advantage of SYMPUTX is its ability to specify the symbol table to which a macro variable should be saved—G for global or L for local. However, despite the so-called "global" macro variables that failed to persist in Program 5.11, RUN_MACRO nevertheless does require a macro variable to be declared as global to communicate with the calling program. Thus, if the L option is specified for SYMPUTX, as demonstrated in Program 5.12, a failure occurs.

Program 5.12: Attempting to Generate a RUN_MACRO Return Value Using SYMPUTX

```
%macro return_sum();
data _null_;
    c = &a + &b;
    call symputx('c', c, 'l');
run;
%put INSIDE;
%put _user_;
%mend;

proc fcmp outlib=work.funcs.test;
    function sum_it(a, b);
        rc = run_macro('return_sum', a, b, c);
        return(c);
        endfunc;
quit;

%put SUM: %sysfunc(sum_it(3, 6));
%put OUTSIDE;
%put _user_;
```

The log demonstrates this failure when &C is declared by SYMPUTX as a local macro variable (denoted by the macro's name prefacing the macro value in the log). Meanwhile, the global macro variable &C is also created by the macro but never explicitly initialized, and thus it is implicitly initialized to a missing value:

```
1083   %put SUM: %sysfunc(sum_it(3, 6));
INSIDE
RETURN_SUM C 9
GLOBAL A 3
GLOBAL B 6
GLOBAL C .
SUM: .
1084   %put OUTSIDE;
OUTSIDE
1085   %put _user_;
```

Within the log, the local macro variable (&C) is prefaced by "RETURN_SUM"—indicating that this &C is local to the RETURN_SUM macro. However, when SUM_IT is called, its RUN_MACRO function in turn creates an identically named global macro variable &C, which is prefaced by "GLOBAL" in the log, and is shown to be missing.

This issue is remedied by changing the L (local) to G (global) within the SYMPUTX subroutine:

```
call symputx('c', c, 'g');
```

With SYMPUTX modified, the SUM_IT call (not shown) correctly sums 3 and 6 because only one &C macro variable is initialized inside the RETURN_SUM macro.

Program 5.12 demonstrates that a macro called via RUN_MACRO can effectively maintain both a local and global instance of identically named macro variables. As demonstrated in the next subsection, this issue can also cause two identically named global macro variables to be maintained simultaneously.

Global Macro Variable Interaction with RUN_MACRO

Given that identically named global and local macro variables &C were simultaneously maintained in the RETURN_SUM macro, as demonstrated in the preceding output, it is important to understand how global macro variables interact with the so-called "global" macro variables that are briefly created inside a RUN_MACRO macro. For example, if a global macro variable exists, and then an identically named argument is passed via RUN_MACRO, what chaos ensues, and which macro variable is being modified inside the called macro?

Consider Program 5.13, which demonstrates the initialization of a global macro variable (&IMPORTANT_VAR), and subsequent modification of that variable inside the TEST_MACRO_SCOPE macro, which is called via the RUN_MACRO function.

Program 5.13: Modify a Global Macro Variable within a RUN_MACRO Macro
```
%macro test_macro_scope();
%put INSIDE;
%let important_var=stool;
%put _user_;
%mend;

proc fcmp outlib=work.funcs.test;
   function test_scope(char $) $;
      rc = run_macro('test_macro_scope', char);
      return(char);
      endfunc;
quit;

%global important_var;
%let important_var=chair;
%put RETURN VALUE: %sysfunc(test_scope(table));
%put OUTSIDE;
%put _user_;
```

The log demonstrates that &IMPORTANT_VAR is initialized to "chair," after which TEST_MACRO_SCOPE modifies its value to "stool":

```
 280  %global important_var;
1281  %let important_var=chair;
1282  %put RETURN VALUE: %sysfunc(test_scope(table));
INSIDE
```

```
GLOBAL CHAR 'table'
GLOBAL IMPORTANT_VAR stool
RETURN VALUE: table
1283  %put OUTSIDE;
OUTSIDE
1284  %put _user_;
GLOBAL IMPORTANT_VAR stool
```

Also note that the return value generated by TEST_SCOPE is "table." This occurs because "table" is the initial value of the CHAR parameter inside TEST_SCOPE, and no attempt is made to modify its argument. This all is expected behavior, in part because the CHAR argument passed by RUN_MACRO is not redundantly named.

However, if RUN_MACRO passes an argument whose name has already been declared as a global macro variable, unintended (or unwanted) results can occur. Consider the revised Program 5.14, whose title alone should evoke angst! In Program 5.14, the CHAR parameter is no longer declared within TEST_SCOPE or passed as an argument via RUN_MACRO. The IMPORTANT_VAR parameter is instead declared using %GLOBAL, and its argument is passed.

Program 5.14: Simultaneous Identically Named Global Macro Variables
```
%macro test_macro_scope();
%put INSIDE;
%put _user_;
%let important_var=stool;
%put _user_;
%mend;

proc fcmp outlib=work.funcs.test;
   function test_scope(important_var $) $;
      rc = run_macro('test_macro_scope', important_var);
      return(important_var);
      endfunc;
quit;

%global important_var;
%let important_var=chair;
%put RETURN VALUE: %sysfunc(test_scope(table));
%put OUTSIDE;
%put _user_;
```

When TEST_SCOPE is invoked, "table" is again passed—this time to the IMPORTANT_VAR parameter. The RUN_MACRO function in turn passes this argument (including its "table" value) to the TEST_MACRO_SCOPE macro, in which the global macro variable &IMPORTANT_VAR is, by default, initialized to "table." Thereafter, the %LET statement reinitializes &IMPORTANT_VAR to "stool"—but wait—which global macro variable is being initialized by the %LET statement?

The log demonstrates this issue and confusion, noting that the first _USER_ automatic list records &IMPORTANT_VAR as both 'table' (with single quotation marks) and "chair" (with no quotation marks):

```
1301   %global important_var;
1302   %let important_var=chair;
1303   %put RETURN VALUE: %sysfunc(test_scope(table));
INSIDE
GLOBAL IMPORTANT_VAR 'table'
GLOBAL IMPORTANT_VAR chair
GLOBAL X 5
GLOBAL IMPORTANT_VAR stool
GLOBAL IMPORTANT_VAR chair
GLOBAL X 5
RETURN VALUE: stool
1304   %put OUTSIDE;
OUTSIDE
1305   %put _user_;
GLOBAL IMPORTANT_VAR chair
```

The second _USER_ automatic list is printed after the %LET reinitialization of &IMPORTANT_VAR to "stool"; thus, 'table' is overwritten by "stool" whereas "chair" persists. In effect, there is no method to specify which of the two identically named global macro variables is being reinitialized, so this usage is too risky to consider viable. Moreover, note that the return value of Program 6.14 is "stool," whereas the return value of Program 6.13 is "table." Thus, because the %LET statement has failed to reinitialize the true global macro variable that was declared and initialized before the TEST_SCOPE function call, the incorrect return value is generated.

As stated previously within this chapter, use extreme caution when calling RUN_MACRO to ensure that arguments passed via this function are unique and not in use elsewhere within the program or SAS session.

Passing Special Characters Using RUN_MACRO

The previous sections demonstrated how RUN_MACRO intrinsically relies on global macro variables to pass values to and from the macro called by RUN_MACRO, as well as how character values are automatically quoted within single quotation marks. The reliance on macro variables can cause complications otherwise unseen in FCMP function design, so this risk is explored in this section. For example, when unmatched quotation marks, commas, ampersands, or percentage signs are maintained in data sets and manipulated only through the DATA step, there is no need to mask these special characters. However, when the same values are encoded within macro variables, functionality could be altered, and data masking might be required.

The DATA step in Program 5.15 generates the Candies data set, which enumerates some candy names that include special characters. The DATALINES statement correctly interprets each of the candy names, despite their flavorful special characters, and the "Chocolate, Nougat, and Nutter" bar has its commas masked within double quotation marks.

Program 5.15: Creating a Special Characters Data Set
```
data candies;
    infile datalines dsd delimiter=',';
    length candy $40;
    input candy $;
    datalines;
M&Ms
Hershey's Kisses
Hershey's Cookies 'n' Cream
"Chocolate, Nougat, and Nutter"
;
```

The MY_FAV_CANDY function, defined in Program 5.16, prepends "My favorite candy is:" to each candy name and returns this value to the calling program. Thus, the subsequent DATA step writes the resultant concatenated values to the log.

Program 5.16: Successful Use of Special Characters in the DATA Step
```
proc fcmp outlib=work.funcs.test;
    function my_fav_candy(fav_candy $) $80;
        return('My favorite candy is: ' || strip(fav_candy));
        endfunc;
quit;

data _null_;
    set candies;
    length combined $80;
    combined = my_fav_candy(candy);
    put combined;
run;
```

When the DATA step executes, the concatenated values are printed to the log without issue:

```
My favorite candy is: M&Ms
My favorite candy is: Hershey's Kisses
My favorite candy is: Hershey's Cookies 'n' Cream
My favorite candy is: Chocolate, Nougat, and Nutter
```

Complexity arises, however, when the RUN_MACRO function is introduced to the MY_FAV_CANDY function. The updated MY_FAV_CANDY function calls the TEST_SPECIAL macro, both of which are demonstrated in Program 5.17. The TEST_SPECIAL macro, in its initial implementation, only prints &FAV_CANDY to the log using the %PUT statement.

Program 5.17: Passing Special Characters Using RUN_MACRO

```
%macro test_special();
%put &fav_candy;
%mend;

proc fcmp outlib=work.funcs.test;
   function my_fav_candy(fav_candy $) $80;
      rc = run_macro('test_special', fav_candy);
      return('My favorite candy is: ' || strip(fav_candy));
      endfunc;
quit;
```

When the DATA step shown in Program 5.16 is rerun, the log alternates values of &FAV_CANDY (shown inside the TEST_SPECIAL macro) and the return value (returned to the DATA step):

```
'M&Ms                                    '
My favorite candy is: M&Ms
'Hershey"s Kisses                        '
My favorite candy is: Hershey's Kisses
'Hershey"s Cookies "n" Cream             '
My favorite candy is: Hershey's Cookies 'n' Cream
'Chocolate, Nougat, and Nutter           '
My favorite candy is: Chocolate, Nougat, and Nutter
```

In addition to leading and trailing single quotation marks and trailing spaces, note that both matched and unmatched quotation marks have been automatically masked inside the TEST_SPECIAL macro. Thus, Hershey's becomes Hershey''s and Cookies 'n' Cream becomes Cookies ''n'' Cream.

At this point, the &FAV_CANDY macro variable is being inspected but not modified. However, as stated previously, the first step in manipulating a character parameter within a macro called by RUN_MACRO is to remove the leading and trailing quotation marks using the DEQUOTE function—and here we find trouble.

For example, when the TEST_SPECIAL macro is modified to print the unquoted, original version of the arguments that contain special characters, failures abound. Program 5.18 displays the updated TEST_SPECIAL macro.

Program 5.18: Attempting to Modify Macro Arguments Containing Special Characters

```
%macro test_special();
%put &fav_candy;
%let fav_candy=%sysfunc(dequote(&fav_candy));
%put &fav_candy;
%mend;
```

When the DATA step in Program 5.16 is rerun a third time, the log demonstrates the failures:

```
'M&Ms                                    '
WARNING: Apparent symbolic reference MS not resolved.
WARNING: Apparent symbolic reference MS not resolved.
M&Ms
My favorite candy is: M&Ms
'Hershey''s Kisses                         '
ERROR: Literal contains unmatched quotation mark.
ERROR: The macro TEST_SPECIAL will stop executing.
My favorite candy is: Hershey's Kisses'
'Hershey''s Cookies ''n'' Cream           '
ERROR: Literal contains unmatched quotation mark.
ERROR: The macro TEST_SPECIAL will stop executing.
My favorite candy is: Hershey's Cookies 'n' Cream'
'Chocolate, Nougat, and Nutter            '
Chocolate, Nougat, and Nutter
My favorite candy is: Chocolate, Nougat, and Nutter
```

When the SAS macro processor encounters "M&Ms" in the first observation, it interprets that the non-existent macro variable &MS is being referenced. And when the macro processor encounters "Hershey's Kisses" in the second argument, it fails to interpret the unmatched single quotation mark. Even the matched single quotation marks in "Cookies 'n' Cream" result in a runtime error.

Several built-in SAS macro functions (such as %STR, %BQUOTE, and %SUPERQ) aid in masking special characters in macro variables and can be relied on to parse arguments passed to macros via RUN_MACRO. Their syntax and usage, however, lie outside the scope of this text. For now, it is important to note the risks that RUN_MACRO can introduce when arguments containing special characters are passed.

Running DATA Steps and SAS Procedures via RUN_MACRO

Because RUN_MACRO enables a macro to be called from within a user-defined function, and because macros can contain not only macro statements but also DATA steps and SAS procedures, it follows that RUN_MACRO facilitates executing DATA steps and SAS procedures inside of a user-defined function—that is, running a DATA step inside of a DATA step, or a procedure inside of a DATA step. Mind. Blown!

Consider the need to compute the average value of some variable across all observations within a data set. Out of habit, we reach for the MEANS procedure for this task, and it performs admirably. Program 5.19 creates the Planets data set, which includes mean diameters (in kilometers) for planets in our solar system, after which the MEANS procedure calculates the average planet diameter. The OUTPUT statement saves this value to the Diam_km variable in the Planet_diameter data set.

Program 5.19: Compute the Average Value of a Variable Using PROC MEANS

```
data planets;
    infile datalines dsd delimiter=',';
    length name $10 diameter 8;
    input name $ diameter;
    format diameter comma8.0;
    datalines;
mercury,4879
venus,12104
earth,12756
mars,6792
jupiter,142984
saturn,120536
uranus,51118
neptune,49528
pluto,2376
;

proc means data=planets noprint;
    var diameter;
    output out=planet_diameter mean=diam_km;
run;
```

MEANS calculates the average diameter to be 44,786 kilometers. But what if you didn't *always* need to compute the average? For example, what if you only needed the average if one or more observations had missing data, and you wanted to impute a value using the average? Or what if you otherwise wanted to compute the average inside the DATA step rather than being forced to run a preceding MEANS statement? RUN_MACRO can assist in both use cases.

Executing a SAS Procedure inside a DATA Step

Program 5.20 defines the COMPUTE_MEAN_MACRO macro that the COMPUTE_MEAN function calls via the RUN_MACRO function. COMPUTE_MEAN declares two parameters—DSN, the data set name, and VAR, the name of the variable to be averaged. COMPUTE_MEAN returns the average to the calling program. In lieu of relying on the MEANS procedure, the COMPUTE_MEAN_MACRO instead uses the built-in AVG function within the SQL procedure.

Program 5.20: Defining the COMPUTE_MEAN Function to Calculate Average

```
%macro compute_mean_macro();
%let dsn=%sysfunc(dequote(&dsn));
%let var=%sysfunc(dequote(&var));
proc sql noprint;
    select avg(&var) into: avg
        from &dsn;
```

```
quit;
%mend;

proc fcmp outlib=work.funcs.stats;
   function compute_mean(dsn $,var $);
       rc=run_macro('compute_mean_macro', dsn, var, avg);
       return(avg);
       endfunc;
quit;
```

With the function and macro defined, the following single statement now generates the identical average that previously required the MEANS procedure in Program 5.19:

```
%put %sysfunc(compute_mean(planets,diameter));
```

The function call is not only readable but can be flexibly incorporated into any DATA step. For example, consider the need to compare the diameters of each individual planet against the mean of all planets. The DATA step in Program 5.21 initializes the Diff variable to the difference between the average diameter and a specific planet's diameter. Statements subsequently relay whether each specific planet's diameter is greater or less than the average.

Program 5.21: Running PROC SQL inside a DATA Step
```
data _null_;
   set planets;
   length statement $40 diff 8;
   diff = diameter - compute_mean('planets', 'diameter');
   if diff > 0 then statement = strip(name) || ' is ' || strip(put(diff, comma8.)) ||
      'km greater than average';
   else statement = strip(name) || ' is ' || strip(put(abs(diff), comma8.)) ||
      'km less than average';
   put statement;
run;
```

The log demonstrates the production of planet-specific statements:

```
mercury is 39,907km less than average
venus is 32,682km less than average
earth is 32,030km less than average
mars is 37,994km less than average
jupiter is 98,198km greater than average
saturn is 75,750km greater than average
uranus is 6,332km greater than average
neptune is 4,742km greater than average
pluto is 42,410km less than average
```

The solution is functional, yet inefficient. Note that Diff is repeatedly calculated for each observation, yet a summary statistic like the mean only needs to be calculated once. Program

5.22 overcomes this inefficiency by only calculating the average once, which is saved to the Avg variable, and retained across observations by the RETAIN statement.

Program 5.22: More Efficiently Running PROC SQL inside a DATA Step

```
data _null_;
   set planets;
   length statement $40 avg diff 8;
   retain avg;
   if _n_ = 1 then avg = compute_mean('planets', 'diameter');
   diff = diameter - avg;
   if diff > 0 then statement = strip(name) || ' is ' || strip(put(diff, comma8.)) ||
      'km greater than average';
   else statement = strip(name) || ' is ' || strip(put(abs(diff), comma8.)) ||
      'km less than average';
   put statement;
run;
```

Programs 5.21 and 5.22 are functionally equivalent; however, the latter is more efficient as it calls COMPUTE_MEAN only once. The STATIC statement, introduced in Chapter 7, also could have been leveraged to use *memoization* to produce a functionally equivalent, efficient function. In this alternate design (not shown), the COMPUTE_MEAN function would be called for each observation, but it would calculate the average only during the first call, after which the function would subsequently return a saved value.

Executing a DATA Step inside a DATA Step

Similar to the previous section, RUN_MACRO can also execute a DATA step inside another DATA step. For example, multiple methods exist within Base SAS to compute the mean of some variable across observations—two have already been shown, the MEANS procedure and SQL procedure—and a third option calculates the average within a DATA step by leveraging RETAIN.

The COMPUTE_MEAN_MACRO macro, defined in Program 5.20 is redefined in Program 5.23, which now leverages the DATA step to calculate the mean, rather than the built-in AVG function within the SQL procedure.

Program 5.23: Redefining the COMPUTE_MEAN Function Using a DATA Step

```
%macro compute_mean_macro();
%let dsn=%sysfunc(dequote(&dsn));
%let var=%sysfunc(dequote(&var));
data _null_;
   set &dsn end=eof;
   retain tot 0;
   tot = sum(tot, &var);
   if eof then call symputx('avg',tot / _n_, 'g');
run;
%mend;
```

As before, COMPUTE_MEAN_MACRO should only be called once per DATA step because the average will remain constant once calculated. Alternatively, the %SYSFUNC macro function can call COMPUTE_MEAN, which in turn calls the updated COMPUTE_MEAN_MACRO macro via RUN_MACRO:

```
data _null_;
   diam = compute_mean(planets, diameter);
   put diam;
run;

%put %sysfunc(compute_mean(planets, diameter));
```

Identical results are printed to the log, demonstrating the average diameter of all planets:

```
44785.888889
44785.888889
```

Most importantly, the impossible has been accomplished—a DATA step has been executed inside a DATA step!

Comparison of RUN_MACRO to DOSUBL Function

Arguably, the question I am most often asked about RUN_MACRO is how its syntax and functionality compare to that of the built-in DOSUBL function. DOSUBL offers somewhat comparable functionality to RUN_MACRO by launching a side session of SAS that executes in real-time. Thus, DOSUBL temporarily transfers program control to SAS statements or to a SAS macro, both of which can include DATA steps and/or SAS procedures. DOSUBL returns program control when the side session terminates.

The primary benefit of DOSUBL over RUN_MACRO is that DOSUBL is called from the DATA step, whereas RUN_MACRO requires an additional FCMP function wrapper to be called. Notwithstanding, RUN_MACRO has several advantages over DOSUBL. For example, RUN_MACRO passes actual delimited arguments in the RUN_MACRO function call, whereas DOSUBL must pass arguments that are commingled in one large text string, similar to how the EXECUTE built-in subroutine (also known as CALL EXECUTE) is called. RUN_MACRO can also return one or more macro variables from the called macro to the user-defined function, whereas DOSUBL cannot natively return values and must instead communicate by initializing a global macro variable or saving data to a SAS data set. Although DOSUBL is appropriate in some use cases, user-defined functions that require bi-directional communication typically are better handled by RUN_MACRO.

Consider Program 5.22, which leverages RUN_MACRO to compute the average diameter of all planets during a DATA step. The DATA step calls the COMPUTE_MEAN function, and the COMPUTE_MEAN function in turn calls COMPUTE_MEAN_MACRO via RUN_MACRO, in which the

SQL procedure calculates the average diameter. This average diameter is subsequently returned to the COMPUTE_MEAN function via a macro variable, and it is here that DOSUBL functionality cannot compete with RUN_MACRO.

For example, Program 5.24 is functionally equivalent to Program 5.22, but leverages DOSUBL to call the SQL procedure directly—that is, inside the DATA step.

Program 5.24: Running PROC SQL inside a DATA Step Using DOSUBL

```
data _null_;
   set planets;
   length statement $40 avg diff 8;
   retain avg;
   if _n_ = 1 then do;
      rc = dosubl('proc sql noprint;
                  select avg(diameter) into: avg
                     from planets;
               quit;');
      avg=input(symget('avg'), comma8.3);
      end;
   diff = diameter - avg;
   if diff > 0 then statement = strip(name) || ' is ' || strip(put(diff, comma8.)) ||
      'km greater than average';
   else statement = strip(name) || ' is ' || strip(put(abs(diff), comma8.)) ||
      'km less than average';
   put statement;
run;

%put &=avg;
```

After DOSUBL calculates the average diameter using the SQL procedure, the average value is saved as the &AVG macro variable, which in turn the SYMGET function initializes into the Avg variable.

The log demonstrates that Avg is used to create the following statements dynamically:

```
mercury is 39,907km less than average
venus is 32,682km less than average
earth is 32,030km less than average
mars is 37,994km less than average
jupiter is 98,198km greater than average
saturn is 75,750km greater than average
uranus is 6,332km greater than average
neptune is 4,742km greater than average
pluto is 42,410km less than average

1871   %put &=avg;
AVG=44785.89
```

The DATA step in Program 5.24 is functional, yet not modular, in that the entire SQL procedure is maintained inside the DATA step. Moreover, the necessity to declare the &AVG global macro variable inside the SQL procedure yields a leaky DATA step because &AVG remains initialized after the DATA step has concluded, as evidenced by the %PUT statement. At issue here is the risk of a macro variable collision if some other process or program is relying on an identically named macro variable.

Thus, after the DATA step executes, the %SYMDEL macro statement should remove &AVG from the global symbol table:

```
%symdel avg;
```

A far better design would instead leverage DOSUBL to call a macro that computes the average diameter, thus enabling the SQL procedure to be wrapped inside of the macro rather than the DOSUBL function call. Program 5.25 attempts to implement DOSUBL using this more modular design, yet it fails because DOSUBL is incapable of returning a macro variable (natively) from the COMPUTE_MEAN_MACRO_DOSUBL macro.

Program 5.25: Attempting (and Failing at) Modular Design Using the DOSUBL Function

```
%macro compute_mean_macro_dosubl(dsn, var);
proc sql noprint;
   select avg(&var) into: avg
      from &dsn;
quit;
%put &=avg;
%mend;

data _null_;
   set planets;
   length statement $40 avg diff 8;
   retain avg;
   if _n_ = 1 then do;
      rc = dosubl('%compute_mean_macro_dosubl(planets, diameter);');
      avg=input(symget('avg'), comma8.3);
      end;
   diff = diameter - avg;
   if diff > 0 then statement = strip(name) || ' is ' || strip(put(diff, comma8.)) ||
      'km greater than average';
   else statement = strip(name) || ' is ' || strip(put(abs(diff), comma8.)) ||
      'km less than average';
   put statement;
run;

%put &=avg;
```

The log demonstrates the failure in which &AVG is successfully calculated inside the macro, as shown by the &AVG value printed to the log, but it cannot be returned to the calling DATA step. Thus, &AVG cannot be leveraged by the SYMGET function to initialize the Avg variable:

```
AVG=44785.89
NOTE: Invalid argument to function SYMGET('avg') at line 1789 column 17.
mercury is .km less than average
name=mercury diameter=4,879 statement=mercury is .km less than average
avg=. diff=. rc=0
_ERROR_=1 _N_=1
venus is .km less than average
earth is .km less than average
mars is .km less than average
jupiter is .km less than average
saturn is .km less than average
uranus is .km less than average
neptune is .km less than average
pluto is .km less than average
NOTE: Missing values were generated as a result of performing an operation
on missing values.
      Each place is given by: (Number of times) at (Line):(Column).
      9 at 1791:18    9 at 1794:54


1903    %put &=avg;
WARNING: Apparent symbolic reference AVG not resolved.
avg
```

Thus, although the first %PUT statement inside the macro can access &AVG, the second %PUT statement after the DATA step cannot reference &AVG because it was not saved as a global macro variable.

At this point, the solution should be clear—declare &AVG as a global macro variable inside the macro and subsequently access this macro variable from the calling DATA step. Program 5.26 demonstrates this final approach and redefines the COMPUTE_MEAN_MACRO_DOSUBL macro, in which the %GLOBAL statement declares &AVG as a global macro variable.

Program 5.26: Returning a Global Macro Variable from a DOSUBL Macro Call

```
%macro compute_mean_macro_dosubl(dsn, var);
%global avg;
proc sql noprint;
   select avg(&var) into: avg
      from &dsn;
quit;
%mend;
```

When the preceding DATA step in Program 5.25 is now run, DOSUBL calls the redefined macro. The macro successfully initializes the &AVG global macro variable, which is subsequently leveraged by SYMGET to initialize the Avg variable in the DATA step. The results printed to the log (not shown) are successful and identical to those of Program 5.24.

Unfortunately, the need to rely on global macro variables to return values increases the risk of macro variable collisions, and the %SYMDEL macro statement should again be run to remove

&AVG from the global symbol table. Notwithstanding, DOSUBL was successful in calling the COMPUTE_MEAN_MACRO_DOSUBL macro, and where implemented, calling a macro from DOSUBL can increase software modularity by removing complex operations from the calling DATA step.

RUN_SASFILE

Although this chapter has focused primarily on the RUN_MACRO function, the RUN_SASFILE built-in function has similar functionality, even though it executes a SAS program file inside a user-defined function, rather than executing a SAS macro. Thus, RUN_SASFILE somewhat increases software modularity because code is executed that does not reside in the current program. However, use this modularity with caution because the user-defined function remains intertwined with, and dependent on, its referenced program file.

For example, note that in each of the previous user-defined functions that uses RUN_MACRO, the macro is defined immediately before the function definition—because the two must coexist. By removing macro functionality and placing this code inside an external program file, some flexibility could be gained, but you also could lose track of that external file. It is considered a best practice to place user-defined functions within their own program files—because this maximizes modularity and reuse, as different users and programs can call a centralized, curated version of the function. However, given the tight coupling between user-defined functions that leverage either RUN_MACRO or RUN_SASFILE, the function definition should be closely bound to the code called by either RUN_MACRO or RUN_SASFILE.

The COMPUTE_MEAN user-defined function and subordinate COMPUTE_MEAN_MACRO macro are demonstrated in Program 5.20 and refactored in Program 5.27 using the RUN_SASFILE function in lieu of RUN_MACRO. The %MACRO and %MEND statements are no longer required, and the remaining code is copied into the Compute_mean_sasfile.sas program file. Note that two %PUT macro statements are optionally shown to illustrate the transmission of the macro variables &DSN and &VAR to the program.

Program 5.27: Compute_mean_sasfile SAS Program File
```
* saved to compute_mean_sasfile.sas;
%put &=dsn;
%put &=var;
%let dsn=%sysfunc(dequote(&dsn));
%let var=%sysfunc(dequote(&var));
proc sql noprint;
   select avg(&var) into: avg
      from &dsn;
quit;
```

The COMPUTE_MEAN function, shown in Program 5.20, is modified in Program 5.28 to reference RUN_SASFILE in lieu of RUN_MACRO. Note that the FILENAME statement must first create the file reference (CMP_FILE) for the program file referenced by RUN_SASFILE, and that it is this file reference—not the filename itself—that is supplied as the first argument within RUN_SASFILE.

Program 5.28: COMPUTE_MEAN_SASFILE User-Defined Function

```
filename cmp_file 'C:\sas\compute_mean_sasfile.sas';

proc fcmp outlib=work.funcs.stats;
   function compute_mean_sasfile(dsn $, var $);
      rc=run_sasfile('cmp_file', dsn, var, avg);
      return(avg);
      endfunc;
quit;
```

COMPUTE_MEAN_SASFILE can be called similarly to COMPUTE_MEAN, including from within a DATA step, or as shown, using %SYSFUNC:

```
%put %sysfunc(compute_mean_sasfile(planets,diameter));
```

The output demonstrates the values of &DSN and &VAR shown inside the COMPUTE_MEAN_SASFILE macro, and the return value returned to the calling program (the %SYSFUNC function):

```
DSN='planets'
VAR='diameter'
44785.89
```

As demonstrated previously, the user-defined function computes the average (mean) diameter of planets in our solar system to be 44,786 kilometers.

COMPUTE_MEAN (shown in Program 5.20) and COMPUTE_MEAN_SASFILE (shown in Program 5.27) are functionally equivalent, with the former relying on RUN_MACRO and the latter leveraging RUN_SASFILE. Note the complexity and risk, however, that even the compiled version of COMPUTE_MEAN_SASFILE will fail if its dependent program (Compute_mean_sasfile.sas) is renamed, moved, or deleted.

For example, when Compute_mean_sasfile.sas is renamed to Compute_mean_sasfile_RENAMED.sas and %SYSFUNC is again used to call the COMPUTE_MEAN_SASFILE function, this attempt will fail:

```
WARNING: Physical file does not exist,
         C:\sas\compute_mean_sasfile.sas.
ERROR: Cannot open %INCLUDE file CMP_FILE.
135
136  %put %sysfunc(compute_mean_sasfile(planets,diameter));
```

Thus, it is not the case that the dependent program file called by RUN_SASFILE is relied on during compilation, but rather that each execution of the user-defined function requires this program, which is implicitly accessed via the built-in %INCLUDE macro statement. In the end, for most use cases, SAS practitioners would benefit from relying on RUN_MACRO in lieu of RUN_SASFILE, which enables the user-defined function and its subordinate macro to be chained together in the same program file.

Leveraging RUN_MACRO to Overcome FCMP Limitations

Inherent in FCMP are some functional limitations—in part because the nature of function design can differ from DATA step design, and in part because FCMP functionality has been incrementally built and released to maximize its usage and utility. With this in mind, SAS practitioners might arrive at perceived dead ends when functionality achievable within a DATA step is seemingly and tauntingly out of reach within a user-defined function. In some cases, RUN_MACRO or RUN_SASFILE can assist.

For example, in Chapter 4, Table 4.1 lists the hash object components that are available in FCMP—only 15 of the 30 hash components available in the DATA step. The DATA step supports data set options when declaring the data set to be loaded into a hash object; the FCMP hash object does not. So, if you have a password-encrypted data set, the DATA step instance of the DECLARE statement that instantiates a hash object supports data set options, and it can be used to load an encrypted data set into a hash object. Similarly, you can specify OBS, FIRSTOBS, and other data set options when instantiating a hash object inside the DATA step.

The DATA step in Program 5.29 creates a password-encrypted data set that contains usernames, user IDs, and DSM-V diagnostic codes—sensitive health information that likely should be protected.

Program 5.29: Creation of a Password-Encrypted Data Set
```
/* DSM-5 codes:
305.90 = caffeine intoxication
292.0 = opioid withdrawal
291.81 = alcohol withdrawal
*/
data users (encrypt=yes pw="ABCDE");
   infile datalines dsd delimiter=',';
   length name $50 id 8 dsm_dx $10;
   input name $ id dsm_dx $;
   datalines;
John,12,305.90
Sally,18,292.0
Jane,14,291.81
;
```

Consider the need to retrieve the data associated with Sally's ID (18). The DATA step in Program 5.30 again leverages the PW data set option that specifies the password to read the encrypted data set.

Program 5.30: DATA Step Hash Object Lookup

```
data process_users;
   length id 8 name $50 dsm_dx $10;
   * instantiate hash object lookup table;
   if _n_ = 1 then do;
      declare hash h(dataset: 'users (pw="ABCDE")');
      rc = h.defineKey('id');
      rc = h.defineData('name', 'dsm_dx');
      rc = h.defineDone();
      call missing(id, name, dsm_dx);
      end;
   * retrieve info for Sally;
   id = 18;
   rc = h.find();
   put id= name= dsm_dx=;
run;
```

When the DATA step executes, Sally's information is printed to the log:

```
NOTE: There were 3 observations read from the data set WORK.USERS.
id=18 name=Sally dsm_dx=292.0
```

More commonly, however, this type of lookup operation should be performed within a hash object instantiated within a user-defined function—not the DATA step—so it can be reused to retrieve other users' information. Unfortunately, the FCMP version of the DECLARE statement is substantially curtailed, and it does not support any data set options. No OBS, no FIRSTOBS, and no PW. At this juncture, it would *prima facie* appear that user-defined functions cannot leverage encrypted data sets to instantiate hash objects.

Enter RUN_MACRO to the rescue! Because RUN_MACRO can facilitate calling a DATA step from a user-defined function, the full extent of DATA step hash functionality can indirectly be leveraged. The GET_DX function and subordinate GET_DX_MACRO macro, which is called via RUN_MACRO, are demonstrated in Program 5.31. Note that because the hash object is instantiated inside a DATA step, the PW option can be specified in the hash declaration. That is, all 30 hash components listed in Table 4.1 are available inside a DATA step called by RUN_MACRO or RUN_SASFILE.

Program 5.31: Poorly Instantiating a Hash Object Using RUN_MACRO

```
%macro get_dx_macro();
%let dsn=%sysfunc(dequote(&dsn));
data _null_;
   length id 8 name $50 dsm_dx $10;
   * instantiate hash object lookup table;
   if _n_ = 1 then do;
      declare hash h(dataset: "&dsn (pw='ABCDE')");
      rc = h.defineKey('id');
      rc = h.defineData('dsm_dx');
      rc = h.defineDone();
```

```
      call missing(id, name, dsm_dx);
      end;
   * retrieve info for user;
   Id = &id;
   Rc = h.find();
   call symputx('dx', dsm_dx, 'g');
run;
%mend;

proc fcmp outlib=work.funcs.dsm;
   function get_dx(dsn $,id) $10;
      length dx $10;
      rc = run_macro('get_dx_macro', dsn,id, dx);
      return(dx);
      endfunc;
quit;
```

Program 5.31 is functional, but terribly inefficient. Do you see the issue?

DATA step hash objects are ephemeral and last only for the duration of the DATA step in which they are instantiated. Thus, each time GET_DX is called, it must re-create the entire hash object. For comparison, hash objects instantiated inside the FCMP procedure are created once, and thereafter reside in memory for all subsequent lookup operations.

For example, the DATA steps in Program 5.32 call the GET_DX function twice—for both John and Sally. However, both function calls create, search, and delete the hash object, and this redundancy generates enormous inefficiency when the number of lookup observations is increased.

Program 5.32: Calling the Inefficient GET_DX Function to Retrieve Diagnostic Codes

```
data two_ids;
   length id 8;
   id = 12; output;
   id = 18; output;
run;

data _null_;
   set two_ids;
   length dsm_dx $10;
   dsm_dx = get_dx('users', id);
   put id= dsm_dx=;
run;
```

The output demonstrates the two user IDs and respective diagnostic codes:

```
id=12 dsm_dx=305.90
id=18 dsm_dx=292.0
```

Despite this new limitation, RUN_MACRO is not the issue, and a functional and efficient solution is waiting around the corner. Although this example demonstrates why hash objects should never be created inside a macro called via RUN_MACRO or RUN_SASFILE, a more refined DATA step hash instantiation will provide the most efficient function-based solution, given the constraint that a password-encrypted data set must be accessed.

To start, Program 5.33 re-creates the Users data set; it remains password-encrypted, but now incorporates an index that names ID as the unique key. This index facilitates faster lookup operations, such as those that leverage the WHERE data set option.

Program 5.33: Re-creating the Users DATA Step with an Index
```
data users (index=(id) encrypt=yes pw="ABCDE");
   infile datalines dsd delimiter=',';
   length name $50 id 8 dsm_dx $10;
   input name $ id dsm_dx $;
   datalines;
John,12,305.90
Sally,18,292.0
Jane,14,291.81
;
```

With the lookup data set now indexed, Program 5.34 demonstrates a redesigned GET_DX_ MACRO that now leverages this index to retrieve the single observation corresponding to the specified key value using the WHERE data set option.

Program 5.34: Efficiently Performing an Encrypted Lookup Operation
```
%macro get_dx_macro();
%let dsn=%sysfunc(dequote(&dsn));
data _null_;
   set &dsn (pw='ABCDE' where=(id=&id) keep=id dsm_dx);
   call symputx('dx', dsm_dx, 'g');
run;
%mend;

proc fcmp outlib=work.funcs.dsm;
   function get_dx(dsn $, id) $10;
      length dx $10;
      rc = run_macro('get_dx_macro', dsn,id,dx);
      return(dx);
      endfunc;
quit;
```

Thus, GET_DX_MACRO ensures that only the relevant (that is, matching) observation is retrieved and that only relevant variables are maintained. No, the GET_DX function will never be as fast or as efficient as a functionally equivalent function that instantiates the hash object inside the FCMP procedure itself. However, as encrypted data sets cannot be instantiated by the FCMP DECLARE statement inside the FCMP procedure, this RUN_MACRO solution is the next fastest method—far faster and more efficient than the version shown in Program 5.31.

Program 5.35 again calls the GET_DX function to retrieve encrypted diagnostic codes for both John and Sally.

Program 5.35: Calling the Efficient GET_DX Function to Retrieve Diagnostic Codes

```
data _null_;
   set two_ids;
   length dsm_dx $10;
   dsm_dx = get_dx('users', id);
   put id= dsm_dx=;
run;
```

As before, the DATA step returns the DSM-V codes for both users (not shown).

Thus, when it appears that a roadblock in FCMP functionality has been reached, always consider how RUN_MACRO or RUN_SASFILE could lend a helping hand—in part, by unleashing the full functionality of the DATA step or SAS procedure inside a user-defined function.

Conclusion

This chapter introduced RUN_MACRO and RUN_SASFILE, two extraordinary, built-in functions that offer matchless functionality. Both functions enable SAS macro statements, DATA steps, and SAS procedures to be executed from inside a user-defined function call. Some complexities of RUN_MACRO and RUN_SASFILE were discussed, such as the risks incurred when parameter names are reused or when arguments containing special characters are passed. However, with an understanding of RUN_MACRO and RUN_SASFILE limitations, tremendous feats can be achieved, and seemingly impossible functionality can be delivered through user-defined functions. Finally, the DOSUBL built-in function was contrasted with RUN_MACRO, as both methods enable users to run side sessions of SAS. The next chapter continues to explore RUN_MACRO and how it can support "getter" and "setter" functionality—user-defined functions that retrieve or modify key-value pairs in lookup tables.

Chapter 6: Getters and Setters

Variables are a core component of every programming language. They allow data to be stored, transformed, and otherwise manipulated during program execution. The SAS language is no different, and it defines both DATA step variables and macro variables. DATA step variables correspond to columns in a data set and do not persist across DATA steps. Macro variables, on the other hand, do persist across DATA steps, SAS procedures, and other statements, and thus fulfill a critical niche that DATA step variables cannot perform—communication across and among processes.

For example, consider the need within a program to evaluate today's date and use it repeatedly across multiple DATA steps. The typical SAS solution is to declare a macro variable, initialize the macro variable to today's date, and subsequently reference the macro variable (in lieu of the literal date value) within DATA step statements or SAS procedures. Macro variables are limited, however, in that only the character data type is supported. Thus, dates and other numeric data must be stored as character values.

An alternative solution maintains persistent values not within macro variables and macro symbol tables, but instead within lookup tables—SAS data sets that are indexed by one or more unique keys, and whose corresponding values can be retrieved. These key-value pairs enable user-defined lookup operations to initialize, retrieve, modify, or delete values maintained in a lookup table. Within this paradigm, *getter* functions retrieve (or *get*) a value based on its associated key, and *setter* functions initialize (or *set*) a value associated with some key. The FCMP procedure enables SAS practitioners to build user-defined getters and setters that can eliminate the reliance on macro variables in many circumstances—all while maintaining data within a built-in data structure, the SAS data set.

This chapter introduces getters and setters and demonstrates several methods to operationalize them using the FCMP procedure. The RUN_MACRO function, a built-in SAS function introduced in Chapter 5, is used to operationalize setters because it can facilitate user-defined functions that execute DATA steps. One of the primary benefits of getters and setters is their ability to represent mathematical expressions algorithmically—that is, as single SAS statements—rather than procedurally.

A Business Case for Evaluating Nutritional Data

Consider the need to evaluate nutritional data for various recipes. In the most basic sense, this entails multiplying each ingredient's mass by its nutritional value per unit of mass and subsequently aggregating this product across all ingredients. For example, frying up some garlic broccoli might yield the following individual ingredients, which sum to 300.5 calories:

- 100 grams of raw broccoli (at 0.34 calories per gram) is 34 calories
- 30 grams of extra virgin olive oil (at 7.89 calories per gram) is 236.7 calories
- 20 grams of raw garlic (at 1.49 calories per gram) is 29.8 calories

The following statement initializes Total_cal to the total number of calories:

```
total_cal = (100 * .34) + (30 * 7.89) + (20 * 1.49);
```

However, individual nutritional metrics (for example, the number of calories per gram of broccoli or the quantity of fat per gram of olive oil) represent master data. They are typically maintained in lookup tables. That is, different recipes should be able to use the same master data by accessing the lookup table, in which case these nutritional values would be represented by variables rather than literal values:

```
total_cal = (100 * cal_broc) + (30 * cal_oil) + (20 * cal_garlic);
```

The difficulty with this setup is it requires the three calorie-specific variables (master data) to be initialized in the same recipe-specific data set (transactional data). Thus, master data are commingled with transactional data.

To explore possible solutions that operationalize this algorithm, Program 6.1 initializes three variables that represent caloric content. These variables are the master data that should be queried for any recipe using one or more of these ingredients. An actual caloric master table might comprise thousands of observations representing the breadth of culinary diversity.

Program 6.1: Caloric Master Table
```
data calories;
   length item $20 cal 8;
   item = 'broccoli';   cal = .34;  output;
   item = 'olive oil'; cal = 7.89; output;
   item = 'garlic';    cal = 1.49; output;
run;
```

The caloric calculation for all three ingredients must incorporate values maintained across multiple observations; that is, the caloric values within three observations are required to calculate the caloric content of garlic-fried broccoli. Thus, some data transposition or other transformation must precede the calculation.

For example, Program 6.2 demonstrates this data transformation by relying on the RETAIN statement to aggregate the Total_cal variable across all observations. When the DATA step reaches the final observation (denoted by EOF), the final value of Total_cal (representing the total calories for all ingredients) is printed to the log.

Program 6.2: Calculating Calories Using DATA Step Variables

```
data calculate;
   set calories end=eof;
   retain total_cal 0;
   if item = 'broccoli' then total_cal = total_cal + (100 * cal);
   else if item = 'olive oil' then total_cal = total_cal + (30 * cal);
   else if item = 'garlic' then total_cal = total_cal + (20 * cal);
   if eof then put total_cal=;
run;
```

Consider the need, however, to evaluate other nutritional aspects of the recipe besides caloric content (for example, total carbohydrates, fat, or protein). Each of these calculations would require additional RETAIN statements, as well as conditional logic to calculate the metrics. A preferred design would instead aggregate each metric using a single SAS statement.

Because of the complexity of summing variables across observations, SAS practitioners commonly rely on macro variables rather than DATA step variables. For example, Program 6.3 first initializes three global macro variables to the number of calories per gram of food, after which the macro variables can be substituted in the recipe's single-statement calculation.

Program 6.3: Calculating Calories Using Macro Variables

```
%let cal_broc=.34;
%let cal_oil=7.89;
%let cal_garlic=1.49;

data _null_;
   total_cal = (100*&cal_broc) + (30*&cal_oil) + (20*&cal_garlic);
   put total_cal=;
run;
```

The simplicity of using macro variables in this fashion is undeniably attractive; however, as the quantity and complexity of the master data increase, it becomes less convenient to maintain data as macro variables. Moreover, this unnecessarily converts a built-in data structure (the SAS data set) to multiple macro variables. And finally, if multiple metrics such as calories, carbohydrates, and fat content are being maintained for each variable, this effectively requires macro variables to represent a tabular matrix—something that they were never intended to do.

Thus, the ideal methodology is one in which both requirements are met—master data can be maintained natively within SAS data sets, and values can be extracted for use in single-statement DATA step calculations. For example, the following code meets these requirements, repeatedly calling a user-defined function (GET_CAL) that returns the caloric content of the parameterized ingredient:

```
total_cal = (100*get_cal('broccoli')) + (30*get_cal('olive oil')) + (20*get_
cal('garlic'));
```

This is the advantage of getters and setters—a key can be passed to a getter function and its value returned, or passed to a setter function and its value modified. The remainder of this chapter demonstrates the design of getters and setters, with examples representing increasingly more complex nutritional data and calculations.

GET_CAL Getter to Retrieve Caloric Content

The GET_CAL user-defined function (Program 6.4) performs a straightforward hash object lookup on the previously created Calories data set. A single parameter (ITEM) is declared, which also acts as the hash object key. When GET_CAL is called and the argument is located, the associated value of the key-value pair is returned to the calling program. Usage of hash objects within functions and subroutines is introduced in Chapter 4.

Program 6.4: Defining the GET_CAL Getter Function

```
proc fcmp outlib=work.funcs.food;
   function get_cal(item $);
      length cal 8;
      declare hash h(dataset: 'calories');
      rc = h.defineKey('item');
      rc = h.defineData('cal');
      rc = h.defineDone();
      rc = h.find();
      return(cal);
      endfunc;
quit;
```

GET_CAL can now be called from the DATA step to calculate the caloric content of the garlic-fried broccoli, as shown in Program 6.5, which again yields 300.5 calories. Note that no SET statement is required, as all data that are evaluated are retrieved by the getter function.

Program 6.5: Calling the GET_CAL Getter Function

```
options cmplib=work.funcs;

data calculate;
   total_cal = (100*get_cal('broccoli')) + (30*get_cal('olive oil')) +
      (20*get_cal('garlic'));
   put total_cal=;
run;
```

Unlike Program 6.2, the calculation is now encapsulated within a single SAS statement, and unlike Program 6.3, the master data of caloric content is maintained within a built-in data structure, the Calories data set. Because the master data are maintained in a SAS data set, their native data type (numeric) is retained throughout the entire lookup operation.

Another benefit of SAS getters is their ability to be called directly using the %SYSFUNC function. For example, the following statement retrieves the caloric content of olive oil (7.89 calories per gram) and prints this result to the log:

```
%put %sysfunc(get_cal(olive oil));
```

The GET_CAL function returns caloric count for ingredients contained in the Calories data set, but what occurs when an ingredient has not yet been indexed? For example, if the garlic is substituted with ginger due to personal preference, as shown in Program 6.6, a new use (or misuse) case for the getter is effectively defined—the functionality of GET_CAL when an argument is *not* found in the hash object.

Program 6.6: Calling GET_CAL on Missing Keys
```
data calculate;
   total_cal = (100*get_cal('broccoli')) + (30*get_cal('olive oil')) +
      (20*get_cal('ginger'));
   put total_cal=;
run;
```

The output demonstrates the missing value that is generated by GET_CAL when ginger is not found in the Calories data set, and a missing value is returned to the DATA step. Subsequently, the addition of the missing value—when performed by the + operator—yields only a missing value as the total:

```
total_cal=.
NOTE: Missing values were generated as a result of performing an operation
on missing values.
      Each place is given by: (Number of times) at (Line):(Column).
      1 at 1872:70
```

This functionality might be desired, as it alerts the user that the key was not found in the hash object. However, in other cases, a user might want the value to be calculated for the remaining ingredients—thus, only adding the calories resulting from broccoli and olive oil. This could be accomplished by modifying the calculation statement to use the built-in SUM function rather than the + operator:

```
total_cal = sum((100*get_cal('broccoli')), (30*get_cal('olive oil')),
   (20*get_cal('ginger')));
```

When the DATA step executes with this modification, SUM denotes the missing value for ginger, but nevertheless adds the remaining values for broccoli and olive oil:

```
total_cal=270.7
NOTE: Missing values were generated as a result of performing an operation
on missing values.
      Each place is given by: (Number of times) at (Line):(Column).
      1 at 1883:77
```

However, if the desired functionality is that ingredients not found in the hash object should *always* enable the remainder of the calories to be counted, as occurred when using SUM, an alternative solution would be to return a 0 from the GET_CAL function when a key is not found. Program 6.7 modifies GET_CAL to return one of two possible values—the associated value, when a key is found, or a 0, if the key is not found.

Program 6.7: Redefining the GET_CAL Getter Function to Return 0 for Missing Key
```
proc fcmp outlib=work.funcs.food;
   function get_cal(item $);
      length cal 8;
      declare hash h(dataset: 'calories');
      rc=h.defineKey('item');
      rc=h.defineData('cal');
      rc=h.defineDone();
      if h.find()=0 then return(cal);
      else return(0);
      endfunc;
quit;
```

Now, when Program 6.6 calls the redefined GET_CAL function, the calculation succeeds and sums the total calories, despite relying on the + operator, because no missing values are returned from GET_CAL. Alternatively, the second RETURN statement could be modified to instead return a missing value:

```
else return(.);
```

So, if the default behavior of the GET_CAL function in Program 6.4 is to return a missing value when a key is not found, why explicitly return a missing value using a second RETURN statement, as in Program 6.7? For one reason only—because this explicit return of a missing value demonstrates that the software developer has accounted for not only *use cases* but also *misuse* cases. That is, two RETURN statements convey an intentionality both for keys that are found and for those that are not. No user reading GET_CAL will have to wonder, *Did the developer intend for a missing key to result in a missing value, or was that accidental or an oversight?*

DATA Step Setter to Initialize Caloric Content

Behind every successful getter is an equally powerful setter that initializes the values to be retrieved. As shown in the previous section, SAS getters can be used in isolation, in which their lookup tables represent hash objects that are instantiated from data sets. For example, in Programs 6.4 and 6.7, the DATASET option in the DECLARE statement reads the Calories data set into the H hash object. In other cases, however, you might want to load key-value pairs incrementally into a lookup table or modify existing key-value pairs. Setter functions provide this functionality.

Fundamental to setter functions in any language is their ability to modify the data that getters return. This makes them intrinsically more complex than getters because setters must specify not only the key but also the new value to associate with that key in a key-value pair.

The following code uses the GET_CAL function to retrieve the number of calories per gram of broccoli to calculate the number of calories in 100 grams:

```
Total_cal_100g = 100 * get_cal('broccoli');
```

However, an equivalent setter function that initializes the number of calories per gram of food must specify both the food *and* its new caloric value—two arguments. For example, the following statement calls the SET_CAL_FUNC function (which has yet to be defined) to initialize the "broccoli" key to 0.38 calories per 100 grams:

```
rc = set_cal_func('broccoli', .38);
```

Note that setter functions—like all functions—produce a return code, which typically corresponds to the success of the setter. For example, a setter might be engineered so that a missing key (that is, an argument not found in the lookup table referenced by the setter) produces an exception, flagged by a return code of -1. In this way, the DATA step calling the setter could programmatically evaluate its success or failure.

In addition to setter *functions*, setter *subroutines* can also be engineered in SAS, which produce identical functionality to setter functions with the exception that no return value is generated. An equivalent setter subroutine could be called using the CALL statement:

```
call set_cal_sub('broccoli', .38);
```

The hash REPLACE method is instrumental to setter functions and subroutines that leverage hash objects. REPLACE modifies the value(s) in a key-value pair when the key is found in the hash object. If the key is not found, the key and associated value(s) are added to the hash object. Program 6.8 demonstrates use of REPLACE within a DATA step to modify broccoli's key-value pair by changing broccoli's caloric content from 0.34 calories to 0.38 calories.

Program 6.8: REPLACE Hash Method inside DATA Step
```
data _null_;
   if _n_=1 then do;
      declare hash h(dataset: 'calories');
      rc = h.definekey('item');
      rc = h.definedata('cal');
```

```
      rc = h.definedone();
      call missing(cal);
      end;
   length item $20 cal 8;
   item = 'broccoli';
   cal = .38;
   rc = h.replace();
run;
```

When REPLACE is called without arguments, it implicitly passes the values of Item and Cal, which had been declared using DEFINEKEY and DEFINEDATA, respectively. Because the "broccoli" key is found in the hash object, its associated caloric value is updated to 0.38.

Despite this successful implementation of REPLACE to update the hash object, when the Calories data set is reopened, the prior caloric value for broccoli (0.34) persists. Although REPLACE appears to have failed, the hash object "broccoli" entry was updated in the DATA step. However, when the DATA step terminated, the hash object was removed from memory without explicit instruction to save the Calories data set and the updated "broccoli" value of 0.38.

The solution is to use the hash OUTPUT method, which saves the hash object to disk and optionally to the data set specified in the DATASET option of the DECLARE statement. This method effectively overwrites the input data set with any new or modified values. Program 6.9 incorporates the OUTPUT method to update Calories permanently from 0.34 to 0.38.

Program 6.9: OUTPUT Hash Method inside DATA Step

```
data _null_;
   if _n_ = 1 then do;
      declare hash h(dataset: 'calories');
      rc = h.definekey('item');
      rc = h.definedata('item', 'cal');
      rc = h.definedone();
      call missing(cal);
      end;
   length item $20 cal 8;
   item = 'broccoli';
   cal = .38;
   rc = h.replace();
   rc = h.output(dataset: 'calories');
run;
```

Also note that the DEFINEDATA method now must enumerate both Item and Cal, whereas Program 6.8 declared only Cal. This change is required because OUTPUT cannot write a variable unless it is referenced by the DEFINEDATA method. When the Calories data set is viewed, the "broccoli" caloric value has now been modified from 0.34 to 0.38.

This brief foray into DATA step hash operations is necessary so that limitations of hash operations within the FCMP procedure can be better understood. Because the OUTPUT method is unavailable in the FCMP implementation of the hash object, FCMP functions cannot create or update data sets based on modifications made to a hash object. And although Program 6.9 is functional, it does not define a callable, reusable process. Thus, in the next section, Program 6.9 is morphed into a user-defined subroutine that meets these criteria.

FCMP Procedure Setter to Initialize Caloric Content

Program 6.9 succeeds in modifying the Calories data set by loading the data set into the hash object (H) and modifying the hash object using the REPLACE method. However, as the hash object is declared within the DATA step—rather than an FCMP function—this functionality is neither modular nor reusable. The FCMP implementation of the hash object does not support the hash OUTPUT method, as shown in Program 6.9. Two alternative methods do exist to modify a data set within FCMP; these include the OUT option of the PROC FCMP statement and the WRITE_ARRAY function, which was demonstrated in Chapter 3. However, neither of these methods can produce a function capable of updating the Calories data set.

The OUT option can be specified in the PROC FCMP statement to optionally create an output data set. However, note that this occurs in the FCMP wrapper, not within the confines of a function or subroutine definition (that is, between the FUNCTION and ENDFUNC statements, or the SUBROUTINE and ENDSUB statements). For this reason, OUT is not designed to write a data set when a user-defined function or subroutine is called.

WRITE_ARRAY can be called within a user-defined function, and it does write an array to a data set during a function call. However, because SAS arrays by definition contain same-type values, an array can contain all numeric data or all character data, but it cannot contain character and numeric variables. Thus, WRITE_ARRAY cannot be used to create or modify the Calories data set, which includes one character variable (Item) and one numeric variable (Cal).

But FCMP does have a trick up its sleeve, and that trick is the ever-capable RUN_MACRO function, which was introduced in Chapter 5. If ever there were a SAS multiverse, RUN_MACRO is the portal to transport you there, with its awe-inspiring, seemingly limitless functionality.

Because the RUN_MACRO function can call a SAS macro, and because that macro can contain either a hash object or a DATA step, RUN_MACRO can update a data set during a user-defined function call. In other words, RUN_MACRO independently enables SAS setters!

Program 6.10 demonstrates the SET_CAL subroutine and its subordinate SET_CAL macro, which is called by the RUN_MACRO function within the subroutine.

Program 6.10: FCMP SET_CAL Setter to Initialize Caloric Content

```
%macro set_cal();
%let attribute=%sysfunc(dequote(&attribute));
data calories;
   modify calories;
   if item = "&attribute" then cal = &value;
```

```
run;
%mend;

proc fcmp outlib=work.funcs.food;
   subroutine set_cal(attribute $, value);
      rc = run_macro('set_cal', attribute, value);
      endsub;
quit;
```

The SET_CAL subroutine declares two parameters: ATTRIBUTE, which defines the key for which to search, and VALUE, which defines the new value to ascribe to that key. When SET_CAL is called, the RUN_MACRO function calls the SET_CAL macro and passes the same ATTRIBUTE and VALUE values as arguments:

```
rc = run_macro('set_cal', attribute, value);
```

Macros called by the RUN_MACRO function do not need to declare parameters, unlike ordinary macros. Thus, despite retrieving two arguments, the %MACRO statement does not declare these parameters, yet it creates the &ATTRIBUTE and &VALUE macro variables:

```
%macro set_cal();
```

Note that character arguments (but not numeric arguments) passed via RUN_MACRO are quoted automatically, so these quotation marks typically must be removed with the DEQUOTE built-in function:

```
%let attribute=%sysfunc(dequote(&attribute));
```

The DATA step overwrites the Calories data set using the MODIFY statement rather than SET, and it replaces the Cal variable only if the Item variable matches the &ATTRIBUTE value:

```
data calories;
   modify calories;
   if item = "&attribute" then cal = &value;
run;
```

When the DATA step terminates, control returns from the SET_CAL macro to the SET_CAL subroutine, at which point the subroutine terminates and returns control to the calling program. Program 6.11 demonstrates a DATA step that calls the SET_CAL subroutine, which in turn calls the SET_CAL macro to initialize the Cal value in the Calories data set to 0.39 calories.

Program 6.11: Calling the SET_CAL Subroutine
```
data _null_;
   call set_cal('broccoli', .39);
run;
```

With a callable, reusable user-defined subroutine now defined, it is important to contrast the previous DATA step setter, demonstrated in Program 6.9. For example, why does Program 6.9 use a hash object and hash OUTPUT method to operationalize a setter, whereas the SET_CAL subroutine relies on a DATA step and MODIFY statement? In short, this design shift maximizes efficiency.

When RUN_MACRO executes inside the SET_CAL subroutine, it runs the subordinate DATA step inside the SET_CAL macro one time per subroutine call. Thus, if Program 6.11 instead called the SET_CAL subroutine multiple times to initialize multiple values, a hash-based approach in which the subordinate DATA step inside the SET_CAL macro instead relied on a hash object lookup is demonstrably slower than relying on the MODIFY statement. This is in large part because the hash object, once initialized, does not persist across subsequent subroutine calls, so it must be rebuilt as many times as the SET_CAL subroutine is called. Thus, in this instance, and especially as the size of a lookup table grows, the MODIFY statement will outperform a hash lookup operation.

Also notice a second discrepancy between Program 6.9 and the SET_CAL subroutine, demonstrated in Program 6.10. Program 6.9 implicitly adds new key-value pairs when new keys are encountered. This difference is explored in the next section.

FCMP Procedure Setter to Initialize and Add Caloric Content

The SET_CAL subroutine, demonstrated in Program 6.10, is excellent at reinitializing key-value pairs that already exist, as demonstrated in Program 6.11. For example, in Program 6.6, a user attempted to evaluate a recipe that included ginger—an ingredient not yet defined in the Calories data set. According to the USDA FoodData Central database, one gram of raw ginger root contains 0.8 calories. However, Program 6.12 fails to add a key-value entry to Calories for ginger because the SET_CAL macro can only modify existing entries—it cannot add new key-value pairs.

Program 6.12: Attempting to Add a New Key-Value Pair
```
data _null_;
   call set_cal('ginger', .8);
run;
```

The SET_CAL call in Program 6.12 does not alter the Calories data set. Rather, to extend the functionality of the SET_CAL subroutine, the SET_CAL macro must be changed so that it can both modify and add key-value pairs.

Program 6.13 defines the SET_ADD_CAL subroutine and macro and extends the functionality of the previous SET_CAL subroutine and macro by modifying the SET_ADD_CAL macro to include both REPLACE and OUTPUT statements.

Program 6.13: FCMP SET_ADD_CAL Setter to Initialize and Add Caloric Content
```
%macro set_add_cal();
%let attribute=%sysfunc(dequote(&attribute));
```

```
data calories;
   retain found 0;
   modify calories end = eof;
   if item = "&attribute" then do;
      cal = &value;
      found = 1;
      replace;
      end;
   if eof and found = 0 then do;
      item = "&attribute";
      cal = &value;
      output;
      end;
run;
%mend;

proc fcmp outlib=work.funcs.food;
   subroutine set_add_cal(attribute $, value);
      rc=run_macro('set_add_cal', attribute, value);
      endsub;
quit;
```

As before, the RUN_MACRO function within the SET_ADD_CAL subroutine calls the SET_ADD_CAL macro. However, the DATA step within the SET_ADD_CAL macro is substantially overhauled so that it can both modify existing key-value pairs and add new key-value pairs. The RETAIN statement initializes the Found variable to 0, which indicates that no key has been found yet:

```
retain found 0;
```

The MODIFY statement is updated to include the END option, which enables the Found variable to be evaluated after all observations have been read:

```
modify calories end = eof;
```

The first IF block evaluates the Item variable against the &ATTRIBUTE macro variable and, if their values match, performs three actions: the Cal variable is overwritten, the Found variable is reinitialized to denote the successful match, and the REPLACE statement overwrites the updated Cal variable in the Calories data set:

```
if item = "&attribute" then do;
   cal = &value;
   found = 1;
   replace;
   end;
```

The second IF block evaluates the final observation (denoted by EOF = 0). If the ingredient could not be found (represented by FOUND = 0), the key and value (&ATTRIBUTE and &VALUE, respectively) are initialized, after which the OUTPUT statement creates the new observation:

```
if eof and found = 0 then do;
   item = "&attribute";
   cal = &value;
   output;
   end;
```

If Program 6.12 is rerun and now instead calls the SET_ADD_CAL subroutine, the key-value pair for ginger is successfully added to the Calories data set, and the Cal variable is set to 0.8 calories for this new ingredient.

Differentiating Attributes in Getter Functions

Thus far, the previous examples have each demonstrated getting and setting only the caloric value for each ingredient. However, an expanded data model could incorporate not only calories but also fat per gram, protein per gram, or carbohydrates per gram. Program 6.14 creates the Food data set, which includes some of these metrics for broccoli, olive oil, and garlic. The Item variable defines the ingredient; Metric defines the nutritional metric; and Val defines the value of the specific metric.

Program 6.14: Incorporating Multiple Nutritional Attributes and Metrics

```
data food;
   infile datalines dsd delimiter=',';
   length item $20 metric $20;
   input item $ metric $ val;
   datalines;
broccoli,cal,0.34
broccoli,protein,0.0282
broccoli,carbs,0.0664
broccoli,fiber,0.026
olive oil,cal,7.8916666667
olive oil,protein,0
olive oil,carbs,0
olive oil,fiber,0
olive oil,fat,0.947
garlic,cal,1.49
garlic,protein,0.0636
garlic,fat,0.005
garlic,carbs,0.331
garlic,fiber,0.021
;
```

The GET_METRIC getter function is defined in Program 6.15. It now declares two parameters—ITEM represents the ingredient to be evaluated, and METRIC represents the nutritional value to be returned.

Program 6.15: Defining the GET_METRIC Getter Function

```
proc fcmp outlib=work.funcs.food;
   function get_metric(item $, metric $);
      length val 8;
```

```
        declare hash h(dataset: 'food');
        rc = h.defineKey('item', 'metric');
        rc = h.defineData('val');
        rc = h.defineDone();
        if h.find() = 0 then return(val);
        else return(0);
        endfunc;
quit;
```

GET_METRIC is nearly identical to GET_CAL with the exception that the DEFINEKEY method now declares two keys—Item and Metric. Note also that a more generic Val (value) is returned, rather than the more specific Cal (calorie), representing that the function can get not only caloric values but also other nutritional metrics.

The DATA step in Program 6.16 calls the GET_METRIC function repeatedly to calculate the total number of calories occurring in garlic-fried broccoli.

Program 6.16: Calling the GET_METRIC Getter Function
```
data calculate;
   total_cal = (100*get_metric('broccoli','cal')) + (30*get_metric('olive oil','cal'))
      + (20*get_metric('garlic','cal'));
   put total_cal=;
run;
```

The log demonstrates that Total_cal is again initialized to 300.55 calories:

```
total_cal=300.55
```

Thus, GET_METRIC extends the functionality of the GET_CAL getter function because it can return not only calories but all nutritional metrics. For example, Program 6.17 calls GET_METRIC to evaluate the number of carbohydrates in the garlic-fried broccoli recipe.

Program 6.17: Calling the GET_METRIC Getter Function to Calculate Carbohydrates
```
data calculate;
   total_carbs = (100*get_metric('broccoli','carbs'))
      + (30*get_metric('olive oil','carbs')) + (20*get_metric('garlic','carbs'));
   put total_carbs=;
run;
```

The output demonstrates that the recipe contains 13.26 carbohydrates:

```
total_carbs=13.26
```

Differentiating Attributes in Setter Functions

The previous section demonstrated how to extend the data model to incorporate not only caloric data but other nutritional data. This expansion added the Metric variable to the Food data set, which required the GET_METRIC function (demonstrated in Program 6.15) to add METRIC as a second parameter. Similarly, setter functions operating on the Food data set must also specify the METRIC argument.

The SET_METRIC setter subroutine, shown in Program 6.18, initializes nutritional metrics based on three parameters: ITEM represents the ingredient, METRIC represents the nutritional metric, and VALUE represents the value to add or update.

Program 6.18: Defining the SET_METRIC Setter Subroutine
```
%macro set_metric();
%let item=%sysfunc(dequote(&item));
%let metric=%sysfunc(dequote(&metric));
data food;
   retain found 0;
   modify food end = eof;
   if item = "&item" and metric = "&metric" then do;
      val = &value;
      found = 1;
      replace;
      end;
   if eof and found = 0 then do;
      item = "&item";
      metric = "&metric";
      val = &value;
      output;
      end;
run;
%mend;

proc fcmp outlib=work.funcs.food;
   subroutine set_metric(item $, metric $, value);
      rc=run_macro('set_metric', item, metric, value);
      endsub;
quit;
```

The SET_METRIC subroutine differs from the SET_CAL function in that two variables (Item and Metric) now must match two arguments (&ITEM and &METRIC) that are passed from the SET_METRIC subroutine to the SET_METRIC macro via the RUN_MACRO function.

For example, Program 6.19 calls SET_METRIC to add the number of calories and number of grams of protein found in raw ginger.

Program 6.19: Calling the SET_METRIC Setter Subroutine
```
data _null_;
   call set_metric('ginger', 'cal', .8);
   call set_metric('ginger', 'protein', 1.82);
run;
```

The DATA step appends two observations to the Food data set, which can subsequently be retrieved using the GET_METRIC function, or updated using the SET_METRIC subroutine.

Differentiating Data Types in Getter Functions

The previous getters and setters have all operated on numeric values; that is, numeric values are returned by getters, and modified (or initialized) by setters. However, one final expansion of the underlying data model can support both numeric and character values. For example, with broccoli defined as the first attribute, it could be important to associate the specific entry name within the USDA FoodData Central database ("broccoli, raw"), as well as the URL at which the metrics are maintained (https://fdc.nal.usda.gov/fdc-app.html#/food-details/170379/nutrients).

The updated data model now includes both numeric and character values, which are recorded in the Val_num and Val_char variables, respectively. The DATA step in Program 6.20 creates the Food_n_stuff lookup table on which updated getters and setters rely.

Program 6.20: Incorporating Character Attributes into the Data Model
```
data food_n_stuff;
   infile datalines dsd delimiter=',';
   length item $20 metric $20 val_num 8 val_char $100;
   input item $ metric $ val_num val_char $;
   datalines;
broccoli,name,,"broccoli, raw"
broccoli,url,,https://fdc.nal.usda.gov/fdc-app.html#/food-details/170379/
nutrients
broccoli,cal,0.34,
broccoli,protein,0.0282,
broccoli,carbs,0.0664,
broccoli,fiber,0.026,
olive oil,name,,"oil, olive, extra virgin"
olive oil,url,,https://fdc.nal.usda.gov/fdc-app.html#/food-details/748608/
nutrients
olive oil,cal,7.8916666667,
olive oil,protein,0,
olive oil,carbs,0,
olive oil,fiber,0,
olive oil,fat,0.947,
garlic,name,,"garlic, raw"
garlic,url,,https://fdc.nal.usda.gov/fdc-app.html#/food-details/1104647/
nutrients
garlic,cal,1.49,
```

```
garlic,protein,0.0636,
garlic,fat,0.005,
garlic,carbs,0.331,
garlic,fiber,0.021,
;
```

Getters now must be differentiated based on the data type of their return value. Thus, a character getter can extract the Name and URL variables from the Food_n_stuff data set, and a numeric getter can extract the remaining numeric metrics from the data set. The GET_FOOD_NUM function, shown in Program 6.21, extracts numeric values from Food_n_stuff, displaying identical functionality to the GET_METRIC getter function demonstrated in Program 6.15.

Program 6.21: Defining the GET_FOOD_NUM Numeric Getter Function

```
proc fcmp outlib=work.funcs.food;
   function get_food_num(item $, metric $);
      length val_num 8;
      declare hash h(dataset: 'food_n_stuff');
      rc = h.defineKey('item', 'metric');
      rc = h.defineData('val_num');
      rc = h.defineDone();
      if h.find() = 0 then return(val_num);
      else return(0);
      endfunc;
quit;
```

The equivalent character getter function (GET_FOOD_CHAR) is demonstrated in Program 6.22. Note that the function returns a 100-character value when the key is found in the Food_n_stuff dataset; otherwise, a missing value is returned.

Program 6.22: Defining the GET_FOOD_CHAR Character Getter Function

```
proc fcmp outlib=work.funcs.food;
   function get_food_char(item $, metric $) $;
      length val_char $100;
      declare hash h(dataset: 'food_n_stuff');
      rc = h.defineKey('item', 'metric');
      rc = h.defineData('val_char');
      rc = h.defineDone();
      if h.find() = 0 then return(val_char);
      else return('');
      endfunc;
quit;
```

Program 6.23 first calculates the total calories using the familiar formula, after which the DO loop prints the USDA sources for the three ingredients.

Program 6.23: Calling the GET_METRIC Getter Function

```
data calculate;
   total_cal = (100*get_food_num('broccoli','cal')) +
      (30*get_food_num('olive oil','cal')) + (20*get_food_num('garlic','cal'));
   put total_cal=;
```

```
    length items origin $100 item $20;
    items = 'broccoli,olive oil,garlic';
    do i=1 to countw(items, ',');
        item = scan(items, i, ',');
        origin = strip(get_food_char(item, 'name')) || ': ' || get_food_char(item, 'url');
        put origin;
        end;
run;
```

The log demonstrates the number of calories in garlic-fried broccoli, after which USDA sources are listed:

```
total_cal=300.55
broccoli, raw: https://fdc.nal.usda.gov/fdc-app.html#/food-details/170379/
nutrients
oil, olive, extra virgin: https://fdc.nal.usda.gov/fdc-app.html#/food-
details/748608/nutrients
garlic, raw: https://fdc.nal.usda.gov/fdc-app.html#/food-details/1104647/
nutrients
```

In the future, if the caloric content for a specific ingredient needs to be modified (for example, from its USDA value to a different value originating from a separate data source), a numeric setter function could be called to modify the metric, and a character setter function could be called to modify the source URL. These setter functions are introduced in the next section.

Differentiating Data Types in Setter Functions

Finally, whenever a getter function has been modified to support an extended data model, the accompanying setter subroutine also must be modified. Thus, just as the GET_METRIC function was refactored into the GET_FOOD_NUM and GET_FOOD_CHAR functions, the SET_METRIC subroutine also must be refactored so that it can support both character and numeric data types.

The SET_FOOD_NUM subroutine, demonstrated in Program 6.24, is identical to the SET_METRIC subroutine (Program 6.18), with the exception that it accesses and modifies the FOOD_N_STUFF data set. Thus, SET_FOOD_NUM modifies a numeric value.

Program 6.24: Defining the SET_FOOD_NUM Numeric Setter Subroutine

```
%macro set_food_num();
%let item=%sysfunc(dequote(&item));
%let metric=%sysfunc(dequote(&metric));
data food_n_stuff;
    retain found 0;
    modify food_n_stuff end = eof;
    if item = "&item" and metric = "&metric" then do;
        val_num = &value;
```

```
        found = 1;
        replace;
        end;
     if eof and found = 0 then do;
        item = "&item";
        metric = "&metric";
        val_num = &value;
        output;
        end;
run;
%mend;


proc fcmp outlib=work.funcs.food;
    subroutine set_food_num(item $, metric $, value);
        rc=run_macro('set_food_num', item, metric, value);
        endsub;
quit;
```

For example, Program 6.25 calls SET_FOOD_NUM to modify the number of calories associated with one gram of broccoli from 0.34 to 0.38.

Program 6.25: Calling the GET_FOOD_NUM Subroutine
```
data _null_;
    call set_food_num('broccoli', 'cal', .38);
run;
```

GET_FOOD_CHAR is the final setter function, which modifies a character variable within the Food_n_stuff data set. The GET_FOOD_CHAR subroutine is demonstrated in Program 6.26.

Program 6.26: Defining the SET_FOOD_CHAR Character Setter Subroutine
```
%macro set_food_char();
%let item=%sysfunc(dequote(&item));
%let metric=%sysfunc(dequote(&metric));
%let value=%sysfunc(dequote(&value));
data food_n_stuff;
    retain found 0;
    modify food_n_stuff end = eof;
    if item = "&item" and metric = "&metric" then do;
        val_char = "&value";
        found = 1;
        replace;
        end;
     if eof and found = 0 then do;
        item = "&item";
        metric = "&metric";
        val_char = "&value";
        output;
        end;
run;
%mend;
```

```
proc fcmp outlib=work.funcs.food;
   subroutine set_food_char(item $, metric $, value $);
      rc=run_macro('set_food_char', item, metric, value);
      endsub;
quit;
```

For example, to change the name of the broccoli entry from "broccoli, raw" to "broccoli," SET_
FOOD_CHAR could be called. Program 6.27 calls this subroutine to modify the Name variable
associated with the "broccoli" key.

Program 6.27: Calling the GET_FOOD_CHAR Subroutine
```
data _null_;
   call set_food_char('broccoli','name','broccoli');
run;
```

The subroutine call successfully modifies the observation that matches the name of broccoli, and
the updated key-value pair is saved to the Food_n_stuff data set.

Conclusion

The notion of getters and setters is uncommon within the SAS language, as SAS practitioners are
far more likely to perform a DATA step MERGE or a SQL procedure JOIN when master data and
transactional data need to be compared or evaluated within a single algorithm. However, the
analysis of lookup tables may require the extraction of only one or two values from a table, in
which case a lookup operation can be more efficient than an equivalent merge or join. Similarly,
the modification of a lookup table often requires altering only one value—that is, one variable
within a single observation. Finally, the use of getters and setters facilitates writing equations
and other expressions algorithmically in a single statement rather than relying on multi-line
processes that can obscure the intent of the expression. This chapter introduced getters and
setters, operationalized within user-defined functions and subroutines, and demonstrated their
advantage in interacting with lookup tables.

Chapter 7: Recursion and Memoization

This chapter introduces two software design concepts, recursion and memoization, and demonstrates how they can be operationalized within the FCMP procedure. A recursive function is one that repeatedly calls itself, and in doing so, decomposes a larger problem into a simpler one. When a recursive function finally terminates and stops calling itself, the final solution is returned to the calling program. Both user-defined functions and subroutines can be designed to be recursive, but not all functionality can be achieved through recursion. The aim of recursion is typically to simplify software design and improve readability, as opposed to increasing performance or efficiency.

Memoization, on the other hand, does aim to improve both software performance and efficiency by reducing both runtime and system resource utilization. Memoization stores the results of predictable, complex computations for future reuse. Thus, rather than repeatedly computing some value, the value can be saved in memory and retrieved directly (rather than recalculated) the next time the value is required. Within the FCMP procedure, the STATIC statement, hash object, and dictionary object each facilitates memoization objectives, and each is demonstrated in this chapter.

Introducing the FCMP STATIC Statement

The STATIC statement, available only inside the FCMP procedure, declares and optionally initializes one or more variables whose values are retained across successive function calls. If you call a user-defined function once, STATIC can remember a value for you, and when calling the same function a second time, that value can be recalled and used. To introduce STATIC, it is best to first demonstrate how the built-in OPEN function retains values across successive function calls.

Consider the ubiquitous OPEN function, which opens a SAS data set. OPEN is commonly implemented prior to leveraging subsequent input/output (I/O) built-in functions that evaluate data set structure, size, and other attributes. The OPEN function generates a return code that demonstrates whether the data set could be opened—a 0 value indicates failure, whereas a positive integer (starting with 1) indicates success. The OPEN return code, by tradition, is referenced as the data set ID (DSID), and subsequent built-in I/O functions must reference each data set's specific DSID to extract information about the open data set. Thus, when a DATA step opens its first data set, OPEN will ascribe a DSID of 1. When the same DATA step opens a second data set, OPEN will ascribe a DSID of 2. Thus, OPEN remembers from one call to the next how many data sets have been opened, and user-defined functions can demonstrate equivalent functionality by leveraging the STATIC statement.

Program 7.1 creates the Some_fruit and Some_vegetables data sets. They contain no actual data because only their respective variable names are analyzed.

Program 7.1: Opening Fruits and Vegetables

```
data some_fruit;
   length apples bananas pears mangoes 8;
   call missing(apples, bananas, pears, mangoes);
run;

data some_vegetables;
   length bok_choi onion garlic broccoli 8;
   call missing(bok_choi, onion, garlic, broccoli);
run;

data get_vars;
   dsid1 = open('some_fruit', 'i');
   put dsid1=;
   do i=1 to attrn(dsid1, 'nvars');
      var = varname(dsid1, i);
      put var=;
      end;
   dsid2 = open('some_vegetables', 'i');
   put dsid2=;
   do i=1 to attrn(dsid2, 'nvars');
      var = varname(dsid2, i);
      put var=;
      end;
run;
```

When the third DATA step executes, it opens Some_fruit, and initializes DSID1 to 1, after which it opens Some_vegetables, and initializes DSID2 to 2. Thus, the ATTRN function that references DSID1 evaluates the number of variables in the Some_fruit data set, whereas the subsequent ATTRN function that references DSID2 evaluates the number of variables in the Some_vegetables data set.

The log demonstrates that DSID is incremented with each successive call to the OPEN function. DSID1 is printed, followed by the list of variables in Some_fruit. Then DSID2 is printed, followed by the list of variables in Some_vegetables:

```
dsid1=1
var=apples
var=bananas
var=pears
var=mangoes
dsid2=2
var=bok_choi
var=onion
var=garlic
var=broccoli
```

Within the OPEN function, the retention of the previous DSID value is essential, as this enables subsequent data sets to be opened and assigned incremental DSID values. This same functionality can be operationalized through STATIC within the FCMP procedure.

The STATIC statement supports recursive functions because a value can be retained from one function call to the next, including when a function calls itself. Similarly, STATIC supports memoization because an expensive calculation—that is, one that is resource intensive—can be calculated once and retained thereafter in case the function is subsequently called. These two use cases are explored in detail later in this chapter.

Using STATIC to Count Function Calls

In its most straightforward implementation STATIC can be used to count how many times a user-defined function has been called by initializing a counter, retaining that counter across function calls, and incrementing the counter value during each subsequent function call.

Within Program 7.2, STATIC declares the Cnt numeric variable and initializes it to 1 during the first function call. On all subsequent function calls, however, STATIC does not reinitialize Cnt, so the value is retained from one function call to the next. Thus, the Cnt variable can be incremented during each function call. The incremented value is retained internally without passing Cnt as a parameter and without exposing Cnt to the calling program.

Program 7.2: Counting Function Calls with STATIC

```
proc fcmp outlib=work.funcs.test;
   function count_calls(char $) $;
      file log;
      static cnt 0;
      cnt+1;
      put cnt=;
      return(char);
      endfunc;
quit;
```

The DATA step in Program 7.3 calls COUNT_CALLS twice. STATIC enables COUNT_CALLS to count how many times the function has been called from the same DATA step.

Program 7.3: Calling the COUNT_CALLS Function

```
options cmplib=work.funcs;
data _null_;
   length char_val $20;
   char_val = count_calls('hello');
   put char_val=;
   char_val = count_calls('goodbye');
   put char_val=;
run;
```

The log demonstrates that COUNT_CALLS initializes Cnt to 1 in the first function call, after which Cnt is incremented in subsequent function calls:

```
cnt=1
char_val=hello
cnt=2
char_val=goodbye
```

Note, however, that STATIC releases all retained values when the DATA step terminates. Thus, if two function calls occur in two separate DATA steps, each function call is considered to be the first, and STATIC reinitializes all counter (or other retained) values.

For example, Program 7.4 calls COUNT_CALLS twice, but because the calls occur in separate DATA steps, STATIC initializes Cnt to 1 in both DATA steps and does not increment Cnt to 2.

Program 7.4: Reinitialization of STATIC Counter Across Multiple DATA Steps

```
data _null_;
   length char_val $20;
   char_val = count_calls('hello');
   put char_val=;
run;

data _null_;
   length char_val $20;
   char_val = count_calls('goodbye');
   put char_val=;
run;
```

The log demonstrates that STATIC initializes Cnt during both function calls because the function calls occur in separate DATA steps:

```
304  data _null_;
305     length char_val $20;
306     char_val=count_calls('hello');
307     put char_val=;
308  run;
```

```
cnt=1
char_val=hello

309
310  data _null_;
311     length char_val $20;
312     char_val=count_calls('goodbye');
313     put char_val=;
314  run;

cnt=1
char_val=goodbye
```

Calling STATIC Functions and Subroutines Using %SYSFUNC and %SYSCALL

When a function containing STATIC is called from successive %SYSFUNC functions or a subroutine containing STATIC is called from successive %SYSCALL statements, the behavior of STATIC differs from that of DATA step function calls. Specifically, STATIC values are retained across multiple function calls, unlike STATIC values that are *not* retained across multiple DATA steps.

Moreover, when a function that leverages STATIC is concurrently called from both the DATA step and %SYSFUNC, it becomes apparent that STATIC maintains two separate variable stacks—one for the DATA step and one for the SAS macro language. This behavior is demonstrated here so as not to surprise unsuspecting SAS practitioners.

For example, consider three successive calls to COUNT_CALLS, defined in Program 7.2, via the %SYSFUNC macro function:

```
%put %sysfunc(count_calls('hey there'));
%put %sysfunc(count_calls('hi there'));
%put %sysfunc(count_calls('ho there'));
```

The log demonstrates that STATIC initializes Cnt to 1 during the first function call, and subsequent calls increment this value to 2 and 3:

```
2103  %put %sysfunc(count_calls('hey there'));
'hey there'
2104  %put %sysfunc(count_calls('hi there'));
'hi there'
2105  %put %sysfunc(count_calls('ho there'));
'ho there'
cnt=1
cnt=2
cnt=3
```

One might expect a subsequent DATA step call to COUNT_CALLS to evaluate Cnt as 4, given that the last %SYSFUNC call to COUNT_CALLS yielded a Cnt value of 3. However, because the DATA step maintains a separate stack of STATIC variables, when COUNT_CALLS is called from the DATA step in Program 7.5, the Cnt variable is reinitialized to 1.

Program 7.5: Calling STATIC Function from DATA Step After %SYSFUNC

```
data _null_;
   length char_val $20;
   char_val = count_calls('hello');
   put char_val=;
run;
```

The log demonstrates this reinitialization of Cnt to 1, which occurs because the DATA step is not tracking when COUNT_CALLS is invoked using the SAS macro language:

```
2106   data _null_;
2107      length char_val $20;
2108      char_val = count_calls('hello');
2109      put char_val=;
2110   run;

cnt=1
char_val=hello
```

At this point, with the realization that two variable stacks are being maintained by STATIC, it is fairly predictable that subsequent calls to COUNT_CALLS using %SYSFUNC will continue to increment the macro stack. For example, when COUNT_CALLS is invoked three more times, Cnt is incremented to 4, 5, and 6:

```
%put %sysfunc(count_calls('hey there'));
%put %sysfunc(count_calls('hi there'));
%put %sysfunc(count_calls('ho there'));
```

The log demonstrates these successive calls:

```
2111   %put %sysfunc(count_calls('hey there'));
'hey there'
2112   %put %sysfunc(count_calls('hi there'));
'hi there'
2113   %put %sysfunc(count_calls('ho there'));
'ho there'
cnt=4
cnt=5
cnt=6
```

At this point, it might appear that STATIC is a runaway process and that you will need to restart the SAS application to reinitialize Cnt to 1—at least where COUNT_CALLS is called via %SYSFUNC.

Never fear, however, because recompiling the COUNT_CALLS function by rerunning the FCMP procedure in Program 7.2 resets all STATIC variables.

After rerunning the FCMP procedure (not shown), COUNT_CALLS is called one final time using %SYSFUNC:

```
%put %sysfunc(count_calls('hey there'));
```

The log demonstrates that Cnt has been reinitialized to 1:

```
2125   %put %sysfunc(count_calls('hey there'));
'hey there'
cnt=1
```

Thus, within a DATA step, STATIC initializes a variable once. Across multiple DATA steps, STATIC initializes a variable once per DATA step. However, STATIC maintains an entirely separate variable stack when a function containing the STATIC statement is called via %SYSFUNC or a subroutine is called via %SYSCALL. Given this divergence of functionality, end users must be made aware whenever a user-defined function leverages STATIC to ensure that the function is appropriately invoked. For example, in some cases, a user-defined function might be able to be called from the DATA step, but not via the %SYSFUNC function. This is OK, as long as this caveat is documented.

Recursion

Recursion. *See* Recursion. It's the oldest, and arguably most esoteric, joke among programmers. *Recursion*, all levity aside, describes a callable software module such as a procedure, function, or subroutine that calls itself repeatedly until some definite, calculated, or evaluated termination. Recursive operations should not call themselves *ad infinitum*. Just like loops, recursive operations must also have exit criteria upon which they terminate. Recursion decomposes a problem into multiple, successive calls to some operation, and after all calls have terminated, the combined output of all calls forms the aggregate solution that is returned to the calling program.

Both loops and recursive functions operate iteratively, although this iteration is operationalized through different mechanisms. Because of this shared iteration, it is often touted that *any software loop can be rewritten as a recursive function*. Using this adage as a guide (rather than decrying it as universal truth), this chapter refactors two looping operations into recursive functions. Note that in both cases, the output (whether an actual return value or multiple values that are passed by reference via the OUTARGS statement) from one call of a recursive function must be passed as input to the next call of that function. Thus, despite a recursive function repeatedly calling itself, it typically passes different arguments to itself during each successive call.

Calculating a Factorial

Calculating a factorial is one of the most elemental of all recursive functions, as it only requires the return value from each function call to be multiplied by the return values of all successive function calls. For example, "5 factorial" (written as 5!) equals 120 and is described in the following equations:

```
5! = 5 X 4 X 3 X 2 X 1

5! = 120
```

Clearly, no one wants a reusable function that *only* calculates 5!, so a function can be conceptualized in which the base number (5) is passed flexibly as an argument. Program 7.6 defines the FACTORIAL_LOOP function, which calculates the factorial in a DO loop that iterates (in reverse) from the base number to 1.

Program 7.6: Calculating Factorial in a Loop

```
proc fcmp outlib=work.funcs.maths;
   function factorial_loop(base);
      factorial = 1;
      do cnt = base to 1 by -1;
         factorial = factorial * cnt;
         end;
      return(factorial);
      endfunc;
quit;

options cmplib=work.funcs;

data _null_;
   value = factorial_loop(5);
   put value=;
run;
```

The log demonstrates that 5! was calculated to be 120:

```
value=120
```

However, rather than looping, a functionally equivalent solution can instead leverage recursion, which requires the user-defined function to call itself until it arrives at the final solution.

The FACTORIAL_RECURSIVE function in Program 7.7 relies on recursion rather than looping, and the simplicity that is achieved requires only a single variable—the BASE parameter.

Program 7.7: Calculating a Factorial in a Recursive Function

```
proc fcmp outlib=work.funcs.maths;
   function factorial_recursive(base);
      file log;
      put base=;
      if base = 1 then return(1);
      else return(base * factorial_recursive(base-1));
      endfunc;
quit;

data _null_;
   value = factorial_recursive(5);
   put value=;
run;
```

FACTORIAL_RECURSIVE operates by evaluating the value of Base. When Base equals 1, the function exits. Otherwise, FACTORIAL_RECURSIVE calls itself, but passes a Base value that has been decremented by 1. In other words, both the looping functionality demonstrated in Program 7.6 and the recursive functionality demonstrated in Program 7.7 are counting down from the Original Base value to 1.

The FILE and PUT statements are included only to represent the internal workings of the function, and the Base values are printed to the log as the function recursively calls itself:

```
base=5
base=4
base=3
base=2
base=1
value=120
```

Some developers prefer the simplicity of recursion in cases in which it does reduce code complexity, such as by eliminating unnecessary counters or other variables. However, recursion does not simplify *all* iterative functions, and software readability always must be a preeminent design consideration. More complex examples of recursion follow in this chapter.

Making Change Recursively

In Chapter 3, Programs 3.27 through 3.35 demonstrated various functions and subroutines that make change. Given some item price and some amount of currency tendered, the amount of change to be returned was generated in total as well as quantity per bill or coin denomination. Each of the Chapter 3 programs used a DO loop that iterated over an array of U.S. currency denominations. For example, should the change to be returned include a $1 bill, and if so, how many bills? Should the change to be returned include a 50-cent piece, and if so, how many coins?

The MAKE_CHANGE subroutine, shown in Program 7.8, declares three numeric parameters:

- PRICE describes the item price.
- PAID is the amount tendered.
- CHANGE is the difference to be returned to the customer.

Two numeric arrays are also declared:

- CURR_VAL enumerates a list of currency values for bills and coins.
- CURR_CNT enumerates the quantity of each bill or coin to be returned to the customer.

The OUTARGS statement specifies that CHANGE and CURR_CNT are passed by reference, which provides the calling program access to their modified values after the subroutine terminates. Finally, the Cnt variable facilitates iteration by counting the number of loops that have occurred.

Program 7.8: Defining the MAKE_CHANGE Subroutine to Calculate Change and Currency Values

```
proc fcmp outlib=work.funcs.change;
   subroutine make_change(price, paid, change, curr_val[*], curr_cnt[*]);
      outargs change, curr_cnt;
      change=paid - price;
      amt=change;
      do cnt=1 to dim(curr_val);
         curr_cnt[cnt] = floor(amt/curr_val[cnt]);
         amt = mod(amt, curr_val[cnt]);
         end;
      endsub;
quit;
```

The DATA step in Program 7.9 calls MAKE_CHANGE to calculate the change that should be returned when $10.00 is tendered for an item that costs $7.67.

Program 7.9: Calling the MAKE_CHANGE Subroutine

```
data _null_;
   length change 8;
   array curr_val[9] 8 (20 10 5 1 .50 .25 .10 .05 .01);
   array curr_cnt[9] 8;
   format change curr_val1-curr_val9 dollar8.2;
   call missing(change);
   call make_change(7.67, 10, change, curr_val, curr_cnt);
   put change=;
   do cnt=1 to dim(curr_val);
      put curr_val[cnt] @10 curr_cnt[cnt] ;
      end;
run;
```

The output first lists the amount to be returned ($2.33), after which the quantities of specific currency denominations are enumerated:

```
change=$2.33
$20.00   0
$10.00   0
$5.00    0
$1.00    2
$0.50    0
$0.25    1
$0.10    0
$0.05    1
$0.01    3
```

The change should include two $1 bills, one quarter, one nickel, and three pennies.

Rather than iterating a loop, however, a functionally equivalent recursive subroutine could instead repeatedly call itself until the type and quantity of change had been generated, with each successive call referencing the next, lower currency denomination.

Note that each successive call must track the overall number of calls to ensure that the Curr_val array of currency denominations is correctly iterated. Because the Curr_val array is itself utilized by the calling program and, therefore, cannot be modified inside the subroutine, initialization of an array counter variable is required. Thus, just as the Cnt variable facilitates the iteration and termination in Program 7.8, the CNT parameter facilitates iteration as well as the termination of recursion in Program 7.10.

The MAKE_CHANGE_RECUR recursive subroutine, shown in Program 7.10, is functionally equivalent to MAKE_CHANGE, but it relies on recursion rather than iteration of a loop. In both subroutines, however, the Cnt variable is required to iterate the array of currency denominations, and the DIM function is used to evaluate the exit criterion to determine when iteration should terminate.

Program 7.10: Defining the MAKE_CHANGE_RECUR Recursive Subroutine

```
proc fcmp outlib=work.funcs.change;
   subroutine make_change_recur(price, paid, change, curr_val[*], curr_cnt[*], cnt);
      outargs change, curr_cnt;
      if cnt = 1 then change = paid - price;
      curr_cnt[cnt] = floor((paid - price)/curr_val[cnt]);
      if cnt < dim(curr_val) then
         call make_change_recur(price, paid - (curr_cnt[cnt] * curr_val[cnt]), change,
            curr_val, curr_cnt, cnt+1);
      endsub;
quit;
```

Also note that MAKE_CHANGE_RECUR must pass the current array element position (1 through 9, representing each of the specific currency denominations) to each subroutine call, which requires the declaration of the additional parameter CNT. Thus, when MAKE_CHANGE_RECUR is called in Program 7.11, the invocation requires this extra argument to be passed as 1.

Program 7.11: Calling the MAKE_CHANGE_RECUR Recursive Subroutine
```
data _null_;
   length change 8;
   array curr_val[9] 8 (20 10 5 1 .50 .25 .10 .05 .01);
   array curr_cnt[9] 8;
   format change curr_val1-curr_val9 dollar8.2;
   call missing(change);
   call make_change_recur(7.67, 10, change, curr_val, curr_cnt, 1);
   put change=;
   do cnt=1 to dim(curr_val);
      put curr_val[cnt] @10 curr_cnt[cnt] ;
      end;
run;
```

The DATA steps in Programs 7.9 and 7.11 are functionally equivalent and generate identical output. However, in this specific case, the recursive subroutine requires the declaration of one additional parameter. The STATIC statement overcomes this issue in the next section.

Programs 7.8 and 7.10 demonstrate the reality that functions might need to convey information from one function call to the next call, but not require that information for the final solution. For example, MAKE_CHANGE_RECUR requires some method to track how many times it has been recursively called to ensure that the array is both iterated and terminated. The CNT parameter iterates the Curr_val and Curr_cnt arrays in each successive subroutine call. However, CNT is ugly because it requires a counter variable to be declared as a parameter and passed as an argument, and this design adds unwanted complexity to the subroutine call. Finally, the solution returned to the calling program has no use for CNT—it represents only a means to an end—so it is beneficial to remove it from the list of parameters that MAKE_CHANGE_RECUR declares, and STATIC can facilitate removing this parameter.

Making Change Recursively with STATIC

With STATIC functionality already introduced in this chapter, its application to recursive functions can be demonstrated. Among other operations, STATIC can be used to track the number of times a function has been recursively called. For example, the MAKE_CHANGE_RECUR_STATIC subroutine demonstrated in Program 7.12 refactors the MAKE_CHANGE_RECUR subroutine (Program 7.10) and relies on STATIC to count subroutine calls, which eliminates the need to declare and pass the CNT parameter.

Program 7.12: Defining the MAKE_CHANGE_RECUR_STATIC Recursive Subroutine
```
proc fcmp outlib=work.funcs.change;
   subroutine make_change_recur_static(price, paid, change, curr_val[*], curr_cnt[*]);
      outargs change, curr_cnt;
      static cnt 0;
```

```
      cnt+1;
      if cnt = 1 then change = paid - price;
      curr_cnt[cnt] = floor((paid - price)/curr_val[cnt]);
      if cnt < dim(curr_val) then
         call make_change_recur_static(price, paid - (curr_cnt[cnt] * curr_val[cnt]),
            change, curr_val, curr_cnt);
      endsub;
quit;
```

During the first subroutine call, STATIC initializes CNT to 0, after which CNT is immediately incremented to 1. Thereafter, in subsequent subroutine calls, CNT is not reinitialized, but continues to be incremented by 1; thus, STATIC tracks the number of subroutine calls.

The MAKE_CHANGE_RECUR_STATIC subroutine is called in Program 7.13, which is identical to the DATA step in Program 7.11, except that an argument for CNT no longer needs to be passed. Again, this is possible because the STATIC statement shifts the burden of counting iterations from a parameter to a STATIC variable.

Program 7.13: Calling the MAKE_CHANGE_RECUR_STATIC Recursive Subroutine
```
data _null_;
   length change 8;
   array curr_val[9] 8 (20 10 5 1 .50 .25 .10 .05 .01);
   array curr_cnt[9] 8;
   format change curr_val1-curr_val9 dollar8.2;
   call missing(change);
   call make_change_recur_static(7.67, 10, change, curr_val, curr_cnt);
   put change=;
   do cnt=1 to dim(curr_val);
      put curr_val[cnt] @10 curr_cnt[cnt];
      end;
run;
```

The output is identical to that of Programs 7.9 and 7.11 and lists both the total change to be returned ($2.33) as well as the individual quantities of each specific bill and coin. Most importantly, STATIC has removed complexity from the subroutine's declaration and invocation by eliminating the need to declare and pass CNT as a parameter because Cnt is maintained internally as a variable. Although not demonstrated in this text, STATIC can be used to declare and initialize character variables, as well as character and numeric arrays. Thus, STATIC functionality extends far beyond the limited scope of counting recursive function calls or subroutine calls.

Making Change Recursively without STATIC or a Counter Variable

The previous two sections demonstrate functionally equivalent methods that facilitate iteration within a recursive function, relying on either a variable that iterates the data structure (the array) or a comparable parameter that maintains iteration count (facilitated by the STATIC statement).

It is important to note, however, that many recursive functions effect iteration not through a counter but rather through modification of the data structure itself that is being iterated.

For example, the previous two sections require the Curr_val array—defined in the calling program (the DATA step)—both to call the subroutine and to print the currency denominations iteratively after the subroutine has terminated. And for this reason, Curr_val (the data structure being iterated) cannot be modified by the MAKE_CHANGE_RECUR_STATIC subroutine.

However, a third, more-or-less functionally equivalent solution instead modifies the Curr_val array in each subsequent, recursive call of the subroutine. Doing so eliminates the need to count the number of times the subroutine has been called. The state of the data structure itself becomes the "counter," and when the data structure is empty, the subroutine stops calling itself recursively.

To operationalize this third solution, one helper function and one helper subroutine are required, each of which is called by the primary MAKE_CHANGE_RECUR subroutine. Although this *prima facie* might appear to add complexity to the solution, keep in mind that each helper function can be reused for future, unrelated array operations.

The PUSH_ARRAY_NUM function, demonstrated in Program 7.14, "pushes" a new value to the array "stack." In other words, it adds a value to the right-most empty array element. When successful, PUSH_ARRAY_NUM returns 1, and when unsuccessful (that is, when a full array is encountered), it returns 0.

Program 7.14: Helper Function to "Push" Value into First Empty Array Element

```
* returns 1 for successful push, 0 for failure;
proc fcmp outlib=work.funcs.arrays;
   function push_array_num(arr[*], num);
      outargs arr;
      length rc 3;
      size = dim(arr);
      do i=1 to size;
         if missing(arr[i]) then do;
            arr[i] = num;
            return(1);
            end;
         end;
      return(0);
      endfunc;
quit;
```

The SHIFT_ARRAY_ELEMENTS_LEFT_NUM subroutine, demonstrated in Program 7.15, is the second helper, and it shifts each element of an array to the left. In other words, the left-most (first) element is deleted; the second and subsequent elements are each shifted to the left one position; and the right-most (final) element is initialized to missing.

Program 7.15: Helper Subroutine to Shift All Array Elements Left One Position

```
proc fcmp outlib=work.funcs.arrays;
   subroutine shift_array_elements_left_num(arr[*]);
      outargs arr;
      size = dim(arr);
      do i=1 to (size-1);
         arr[i] = arr[i+1];
         end;
      arr[size] = .;
      endsub;
quit;
```

With these helper functions defined, Program 7.16 defines the updated MAKE_CHANGE_ RECUR subroutine, which again makes change for some purchase. However, note that the subroutine definition contains neither counter nor loop, and that the STATIC statement does not initialize a counter variable. Rather, the Curr_val array is modified each time MAKE_CHANGE_RECUR is called. Thus, the first array element always represents the currency denomination being evaluated. When the first array element is missing, the subroutine stops calling itself because all possible denominations have been evaluated. In this design, the array itself provides both the recursive iteration as well as the condition that causes recursion to terminate.

Program 7.16: Defining a Recursive Function without a Counter

```
proc fcmp outlib=work.funcs.change;
   subroutine make_change_recur(price, paid, change, curr_val[*], curr_cnt[*]);
      outargs change, curr_val, curr_cnt;
      if missing(change) then change = paid - price;
      if ^missing(curr_val[1]) then do;
         quant = floor((paid - price)/curr_val[1]);
         rc = push_array_num(curr_cnt, quant);
         subtract = curr_val[1] * quant;
         call shift_array_elements_left_num(curr_val);
         call make_change_recur(price, paid - subtract, change, curr_val, curr_cnt);
         end;
      endsub;
quit;
```

To parse the MAKE_CHANGE_RECUR subroutine more closely, the CHANGE parameter is passed by reference via the OUTARGS statement and is initialized only the first time MAKE_CHANGE_ RECUR is called. Thus, when MAKE_CHANGE_RECUR is subsequently recursively called, the initial value of Change will persist:

```
outargs change, curr_val, curr_cnt;
if missing(change) then change = paid - price;
```

The second IF statement evaluates whether the Curr_val array is empty, and if so, terminates the recursive calling of the MAKE_CHANGE_RECUR subroutine:

```
if ^missing(curr_val[1]) then do;
```

The number of bills or coins of a particular denomination to be returned is initialized to the Quant variable. If the specific bill or coin denomination exceeds the amount of change remaining, then Quant is initialized to 0:

```
quant = floor((paid - price)/curr_val[1]);
```

The PUSH_ARRAY_NUM function pushes the Quant value to the first empty element within the Curr_cnt array. Although the return value (RC) is not used in this example, it could be used to evaluate programmatically whether PUSH_ARRAY_NUM was successful:

```
rc = push_array_num(curr_cnt, quant);
```

The Subtract variable is initialized to the amount of money to be subtracted from the total to be returned (Change). Thus, Subtract is subtracted from Paid each time the subroutine is recursively called:

```
subtract = curr_val[1] * quant;
```

The SHIFT_ARRAY_ELEMENTS_LEFT_NUM shifts all elements in the Curr_val array to the left. In other words, in each successive call of the MAKE_CHANGE_RECUR subroutine, a smaller denomination value is maintained in the left-most (first) array element, and only that element is evaluated against the remainder of the change to be returned to the customer:

```
call shift_array_elements_left_num(curr_val);
```

Finally, the MAKE_CHANGE_RECUR subroutine is recursively called. Note again that the PAID argument is modified *in situ* inside the subroutine call itself to deduct the amount of change rendered from the current bill or coin denomination:

```
call make_change_recur(price, paid - subtract, change, curr_val, curr_cnt);
```

Despite the added complexity of the helper function and helper subroutine that the refactored MAKE_CHANGE_RECUR subroutine requires, this solution nevertheless demonstrates that iteration—including recursive function design—does not necessitate explicit counter variables or counter parameters.

The DATA step in Program 7.17 calls the MAKE_CHANGE_RECUR subroutine and produces identical output to that of the DATA steps in Programs 7.9, 7.11, and 7.13.

Program 7.17: Calling the MAKE_CHANGE_RECUR Recursive Subroutine

```
data _null_;
   length change 8;
   array curr_val[9] 8 (20 10 5 1 .50 .25 .10 .05 .01);
   array curr_cnt[9] 8;
   format change curr_val1-curr_val9 dollar8.2;
   call missing(change);
   call make_change_recur(7.67, 10, change, curr_val, curr_cnt);
   put change=;
   * reinitialize the array to its initial values;
   i=0;
   do num=20, 10, 5, 1, .50, .25, .10, .05, .01;
      i+1;
      curr_val[i]=num;
      end;
   * print denomination values and quantity values;
   do i=1 to dim(curr_val);
      put curr_val[i] @10 curr_cnt[i] ;
      end;
run;
```

Note that this solution modifies the Curr_val array, which is passed by reference, in each recursive call of the subroutine. Thus, when MAKE_CHANGE_RECUR terminates, Curr_val will always comprise an array of empty elements. For this reason, and because the ARRAY statement cannot be used twice in one DATA step to initialize and reinitialize values, the additional DO loop is required to reinitialize Curr_val to its initial values. This is only required because the values of the array are printed using the PUT statement.

Memoization—No That's Not a Spelling Error!

Memoization describes a calculation or other operation that is run once, after which its output is saved for future use. Memoization aims to improve efficiency by eliminating the unnecessary, repeated calculation of predictable outputs given predictable inputs. It is most commonly implemented when resource-intensive operations can be distilled into their component inputs and outputs. The STATIC statement, demonstrated in the previous section, retains data from one function call to the next and can facilitate only the most basic memoization in which one value (like a variable) or one data structure (like an array) is retained.

For example, STATIC can initialize Y to 5. It can retain, increment, or modify this value from one function call to the next—and this can improve performance and efficiency. Memoization typically, however, requires a key-value pairing of input arguments to output values. For example, when an X argument passed to some function is 3, Y should be initialized to 5. This key-value pairing—of X (3) to Y (5)—is subsequently retained within an in-memory data structure like a hash object. Thereafter, in subsequent function calls, whenever X is evaluated to be 3, the function *remembers* that the corresponding Y value should be 5 and returns this value from memory rather than recalculating it. In so doing, memoization acts as a lookup table in which one or more keys are declared as parameters, and in which one or more associated values are returned—either through an in-memory lookup or, if the arguments are not found in the data structure, through calculation. Note that when memoization methods are used, calculation always occurs only once for each unique key.

The STATIC Statement Supporting Memoization

Within Chapter 5, Program 5.20 demonstrated the use of the RUN_MACRO function to facilitate a user-defined function that calculates the mean of a variable within some data set—that is, the mean across multiple observations. RUN_MACRO enables the mean to be calculated in real-time across observations, even as the SET statement maintains a read-only lock on the same data set within the DATA step. However, in many instances, once a calculation like a variable mean has been performed, this statistic should be saved for future reuse, rather than repeatedly recalculated.

Consider the requirement posed in Chapter 5 that spawned Programs 5.20 through 5.23—that the average (mean) of some variable across all observations should be calculated in real-time during a DATA step. For example, SAS practitioners might want to generate the mean of some variable dynamically and use this to impute missing values, thereby transforming missing values to the calculated mean of nonmissing values. A data set having no missing values for a particular variable would have no need to calculate the variable's average. Thus, logic should dictate that the average should be calculated *only* when the first missing value is encountered.

Program 7.18 generates a data set having 10 million observations in which the Num variable ranges from 0 to 999. For approximately one in 100,000 observations, which will total approximately 100 observations, Num will be subsequently set to missing. In a later DATA step, these missing values can be imputed to the mean that is calculated.

Program 7.18: Generating 10 Million Observations of Random Values
```
data some_data (drop=i);
   call streaminit(123);
   do i=1 to 10000000;
      num = int(1000*rand('uniform'));
      if int(100000*rand('uniform')) = 0 then num = .;
      output;
      end;
run;
```

Program 5.20 is redefined as Program 7.19 to demonstrate an initial solution that lacks the efficiency that memoization can provide. In other words, the COMPUTE_MEAN function will unnecessarily recalculate the mean each time it is called, rather than calculating only when the first missing value is encountered.

Program 7.19: Defining the COMPUTE_MEAN Function (without Memoization)

```
%macro compute_mean_macro();
%let dsn=%sysfunc(dequote(&dsn));
%let var=%sysfunc(dequote(&var));
proc sql noprint;
   select avg(&var) into: avg
      from &dsn;
quit;
%mend;


proc fcmp outlib=work.funcs.stats;
   function compute_mean(dsn $, var $);
      rc = run_macro('compute_mean_macro', dsn, var, avg);
      return(avg);
      endfunc;
quit;
```

Thus, the DATA step in Program 7.20 calls COMPUTE_MEAN for each of the 93 observations for which Num is missing. And during each of these 93 function calls, the average is needlessly recalculated, which requires repeatedly averaging all 10 million observations.

Program 7.20: Calling the COMPUTE_MEAN Function to Calculate Average Repeatedly

```
options fullstimer;
data some_data_imputed;
   set some_data;
   if missing(num) then num=compute_mean('some_data', 'num');
run;
```

With the FULLSTIMER SAS system option activated, the log demonstrates that these repeated calculations take approximately 36 seconds of real time and 34 seconds of CPU time:

```
NOTE: There were 10000000 observations read from the data set WORK.SOME_DATA.
NOTE: The data set WORK.SOME_DATA_IMPUTED has 10000000 observations and 1 variables.
NOTE: DATA statement used (Total process time):
      real time           35.87 seconds
      user cpu time       33.81 seconds
      system cpu time     2.00 seconds
```

The functionally equivalent COMPUTE_MEAN_MEMOIZ function calls the COMPUTE_MEAN_ MEMOIZ_MACRO macro function via RUN_MACRO, but now only calls the macro when the average is missing—that is, if the average has not yet been calculated. Thus, the first call to COMPUTE_MEAN_MEMOIZ within a DATA step causes the function to call the subordinate macro to perform the calculation. However, all subsequent calls to COMPUTE_MEAN_MEMOIZ will instead rely on the Avg variable, which STATIC retains from one function call to the next within a given DATA step. Program 7.21 demonstrates the COMPUTE_MEAN_MEMOIZ user-defined function and its subordinate COMPUTE_MEAN_MEMOIZ_MACRO macro.

Program 7.21: Defining the COMPUTE_MEAN_MEMOIZ Function (with Memoization)

```
%macro compute_mean_memoiz_macro();
%let dsn=%sysfunc(dequote(&dsn));
%let var=%sysfunc(dequote(&var));
proc sql noprint;
    select avg(&var) into: avg
        from &dsn;
quit;
%mend;


proc fcmp outlib=work.funcs.stats;
    function compute_mean_memoiz(dsn $, var $);
        static avg;
        if missing(avg) then rc = run_macro('compute_mean_memoiz_macro', dsn, var, avg);
        return(avg);
        endfunc;
quit;
```

The updated COMPUTE_MEAN_MEMOIZ function can be called using the DATA step shown in Program 7.22. Note that because COMPUTE_MEAN_MEMOIZ has been refactored with backward compatibility in mind, the parameters are identical between Programs 7.19 and 7.21. Thus, identical DATA steps are able to call these two functions in the same manner, which facilitates function reusability.

Program 7.22: Calling the COMPUTE_MEAN_MEMOIZ Function

```
options fullstimer;
data some_data_imputed;
    set some_data;
    if missing(num) then num=compute_mean_memoiz('some_data', 'num');
run;
```

When the DATA step executes, because the average of Num only needs to be calculated once, the log demonstrates the significant decrease in runtime and CPU time—both of which are less than one second!

```
NOTE: There were 10000000 observations read from the data set WORK.SOME_DATA.
NOTE: The data set WORK.SOME_DATA_IMPUTED has 10000000 observations and 1
variables.
NOTE: DATA statement used (Total process time):
      real time           0.97 seconds
      user cpu time       0.73 seconds
      system cpu time     0.17 seconds
```

As demonstrated, the STATIC statement successfully supports memoization in cases for which one value (or a set number of values) is being calculated and retained. In more complex instances, however, the data structure in which values are retained might need to scale infinitely. The next sections demonstrate more complex memoization, which can leverage arrays, hash objects, and dictionary objects.

The Hash Object Supporting Memoization

Hash objects are often used to support memoization because key-value pairs can be stored in which the key(s) represent the input criteria, and the associated value(s) represent the output. That is, when one or more arguments match hash key(s) in the hash object, the corresponding hash value(s) can be returned to the calling program, which foregoes having to redundantly perform the calculation that generated the value(s) in the first place. Conversely, when a hash lookup operation fails to find key(s), the calculation is performed, and its key(s) and associated value(s) are added to the hash object.

For example, consider the requirement to create a factoring function that computes whether some integer is a prime number or not—that is, a prime or a *composite* number. Composite numbers comprise two or more *factors* that, when multiplied, equal the composite. Thus, whereas 11 is a prime number, divisible only by itself and 1, 12 is a composite number, which comprises three factors—2, 2, and 3. In this first scenario, a character return value for the factoring function could denote either "prime," or enumerate the factors comprising the composite number.

The basic functionality of prime and factor determination is demonstrated in Program 7.23, in which the PRIME function is defined. Note that PRIME declares a single numeric parameter (NUM) and returns a character return value (Result) that denotes either "prime" or an enumeration of the composite number's factors. Also note that 1 is neither a prime nor a composite, so it is listed as "N/A" in the Result variable.

Program 7.23: Basic Prime/Composite Computation (without Memoization)

```
proc fcmp outlib=work.funcs.prime;
   function prime(num) $;
      length i max 8 result $100;
      result='';
      max=num;
      do i=1 to max by 1;
         if mod(max, i) = 0 then do;
            if i = num and num ^= 1 then result = 'prime';
            else if num = 1 then result = 'N/A';
            else if i ^= 1 then do;
               if missing(result) then result = 'composite: ' || strip(put(i,8.));
               else result = strip(result) || ', ' || strip(put(i,8.));
               max = max / i;
```

```
                i = 1;
              end;
          end;
        end;
      return(result);
      endfunc;
quit;
```

Yes, there are far more efficient algorithms to determine prime status and to calculate composite factors. However, this example requires a resource-intensive computation, so a bit of inefficiency is welcome, as it provides a greater contrast (and benefit) when memoization methods are embraced.

The DATA step in Program 7.24 calls the PRIME function and evaluates prime versus composite status for the numbers 1 through 6. An outer loop directs that each number should be evaluated by the function twice, which results in inefficiency, because memoization is not being used to retain previously calculated results.

Program 7.24: Calling the PRIME Function (without Memoization)
```
options cmplib=work.funcs;
data test;
   length x 8 x_factors $100;
   do i=1 to 2;
      do x=1 to 6;
         x_factors = prime(x);
         put x= x_factors=;
         end;
      end;
run;
```

When the DATA step executes, the numbers 1 through 6 are each evaluated twice:

```
x=1 x_factors=N/A
x=2 x_factors=prime
x=3 x_factors=prime
x=4 x_factors=composite: 2, 2
x=5 x_factors=prime
x=6 x_factors=composite: 2, 3
x=1 x_factors=N/A
x=2 x_factors=prime
x=3 x_factors=prime
x=4 x_factors=composite: 2, 2
x=5 x_factors=prime
x=6 x_factors=composite: 2, 3
```

The PRIME function fails to incorporate memoization, so if PRIME is called repeatedly to evaluate the prime or composite status of the same number, the calculation will be unnecessarily performed multiple times. With prime number evaluation being a resource-intensive process—especially as the numbers being evaluated grow in size—the addition of memoization can facilitate a far faster and more efficient solution.

Observing the SAS log, the X parameter can represent the hash object key, and the X_factors return value can represent the hash object lookup value. The PRIME_MEMOIZ function, defined in Program 7.25, operationalizes memoization using a hash object in which Num is declared as the key and Result is declared as the associated value.

Program 7.25: Prime/Composite Computation with Memoization

```
proc fcmp outlib=work.funcs.prime;
   function prime_memoiz(num) $;
      length i max 8 result $100;
      declare hash h();
      rc = h.defineKey('num');
      rc = h.defineData('result');
      rc = h.defineDone();
      if h.find() = 0 then return(result);
      result = '';
      max = num;
      do i=2 to max by 1;
         if mod(max, i) = 0 then do;
            if i = num and num ^= 1 then result = 'prime';
            else if num = 1 then result = 'N/A';
            else do;
               if missing(result) then result = 'composite: ' || strip(put(i,8.));
               else result = strip(result) || ', ' || strip(put(i,8.));
               max = max / i;
               i = 1;
               end;
            end;
         end;
      rc = h.add();
      return(result);
      endfunc;
quit;
```

The function declares the hash object (H) and relies on the hash FIND method to query the hash object for the key passed as the NUM argument. FIND returns a value of 0 if the key exists in the hash object, in which case the RETURN statement immediately returns the Result value retrieved from the hash object to the calling program.

However, if FIND fails to locate the key in the hash object, FIND returns a nonzero value, in which case Result is initialized to a missing value. Subsequent logic evaluates whether the number is a prime, and if not, enumerates its factors. Finally, the hash ADD method adds this new key-value pair (the number, as well as its associated prime status or enumerated factors) to the hash object.

The DATA steps, shown in Program 7.26, first call PRIME and subsequently call PRIME_MEMOIZ to demonstrate the clear performance advantages of the latter. Note that each DATA step evaluates each number (between 1 and 50,000) five times by calling the respective user-defined function repeatedly. When PRIME is called, it must calculate and recalculate prime/composite status each time a number is encountered because it fails to remember results from previous function calls. However, PRIME_MEMOIZ only calculates prime/composite status once per unique number, after which is can subsequently retrieve the value from the in-memory hash object.

Program 7.26: Demonstrating Memoization Performance Superiority in Factorization

```
data no_memoiz (drop=i);
   length x 8 x_factors $100;
   do i=1 to 5;
      do x=1 to 50000;
         x_factors = prime(x);
         output;
         end;
      end;
run;

data memoiz (drop=i);
   length x 8 x_factors $100;
   do i=1 to 5;
      do x=1 to 50000;
         x_factors = prime_memoiz(x);
         output;
         end;
      end;
run;
```

The log for both DATA steps is demonstrated, which shows the clear performance advantages of memoization, which requires one-fifth the time as the inefficient PRIME function:

```
NOTE: The data set WORK.NO_MEMOIZ has 250000 observations and 3 variables.
NOTE: DATA statement used (Total process time):
      real time            1:21.75
      user cpu time        1:21.68
      system cpu time      0.06 seconds
      memory               1502.75k
      OS Memory            25080.00k

NOTE: The data set WORK.MEMOIZ has 250000 observations and 3 variables.
NOTE: DATA statement used (Total process time):
      real time            16.18 seconds
      user cpu time        16.17 seconds
      system cpu time      0.09 seconds
      memory               9299.75k
      OS Memory            35864.00k
```

Thus, because PRIME unnecessarily performs five times the work, it takes five times longer than PRIME_MEMOIZ.

The hash object can map one or more keys to one or more values, and keys and values can comprise a mix of character or numeric data types. However, what if you instead want to return a numeric array that enumerates all factors for composite data and an empty array to represent prime numbers? A hash object cannot hold an array, but a dictionary object can, as demonstrated in the next section.

The Dictionary Object Supporting Memoization

The SAS dictionary object is the second built-in data structure (in addition to the hash object) that can be leveraged within the FCMP procedure to facilitate in-memory lookup operations. Dictionary objects are prevalent in many other languages and are typically referred to as *dictionaries*. Within SAS nomenclature, however, *dictionary* more commonly refers to a user-defined *data dictionary* or to the SAS built-in *dictionary tables* that are created automatically within the read-only DICTIONARY library. Thus, in part because the FCMP dictionary object is eclipsed by these far more prevalent "dictionaries" (within SAS nomenclature, documentation, and other publications), and in part because the dictionary object is a relative newcomer to the FCMP procedure's syntax, the dictionary object is not widely used by SAS practitioners.

Despite its unfortunate uncommonness, the dictionary object can deliver functionality and flexibility not otherwise found within the FCMP procedure. For example, whereas a hash object (defined in the FCMP procedure) requires that all key variables and data variables be declared as character literals, dictionary key-value pairs can be dynamically declared. Thus, a dictionary can be flexibly designed to maintain mutable variables, variable names, and variable data types.

Moreover, dictionary key-value pairs can maintain not only character and numeric data types— like a hash object—but also arrays, hash objects, and even other dictionaries! For example, given the ability of a dictionary object to maintain key-associated arrays, the dictionary is the preferred—nay, *only*—method to achieve the desired functionality described in the previous section in which a user-defined function should return an array containing the factorization of some number.

The revised subroutine is demonstrated in Program 7.27 and is decomposed and discussed later in this section. For now, it is important to understand only that the dictionary object facilitates memoization through in-memory lookup operations.

Program 7.27: Prime/Composite Computation with Dictionary Memoization

```
proc fcmp outlib=work.funcs.prime;
   subroutine prime_dict_memoiz(num, arr_factors[*]);
      outargs arr_factors;
      length i j max num_items 8;
      declare dictionary d;
```

```
            data_type = d.describe(is_arr, num);
            file log;                                    * FOR DEMONSTRATION ONLY *;
            put data_type= is_arr=;                      * FOR DEMONSTRATION ONLY *;
            if data_type = 1 and is_arr = 1 then arr_factors = d[num];
            else do;
                put 'calculating' num;                   * FOR DEMONSTRATION ONLY *;
                type = '';
                max = num;
                j = 0;
                do i=2 to max by 1;
                    if mod(max, i) = 0 and i ^= num then do;
                        j+1;
                        arr_factors[j] = i;
                        max = max / i;
                        i = 1;
                        end;
                    end;
                rc = d.clone(arr_factors, num);
                end;
            endsub;
quit;
```

The DATA step in Program 7.28 generates the numbers to be evaluated, after which the FCMP procedure calls the PRIME_DICT_MEMOIZ subroutine. Note that due to limitations of the dictionary component object, PRIME_DICT_MEMOIZ should not be called from the DATA step and should instead be called from the FCMP procedure, as demonstrated.

Program 7.28: Generating Sample Data and Calling PRIME_DICT_MEMOIZ

```
data numbers (drop=i);
    length x 8;
    do i=1 to 2;
        do x=1 to 6;
            output;
            end;
        end;
run;

proc fcmp data=numbers out=numbers_calculated;
    drop i;
    array factors[8];
    do i=1 to 8;
        factors[i] = .;
        end;
    call prime_dict_memoiz(x, factors);
run;
```

The log demonstrates that for the first six observations, PRIME_DICT_MEMOIZ was forced to calculate whether each number (ranging 1 one to 6) is a prime or a composite. However, for the seventh through twelfth observations, which represent duplicate numbers already saved in the dictionary object, this calculation is not required. PRIME_DICT_MEMOIZ instead returns the associated array maintained within the dictionary object:

```
data_type=. is_arr=.
calculating 1
data_type=. is_arr=.
calculating 2
data_type=. is_arr=.
calculating 3
data_type=. is_arr=.
calculating 4
data_type=. is_arr=.
calculating 5
data_type=. is_arr=.
calculating 6
data_type=1 is_arr=1
data_type=1 is_arr=1
data_type=1 is_arr=1
data_type=1 is_arr=1
data_type=1 is_arr=1
data_type=1 is_arr=1
NOTE: There were 12 observations read from the data set WORK.NUMBERS.
NOTE: The data set WORK.NUMBERS_CALCULATED has 12 observations and 9
variables.
```

Within Program 7.23, the FCMP statement initiates the FCMP procedure, after which the SUBROUTINE statement names the subroutine (PRIME_DICT_MEMOIZ) and declares the NUM numeric parameter and ARR_FACTORS numeric array parameter:

```
proc fcmp outlib=work.funcs.prime;
   subroutine prime_dict_memoiz(num, arr_factors[*]);
```

Whenever a function needs to modify an array and make that array available to the calling program, the array must be declared as a parameter, and the OUTARGS statement must further declare the array as being passed by reference—not value:

```
outargs arr_factors;
```

The LENGTH statement is optional here, but it helps convey to the user the numeric variables that will be used to generate the solution:

```
length i j max num_items 8;
```

Similar to a hash object, a dictionary object is declared using the DECLARE statement, which both names and instantiates the dictionary data structure:

```
declare dictionary d;
```

The DESCRIBE method initializes a variable (Data_type) to the data type code of the data associated with the particular key (Num) and initializes a variable (Is_arr) to the array indicator code:

```
data_type=d.describe(is_arr, num);
```

Data type codes and array indicator codes are described fully in SAS FCMP documentation. As indicated in the log, a missing data type represents that the key could not be found in the dictionary, whereas a data type of 1 represents both that the key was found and that the associated data type is *double*, which corresponds to numeric data within the DATA step. However, the data type code represents only the data type, and not whether the data structure is a *scalar* (a single value) or an array.

Thus, the array indicator code also should be examined. A missing array indicator code represents that the key could not be found in the dictionary, a code of 0 represents that the key-associated value is not an array, and a code of 1 represents that the key-associated value is an array. Thus, as demonstrated previously in the log, both the data type code and the array indicator code are missing when the first six observations are evaluated (whose keys are not yet maintained in the dictionary), and both the data type code and array indicator code are 1 when the keys are found, and their associated values are evaluated to be numeric arrays.

The IF statement evaluates whether the key and its associated array are found, and if so, initializes the Arr_factors numeric array to the key-associated array within the dictionary. This statement performs the memoization by avoiding resource-intensive calculations that have already been performed:

```
if data_type = 1 and is_arr = 1 then arr_factors = d[num];
```

The next several statements are identical to previous versions, and they evaluate whether the number is a prime, and if not, calculate the factorization of the number:

```
type = '';
max = num;
j = 0;
   do i=2 to max by 1;
   if mod(max, i) = 0 and i ^= num then do;
      j+1;
      arr_factors[j] = i;
      max = max / i;
      i = 1;
      end;
   end;
```

At this point, the Arr_factors array will remain empty if the number was evaluated to be a prime, and if not, will contain values representing each factor of the composite. For example, when six (a composite number) is evaluated, Arr_factors1 will be initialized to 2 and Arr_factors2 will be initialized to 3, representing the factorization of six. However, when five (a prime number) is evaluated, all elements of the Arr_factors array will remain empty.

Finally, the CLONE method stores the key and key-associated numeric array—Num and Arr_factors, respectively—within the dictionary:

```
rc = d.clone(arr_factors, num);
```

The CLONE method directs that the key-value pair should be stored *by value* as opposed to *by reference* and is fully described in SAS documentation.

The FCMP procedure in Program 7.28 generates the Numbers_calculated data set, the first six observations of which are printed by the DATA step shown in Program 7.29.

Program 7.29: Examining the Array Data Structure Returned by PRIME_DICT_MEMOIZ
```
data _null_;
   set numbers_calculated (obs=6);
   put x= factors1= factors2= factors3=;
run;
```

The log demonstrates that primes (and the number 1) are represented by an empty array, whereas the factors of composite numbers fill array elements from left to right:

```
x=1 factors1=. factors2=. factors3=.
x=2 factors1=. factors2=. factors3=.
x=3 factors1=. factors2=. factors3=.
x=4 factors1=2 factors2=2 factors3=.
x=5 factors1=. factors2=. factors3=.
x=6 factors1=2 factors2=3 factors3=.
```

The FCMP procedure in Program 7.28 declares the Factors array to have eight elements, which can safely accommodate factoring numbers that have no more than eight factors (that is, numbers lower than 512). Thus, as larger numbers need to be factored, correspondingly larger arrays must be declared in which to maintain their additional factors.

Finally, note that the memoization demonstrated across these sections is local only—that is, the in-memory STATIC variable, hash object, or dictionary object is initialized once during the DATA step, and when the DATA step terminates, that in-memory data structure is no longer available. More advanced methods could be engineered within the FCMP procedure to effectively retain values across DATA steps by saving hash objects or dictionary objects to disk immediately prior to DATA step termination. However, these solutions lie beyond the scope of this text.

Conclusion

This chapter demonstrated two software design patterns: recursion and memoization. Within the FCMP procedure, recursion is achieved by defining functions or subroutines that call themselves.

DO loops and other iterative methods can often be converted to recursive functions. In some instances, recursion can simplify syntax (for example, by facilitating the removal of counter variables and other control data). However, in other cases, recursion can complicate function design and force previously hidden variables into sight by requiring that they be declared as parameters. In the end, SAS practitioners will need to evaluate when and how recursion can yield greater functionality or performance.

This chapter also demonstrated memoization, in which the results from resource-intensive computations are stored for future reuse and retrieval. Memoization is commonly used when a function yields predictable output given predictable input and when those input-output pairings can be stored within in-memory data structures, such as the hash object or dictionary object. This chapter also introduced the STATIC statement, which saves one or more variables across subsequent function calls. STATIC can facilitate simpler memoization techniques where only one or a few variables must be maintained, rather than entire data structures.

Chapter 8: Python Component Object

The Python language has become one of the most versatile, widely distributed programming languages in the world. Can I say that in a SAS book? Yes! Because the SAS Institute is not only aware of this success—they are capitalizing on it, as they continue their commitment to platform and software interoperability. The FCMP procedure helps facilitate the integration of Python and the SAS application through the Python Component Object, which enables Python functions to be executed inside user-defined SAS functions and subroutines.

Starting in SAS 9.4M6, the Python Component Object has supported the native execution of Python code inside the SAS application; that is, Python code that is run not by the SAS application, but rather by a locally installed Python interpreter. This functionality flexibly enables developers to run user-defined Python functions and select their preferred Python version, as well as preferred Python libraries and packages.

The Python Component Object supports two primary methods to import Python code into an object that is subsequently run in Python. Python code can be defined or created inside the FCMP procedure itself, or it can be defined inside an external program file that is called by the FCMP procedure. Both approaches effectively create a user-defined FCMP function that operates as a wrapper by encapsulating the inner Python function. Arguments passed to the user-defined FMCP function during invocation can subsequently be passed to the derivative Python function, allowing Python to provide the base functionality, after which the FCMP function returns values or other results to the calling program.

The Python Component Object is especially exciting because it allows Python developers to continue to develop within the integrated development environment (IDE) of their choosing (such as Spyder, Visual Studio Code, or old-school IDLE) and to take advantage of the inherent functionality of Python-specific IDEs. These benefits include automatic code highlighting, linting (static code analysis), autocorrection, and debugging, just to name a few familiar capabilities. Neither SAS developers nor Python developers are required to compromise in development best practices; they can all enjoy their comfortable IDEs, and in the end, the Python Component Object joins the collective modules into a cohesive software product.

All examples in this chapter are run on Python 3.11.5. Note that as Python syntax is case sensitive, within the text, Python variables, objects, functions, and other components are highlighted in monospaced font. For example, later in the chapter, the GET_DISTANCE SAS function and the `get_distance` Python function are introduced. Although this chapter does not aim to introduce the Python language or its syntax, high-level concepts and objectives convey the basic functionality of the user-defined Python functions that are demonstrated.

The first few examples demonstrate methods to call a Python function from the FCMP procedure—no glitz, no glamour, just straightforward functionality. However, the final example comprises two-thirds of the chapter and demonstrates a SAS-Python hybrid solution that geocodes street addresses, calculates walking and driving distances, and dynamically builds a keyhole markup language (KML) file that can be uploaded into Google Maps or Google Earth. So, if you stick around until the end, you'll see some "wow" factor that depicts why you would want to call existing Python functions, rather than needlessly re-creating them in the SAS language.

Special thanks to Matthew Slaughter and Isaiah Lankham for their incalculable contributions— through papers, posters, and trainings—to the nexus of SAS and Python, in describing not only the Python Component Object demonstrated in this chapter, but also the PYTHON SAS procedure and the SASPy open-source Python package. Their work was invaluable in writing this chapter, and it will be invaluable to you as you integrate Python into your SAS world. And yes, if that name sounds familiar, Matt's mother is one half of the legendary Susan Slaughter and Lora Delwiche duo who authored all nineteen editions of *The Little SAS® Book*! #legacy

Requirements and Setup

The Python Component Object relies on a locally installed Python interpreter (the Python.exe executable) and the declaration of two environment variables that instruct the SAS application how to connect SAS and Python. Both environment variables must be initialized prior to starting the SAS application.

The first environment variable (MAS_M2PATH) must be set to the location of the mas2py.py file, which is included as part of the SAS installation. For example, the default file location for the SAS 9.4 Windows installation is:

```
MAS_M2PATH = C:\Program Files\SASHome\SASFoundation\9.4\tkmas\sasmisc\
mas2py.py
```

The second environment variable (MAS_PYPATH) instructs SAS where to find the Python.exe executable:

```
MAS_PYPATH = C:\Users\papacito\AppData\Local\Programs\Python\Python311\
python.exe
```

These requirements are detailed in the SAS documentation "Configuring SAS to Run the Python Language" (SAS Institute Inc. 2023).

Defining a Python Function inside a Python Program File

The ideal environment to write Python functions—and Python software in general—is inside any of the myriad IDEs that support the Python language. Benefits include real-time development tools such as autocorrect, autocomplete, color-coded text highlighting, and static code analysis. Additional code analysis tools, debugging tools, and stepping (in which software executes incrementally, line by line) are common features of all leading IDE applications. IDEs represent an effective, efficient, cohesive platform in which to write, debug, test, and execute Python software; however, although typically inadvisable, Python programs can be written in the SAS application.

Chapter 1 began with a user-defined function, as hackneyed as it is ubiquitous, that converts Fahrenheit temperatures to Celsius. The FAHR_TO_CEL function is reprised in Program 8.1. Its straightforward functionality inputs a Fahrenheit temperature and outputs the equivalent Celsius temperature.

Program 8.1: Fahrenheit-to-Celsius (FAHR_TO_CEL) User-Defined Function
```
proc fcmp outlib=work.funcs.num;
   function fahr_to_cel(f);
      c = (f - 32) * (5 / 9);
      return(c);
      endfunc;
quit;
```

The function's functionality—that is, all the bits that perform the conversion—can be operationalized using Python. Program 8.2 defines the functionally equivalent `fahr_to_cel` Python function. Note that Python comments are prefaced with a number sign (octothorpe), and Python statements are not terminated with a semicolon.

Program 8.2: Defining the Python fahr_to_cel Function
```
# saved as c:\sas\fahr_to_cel.py
def fahr_to_cel(f):
    "Output: f_key"
    c = (f - 32) * (5 / 9)
    return c
```

The `def` statement names and defines a function. Function parameters are declared parenthetically, with multiple parameters delimited by commas. A terminal colon ends the declaration. Here, the `fahr_to_cel` function is defined, which declares a single parameter (`f`):

```
def fahr_to_cel(f):
```

The "output string" follows, and it is a SAS convention that is required for Python functions that are called via the FCMP procedure. The statement must follow the `def` statement, be enclosed in double quotation marks, and include "Output:" followed by a comma-delimited list of case-sensitive output keys:

```
"Output: f_key"
```

Within the SAS application, Python functions generate a tuple of return values, so output keys provide the mechanism through which multiple return values can be differentiated and retrieved from a function's output. The output tuple is subsequently assigned to a dictionary—the RESULTS dictionary, by default. The dictionary elements can subsequently be extracted by referencing the respective dictionary key values.

The conversion expression follows the output string and initializes the return value (c):

```
c = (f - 32) * (5 / 9)
```

Finally, the return statement denotes the return value (c) to be returned to the FCMP procedure:

```
return c
```

For example, the world-record high temperature, recorded at Death Valley's Furnace Creek on July 10, 1913, is 134°F (US National Park Service 2023). The following Python code can be run by Python to convert this temperature to the equivalent 56.67°C:

```
death_valley_high = 134
print(fahr_to_cel(death_valley_high))
```

With this baseline Python function built, the next sections demonstrate how to redefine this function inside the FCMP procedure, and how to call this function from a user-defined FCMP function.

Importing a Python Program File in the FCMP Procedure

Although the fahr_to_cel function demonstrates simple, concise functionality—converting from Fahrenheit to Celsius—the complexity of other functions can surpass many screens of text, and especially in these cases, software reuse will always be preferred to software reproduction. Because the fahr_to_cel function has already been built in Python and saved to a Python program file, there is no need to re-create it or its functionality within SAS. Doing so would be time-consuming and needlessly risk the introduction of errors.

Two FCMP techniques—the INFILE method and the SUBMIT INTO statement—facilitate the reuse of Python functions where those functions are defined within Python program files. *Prima facie*, these techniques might appear identical, as they each enable the DATA step to call a user-defined

FCMP function, which in turn executes a Python function natively by the Python interpreter. However, their functionality and flexibility do differ, and those differences must be understood so that the correct reuse technique can be selected.

The INFILE method retains only the path and filename of a Python program file. Thus, when the FCMP function is compiled, it does not contain static Python code, but rather contains a reference to the Python function that will be dynamically executed. This technique maximizes flexibility because updates to that Python program file will be reflected when the FCMP function executes and calls the Python function. However, note the risk that unintended or accidental changes to that Python program file, too, will be absorbed each time the FCMP function is executed.

The INFILE method is especially useful during development, testing, and debugging because changes made on the fly within a Python program file will be immediately incorporated into the FCMP function (calling Python functions in the program file) as soon as the Python program is saved and the FCMP function is recompiled. On the other hand, this real-time, recurring Python compilation does incur higher resource utilization, as compared to the SUBMIT INTO statement.

The SUBMIT INTO statement, on the other hand, is the less flexible (although more stable and less risky) technique to reuse Python functions saved in Python program files. SUBMIT INTO is stable because it imports the body of the Python program file into a Python Component Object. Thus, whereas INFILE maintains only a *reference* linked to a Python program file, SUBMIT INTO maintains the *full text* of the program file itself. And where INFILE requires that a program file is imported at each FCMP *execution*, SUBMIT INTO instead imports the program only during FCMP *compilation*. Thus, SUBMIT INTO supports a development paradigm in which the external Python program file is frozen in time at FCMP compilation. Even if that program file is subsequently modified, its representation inside FCMP will remain stable—at least until the next compilation of the FCMP function. These two techniques that facilitate Python program reuse are demonstrated in the next two sections.

Software modularity is a primary benefit of leveraging these techniques, as developers can write and maintain Python functions within an IDE and choose to run them natively within the IDE or via the FCMP procedure. When a Python function needs to be updated, possibly to expand its functionality or to improve its performance, this maintenance can be performed only on the Python code without risk to the FCMP wrapper or larger SAS program that might call the Python function.

Using the INFILE Method to Import a Python Program File

The FCMP procedure in Program 8.3 defines the F_TO_C function, in which the Fahr_to_cel.py program file is ingested, which contains the `fahr_to_cel` Python function. The INFILE method saves a reference to this program file inside the Python Component Object (PY), after which the Python function can be called from the FCMP function. Note that the path and filename passed by INFILE are not case sensitive, whereas the function name passed by CALL (`fahr_to_cel`) and the RESULTS dictionary key (`f_key`) are both case sensitive.

Program 8.3: Importing a Python Program File into an FCMP Function

```
proc fcmp outlib = work.funcs.py;
   function f_to_c(fahr);
      declare object py(python);
      rc = py.infile("c:\sas\fahr_to_cel.py");
      rc = py.publish();
      rc = py.call("fahr_to_cel", fahr);
      cel = py.results["f_key"];
      return(cel);
      endfunc;
quit;
```

The DECLARE OBJECT statement names and instantiates a Python object (PY), which is denoted by the reserved keyword PYTHON:

```
      declare object py(python);
```

The INFILE method imports a Python program file into a Python Component Object, enabling Python functions defined within the program file to be called from the FCMP procedure:

```
      rc = py.infile("c:\sas\fahr_to_cel.py");
```

Note that the INFILE argument must include the location and name of the Python program file being imported, and the argument must be enclosed in double quotation marks.

The PUBLISH method submits all Python code contained in a Python object to the Python interpreter. It is required after a Python object has been instantiated and prior to calling any functions contained inside the object:

```
      rc = py.publish();
```

The CALL method invokes a Python function that has been both defined in (or imported into) a Python object and published to the Python interpreter:

```
      rc = py.call("fahr_to_cel", fahr);
```

The first argument of the CALL method is required, case sensitive, enclosed in double quotation marks, and specifies the name of the Python function that is being invoked. This Python function must be defined within the Python object that is being called. For example, the previous statement requires that the fahr_to_cel function is contained within the Python object (PY) and that PY has been published.

Subsequent (optional) arguments of the CALL method are comma delimited and specify values to be passed to the Python function. These arguments must correspond to parameters declared within the Python function. For example, the previous CALL method passes the SAS variable Fahr to the numeric parameter (f) declared within the fahr_to_cel Python function.

The RESULTS dictionary stores and retrieves a return value from a Python function. More precisely, RESULTS specifies a case-sensitive dictionary key that must be enclosed within double quotation marks and retrieves the associated value from the SAS Results dictionary:

```
cel = py.results["f_key"];
```

Here, the key (`f_key`) must correspond to the output string (`f_key`) defined inside the `fahr_to_cel` Python function. Where the output string defines multiple keys within the Python function, separate implementations of the RESULTS dictionary must be used to retrieve each individual return value.

Also note that the optional first argument of the CALL method (not yet demonstrated) names a SAS dictionary in which one or more return values from a Python function are to be saved. However, when this optional argument is omitted, return values are instead saved to the default RESULTS dictionary object. Thus, in this example, the `fahr_to_cel` Python function specifies that the return value (`c`) should be saved to the RESULTS dictionary value corresponding to the "`f_key`" key.

Finally, with the Cel variable initialized to the return value of the `fahr_to_cel` Python function, the RETURN statement returns Cel to the calling program that invoked the F_TO_C FCMP function:

```
return(cel);
```

Thus, whenever the INFILE method is used to import one or more Python programs, the FCMP function operates as a wrapper for the Python function. Consider the DATA step in Program 8.4 in which the F_TO_C FCMP function is called again to convert 134° F.

Program 8.4: Calling the F_TO_C FCMP Function to Call the fahr_to_cel Python Function

```
options cmplib = work.funcs;

data temp;
   length temp_f temp_c 8;
   temp_f = 134;
   temp_c = f_to_c(temp_f);
   put temp_f= temp_c=;
run;
```

The DATA step executes and prints the converted temperature (56.67°C) to the log. To recap, the F_TO_C invocation passes 134 to the F_TO_C function's parameter (FAHR), after which the CALL method passes 134 to the `fahr_to_cel` function's parameter (`f`). The Python interpreter natively converts the Fahrenheit value to Celsius inside the `fahr_to_cel` Python function, after which the return value (`c`) is returned to the F_TO_C function, after which the return value (Cel) is returned to the DATA step, where Temp_c is initialized to 56.67°C. Easy as pie!

Using the SUBMIT INTO Statement to Import a Python Program File

The SUBMIT INTO statement imports Python code into a Python Component Object and has two constructions. When the Python object named by SUBMIT INTO optionally specifies a path and filename, the functions inside that Python program file are imported into the Python object when the FCMP procedure is compiled:

```
submit into py("c:\sas\fahr_to_cel.py");
```

Alternatively, when the optional argument is omitted, Python functions can be defined directly inside the FCMP procedure:

```
submit into py;
```

The first usage of SUBMIT INTO is demonstrated in Program 8.5, in which the SUBMIT INTO statement imports the `fahr_to_cel` Python function.

Program 8.5: Importing a Python Program File into an FCMP Function
```
proc fcmp outlib = work.funcs.py;
   function f_to_c(fahr);
      declare object py(python);
      submit into py("c:\sas\fahr_to_cel.py");
      rc = py.publish();
      rc = py.call("fahr_to_cel",fahr);
      cel = py.results["f_key"];
      return(cel);
      endfunc;
quit;
```

The syntax in Program 8.5 differs from that of Program 8.3 only in that the SUBMIT INTO statement is used to import the Python program file rather than the INFILE method. Note again that during FCMP compilation, whereas the INFILE method imports only a reference to the filename, SUBMIT INTO imports the entire Python program file.

The DATA step in Program 8.6 calls the F_TO_C function to convert Death Valley's record high temperature from Fahrenheit to Celsius.

Program 8.6: Calling the F_TO_C FCMP Function to Call the fahr_to_cel Python Function
```
data temp;
   length temp_f temp_c 8;
   temp_f = 134;
   temp_c = f_to_c(temp_f);
   put temp_f= temp_c=;
run;
```

The results of Program 8.6 are identical to those of Program 8.4. The next section demonstrates the second usage of the SUBMIT INTO statement in which the optional argument that specifies a filename is omitted.

Defining a Python Function inside the FCMP Procedure

Only in rare instances should Python software—including Python functions—be written outside of a Python-specific IDE. To do so is pure folly. However, for those instances in which a Python function needs to be dynamically defined inside SAS itself, the SUBMIT INTO statement facilitates the dynamic import of Python functions into a Python object. The recognizable limitation, referenced previously, is that this method robs the Python developer of the rich experience, benefits, and best practice that IDE development provides.

For a third time, the F_TO_C FCMP function is defined and calls the `fahr_to_cel` Python function. However, in Program 8.7, the Python function is maintained not within an external Python program file but rather inside the FCMP procedure itself. That is, the entire `fahr_to_cel` Python function can be copied into the definition of the F_TO_C FCMP function. Program 8.7 demonstrates the F_TO_C FCMP function, in which the `fahr_to_cel` Python function is both defined and called.

Program 8.7: Defining a Python Function Inside an FCMP Function
```
proc fcmp outlib = work.funcs.py;
   function f_to_c(fahr);
      declare object py(python);
      submit into py;
         def fahr_to_cel(f):
            "Output: f_key"
            c = (f - 32) * (5 / 9)
            return c
         endsubmit;
      rc = py.publish();
      rc = py.call("fahr_to_cel", fahr);
      cel = py.results["f_key"];
      return(cel);
      endfunc;
quit;
```

The DECLARE statement instantiates the Python Component Object (PY):

```
      declare object py(python);
```

The SUBMIT INTO statement inserts Python code into a Python object. Because the optional argument is omitted, all code must be inserted within the *SUBMIT block*—that is, between the SUBMIT INTO and ENDSUBMIT statements:

```
      submit into py;
```

The `fahr_to_cel` function, demonstrated in Program 8.2, can be copied verbatim into the body of the SUBMIT block, including the required output string, which must immediately follow the `def` statement:

```
def fahr_to_cel(f):
    "Output: results_key"
    c = (f - 32) * (5 / 9)
    return c
```

The ENDSUBMIT statement terminates the SUBMIT block and signifies the end of Python code that has been included:

```
endsubmit;
```

The PUBLISH method, CALL method, and RESULTS dictionary key lookup are identical to previous examples. They collectively call the `fahr_to_cel` Python function and initialize its return value to a SAS variable (Cel):

```
rc = py.publish();
rc = py.call("fahr_to_cel", fahr);
cel = py.results["f_key"];
```

Thereafter, Cel is returned to the calling program, the function ends, and the FCMP procedure terminates:

```
    return(cel);
    endfunc;
quit;
```

For a third time, the DATA step in Program 8.8 is executed, and the F_TO_C function is called to convert Fahrenheit to Celsius.

Program 8.8: Calling the F_TO_C FCMP Function to Call the fahr_to_cel Python Function

```
data temp;
    length temp_f temp_c 8;
    temp_f = 134;
    temp_c = f_to_c(temp_f);
    put temp_f= temp_c=;
run;
```

The result of Program 8.8 is identical to that of Programs 8.4 and 8.6. Thus, the only difference is the manner in which the `fahr_to_cel` Python function is defined. In the case of Program 8.7, its definition occurs inside the FCMP procedure. However, for the vast majority of use cases, Python functions should be written inside Python-specific IDEs, and not the SAS application, as is demonstrated throughout the remainder of this chapter.

Creating KML Files Using PROC FCMP and Python Geocoding

This chapter introduced the Python Component Object and demonstrated three functionally equivalent methods that call a Python function to convert Fahrenheit values to Celsius. It would be wholly inexcusable, however, to leave readers with the perception that the FCMP procedure only facilitates elementary calculations that you can do in your head. In fact, one of the most practical applications of the Python Component Object is the need to run a Python program whose complexity favors maintaining the functionality in Python—rather than converting the code to SAS. The remainder of this chapter introduces a real-world scenario in which existing user-defined Python functions are refactored so that they can be called via the FCMP procedure, thus preventing the unnecessary reprogramming of the functionality in SAS.

Scenario Setup, Requirements, and Data Ingestion

You're helping organize SAS Innovate 2024, held in exhilarating Las Vegas, and billed as the preeminent SAS user conference of the year. Prior to the conference, you want to solicit input from attendees about their favorite Las Vegas restaurants and distribute the results to all attendees to provide some user-supplied recommendations. Realizing that restaurant proximity is often an important factor in grub selection, you want to provide attendees with not only the restaurant address but also its distance from the Aria Resort and Casino, where SAS Innovate is being held. Finally, to render these data as useful as possible, you want to visualize responses in a keyhole markup language (KML) file, which attendees can download from the conference website and overlay onto their Google Maps or Google Earth mobile apps.

Some sample restaurant data, similar to those supplied by attendees, are maintained in a comma-separated values (CSV) file (c:\sas\restaurants.csv). It contains ten recommendations and comprises two variables—Restaurant and Addy:

```
restaurant,addy
Gordon Ramsay Steak,"3655 S Las Vegas Blvd, Las Vegas, NV 89109"
Gordon Ramsay Hell's Kitchen,"3570 Las Vegas Blvd S, Las Vegas, NV 89109"
Gordon Ramsay Burger,"3667 S Las Vegas Blvd, Las Vegas, NV 89109"
Gordon Ramsay Fish and Chips,"3545 S Las Vegas Blvd, Las Vegas, NV 89109"
Ramsay's Kitchen,"3475 S Las Vegas Blvd, Las Vegas, NV 89109"
Eiffel Tower Restaurant,"3655 S Las Vegas Blvd, Las Vegas, NV 89109"
Margaritaville,"3555 S Las Vegas Blvd, Las Vegas, NV 89109"
Heart Attack Grill,"450 E Fremont St #130, Las Vegas, NV 89101"
Gordon Ramsay Hell's Kitchen,"3570 Las Vegas Blvd S, Las Vegas, NV 89109"
Gordon Ramsay Burger,"3667 S Las Vegas Blvd, Las Vegas, NV 89109"
```

Note the overwhelming popularity of Gordon Ramsay is already highlighted, as Hell's Kitchen is duplicated in observations two and nine, and Gordon Ramsay Burger, in observations three and ten. Moreover, when thousands of attendees have reported their favorite restaurants, dozens if not hundreds of duplicate entries will exist.

The first step is to ingest the Restaurants file into a SAS data set. The &LOC macro variable defines the path; the &FIL macro variable defines the filename; and the &PY_FIL macro variable defines the Python program file in which all Python functions will be saved:

```
%let loc=c:\sas\;
%let fil=restaurants.csv;
%let py_fil=las_vegas_gis.py;
```

A DATA step next reads the CSV file to create the Restaurants data set, which contains ten observations:

```
data restaurants;
    infile "&loc&fil" dsd delimiter=',' firstobs=2;
    length restaurant $50 addy $100;
    input restaurant $ addy $;
run;
```

The software requirements can be functionally decomposed and modularized into discrete functions. After the Restaurants data have been ingested, the first function should transform each address into its associated latitude and longitude coordinates—a process known as *geocoding*. The geocoding function can generate the coordinates for the Aria hotel, the origin, and for each of the restaurants, the respective destinations.

Thereafter, a second function is conceptualized that accepts origin and destination coordinates and calculates the distance between the hotel and each restaurant. Realizing some attendees will walk while others will drive or take ride sharing (for example, a taxi, Uber, or Lyft), you should calculate both walking and driving distances.

Finally, a third module should dynamically build a KML file from the transformed data, which will map the coordinates for each restaurant, as well as display the walking and driving distances to each restaurant. Because you're anticipating that many attendees will select the same restaurants, a voting score should denote in the KML how many people recommended each restaurant.

As if by a stroke of luck, you happen to have a former U.S. Navy geospatial analyst (that is, a *geo*) on your conference planning committee, so you task him with building the application that transforms the raw data and generates the derivative KML file. He gives you two options—he can build and test the application in Python in two hours, or he can spend several days learning SAS and the GEOCODE procedure. This isn't to say that one language is more or less desirable or comprehensible—only that all developers have their preferred languages, and successfully supporting developers should respect those preferences, where possible.

Clearly, you let him work in Python—the programming language in which he's competent— in part because you're confident that the FCMP procedure can run his code, seamlessly integrating complex Python functionality into a SAS program. And with that roadmap, development can begin!

Creating a PROC FCMP Wrapper to Invoke Python Geocoding

At this point, a subsequent DATA step will need to call a user-defined function or subroutine, pass the restaurant address as a character value, and retrieve the latitude and longitude coordinates. Because the callable module is required to return two values—latitude and longitude—these arguments must be passed by reference, and cannot be returned as a return value.

Thus, the GET_COORDS_SUB subroutine is declared, including the ADDY character parameter and the LAT and LON numeric parameters. The OUTARGS statement completes the subroutine's signature and prescribes that LAT and LON will be passed by reference so that their computed values are available in the calling DATA step:

```
proc fcmp outlib=work.funcs.py;
   subroutine get_coords_sub(addy $, lat, lon);
      outargs lat, lon;
```

The subroutine continues, and the DECLARE statement instantiates the Python Component Object; the INFILE method reads the Python source code; and the PUBLISH method submits the Python code to the Python interpreter:

```
      declare object py(python);
      rc = py.infile("&loc&py_fil");
      rc = py.publish();
```

The CALL method instructs SAS to call the `get_coords` Python function (whose capitalization must match its definition in the Python program file) and to pass the Addy variable as the lone argument:

```
      rc = py.call("get_coords", addy);
```

The RESULTS dictionary first initializes Lat to the latitude return value and next initializes Lon to the longitude return value:

```
      lat = py.results["lat_key"];
      lon = py.results["lon_key"];
```

Finally, the subroutine ends with the ENDSUB and QUIT statements:

```
      endsub;
quit;
```

Although the `get_coords` Python function has not been written yet, the GET_COORDS_SUB subroutine defines the input (Addy) that `get_coords` will require, as well as the output (Lat and

Lon) that geocoding will produce. Thus, the GET_COORDS_SUB signature signals to the Python developer the specific mechanism through which geocoding function must interact with the subroutine that calls it. Moreover, the SAS developer writing GET_COORDS_SUB does not need to be aware of the Python code that geocodes the addresses.

Program 8.9 presents the preceding SAS code in a single program file, which will subsequently be expanded.

Program 8.9: Ingesting the Restaurants Data and Defining the GET_COORDS_SUB Subroutine

```
%let loc=c:\sas\;
%let fil=restaurants.csv;
%let py_fil=las_vegas_gis.py;

data restaurants;
    infile "&loc&fil" dsd delimiter=',' firstobs=2;
    length restaurant $50 addy $100;
    input restaurant $ addy $;
run;

proc fcmp outlib=work.funcs.py;
    subroutine get_coords_sub(addy $, lat, lon);
        outargs lat, lon;
        declare object py(python);
        rc = py.infile("&loc&py_fil");
        rc = py.publish();
        rc = py.call("get_coords", addy);
        lat = py.results["lat_key"];
        lon = py.results["lon_key"];
        endsub;
quit;
```

Geocoding in Python Using the Google Maps API

Geocoding is a resource-intensive process, in part because most solutions require real-time connectivity to a service to return latitude and longitude coordinates. Google Maps, which is recognized as the industry leader for commercial mapping, provides fee-for-service geocoding, as well as other geographic information system (GIS) functionality, such as mapping and distance calculation (Google 2023). The `googlemaps` Python package, available on GitHub, provides documentation for all Google GIS Python functionality (Google 2023). After obtaining a client key, a user or organization can leverage the `googlemaps` package within custom-built Python applications, relying on the same trusted undercarriage that powers Google Maps and Google Earth.

A Python program file can define multiple functions, so `las_vegas_gis` (c:\sas\las_vegas_gis.py) can contain all of the GIS functions that will be separately called from SAS.

First, the `googlemaps` package must be imported so that its methods and functions are made available to the Python session:

```
import googlemaps
```

Next, to access the Google Maps API, a *Google API key* must be specified, which uniquely ties each API call to a user or organization, and which facilitates a pay-as-you-go pricing model (Google 2023). Although each API call costs only a fraction of a penny, over time, and with a sufficiently large user base, these API calls can add up to real dollars. Fortunately, Google credits each account with an allotted number of free API calls per month and also supports a number of various pricing models (Google 2023).

The `Client` method specifies YOUR unique Google Maps key and instantiates a `Client` object as `gmaps_key`:

```
gmaps_key = googlemaps.Client(key="YOUR_GOOGLE_MAPS_KEY_GOES_HERE")
```

The `get_coords` function is declared, in which the `addy` parameter is declared:

```
def get_coords (addy):
```

As discussed previously, the first line of a Python function called from the FCMP procedure must declare the `Output` key(s) that will be written to the RESULTS dictionary:

```
    "Output: lat_key, lon_key"
```

Next, the `geocode` method calls the Google Maps API and returns a geographic object, which contains not only the latitude and longitude of the location, but also a host of other metadata that are embedded hierarchically inside Python dictionaries. These metadata lie outside the scope of this text, and because only the latitude and longitude values are required in this straightforward example, the following two statements extract latitude and longitude values from the geographic object and initialize `lat` and `lon`, respectively:

```
    lat = g[0]['geometry']['location']['lat']
    lon = g[0]['geometry']['location']['lng']
```

Finally, the `return` statement returns a tuple that includes latitude and longitude values:

```
    return lat, lon
```

That is, the value of `lat` corresponds to the `lat_key` key of the RESULTS dictionary, and the value of `lon` corresponds to the `lon_key` key of the RESULTS dictionary. It is for this reason that the RESULTS dictionary must reference `lat_key` to initialize Lat and must reference `lon_key` to initialize Lon.

Program 8.10 demonstrates the preceding Python code in the las_vegas_gis.py program file.

Program 8.10: Defining the get_coords User-Defined Python Function

```
import googlemaps

gmaps_key = googlemaps.Client(key="YOUR_GOOGLE_MAPS_KEY_GOES_HERE")

def get_coords(addy):
    "Output: lat_key, lon_key"
    g = gmaps_key.geocode(addy)
    lat = g[0]['geometry']['location']['lat']
    lon = g[0]['geometry']['location']['lng']
    return lat, lon
```

Calculating Latitude and Longitude Coordinates in SAS

At this point, the GET_COORDS_SUB subroutine has been defined inside the FCMP wrapper, and the subroutine in turn calls the `get_coords` Python function. Program 8.11 demonstrates the final DATA step that reads the Restaurants data set and calls the GET_COORDS_SUB subroutine, which initializes the Lat and Lon values for each restaurant. Because Lat and Lon are being passed by reference, and because neither is initialized prior to the subroutine call, the MISSING subroutine call initializes both variables to a missing value before the subroutine call.

Program 8.11: Calling the GET_COORDS_SUB Subroutine to Geocode Restaurant Addresses

```
options cmplib=work.funcs;

data restaurant_coords;
   set restaurants;
   length lat 8 lon 8;
   format lat lon 12.7;
   call missing(lat, lon);
   call get_coords_sub(addy, lat, lon);
run;
```

Note that the SAS log demonstrates results for only the SAS code that was executed—not for the Python function that was indirectly called:

```
600  data restaurant_coords;
601     set restaurants;
602     length lat 8 lon 8;
603     format lat lon 12.7;
604     call missing(lat, lon);
605     call get_coords_sub(addy, lat, lon);
606  run;

NOTE: There were 10 observations read from the data set WORK.RESTAURANTS.
NOTE: The data set WORK.RESTAURANT_COORDS has 10 observations and 4
variables.
```

It is possible to separately save logs from Python functions that are executed from the FCMP procedure as well as to implement exception handling that generates return codes for warnings or errors. However, these methods lie outside the scope of this example.

The Restaurant_coords data set, displayed in Table 8.1, includes the geocoding results—the latitude and longitude for each restaurant.

With each restaurant's coordinates calculated, more advanced GIS functions can be performed, such as calculating driving directions and distances. However, note that the Google Maps API was unnecessarily called twice for Hell's Kitchen and twice for Gordon Ramsay Burger. This inefficiency not only slows processing, but it incurs real costs where one restaurant might be geocoded dozens or hundreds of times—given that many conference attendees would have suggested these popular establishments. This inefficiency is addressed in subsequent sections.

One final location must be geocoded—the Aria Resort—so that it can be incorporated in subsequent distance calculations. Program 8.12 initializes the &ADDY_ORIGIN macro variable to the street address of the Aria and initializes &LAT_ORIGIN and &LON_ORIGIN to missing values. These last two assignments are equivalent to calling the MISSING subroutine in Program 8.11

Table 8.1: Restaurant_coords Data Set Containing Resolved Latitude and Longitude Coordinates

	restaurant	addy	lat	lon
1	Gordon Ramsay Steak	3655 S Las Vegas Blvd, Las Vegas, NV 89109	36.1121506	-115.17155
2	Gordon Ramsay Hell's Kitchen	3570 Las Vegas Blvd S, Las Vegas, NV 89109	36.1157297	-115.17323
3	Gordon Ramsay Burger	3667 S Las Vegas Blvd, Las Vegas, NV 89109	36.1111576	-115.16861
4	Gordon Ramsay Fish and Chips	3545 S Las Vegas Blvd, Las Vegas, NV 89109	36.117735	-115.17236
5	Ramsay's Kitchen	3475 S Las Vegas Blvd, Las Vegas, NV 89109	36.1194161	-115.17076
6	Eiffel Tower Restaurant	3655 S Las Vegas Blvd, Las Vegas, NV 89109	36.1121506	-115.17155
7	Margaritaville	3555 S Las Vegas Blvd, Las Vegas, NV 89109	36.1160446	-115.16858
8	Heart Attack Grill	450 E Fremont St #130, Las Vegas, NV 89101	36.169458	-115.14075
9	Gordon Ramsay Hell's Kitchen	3570 Las Vegas Blvd S, Las Vegas, NV 89109	36.1157297	-115.17323
10	Gordon Ramsay Burger	3667 S Las Vegas Blvd, Las Vegas, NV 89109	36.1111576	-115.16861

prior to calling the GET_COORDS_SUB subroutine. Finally, GET_COORDS_SUB is called; three arguments are passed; and &LAT_ORIGIN and &LON_ORIGIN are initialized to the values calculated by the Google Maps API.

Program 8.12: Calling the GET_COORDS_SUB Subroutine Using the %SYSCALL Statement

```
%let addy_origin=3730 S Las Vegas Blvd, Las Vegas, NV 89158;
%let lat_origin=.;
%let lon_origin=.;

%syscall get_coords_sub(addy_origin, lat_origin, lon_origin);

%put &=lat_origin;
%put &=lon_origin;
```

The log demonstrates the geocoded coordinates for the Aria, &LAT_ORIGIN and &LON_ORIGIN:

```
632   %put &=lat_origin;
LAT_ORIGIN=36.1073485
633   %put &=lon_origin;
LON_ORIGIN=-115.1765836
```

In the next section, these values are used to calculate distances to and from the hotel and each restaurant.

Creating a PROC FCMP Wrapper to Invoke Python Distance Calculations

In the previous section, the Google Maps API, accessed through the `googlemaps` Python package, geocoded street addresses into their latitude and longitude coordinates. Next, the walking and driving distances can be calculated from these coordinates by creating an FCMP function that calls a user-defined Python function that leverages the `googlemaps` package. Thus, as before, the SAS developer and Python developer are able to work in their respective preferred languages, and they only need to know the arguments being passed to and the values being returned from their respective user-defined functions.

Whereas the GET_COORDS_SUB subroutine (demonstrated in Program 8.9) was required to return two values, latitude and longitude, the GET_DISTANCE function returns only a single value. For this reason, GET_DISTANCE is best defined as a function as opposed to a subroutine.

The FUNCTION statement declares the GET_DISTANCE function and five parameters:

- LAT_ORIGIN and LON_ORIGIN describe the latitude and longitude of the hotel.
- LAT_DEST and LON_DEST describe the latitude and longitude of the restaurant.

- MODE describes the method of transportation and can be set to `walking` or `driving`—values that are specified in the `distance_matrix` Python method and its GitHub documentation. (Google 2023)

The Dist variable, which is calculated and returned to the DATA step, is the final component of the GET_DISTANCE signature:

```
proc fcmp outlib=work.funcs.py;
   function get_distance(lat_origin, lon_origin, lat_dest, lon_dest, mode $);
      length dist 8;
```

Note that as MODE will be transmitted directly to the Python function that is subsequently called, its values are case sensitive and must be passed precisely. Thus, per the GitHub documentation, `walking`, `driving`, `transit`, and `bicycling` are each valid values for the `mode` parameter; however, `Walking` or `Driving` would fail due to invalid capitalization.

The function definition continues, and the DECLARE statement instantiates the Python Component Object; the INFILE method reads the Python source code; and the PUBLISH method submits the Python code to the Python interpreter:

```
        declare object py2(python);
        rc = py2.infile("&loc&py_fil");
        rc = py2.publish();
```

Note that although the INFILE statement references the same Python program file as the INFILE statement in the GET_COORDS_SUB subroutine (demonstrated in Program 8.9), a new Python Component Object (PY2) must be instantiated. Thus, although both Python user-defined functions are being saved in a single program file, and both INFILE statements reference that single file, two Python Component Objects are required.

The CALL method instructs SAS to call the Python `get_distance` function (whose capitalization must match its definition in the Python program file) and to pass the five arguments already described:

```
        rc = py2.call("get_distance", lat_origin, lon_origin, lat_dest,
        lon_dest, mode);
```

The RESULTS dictionary initializes Dist to the single value returned from the `get_distance` Python function:

```
        dist = py2.results["dist_key"];
```

Finally, the function ends with the ENDFUNC and QUIT statements:

```
        endfunc;
quit;
```

Program 8.13 combines the preceding statements into the cohesive GET_DISTANCE user-defined SAS function.

Program 8.13: Defining the GET_DISTANCE User-Defined SAS Function

```
proc fcmp outlib=work.funcs.py;
   function get_distance(lat_origin, lon_origin, lat_dest, lon_dest, mode $);
      length dist 8;
      declare object py2(python);
      rc = py2.infile("&loc.&py_fil");
      rc = py2.publish();
      rc = py2.call("get_distance", lat_origin, lon_origin, lat_dest, lon_dest, mode);
      dist = py2.results["dist_key"];
      return(dist);
      endfunc;
quit;
```

Note that in this case, the SAS function (GET_DISTANCE) has the same name as the Python function (`get_distance`). This is syntactically acceptable, but it can present a difficulty when discussing the identically named SAS and Python functions. It was for this reason that the GET_COORDS_SUB subroutine (demonstrated in Program 8.9) was named differently than the `get_coords` Python function (demonstrated in Program 8.10). Ultimately, software readability should prescribe the naming of all user-defined functions—in any language.

Calculating Distance in Python Using the Google Maps API

With the GET_DISTANCE SAS function defined, the `get_distance` Python function is next defined, which leverages the Google Maps API to call the `googlemaps distance_matrix` method to calculate walking and driving distances. Within the Python program file (las_vegas_gis.py), the `def` statement declares the get_distance function, and declares its five parameters—each of which is passed verbatim from the GET_DISTANCE SAS function (demonstrated in Program 8.13):

```
def get_distance(lat_start, lon_start, lat_end, lon_end, travel_mode):
```

All Python programs called from the FCMP procedure must declare the return value(s) in the next statement by specifying the dictionary key(s) into which the return value(s) will be saved:

```
   "Output: dist_key"
```

Next, the origin coordinates are bound together in the `coords_origin` tuple, and the destination coordinates are bound together in the `coords_dest` tuple:

```
   coords_origin = (lat_start, lon_start)
   coords_dest = (lat_end, lon_end)
```

These two tuple assignment statements are not necessary, but they arguably improve the readability of the `distance_matrix` method when it is subsequently called. Thus, `distance_matrix` next passes the origin coordinates, destination coordinates, and travel mode (`walking` or `driving`), and retrieves the distance (in meters) between the two locations:

```
dist = gmaps_key.distance_matrix(coords_origin, coords_dest,
        mode=travel_mode)['rows'][0]['elements'][0]['distance']['value']
```

Finally, the distance is converted from meters to miles, and the `return` statement sends the distance value back to the calling FCMP function by saving the value in the RESULTS dictionary `dist_key` entry:

```
dist = round(dist * 0.000621371, 1)
```

Program 8.14 combines the preceding Python statements into the user-defined `get_distance` Python function:

Program 8.14: Defining the get_distance User-Defined Python Function
```
# travel_mode: walking or driving
def get_distance(lat_start, lon_start, lat_end, lon_end, travel_mode):
    "Output: dist_key"
    coords_origin = (lat_start, lon_start)
    coords_dest = (lat_end, lon_end)
    # generates distances in meters
    dist = gmaps_key.distance_matrix(coords_origin, coords_dest,
            mode=travel_mode)['rows'][0]['elements'][0]['distance']['value']
    # converts meters to miles
    dist = round(dist * 0.000621371, 1)
    return dist
```

When the GET_DISTANCE SAS function (shown in Program 8.13) is called, it invokes the Python `get_distance` function, which calculates either the walking or driving distance and returns this value to FCMP, and subsequently to the DATA step. In this sense, to generate both walking and driving distances, GET_DISTANCE must be called twice—once specifying the `travel_mode` as `walking`, and once specifying the `travel_mode` as `driving`.

Calculating Coordinates and Calculating Distances in SAS

Program 8.11, which calls the GET_COORDS_SUB subroutine, and Program 8.12, which calculates the coordinates of the Aria Resort, are refactored to call both GET_COORDS_SUB and the GET_DISTANCE SAS function. Thus, in Program 8.15, GET_COORDS_SUB is first called to generate latitude and longitude coordinates for the Aria Resort. GET_COORDS_SUB is subsequently called inside the DATA step to generate coordinates for each restaurant. GET_DISTANCE is called twice to generate both walking and driving distances for each restaurant.

Program 8.15: Calling GET_COORDS_SUB and GET_DISTANCE to Calculate Coordinates and Distance

```
%let addy_origin=3730 S Las Vegas Blvd, Las Vegas, NV 89158;
%let lat_origin=.;
%let lon_origin=.;

%syscall get_coords_sub(addy_origin, lat_origin, lon_origin);

data restaurant_coords_distances;
   set restaurants;
   length lat_origin lon_origin lat lon dist_walking dist_driving 8;
   format lat_origin lon_origin lat lon 12.7 dist_walking dist_driving 8.1;
   lat_origin=&lat_origin;
   lon_origin=&lon_origin;
   call missing(lat, lon);
   call get_coords_sub(addy, lat, lon);
   dist_walking = get_distance(lat_origin, lon_origin, lat, lon, 'walking');
   dist_driving = get_distance(lat_origin, lon_origin, lat, lon, 'driving');
run;
```

The Restaurant_coords_distances data set is demonstrated in Table 8.2. May I just add that despite the five-mile trek to the Heart Attack Grill, it is well worth the effort!

At this point, the coordinates and distances have been calculated for each restaurant. However, recall the previously mentioned inefficiency that GET_COORDS_SUB is redundantly called when

Table 8.2: Restaurants, Their Coordinates, and Distances from the Aria Resort

	restaurant	addy	lat_origin	lon_origin	lat	lon	dist_walking	dist_driving
1	Gordon Ramsay Steak	3655 S Las Vegas Blvd, Las Vegas, NV 89109	36.1073485	-115.176584	36.112151	-115.17155	0.6	0.7
2	Gordon Ramsay Hell's Kitchen	3570 Las Vegas Blvd S, Las Vegas, NV 89109	36.1073485	-115.176584	36.11573	-115.173232	0.9	1.1
3	Gordon Ramsay Burger	3667 S Las Vegas Blvd, Las Vegas, NV 89109	36.1073485	-115.176584	36.111158	-115.168611	0.8	0.8
4	Gordon Ramsay Fish and Chips	3545 S Las Vegas Blvd, Las Vegas, NV 89109	36.1073485	-115.176584	36.117735	-115.172356	1	1
5	Ramsay's Kitchen	3475 S Las Vegas Blvd, Las Vegas, NV 89109	36.1073485	-115.176584	36.119416	-115.170759	1.2	1.2
6	Eiffel Tower Restaurant	3655 S Las Vegas Blvd, Las Vegas, NV 89109	36.1073485	-115.176584	36.112151	-115.17155	0.6	0.7
7	Margaritaville	3555 S Las Vegas Blvd, Las Vegas, NV 89109	36.1073485	-115.176584	36.116045	-115.168582	1.1	1.2
8	Heart Attack Grill	450 E Fremont St #130, Las Vegas, NV 89101	36.1073485	-115.176584	36.169458	-115.140751	5.1	6.9
9	Gordon Ramsay Hell's Kitchen	3570 Las Vegas Blvd S, Las Vegas, NV 89109	36.1073485	-115.176584	36.11573	-115.173232	0.9	1.1
10	Gordon Ramsay Burger	3667 S Las Vegas Blvd, Las Vegas, NV 89109	36.1073485	-115.176584	36.111158	-115.168611	0.8	0.8

a restaurant is repeated. Moreover, GET_DISTANCE is also now redundantly called. For example, because Hell's Kitchen is listed both in the second and ninth observations, GET_COORDS_SUB should be called to geocode only the first instance of Hell's Kitchen, and SAS should instead "remember" these coordinates for all subsequent Hell's Kitchen observations. Again, as coded currently, real time and money are being wasted by the inefficiency of GET_COORDS_SUB and GET_DISTANCE.

Introducing Memoization for Geocoding

Memoization, which is introduced and explored in Chapter 7, enables a function to "remember" past calculations, and it can be used where costly (that is, resource-intensive) functions would otherwise need to recalculate some value using previously observed input criteria. For example, Table 8.2 demonstrates that the address for Hell's Kitchen is geocoded twice—in the second and ninth observations—and this is both inefficient and literally more expensive, given that each call to the Google Maps API incurs a nominal expense. Thus, a more pragmatic approach to defining the GET_COORDS_SUB subroutine would instead call the `get_coords` Python function *only* when the function encounters a given address for the first time.

Program 8.16 demonstrates the GET_COORDS_MEM_SUB subroutine, which extends the GET_COORDS_SUB subroutine demonstrated in Program 8.9. The subroutine is demonstrated in its entirety, after which individual statements are explored.

Program 8.16: Defining the GET_COORDS_MEM_SUB Subroutine to Geocode Efficiently

```
proc fcmp outlib=work.funcs.py;
   subroutine get_coords_mem_sub(addy $, lat, lon, method $);
      outargs lat, lon, method;
      length hex_md5 $32;
      hex_md5 = hashing('md5', addy);
      * statements only used to demonstrate hash values;
      file log;
      put hex_md5=;
      * instantiate hash object;
      declare hash h();
      rc = h.defineKey('hex_md5');
      rc = h.defineData('lat', 'lon');
      rc = h.defineDone();
      * instantiate python object;
      declare object py(python);
      rc = py.infile("&loc&py_fil");
      rc = py.publish();
      * test hash object and return results;
      if h.find() = 0 then method='hash';
      * call python only for new addresses;
      else do;
         rc = py.call("get_coords", addy);
```

```
            lat = py.results["lat_key"];
            lon = py.results["lon_key"];
            rc = h.add();
            method='geocode';
            end;
        endsub;
quit;
```

To illustrate the dynamic functionality of GET_COORDS_MEM_SUB, a new parameter (METHOD) is declared, which records whether a given pair of coordinates were retrieved from the hash object or calculated using the `get_coords` function. Thus, METHOD is unnecessary and would be removed from a production version of the subroutine:

```
proc fcmp outlib=work.funcs.py;
    subroutine get_coords_mem_sub(addy $, lat, lon, method $);
        outargs lat, lon, method;
```

Because hash object keys are limited to a length of 33 characters, and because addresses will exceed this threshold, the MD5 hash of each address is calculated using the built-in HASHING function. Each MD5 hash generates a 16-byte (32-character) hexadecimal value, so street address hashes—rather than the addresses themselves—are loaded into the hash object as keys. Thus, a new variable (Hex_MD5) is calculated as the MD5 hash of each address:

```
        length hex_md5 $32;
        hex_md5 = hashing('md5', addy);
        * statements only used to demonstrate hash values;
        file log;
        put hex_md5=;
```

The FILE statement and PUT statement print the 32-character hexadecimal hash value to the log for demonstration purposes only. Thus, these statements would be removed from a production version of the subroutine.

The hash object (H) is instantiated, in which the Hex_MD5 hash value represents the key, and the Lat and Lon values represent the associated data values:

```
        declare hash h();
        rc = h.defineKey('hex_md5');
        rc = h.defineData('lat', 'lon');
        rc = h.defineDone();
```

Next, the Python Component Object (PY) is instantiated, as previously described:

```
        declare object py(python);
        rc = py.infile("&loc&py_fil");
        rc = py.publish();
```

The hash FIND method tests whether the address (that is, the MD5 hash representation of the address) is found in the hash object and returns a 0 when the key is found. Moreover, when a key is found, the Lat and Lon values are retrieved from the associated data values in the hash object. Finally, because the OUTARGS statement declares the LAT and LON parameters as being passed by reference, when the Lat and Lon values are updated by the FIND method, those values are made available to the calling program, the DATA step:

```
if h.find() = 0 then method='hash';
```

However, if the FIND method returns a nonzero value (representing that the address is being observed for the first time and does not appear in the hash object), the ELSE block executes and calls the get_coords Python function to generate latitude and longitude values via the Google Maps API:

```
else do;
   rc = py.call("get_coords", addy);
   lat = py.results["lat_key"];
   lon = py.results["lon_key"];
   rc = h.add();
   method='geocode';
   end;
```

Note that when a key is not found in the hash object, the hash ADD method now adds the Hex_MD5 value as a new key and the Lat and Lon values as its associated data values.

The GET_COORDS_MEM_SUB subroutine can now be called, as demonstrated in Program 8.17. Note that no changes were required to be made to the underlying get_coords Python function that is called. Thus, in this example, all memoization occurs directly in the FCMP procedure, as opposed to in Python.

Program 8.17: Calling the GET_COORDS_MEM_SUB Subroutine to Geocode Addresses

```
%let loc=c:\sas\;
%let fil=restaurants.csv;

%let py_fil=las_vegas_gis.py;

data restaurants;
   infile "&loc&fil" dsd delimiter=',' firstobs=2;
   length restaurant $50 addy $100;
   input restaurant $ addy $;
run;

data restaurant_coords_mem;
   set restaurants;
   length lat 8 lon 8 method $10;
   format lat lon 12.7;
```

```
    call missing(lat, lon, method);
    call get_coords_mem_sub(addy, lat, lon, method);
run;
```

When Program 8.17 is run, the log demonstrates the ten hexadecimal keys that the HASHING built-in function calculates, one for each restaurant street address:

```
hex_md5=DF8064365E611283F6EC543F9519A2E9
hex_md5=C8050AB66A32B3043499845C45E6A1AD
hex_md5=D40C4610D1B3E8DE2CA50612D5127283
hex_md5=1B1268ADDD724B6FCB2C08712E99DA27
hex_md5=A650D7A65598ED5665304A21A2AE4843
hex_md5=DF8064365E611283F6EC543F9519A2E9
hex_md5=8DDB8E3D626777AAF517AB2D1A2506E0
hex_md5=BFB0C11377D2F50F471B11097D7836AA
hex_md5=C8050AB66A32B3043499845C45E6A1AD
hex_md5=D40C4610D1B3E8DE2CA50612D5127283
NOTE: There were 10 observations read from the data set WORK.RESTAURANTS.
```

As expected, because the Hell's Kitchen address is repeated in the second and ninth observations, the second and ninth keys are identical. Similarly, because the Gordon Ramsay Burger address is repeated in the third and tenth observations, the third and tenth keys are identical.

Somewhat surprisingly, however, the first and sixth key values are also identical—and this occurs because both Gordon Ramsay Steak and the Eiffel Tower Restaurant are located inside the Paris Resort, whose address is 3655 South Las Vegas Boulevard.

The resultant Restaurant_coords_mem data set is demonstrated in Table 8.3, in which the Method variable indicates whether the Google Maps API is called to geocode the address, or the coordinates are instead pulled from the hash object. For example, the first five addresses must be geocoded using the `get_coords` Python function because they are observed for the first time. However, the latitude and longitude values for the sixth observation are instead retrieved from the hash object because the address had already been geocoded for Gordon Ramsay Steak.

The revised solution, which uses memoization operationalized through a hash object, is both more efficient and cost effective, as three of the ten addresses no longer require geocoding.

Introducing Memoization for Distance Calculations

The GET_COORDS_SUB subroutine was extended in the previous section to the GET_COORDS_MEM_SUB subroutine. This extension supported memoization by caching addresses and their associated coordinates. In this section, the GET_DISTANCE function is redefined as the GET_DISTANCE_MEM function, which similarly leverages the hash object to remember walking and driving distances.

Table 8.3: Memoization of Geocoded Addresses

	restaurant	addy	lat	lon	method
1	Gordon Ramsay Steak	3655 S Las Vegas Blvd, Las Vegas, NV 89109	36.1121506	-115.17155	geocode
2	Gordon Ramsay Hell's Kitchen	3570 Las Vegas Blvd S, Las Vegas, NV 89109	36.1157297	-115.173232	geocode
3	Gordon Ramsay Burger	3667 S Las Vegas Blvd, Las Vegas, NV 89109	36.1111576	-115.168611	geocode
4	Gordon Ramsay Fish and Chips	3545 S Las Vegas Blvd, Las Vegas, NV 89109	36.117735	-115.172356	geocode
5	Ramsay's Kitchen	3475 S Las Vegas Blvd, Las Vegas, NV 89109	36.1194161	-115.170759	geocode
6	Eiffel Tower Restaurant	3655 S Las Vegas Blvd, Las Vegas, NV 89109	36.1121506	-115.17155	hash
7	Margaritaville	3555 S Las Vegas Blvd, Las Vegas, NV 89109	36.1160446	-115.168582	geocode
8	Heart Attack Grill	450 E Fremont St #130, Las Vegas, NV 89101	36.169458	-115.140751	geocode
9	Gordon Ramsay Hell's Kitchen	3570 Las Vegas Blvd S, Las Vegas, NV 89109	36.1157297	-115.173232	hash
10	Gordon Ramsay Burger	3667 S Las Vegas Blvd, Las Vegas, NV 89109	36.1111576	-115.168611	hash

Program 8.18 extends the GET_DISTANCE function, demonstrated in Program 8.13. Note that a hash object now supports memoization, and the `get_distance` Python function needs to be called only for those origin-destination combinations that have not been observed. This expansion of GET_DISTANCE into GET_DISTANCE_MEM requires no updates to the `get_distance` Python function that it calls.

Program 8.18: Incorporating Memoization in Distance Calculations

```
proc fcmp outlib=work.funcs.py;
   function get_distance_mem(lat_origin, lon_origin, lat_dest, lon_dest,
         mode $, method $);
      outargs method;
      length dist 8;
      * instantiate hash object;
      declare hash h();
      rc = h.defineKey('lat_origin', 'lon_origin', 'lat_dest', 'lon_dest', 'mode');
      rc = h.defineData('dist');
      rc = h.defineDone();
      * instantiate python object;
      declare object py2(python);
      rc = py2.infile("&loc.&py_fil");
      rc = py2.publish();
      * test hash object and return results;
```

```
            if h.find() = 0 then method='hash';
            * call python function if not in hash;
            else do;
               rc = py2.call("get_distance", lat_origin, lon_origin,
                  lat_dest, lon_dest, mode);
               dist = py2.results["dist_key"];
               rc = h.add();
               method = 'calculated';
               end;
            return (dist);
            endfunc;
quit;
```

As was demonstrated in the GET_COORDS_MEM_SUB subroutine, the method of data retrieval—whether hash or calculation—is maintained only for demonstration purposes. Thus, in a production version of this function, all references to the METHOD parameter and Method variable should be removed.

The FUNCTION statement declares the GET_DISTANCE_MEM function and its parameters. Note that both the OUTARGS statement and LENGTH statement are considered to be part of the function's signature as they define the return value (Dist) and the parameter passed by reference (METHOD):

```
proc fcmp outlib=work.funcs.py;
   function get_distance_mem(lat_origin, lon_origin, lat_dest, lon_dest,
         mode $, method $);
      outargs method;
      length dist 8;
```

The hash object (H) is instantiated, and the DEFINEKEY method defines five keys—four numeric keys representing the origin coordinates and the destination coordinates, and a character key (Mode) representing whether the walking or driving distance is being calculated. Because the solitary character key is fewer than 33 characters and the remaining keys are numeric, no MD5 hash is required to transform the key, as was necessary in the GET_COORDS_MEM_SUB subroutine:

```
      declare hash h();
      rc = h.defineKey('lat_origin', 'lon_origin', 'lat_dest', 'lon_dest', 'mode');
      rc = h.defineData('dist');
      rc = h.defineDone();
```

The Python Component Object (PY2) is instantiated, and the Python code published:

```
      declare object py2(python);
      rc = py2.infile("&loc.&py_fil");
      rc = py2.publish();
```

The hash FIND method evaluates whether a matching record with the five keys exists in the hash object. If it does, the `get_distance` Python function is skipped, and the GET_DISTANCE_MEM function instead returns the distance value (Dist) maintained in the hash object:

```
if h.find() = 0 then method='hash';
```

On the other hand, if the five keys do not match a record in the hash object, the `get_distance` Python function is called, the Dist return value is initialized to the value returned by `get_distance`, and Method is set to "calculated" to denote that a calculation (in lieu of an in-memory lookup) was required:

```
else do;
   rc = py2.call("get_distance", lat_origin, lon_origin,
      lat_dest, lon_dest, mode);
   dist = py2.results["dist_key"];
   rc = h.add();
   method = 'calculated';
   end;
```

Finally, the RETURN statement returns the Dist return value to the calling DATA step; ENDFUNC terminates the function; and QUIT terminates the FCMP procedure:

```
   return (dist);
   endfunc;
quit;
```

At this point, both the geocoding functionality (GET_COORDS_MEM_SUB subroutine) and distance calculation (GET_DISTANCE_MEM function) have been recoded to take advantage of memoization, as operationalized through two hash objects.

Thus, for one final time, the DATA step in Program 8.19 ingests the Restaurants data set, calls GET_COORDS_MEM_SUB and GET_DISTANCE_MEM, and produces a data set that includes geocoded coordinates for each restaurant, as well as walking and driving distances from the Aria Resort.

Program 8.19: Calling the GET_COORDS_MEM_SUB Subroutine and GET_DISTANCE_MEM Function

```
%let addy_origin=3730 S Las Vegas Blvd, Las Vegas, NV 89158;

data restaurant_coords_distances_mem;
   set restaurants;
   length lat_origin lon_origin lat lon dist_walking dist_driving 8
      method1 method2 method3 $12;
   format lat_origin lon_origin lat lon 12.7 dist_walking dist_driving 8.1;
   retain lat_origin lon_origin;
   if _n_ = 1 then do;
      call missing(lat_origin, lon_origin, method1);
```

```
      call get_coords_mem_sub("&addy_origin", lat_origin, lon_origin, method1);
      end;
   call missing(lat, lon, method1);
   call get_coords_mem_sub(addy, lat, lon, method1);
   call missing(method2);
   dist_walking = get_distance_mem(lat_origin, lon_origin, lat, lon,
      'walking', method2);
   call missing(method3);
   dist_driving = get_distance_mem(lat_origin, lon_origin, lat, lon,
      'driving', method3);
run;
```

Note that in lieu of initializing Lat_origin and Lon_origin via the %SYSCALL statement, as Program 8.15 demonstrates, Program 8.19 instead initializes these values in the DATA step and relies on the RETAIN statement to retain these values across all observations.

The Restaurant_coords_distances_mem data set is displayed in Table 8.4, which now includes three variables that peek under the covers to reveal the memoization mechanics. Method1 displays "geocode" when the get_coords Python function is called, and "hash" when the coordinate values are returned from the hash object. Method2 and Method3 each display "calculated" when the get_distance Python function is called, and they display "hash" when the Dist value is returned from the hash object. Again, Method1, Method2, and Method3 are only created to demonstrate those observations that benefit from memoization—that is, when the hash FIND method successfully locates the key(s) in the hash object.

Creating a KML File for Las Vegas Restaurants

So many pages ago, the requirements for this project were described as the need for a keyhole markup language (KML) file that contains attendee-supplied restaurant recommendations.

Table 8.4: Restaurant_coords_distances_mem Data Set Demonstrating Memoization

	restaurant	addy	lat_origin	lon_origin	lat	lon	dist_walking	dist_driving	method1	method2	method3
1	Gordon Ramsay Steak	3655 S Las Vegas Blvd, Las Vegas, NV 89109	36.1073485	-115.1765836	36.1121506	-115.17155	0.6	0.7	geocode	calculated	calculated
2	Gordon Ramsay Hell's Kitchen	3570 Las Vegas Blvd S, Las Vegas, NV 89109	36.1073485	-115.1765836	36.1157297	-115.173232	0.9	1.1	geocode	calculated	calculated
3	Gordon Ramsay Burger	3667 S Las Vegas Blvd, Las Vegas, NV 89109	36.1073485	-115.1765836	36.1111576	-115.168611	0.8	0.8	geocode	calculated	calculated
4	Gordon Ramsay Fish and Chips	3545 S Las Vegas Blvd, Las Vegas, NV 89109	36.1073485	-115.1765836	36.117735	-115.172356	1	1	geocode	calculated	calculated
5	Ramsay's Kitchen	3475 S Las Vegas Blvd, Las Vegas, NV 89109	36.1073485	-115.1765836	36.1194161	-115.170759	1.2	1.2	geocode	calculated	calculated
6	Eiffel Tower Restaurant	3655 S Las Vegas Blvd, Las Vegas, NV 89109	36.1073485	-115.1765836	36.1121506	-115.17155	0.6	0.7	hash	hash	hash
7	Margaritaville	3555 S Las Vegas Blvd, Las Vegas, NV 89109	36.1073485	-115.1765836	36.1160446	-115.168582	1.1	1.2	geocode	calculated	calculated
8	Heart Attack Grill	450 E Fremont St #130, Las Vegas, NV 89101	36.1073485	-115.1765836	36.169458	-115.140751	5.1	6.9	geocode	calculated	calculated
9	Gordon Ramsay Hell's Kitchen	3570 Las Vegas Blvd S, Las Vegas, NV 89109	36.1073485	-115.1765836	36.1157297	-115.173232	0.9	1.1	hash	hash	hash
10	Gordon Ramsay Burger	3667 S Las Vegas Blvd, Las Vegas, NV 89109	36.1073485	-115.1765836	36.1111576	-115.168611	0.8	0.8	hash	hash	hash

With this information, all SAS Innovate attendees can benefit from recommendations through a navigable format that displays walking and driving distances from the Aria Resort, as well as the number of users who voted for each restaurant.

The structure and format of KML files fall outside the scope of this text. However, Program 8.20 first sorts the Restaurant_coords_distances_mem data set by restaurant name and street address and subsequently builds the KML file (c:\sas\vegas_restaurants.kml). The SORT procedure is required so that duplicate restaurants can be counted, and only the final restaurant observation containing the highest Cnt (the total count of votes for that restaurant) is written to the KML file.

Program 8.20: Dynamically Creating a KML File from a SAS Data Set

```
proc sort data=restaurant_coords_distances_mem (keep=restaurant addy
      dist_walking dist_driving lat lon) out=kml_data;
   by restaurant addy;
run;
data _null_;
   set kml_data end=eof;
   by restaurant addy;
   file "&loc.vegas_restaurants.kml";
   if _n_ = 1 then do;
      put "<?xml version='1.0' encoding='UTF-8'?>";
      put "<kml xmlns='http://www.opengis.net/kml/2.2'>";
      put "<Document>";
      end;
   retain cnt;
   if first.addy then cnt=1;
   else cnt+1;
   if last.addy then do;
      put "  <Placemark>";
      put "    <name><![CDATA[" restaurant "]]></name>";
      put "      <description><![CDATA[" addy "<p>";
      put "        votes: " cnt "<p>";
      put "         miles walking: " dist_walking "<p>";
      put "         miles driving: " dist_driving "]]></description>";
      put "        <Point>";
      put "        <coordinates>" lon "," lat  ",0 </coordinates>";
      put "        </Point>";
      put "    </Placemark>";
      end;
   if eof then do;
   put "</Document>";
   put "</kml>";
   end;
run;
```

The DATA step creates the KML file (c:\sas\vegas_restaurants.kml), which is demonstrated (yet not described) in Program 8.21.

Program 8.21: Vegas_restaurants.kml File

```
<?xml version='1.0' encoding='UTF-8'?>
<kml xmlns='http://www.opengis.net/kml/2.2'>
<Document>
  <Placemark>
    <name><![CDATA[Eiffel Tower Restaurant ]]></name>
      <description><![CDATA[3655 S Las Vegas Blvd, Las Vegas, NV 89109 <p>
        votes: 1 <p>
        miles walking: 0.6 <p>
        miles driving: 0.7 ]]></description>
      <Point>
        <coordinates>-115.1715500 ,36.1121506 ,0 </coordinates>
      </Point>
  </Placemark>
  <Placemark>
    <name><![CDATA[Gordon Ramsay Burger ]]></name>
      <description><![CDATA[3667 S Las Vegas Blvd, Las Vegas, NV 89109 <p>
        votes: 2 <p>
        miles walking: 0.8 <p>
        miles driving: 0.8 ]]></description>
      <Point>
        <coordinates>-115.1686113 ,36.1111576 ,0 </coordinates>
      </Point>
  </Placemark>
  <Placemark>
    <name><![CDATA[Gordon Ramsay Fish and Chips ]]></name>
      <description><![CDATA[3545 S Las Vegas Blvd, Las Vegas, NV 89109 <p>
        votes: 1 <p>
        miles walking: 1.0 <p>
        miles driving: 1.0 ]]></description>
      <Point>
        <coordinates>-115.1723560 ,36.1177350 ,0 </coordinates>
      </Point>
  </Placemark>
  <Placemark>
    <name><![CDATA[Gordon Ramsay Hell's Kitchen ]]></name>
      <description><![CDATA[3570 Las Vegas Blvd S, Las Vegas, NV 89109 <p>
        votes: 2 <p>
        miles walking: 0.9 <p>
        miles driving: 1.1 ]]></description>
      <Point>
        <coordinates>-115.1732319 ,36.1157297 ,0 </coordinates>
      </Point>
  </Placemark>
  <Placemark>
    <name><![CDATA[Gordon Ramsay Steak ]]></name>
      <description><![CDATA[3655 S Las Vegas Blvd, Las Vegas, NV 89109 <p>
```

```
       votes: 1 <p>
       miles walking: 0.6 <p>
       miles driving: 0.7 ]]></description>
       <Point>
       <coordinates>-115.1715500 ,36.1121506 ,0 </coordinates>
       </Point>
   </Placemark>
 <Placemark>
   <name><![CDATA[Heart Attack Grill ]]></name>
     <description><![CDATA[450 E Fremont St #130, Las Vegas, NV 89101 <p>
       votes: 1 <p>
       miles walking: 5.1 <p>
       miles driving: 6.9 ]]></description>
       <Point>
       <coordinates>-115.1407514 ,36.1694580 ,0 </coordinates>
       </Point>
   </Placemark>
 <Placemark>
   <name><![CDATA[Margaritaville ]]></name>
     <description><![CDATA[3555 S Las Vegas Blvd, Las Vegas, NV 89109 <p>
       votes: 1 <p>
       miles walking: 1.1 <p>
       miles driving: 1.2 ]]></description>
       <Point>
       <coordinates>-115.1685822 ,36.1160446 ,0 </coordinates>
       </Point>
   </Placemark>
 <Placemark>
   <name><![CDATA[Ramsay's Kitchen ]]></name>
     <description><![CDATA[3475 S Las Vegas Blvd, Las Vegas, NV 89109 <p>
       votes: 1 <p>
       miles walking: 1.2 <p>
       miles driving: 1.2 ]]></description>
       <Point>
       <coordinates>-115.1707592 ,36.1194161 ,0 </coordinates>
       </Point>
   </Placemark>
</Document>
</kml>
```

Finally, Figure 8.1 demonstrates the KML file as viewed in Google Earth, with Hell's Kitchen selected.

And just for comparison, Figure 8.2 shows the same KML file imported into Google Maps, demonstrating the ease with which conference attendees could download a KML file and add it to the Google Maps app on their cell phones. As before, Hell's Kitchen is highlighted, and the Aria Resort is shown in the lower left.

Figure 8.1: Viewing the Las Vegas Restaurants KML File in Google Earth

Figure 8.2: Viewing the Las Vegas Restaurants KML File in Google Maps

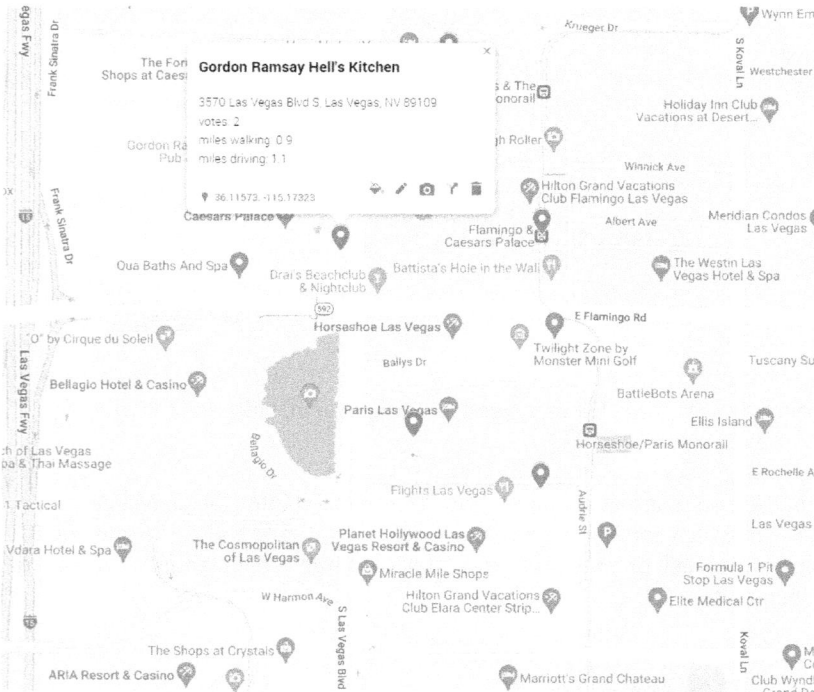

Conclusion

This introduction to the Python Component Object demonstrated how Python user-defined functions can be called natively from within SAS user-defined functions and subroutines. The ability to build a Python function inside the FCMP procedure was demonstrated, as were inarguably superior methods in which external Python program files are imported into the FCMP procedure. This second approach is preferred because it enables Python developers to build software in a native Python environment (and IDE) while not diminishing the ability of the FCMP procedure to run those Python functions using a local Python Interpreter. Finally, despite the subtle complexity of the geocoding example, this has only scratched the surface of capabilities enabled by FCMP Python objects.

Chapter 9: Expanding the Application of Functions

Whereas the first chapter introduced functions and function nomenclature, and other chapters described and demonstrated function design and development, this chapter stands alone in focusing on function invocation. Thus far, myriad examples have demonstrated calling functions and subroutines from the DATA step, as well as calling functions via the %SYSFUNC function and subroutines via the %SYSCALL statement. User-defined functions have also been called from the SQL procedure and the FCMP procedure. This chapter demonstrates two final methods of invoking user-defined functions—using the OTHER option of the FORMAT procedure and inside the COMPUTE block of the REPORT procedure.

SAS formats and informats map values and use key-value pairs to transform data. User-defined formats and informats, created using the FORMAT procedure, are invaluable as they facilitate in-memory lookup operations that transform keys to their paired values. *Multimaps* facilitate many-to-one data mapping and are also supported by the FORMAT procedure, although they are not discussed in this text. User-defined formats are typically designed through one of two modalities—a static enumeration of key-value pairs hardcoded in syntax, or the vastly superior data-driven solution in which the CNTLIN option enables formats and informats to be created from SAS data sets.

The FORMAT procedure also supports a little-known third method of creating user-defined formats and informats, in which the OTHER option is used to call a user-defined *function* (but not a user-defined *subroutine*) from the FORMAT procedure. The result is a format that bears all of the underlying functionality of a user-defined function, which might include hash lookup operations or other complex business rules. Because user-defined formats can be called from not only the DATA step but also numerous built-in SAS procedures, the definition of a user-defined format that calls a user-defined function increases the ways in which that function's functionality can be applied. This chapter demonstrates the creation of both user-defined formats and informats that call user-defined functions.

Finally, user-defined functions can also be called from inside the COMPUTE block of the REPORT procedure. This practice can, in some cases, provide dynamic functionality within REPORT that would otherwise necessitate use of the SAS macro language—for example, to apply dynamic color-coding or other formatting to cells based on some evaluation criteria. In general, calling user-defined functions from the FORMAT procedure and REPORT procedure can yield more flexible software.

User-Defined Functions Applied as Formats and Informats

Throughout the text, user-defined functions and subroutines have been called via two primary methods—from the DATA step, and by using the %SYSFUNC macro function or %SYSCALL macro statement. The FORMAT procedure OTHER option facilitates an additional method of function invocation, in which a user-defined format or informat is created that calls a function—including either a built-in or user-defined function.

This application of FORMAT can greatly extend the utility of a user-defined function because the function can effectively be called anywhere in code that a format can be applied, including within PRINT, MEANS, FREQ, and other procedures that output data. Moreover, user-defined informats that call user-defined functions can validate, standardize, and otherwise transform data easily while obfuscating complex business rules and logic within the user-defined function. Both user-defined formats and user-defined informats are created using the FORMAT procedure OTHER option, as described and demonstrated in the following sections.

Limitations of Functions Called by PROC FORMAT

Prior to demonstrating this functionality, however, several limitations must be discussed regarding the type of user-defined functions that can be called using the FORMAT procedure OTHER option. First, and most importantly, only functions—and not subroutines—can be called in this manner. In fact, if you try to call a user-defined subroutine using the OTHER option, the SAS application will abruptly crash and terminate. Similarly, if you define a function that declares an array parameter and subsequently call the function using the OTHER option, the SAS application will abruptly crash! You will not receive an error message. You will not receive a warning. Go directly to jail and do not pass go!

Other limitations are less pernicious and do at least produce a runtime error from which SAS can recover. Most notably, a function called using the OTHER option can declare only one parameter, which must be either a scalar character parameter or a scalar numeric parameter. Finally, you cannot declare parameters that are passed by reference, so any function called using the OTHER option cannot include the OUTARGS statement. Thus, when conceptualizing what type of functions are compatible with the FORMAT procedure OTHER option calling method, you should only call functions that read a single argument and return a single value—equivalent to how the FORMAT procedure operates when the OTHER option is not being used.

With these few caveats, SAS practitioners absolutely should leverage the flexible manner in which SAS user-defined functions can be called when they are applied using a user-defined format or informat.

User-Defined Format Calling a User-Defined Function

Consider the SAS built-in ROMAN format, which converts Arabic numbers to Roman numerals. For those unfamiliar with this somewhat esoteric format, the DATA step in Program 9.1 iterates from one to five and prints each Arabic number and its Roman numeral equivalent.

Program 9.1: Applying the ROMAN Built-In Format
```
data _null_;
   length rom $20;
   do num = 1 to 5;
      rom = put(num,roman.);
      put num @10 rom;
      end;
run;
```

The log lists the numbers one through five:

```
1        I
2        II
3        III
4        IV
5        V
```

SAS has no reciprocal built-in format that converts Roman numerals to Arabic numbers, but one can be designed easily within FCMP. For example, consider the United_States_Code data set that is created in Program 9.2. It contains Roman numeral representations of the Title, Part, Chapter, and Section of Title 18 U.S. Criminal Code and could benefit from translation of the Roman numerals.

Program 9.2: Creating the United_States_Code Data Set
```
data united_states_code;
   infile datalines dsd delimiter = ',';
   length title part chapter section $20 name $100;
   input title $ part $ chapter $ section $ name $;
   datalines;
XVIII,I,CVII,MMXCVI,'Drunkenness or neglect of duty by seamen'
XVIII,I,L,MLXXXII,'Gambling ships'
XVIII,I,LIII,MCLXVI,'Gambling in Indian Country'
XVIII,I,III,XLVII,'Use of aircraft or motor vehicles to hunt certain wild
horses or burros'
;
```

Program 9.3 first defines the ROM user-defined format, which converts individual Roman numeral letters to their respective Arabic numbers. For example, "X" is converted to 10, and "M" is converted to 1,000. Thereafter, the ROMAN_TO_ARABIC user-defined function is defined in the FCMP procedure and relies on ROM to convert Roman numeral character values to their numeric equivalents.

Program 9.3: Creating the ROM Format and ROMAN_TO_ARABIC Function

```
proc format;
    value $rom
    'I' = 1
    'V' = 5
    'X' = 10
    'L' = 50
    'C' = 100
    'D' = 500
    'M' = 1000;
run;

proc fcmp outlib=work.funcs.math;
    function roman_to_arabic(str $);
        tot = 0;
        do i = 1 to length(str)-1;
            dec1 = input(put(substr(str,i,1),$rom.),8.);
            dec2 = input(put(substr(str,i+1,1),$rom.),8.);
            if dec1 >= dec2 then tot+dec1;
            else tot = tot-dec1;
            end;
        tot+input(put(substr(str,length(str),1),$rom.),8.);
        return(tot);
        endfunc;
quit;
```

The secret to Roman numeral conversion is to assess—from left to right—whether the prior numeral is greater or less than the current numeral. If the prior numeral is greater, it is added to a running total, and if less, it is subtracted from the running total. Finally, the last numeral is always added to the total. For example, in the numeral VI (6), V (5) is greater than I (1), so five is added to the total, after which the terminal one is added to equal six. Conversely, in the numeral IV (4), I (1) is less than V (5), so one is subtracted from the total, after which the terminal five is added to equal four.

The DATA step in Program 9.4 calls the ROMAN_TO_ARABIC function to convert the U.S. Code Title, Part, Chapter, and Section numbers to their numeric representation. Note that the FORMAT procedure requires the CMPLIB option to specify the library and data set in which the function is saved; otherwise, the function will not be located, and the format definition will fail.

Program 9.4: Transforming Roman Numerals Using the ROMAN_TO_ARABIC Function

```
options cmplib=work.funcs;

data _null_;
   set united_states_code;
   length title_num part_num chapter_num section_num 8;
   title_num = roman_to_arabic(title);
   part_num = roman_to_arabic(part);
   chapter_num = roman_to_arabic(chapter);
   section_num = roman_to_arabic(section);
   put 'Title ' title_num 'Part ' part_num 'Chapter ' chapter_num 'Section ' section_num
      name;
run;
```

The log demonstrates the transformed numbers:

```
Title 18 Part 1 Chapter 107 Section 2096 Drunkenness or neglect of duty by seamen
Title 18 Part 1 Chapter 50 Section 1082 Gambling ships
Title 18 Part 1 Chapter 53 Section 1166 Gambling in Indian Country
Title 18 Part 1 Chapter 3 Section 47
Use of aircraft or motor vehicles to hunt certain wild horses or burros
```

The function is powerful, but note the limitation that it must be called only within a DATA step or using %SYSFUNC:

```
%put DCCCLXXXVIII in Arabic numbers is %sysfunc(roman_to_
arabic(DCCCLXXXVIII));
```

The log shows that DCCCLXXXVIII corresponds to 888:

```
DCCCLXXXVIII in Arabic numbers is 888
```

But what if you wanted to convert Roman numerals to Arabic numbers temporarily within a PRINT, MEANS, FREQ, or similar SAS procedure designed to output data? Formats can be applied *in situ* within these procedures using the FORMAT statement, but functions cannot. And this can necessitate that data are first transformed using functions or subroutines in a preliminary DATA step, after which they can be analyzed or displayed using one of many SAS procedures.

The FORMAT procedure, however, can eliminate this sometimes unnecessary step, and the OTHER option facilitates the creation of a user-defined format or informat that calls a user-defined function, as shown in Program 9.5. Note that the name of the user-defined function being transformed into a user-defined format must be enclosed in square brackets. Also note that it is not necessary to specify or pass an argument; thus, the function call includes empty parentheses.

Program 9.5: Creating the FMT_R_TO_A User-Defined Format
```
proc format;
   value $fmt_r_to_a other = [roman_to_arabic()];
run;
```

The OTHER option can be leveraged to create formats using the VALUE statement and informats using the INVALUE statement. However, as only formats can be applied in SAS procedures using the FORMAT statement, Program 9.5 creates the FMT_R_TO_A user-defined character format.

The DATA step in Program 9.6 is functionally equivalent to Program 9.4, but it relies on the PUT statement to apply the FMT_R_TO_A function to each Roman numeral, whereas Program 9.4 directly leveraged the ROMAN_TO_ARABIC function. Also note that because the format yields a character result, the INPUT function converts the character result of the FMT_R_TO_A format to a numeric value.

Program 9.6: Applying the FMT_R_TO_A User-Defined Format
```
data _null_;
   set united_states_code;
   length title_num part_num chapter_num section_num 8;
   title_num = input(put(title, $fmt_r_to_a.),8.);
   part_num = input(put(part, $fmt_r_to_a.),8.);
   chapter_num = input(put(chapter, $fmt_r_to_a.),8.);
   section_num = input(put(section, $fmt_r_to_a.),8.);
   put 'Title ' title_num 'Part ' part_num 'Chapter ' chapter_num 'Section '
      section_num name;
run;
```

This program is not terribly interesting (yet); after all, the ROMAN_TO_ARABIC function could have been directly applied in lieu of its derivative FMT_R_TO_A format. However, Program 9.7 leverages the FMT_R_TO_A format within the PRINT procedure—somewhere that FCMP functions cannot operate—in which the FORMAT statement temporarily transforms all four variables (Title, Part, Chapter, and Section).

Program 9.7: Applying the FMT_R_TO_A User-Defined Format in a SAS Procedure
```
title;
proc print data=united_states_code noobs;
   format title part chapter section $fmt_r_to_a.;
   var title part chapter section name;
run;
```

The output is demonstrated in Table 9.1.

The values of the four variables have now been temporarily transformed by applying the FMT_R_TO_A format; however, the underlying values in the United_States_Code data set remain unchanged.

Table 9.1: Applying the FMT_R_TO_A User-Defined Format inside the PRINT Procedure

title	part	chapter	section	name
18	1	107	2096	Drunkenness or neglect of duty by seamen
18	1	50	1082	Gambling ships
18	1	53	1166	Gambling in Indian Country
18	1	3	47	Use of aircraft or motor vehicles to hunt certain wild horses or burros

User-Defined Function and Format Performance

In all cases, user-defined formats and informats that leverage the OTHER argument to call a user-defined function will incur some performance degradation. This is expected, as the format call to a function call effectively adds a level of abstraction that SAS must process. Calling a function directly will of course run faster than calling that function indirectly via a preceding format application; that format wrapper incurs some overhead. However, in many cases, and especially where data set size is insignificant, this degradation will be negligible if not unnoticeable. Notwithstanding, and when large data sets are being processed, applying a user-defined format that calls a user-defined function can double and even quadruple runtime. This is all to say that despite the wide array of use cases that this design pattern supports, SAS practitioners should evaluate performance to ensure it is not adversely affected.

For example, consider the functionally equivalent ROMAN_TO_ARABIC function and FMT_R_TO_A format that are defined in the previous subsection and the need to transform a large quantity of data using one of these methods. Program 9.8 generates a one-million observation data set of Roman numerals that can subsequently be transformed to compare the performance of these two methods.

Program 9.8: Generating Randomized Roman Numerals
```
data numbers (drop=cnt num);
   length num 8 rom $20;
   call streaminit(123);
   do cnt = 1 to 10000000;
      num = int(1000*rand('uniform'))+1;
      rom = put(num,roman20.);
      output;
      end;
run;
```

Program 9.9 demonstrates two DATA steps. The ROMAN_TO_ARABIC user-defined *function* is first used to transform the Roman numerals, after which the FMT_R_TO_A user-defined *format* performs an identical transformation. Thus, the second method adds a level of abstraction that adds system resource overhead and runtime.

Program 9.9: Calling the ROMAN_TO_ARABIC Function and FMT_R_TO_A Format

```
data transform_function;
   set numbers;
   length arabic 8;
   arabic = roman_to_arabic(rom);
run;

data transform_format;
   set numbers;
   length arabic 8;
   Arabic = input(put(rom, $fmt_r_to_a.),8.);
run;
```

The function completes in approximately half the time that the functionally equivalent format requires, as demonstrated in the log:

```
NOTE: There were 10000000 observations read from the data set WORK.NUMBERS.
NOTE: The data set WORK.TRANSFORM_FUNCTION has 10000000 observations and 2
variables.
NOTE: DATA statement used (Total process time):
      real time              34.72 seconds
      user cpu time          34.42 seconds
      system cpu time        0.21 seconds
      memory                 1605.31k
      OS Memory              24824.00k

NOTE: There were 10000000 observations read from the data set WORK.NUMBERS.
NOTE: The data set WORK.TRANSFORM_FORMAT has 10000000 observations and 2
variables.
NOTE: DATA statement used (Total process time):
      real time              1:06.09
      user cpu time          57.12 seconds
      system cpu time        8.93 seconds
      memory                 1139.75k
      OS Memory              24824.00k
```

However, the ROMAN_TO_ARABIC function is somewhat complex, and application of the equivalent FMT_R_TO_A format requires both an INPUT and PUT function, so this first example does not represent a pristine example upon which to baseline performance.

Rather, the DO_NOTHING_CHAR user-defined function and equivalent DO_NOTHING_CHAR user-defined format are demonstrated in Program 9.10. Both the function and the format transform a value into itself; that is, they return the 20-character string that they are passed. The reduction in complexity also yields a character format that can be applied using the PUT function, and without the additional INPUT function wrapper that the FMT_R_TO_A format requires.

Program 9.10: Defining the DO_NOTHING_CHAR Function and the DO_NOTHING_ CHAR Format

```
proc fcmp outlib=work.funcs.test;
   function do_nothing_char(char $) $;
      return(char);
      endfunc;
quit;

proc format;
   value $ do_nothing_char other = [do_nothing_char()];
run;
```

The first DATA step in Program 9.11 generates a 10-million observation data set that contains 20-character strings of randomized uppercase characters. These "words" are subsequently evaluated by the next two DATA steps. The New_char_var variable is first initialized using the user-defined function, after which the New_char_var variable is subsequently initialized using the equivalent user-defined format. In both cases, New_char_var is being initialized to the current value of New_char; that is, both the function and format effectively perform a copy and paste.

Program 9.11: Compare the DO_NOTHING_CHAR Function and the DO_NOTHING_ CHAR Format

```
data letters (drop=i j);
   length char_var $20;
   call streaminit(123);
   do i = 1 to 10000000;
      char_var = '';
      do j = 1 to 20;
         substr(char_var,j,1) = byte(int(26*rand('uniform'))+65);
         end;
      output;
      end;
run;

data letters_function;
   set letters;
   length new_char_var $20;
   new_char_var = do_nothing_char(char_var);
run;

data letters_format;
   set letters;
   length new_char_var $20;
   new_char_var = put(char_var, $do_nothing_char20.);
run;
```

The log is astounding, and it demonstrates that the second DATA step that applies the user-defined format took 25 times longer than the functionally equivalent first DATA step that calls the user-defined function:

```
NOTE: There were 10000000 observations read from the data set WORK.LETTERS.
NOTE: The data set WORK.LETTERS_FUNCTION has 10000000 observations and 2
variables.
NOTE: DATA statement used (Total process time):
      real time            1.21 seconds
      user cpu time        1.01 seconds
      system cpu time      0.18 seconds
      memory               1436.68k
      OS Memory            20472.00k

NOTE: There were 10000000 observations read from the data set WORK.LETTERS.
NOTE: The data set WORK.LETTERS_FORMAT has 10000000 observations and 2
variables.
NOTE: DATA statement used (Total process time):
      real time            30.51 seconds
      user cpu time        20.96 seconds
      system cpu time      9.53 seconds
      memory               593.18k
      OS Memory            20472.00k
```

Keep in mind, however, that the rationale for applying a user-defined format that calls a user-defined function is to skip an entire DATA step that would otherwise need to apply the function prior to some subsequent SAS procedure. In a real-world scenario, the performance cost of that extra DATA step would need to be evaluated against any performance degradation incurred by applying the user-defined format. In the end, SAS practitioners need to weigh which option delivers the required functionality and performance.

More User-Defined Function and Format Performance

The previous section compared the performance of user-defined functions against their equivalent user-defined formats that dynamically call a user-defined function. No attempt was made, however, to improve the performance of the ROMAN_TO_ARABIC function itself. For example, rather than transforming Roman numerals into Arabic numbers through repeated calculation, a function could instead consult a lookup table that maps all Roman numerals to their equivalents. After all, there are arguably only 3,999 integers that can be represented through Roman numerals (foregoing the placement of a horizontal line above letters, which is not demonstrated in this text).

Program 9.12 builds the Roman_lookup data set, which leverages the built-in ROMAN format to generate corresponding Roman numerals for the numbers between one and 3,999. Thereafter, the ROMAN_TO_ARABIC_HASH format ingests the data set into a hash object and leverages the

FIND hash method to retrieve Arabic numbers based on their corresponding Roman numeral equivalents. Finally, the FORMAT procedure builds a corresponding user-defined format (also ROMAN_TO_ARABIC_HASH) that calls the function.

Program 9.12: Creating a Hash-Based Roman Numeral Conversion Function and Format

```
data roman_lookup;
   length rom $20 num 8;
   do num = 1 to 3999;
      rom = put(num,roman20.);
      output;
      end;
run;

proc fcmp outlib = work.funcs.math;
   function roman_to_arabic_hash(rom $);
      length num 8;
      declare hash h(dataset: 'roman_lookup');
      rc = h.defineKey('rom');
      rc = h.defineData('num');
      rc = h.defineDone();
      rc = h.find();
      return(num);
      endfunc;
quit;

proc format;
   value $roman_to_arabic_hash other = [roman_to_arabic_hash()];
run;
```

With both the ROMAN_TO_ARABIC_HASH function and format defined, the first DATA step in Program 9.13 generates a 10-million observation data set (Numbers) that is transformed by the subsequent two functionally equivalent DATA steps. The second DATA step transforms the Roman numerals by calling the ROMAN_TO_ARABIC_HASH function, and the third DATA step transforms the Roman numerals by applying the ROMAN_TO_ARABIC_HASH character format.

Program 9.13: Generating and Transforming Roman Numerals

```
data numbers (drop=cnt num);
   length num 8 rom $20;
   call streaminit(123);
   do cnt = 1 to 10000000;
      num = int(1000*rand('uniform'))+1;
      rom = put(num,roman20.);
      output;
      end;
run;

data transform_function_hash;
   set numbers;
```

```
   length arabic 8;
   arabic = roman_to_arabic_hash(rom);
run;

data transform_format_hash;
   set numbers;
   length arabic 8;
   arabic = input(put(rom, $roman_to_arabic_hash.),8.);
run;
```

Once again, the log demonstrates the tremendous performance advantages of calling the user-defined function as opposed to applying the equivalent user-defined format, with the function completing ten times faster than the format:

```
NOTE: There were 10000000 observations read from the data set WORK.NUMBERS.
NOTE: The data set WORK.TRANSFORM_FUNCTION_HASH has 10000000 observations
and 2 variables.
NOTE: DATA statement used (Total process time):
      real time            3.23 seconds
      user cpu time        3.09 seconds
      system cpu time      0.14 seconds
      memory               1893.56k
      OS Memory            24060.00k

NOTE: There were 10000000 observations read from the data set WORK.NUMBERS.
NOTE: The data set WORK.TRANSFORM_FORMAT_HASH has 10000000 observations and
2 variables.
NOTE: DATA statement used (Total process time):
      real time            35.53 seconds
      user cpu time        25.56 seconds
      system cpu time      9.90 seconds
      memory               1419.25k
      OS Memory            23804.00k
```

Of course, if it is speed you need, a DATA step solution will often run the fastest because two levels of abstraction are removed—one level to apply the format, and one level to call the function. Thus, as one final performance benchmark, Program 9.14 demonstrates a functionally equivalent DATA step that both ingests the 10-million observation Numbers data set and transforms the Roman numerals—without the need to call a function.

Program 9.14: Performing the Roman Numeral Hash Lookup in the DATA Step
```
data transform_data_step_hash (drop=rc rename=(num=arabic));
   set numbers;
   length num 8;
   if _n_ = 1 then do;
      declare hash h(dataset: 'roman_lookup');
      rc = h.defineKey('rom');
      rc = h.defineData('num');
```

```
        rc = h.defineDone();
        call missing(num);
        end;
    rc = h.find();
run;
```

The functionally equivalent DATA step executes in only 1.2 seconds!

```
NOTE: There were 3999 observations read from the data set WORK.ROMAN_
LOOKUP.
NOTE: There were 10000000 observations read from the data set WORK.NUMBERS.
NOTE: The data set WORK.TRANSFORM_DATA_STEP_HASH has 10000000 observations
and 2 variables.
NOTE: DATA statement used (Total process time):
      real time            1.20 seconds
      user cpu time        1.03 seconds
      system cpu time      0.25 seconds
      memory               1343.28k
      OS Memory            27132.00k
```

This performance annihilates the two format-based solutions, which took 35 and 66 seconds, respectively. Even the ROMAN_TO_ARABIC_HASH function that leverages the hash object completed in 3.2 seconds—more than twice as slow as the equivalent DATA step shown in Program 9.14. However, although applying a format or calling a function do understandably incur overhead system resource utilization, the quality of the code is improved—as it is rendered more readable, more maintainable, and more reusable. The fastest solution is not necessarily the preferred one, and software requirements always should incorporate not only functional requirements but also performance requirements.

User-Defined Informat Calling a User-Defined Function

The previous sections demonstrated how to build a user-defined format that calls a user-defined function, which enables data transformation to occur within not only the DATA step but also SAS procedures that support the FORMAT statement. Similarly, SAS informats can call user-defined functions by supplying the function name to the FORMAT procedure OTHER option. Like formats, informats can standardize and transform data, but by using the INPUT function rather than the PUT function. And unlike formats, informats can be specified by the INPUT statement to validate, clean, or transform data as they are ingested into a data set. Given these diverse use cases, powerful user-defined informats that call user-defined functions can be designed.

Designing a User-Defined Informat to Validate Roman Numerals

In the previous sections, the ROMAN_TO_ARABIC and ROMAN_TO_ARABIC_HASH user-defined functions were created, which convert character Roman numerals to numeric Arabic numbers.

Subsequently, the FMT_R_TO_A and ROMAN_TO_ARABIC_HASH user-defined formats were created, each of which calls its respective user-defined function to transform data. In other cases, however, the requirement might be to validate rather than transform data, and informats can assist here.

The DATA step in Program 9.15 creates the Roman numerals one through 3,999 (again leveraging the built-in ROMAN format), after which the FCMP procedure defines the INF_VALIDATE_ROMAN function that validates whether some character input is a valid Roman numeral.

Program 9.15: Creating the INF_VALIDATE_ROMAN Function to Validate Roman Numerals

```
data roman_lookup;
   length rom $20 num 8;
   do num = 1 to 3999;
      rom = put(num,roman20.);
      output;
      end;
run;

proc fcmp outlib = work.funcs.math;
   function inf_validate_roman(raw_rom $) $;
      length rom $20;
      rom = strip(upcase(raw_rom));
      declare hash h(dataset: 'roman_lookup');
      rc = h.defineKey('rom');
      rc = h.defineDone();
      if h.check() = 0 then return(rom);
      else return('');
      endfunc;
quit;
```

Note that INF_VALIDATE_ROMAN primarily validates Roman numerals, but it also transforms any lowercase characters to uppercase prior to the hash lookup operation. However, because no value is being returned from the hash object, only the DEFINEKEY method is used to import Rom into the hash table, and the DEFINEDATA method is not required. For this reason, the CHECK method is also used in lieu of FIND. CHECK returns a 0 when the hash key (the Roman numeral) is located, after which the value (now uppercase) is returned to the calling program. If the key is not located, a missing value is returned.

The FORMAT procedure in Program 9.16 defines the INF_VALIDATE_ROMAN informat. It is not necessary to name the informat and derivative function identically, although this practice can facilitate readability, as it ties the two modules together. The INVALUE statement declares that an informat rather than format is being created. The DEFAULT option declares that the informat will have a default length of 20 (when not specified), and the OTHER option names the function that is called.

Program 9.16: Creating the INF_VALIDATE_ROMAN User-Defined Informat

```
options cmplib=work.funcs;

proc format;
   invalue $ inf_validate_roman default=20 other=[inf_validate_roman()];
run;
```

The first DATA step in Program 9.17 creates sample data to be evaluated by the INF_VALIDATE_ROMAN function and the INF_VALIDATE_ROMAN format, in which all odd observations are valid, and even observations are invalid.

Program 9.17: Creating Somewhat-Roman Numeral Data

```
data some_romans;
   infile datalines truncover dsd delimiter=',';
   length condition $20 rom $20;
   input condition $ rom $;
   datalines;
valid (upper),LVIII
missing,
valid (lower),mmxxiii
invalid (roman),MILD
valid (mixed),CcXXXviII
invalid (other),12567
;
```

For each observation, the Condition variable describes the Roman numeral data:

1. LVIII – valid (58), uppercase Roman numeral
2. [missing value] – invalid because the text is missing
3. mmxxiii – valid (2023), lowercase Roman numeral
4. MILD – invalid because the Roman numeral characters are meaningless in this order
5. CcXXXviII – valid (238), mixed case Roman numeral
6. 12567 – invalid because Arabic numbers are represented

The DATA step in Program 9.18 calls the INF_VALIDATE_ROMAN function to validate each of the values.

Program 9.18: Calling the INF_VALIDATE_ROMAN Function to Validate Roman Numerals

```
data testing_function;
   set some_romans;
   length func_rom $20;
   func_rom = inf_validate_roman(rom);
   put @1 condition @20 rom @30 func_rom @40;
run;
```

For the valid Roman numerals, the Func_rom variable is initialized to the validated value, and for invalid values, it is initialized as missing:

```
valid (upper)      LVIII     LVIII
missing
valid (lower)      mmxxiii   MMXXIII
invalid (roman)    MILD
valid (mixed)      CcXXXviII CCXXXVIII
invalid (other)    12567
```

Similarly, Program 9.19 applies the INF_VALIDATE_ROMAN informat to validate the same Roman numerals.

Program 9.19: Applying the INF_VALIDATE_ROMAN Informat to Validate Roman Numerals

```
data testing_informat;
   set some_romans;
   length inf_rom $20;
   inf_rom = input(rom, $inf_validate_roman.);
   put @1 condition @20 rom @30 inf_rom @40;
run;
```

The log is identical to that of the functionally equivalent DATA step in Program 9.18.

Designing a User-Defined Informat That Throws Exceptions

The INF_VALIDATE_ROMAN format, defined in the previous section, successfully validates whether a character value represents a Roman numeral. However, it does so only by overwriting the value with a missing value, which must subsequently be evaluated programmatically. A more effective solution can instead initialize the _ERROR_ automatic variable to 1 whenever an invalid value is encountered. An invalid value represents an *exception*—that is, an *exceptional* event, where "exceptional" alludes not to greatness but rather to some unanticipated or unwanted event. Thus, when an invalid value is encountered, the initialization of _ERROR_ to 1 describes *throwing an exception*. The OTHER option in the INVALUE statement can throw an exception during informat processing, which is beneficial because the _ERROR_ value can subsequently be programmatically tested to drive dynamic processing based on the validity of the value.

Consider that Roman numerals are maintained not within a SAS data set but instead within a text file. Third-party data especially require extra vigilance and validation as they are ingested, and informats can facilitate this quality control objective. The following data in the text file (Romans.txt) are identical to those shown in Program 9.17:

```
valid (upper),LVIII
missing,
valid (lower),mmxxiii
```

```
invalid (roman),MILD
valid (mixed),CcXXXviII
invalid (other),12567
```

First, without any exception handling, the DATA step in Program 9.20 ingests the text file. The data are still validated because Rom is only initialized when a valid Roman numeral is evaluated. However, the _ERROR_ automatic variable is not yet incorporated. Note that the INF_VALIDATE_ ROMAN informat is applied to the Rom variable by the INPUT statement, in which a colon must precede the informat name, and a period must follow it.

Program 9.20: Ingesting and Validating Roman Numerals from a Text File
```
%let loc=C:\sas\;
filename f "&loc.romans.txt";
data ingest;
   infile f truncover dsd delimiter = ',';
   length condition $20 rom $20;
   input condition $ rom : $inf_validate_roman.;
run;
```

As before, Rom is initialized to a valid Roman numeral for only the odd-numbered observations, whereas the even-numbered observations are evaluated to be invalid, and thus are initialized to a missing value. Despite the invalid data that are encountered, no notes or warnings are written to the log:

```
NOTE: The infile F is:
      Filename=C:\sas\romans.txt,
      RECFM=V,LRECL=32767,File Size (bytes)=122,

NOTE: 6 records were read from the infile F.
      The minimum record length was 8.
      The maximum record length was 23.
NOTE: The data set WORK.INGEST has 6 observations and 2 variables.
```

Ordinarily, one would leverage the INVALUE statement OTHER=_ERROR_ option to throw exceptions encountered while applying an informat. However, the OTHER option is already occupied because it is calling the user-defined function. Notwithstanding this limitation, by initializing a variable to a missing value, subsequent exception handling can detect and handle these invalid data.

Although FCMP-defined informats are incapable of throwing exceptions, the CNTLIN option of the FORMAT procedure facilitates the creation of more capable informats. The DATA step in Program 9.21 generates a data set that is subsequently read by the FORMAT procedure to create an informat using the CNTLIN option. Note that CNTLIN requires the precise naming of several mandatory variables:

- Fmtname specifies the name of the informat or format.
- Type distinguishes numeric formats (N), character formats (C), numeric informats (I), and character informats (J).

- Start specifies the input value to be evaluated.
- Label specifies the output value to which the input value should be mapped.

Program 9.21 also demonstrates the optional HLO variable that cannot be renamed. "U" (uppercase) denotes that input values are transformed to uppercase prior to evaluation, and "O" (other) denotes the output value to which unmapped input should be transformed.

Program 9.21: Defining an Informat That Throws an Exception Using _ERROR_

```
data roman_cntlin (drop=num);
   set roman_lookup(rename=(rom=start)) end=eof;
   length label $20 fmtname $32 type $2 hlo $2;
   label = start;
   fmtname = 'inf_validate_roman_cntlin';
   type = 'j';
   hlo = 'u';
   output;
   if eof then do;
      start = ' ';
      hlo = 'o';
      label = '_error_';
      output;
      end;
run;

proc format cntlin=roman_cntlin;
run;
```

The FORMAT procedure CNTLIN option specifies the control table (SAS data set) from which the format or informat will be derived.

The DATA step in Program 9.22 applies the updated informat (INF_VALIDATE_ROMAN_CNTLIN) to the Rom variable during data ingestion, and because the informat no longer calls an FCMP function, it ably accommodates implementation of the _ERROR_ automatic variable.

Program 9.22: Applying the INF_VALIDATE_ROMAN_CNTLIN Informat to Throw Exceptions

```
%let loc=c:\sas\;
filename f "&loc.romans.txt";
data ingest;
   infile f truncover dsd delimiter = ',';
   length condition $20 rom $20;
   input condition $ rom : $inf_validate_roman_cntlin.;
run;
```

Note the three exceptions—mmxxiii, MILD, and 12567—are now highlighted in the log:

```
NOTE: The infile F is:
      Filename=C:\sas\romans.txt,
      RECFM=V,LRECL=32767,File Size (bytes)=122,

NOTE: Invalid data for rom in line 2 9-9.
RULE:      ----+----1----+----2----+----3----+----4----+----5----+----6----+----7----+----
8----+-
2           missing, 8
condition=missing rom=  _ERROR_=1 _N_=2
NOTE: Invalid data for rom in line 4 17-20.
4           invalid (roman),MILD 20
condition=invalid (roman) rom=  _ERROR_=1 _N_=4
NOTE: Invalid data for rom in line 6 17-21.
6           invalid (other),12567 21
condition=invalid (other) rom=  _ERROR_=1 _N_=6
NOTE: 6 records were read from the infile F.
      The minimum record length was 8.
      The maximum record length was 23.
NOTE: The data set WORK.INGEST has 6 observations and 2 variables.
```

Moreover, a single line of code could initialize a variable to the value of _ERROR_ to retain it for further programmatic evaluation and action (such as further examination, validation, or deletion of the observation):

```
error_code = _error_;
```

In this example, a user-defined informat derived from a control table has been shown to be more powerful than one derived from a user-defined function because the control table method supports throwing exceptions using the _ERROR_ automatic variable. Despite this limitation, powerful informats can be engineered through the FCMP procedure that cannot be replicated through other means, and these are described in the next section.

Designing a User-Defined Informat That Evaluates Complex Business Rules

The informats demonstrated thus far have equated to lookup tables that map one static input value to one static output value. Far more complex computations, however, can be created where informats call a user-defined function to transform dynamic input values to dynamic output values. For example, consider the chaos that could erupt when a free text form asks users for their phone numbers without any semblance of data input validation. Despite the endless complexity of data that could result from this quality control oversight, a user-defined function—called by a user-defined informat—can validate and standardize these data.

The Phones.txt text file illustrates some variability that might occur in phone number data—the first three numbers are valid, and the fourth is not:

```
valid (11-digit with dashes),1-619-570-1213
valid (11-digit with dots),1.619.570.1213
valid (11-digit compressed),16195701213
invalid (12-digit),1-619-570-12139
```

The CLEAN_PHONE function, demonstrated in Program 9.23, standardizes phone numbers. The COMPRESS function first strips all non-numeric characters, after which the phone number length is evaluated. If the length is 10, the number is evaluated to be valid. If the length is 11 and the first number is a 1, then this 1 is assumed to represent the U.S. country code, the 1 is deleted, and the remaining 10-digit number is evaluated to be valid. Otherwise, the phone number is evaluated to be invalid, and a missing value is returned from the function.

Program 9.23: Encapsulating Data Validation and Standardization Business Rules
```
proc fcmp outlib=work.funcs.phones;
    function clean_phone(phone $) $ 20;
        length phone_cleaned $12 digits $15;
        digits = compress(phone, '0123456789', 'k');
        if lengthn(digits) = 11 and substr(digits, 1, 1)='1'
            then digits = substr(digits, 2);
        if length(digits) = 10 then phone_cleaned=catx('-',substr(digits,1,3),
                substr(digits,4,3),substr(digits,7,4));
        else phone_cleaned = '';
        return(phone_cleaned);
        endfunc;
quit;
```

The DATA step in Program 9.24 ingests the Phones.txt text file and calls the CLEAN_PHONE function to validate and standardize the phone numbers.

Program 9.24: Calling the CLEAN_PHONE Function
```
%let loc=c:\sas\;
filename f "&loc.phones.txt";
data _null_;
    infile f truncover dsd delimiter = ',';
    length condition $30 phone $20 phone_cleaned $15;
    input condition $ phone $;
    phone_cleaned = clean_phone(phone);
    put @1 phone @20 phone_cleaned;
run;
```

The log demonstrates that the first three values of Phone_cleaned are standardized, and the fourth is initialized to missing because it contains 12 digits:

```
1-619-570-1213      619-570-1213
1.619.570.1213      619-570-1213
16195701213         619-570-1213
1-619-570-12139
```

Continuing to extrapolate this example, the business rules inside the CLEAN_PHONE function can be called from a user-defined informat. This can enable the business rules to be applied as the text file is ingested from the INPUT statement rather than in a subsequent statement, as was required in Program 9.24.

The FORMAT procedure in Program 9.25 first creates the CLEAN_PHONE user-defined informat, after which the informat is applied by the INPUT statement as the data are ingested in the DATA step. In theory, this should streamline data ingestion and avoid the two-step process of having to first ingest data and next transform them.

Program 9.25: Attempting to Create a User-Defined Informat from a User-Defined Function

```
proc format;
   invalue $ clean_phone other=[clean_phone()];
run;

data _null_;
   infile f truncover dsd delimiter=',';
   length condition $30 phone_cleaned $15;
   input condition $ phone_cleaned : $clean_phone.;
   put @1 condition @30 phone_cleaned;
run;
```

However, note the discrepancy in the log. The results in the third observation do not match those of Program 9.24—the phone number is valid, but it has been truncated:

```
valid (10-digit with dashes)  619-570-1213
valid (10-digit with dots)    619-570-1213
valid (10-digit compressed)   619-570-121
invalid (12-digit)
```

As it turns out, a defect within the FCMP procedure prevents the full value of the third phone number from being returned. This occurs because the raw value (16195701213) has a length of 11, whereas the standardized value the function is trying to return (619-570-1213) has a length of 12. Thus, the defect causes the FCMP procedure to allocate only enough memory for the length of the raw character value, which causes the 12th position (3) to be truncated from the return value.

No workaround exists for this defect, so SAS practitioners should exercise caution when building user-defined character informats that call user-defined functions. However, in this specific case, as numeric data are essentially being standardized, one possible solution is to return the unformatted (yet standardized) phone number as a numeric value, rather than as a phone number formatted with dashes.

The CLEAN_PHONE_NUM function is defined in Program 9.26. It performs the same standardization as the CLEAN_PHONE function, with the exception that it returns a numeric value—that is, without dashes.

Program 9.26: Returning a Standardized Phone Number as a Numeric Value

```
proc fcmp outlib=work.funcs.phones;
   function clean_phone_num(phone $);
      length phone_cleaned 8 digits $15;
      digits = compress(phone,'0123456789','k');
      if lengthn(digits) = 11 and substr(digits,1,1) = '1'
         then digits = substr(digits,2);
      if length(digits) = 10 then phone_cleaned = input(digits,12.);
      else phone_cleaned = .;
      return(phone_cleaned);
      endfunc;
quit;
```

No longer stymied by the FCMP defect that truncates character return values, CLEAN_PHONE_ NUM returns a numeric value that can be applied using a user-defined numeric informat. The FORMAT procedure in Program 9.27 defines the CLEAN_PHONE_NUM numeric informat, after which the DATA step applies the informat using the INPUT statement during data ingestion.

Program 9.27: Creating a User-Defined Numeric Informat from a User-Defined Function

```
proc format;
   invalue clean_phone_num other = [clean_phone_num()];
run;

data _null_;
   infile f truncover dsd delimiter = ',';
   length condition $30 phone_cleaned 8;
   input condition $ phone_cleaned : clean_phone_num.;
   put @1 condition @30 phone_cleaned;
run;
```

The log demonstrates the successful application of the CLEAN_PHONE_NUM numeric informat, in which the first three values are standardized, and the fourth value is denoted as missing (that is, invalid):

```
phone_cleaned=6195701213
phone_cleaned=6195701213
phone_cleaned=6195701213
invalid (12-digit)           .
```

With the phone numbers now standardized, these values could be reformatted with dashes or other characters as necessary. Or the business rules could be expanded, for example, to validate that the first three digits correspond to a valid U.S. area code. Most importantly, however, this example demonstrates how complex data validation and standardization rules have been encapsulated within a user-defined informat.

Applying User-Defined Functions in PROC REPORT

One final method of calling user-defined functions and subroutines is demonstrated where the invocation occurs inside the COMPUTE block of the REPORT procedure. This powerful functionality enables the text, formatting, and style of report cells to be altered dynamically. For example, a function could transform text within a cell, highlight a cell in various meaningful colors, build an active URL that links from a cell, or construct flyover text that is displayed temporarily when a mouse hovers over a cell. Each of these objectives is demonstrated in the following sections, although this only scratches the surface of how user-defined functions can augment report functionality.

Creating a Basic HTML Report

Consider three hapless souls working in a regional paper supply company—let's call them Jim, Stanley, and Kelly—who must submit quarterly expense reports. Each employee has a maximum for allowable expenses each month, and the Accounting Department is responsible for evaluating whether each employee remained under budget, and if not, by how far the budget was exceeded. The implementation of user-defined functions and subroutines within the REPORT procedure can greatly enhance and streamline reporting capabilities by modularizing business rules and other logic that would otherwise need to be included in the report definition itself.

The DATA step in Program 9.28 creates the Personnel data set, which includes each employee's unique ID, name, maximum allowable expenses per quarter, and link to their virtual personnel file. As this data set maintains a unique ID, this ID can be used as a key in subsequent hash-based lookup operations to retrieve other employee-specific data.

Program 9.28: Creating the Personnel Data Set
```
data personnel;
    infile datalines truncover dsd delimiter = ',';
    length id 8 employee $30 max_expenses 8 employee_profile $100;
    format id 8. employee $30. max_expenses dollar8.2 employee_profile $100.;
    input id employee $ max_expenses employee_profile $;
    datalines;
6,Jim Halpert,2199,https://theoffice.fandom.com/wiki/Jim_Halpert
14,Stanley Hudson,2500,https://theoffice.fandom.com/wiki/Stanley_Hudson
17,Kelly Kapoor,200,https://theoffice.fandom.com/wiki/Kelly_Kapoor
;
```

The DATA step in Program 9.29 creates the Expenses_2022 data set, which enumerates quarterly expense totals for the employees.

Program 9.29: Creating the 2022 Table of Quarterly Expense Totals
```
data expenses_2022;
    infile datalines truncover dsd delimiter=',';
    length id 8 yr 8 qtr 8 submitted 8 exp 8;
```

```
   format id 8. yr 8. qtr 8. submitted mmddyy10. exp dollar8.2;
   input id yr qtr submitted : mmddyy10. exp;
   datalines;
6,2022,1,04-05-2022,1800
6,2022,2,07-02-2022,2149
6,2022,3,10-07-2022,2250
6,2022,4,01-05-2023,1915
14,2022,1,04-10-2022,2300
14,2022,2,07-07-2022,2290
14,2022,3,10-03-2022,1980
14,2022,4,01-08-2023,2510
17,2022,1,04-05-2022,200
17,2022,2,07-05-2022,400
17,2022,3,10-05-2022,600
17,2022,4,01-05-2023,750
;
```

As the Personnel data set maintains a unique ID, it might be beneficial to create a crosswalk that maps employee IDs with their associated names. Program 9.30 uses the CNTLIN option in the FORMAT procedure to create the ID_TO_NAME format, which maps ID to name. This format is subsequently applied in the REPORT procedure so that the report will enumerate employee names rather than IDs.

Program 9.30: Creating the ID_TO_NAME User-Defined Format

```
data id_to_name (keep = start label fmtname type);
   set personnel (rename = (id=start employee=label));
   length fmtname $32 type $2;
   fmtname = 'id_to_name';
   type = 'n';
run;


proc format cntlin = id_to_name;
run;
```

A report is created in Program 9.31 that lists employees and their respective quarterly expenses. Note that the report demonstrates baseline functionality and is incrementally modified in subsequent examples.

Program 9.31: Baseline Expense Report Functionality

```
%let loc = c:\sas\;
ods html path = "&loc";
title;
proc report data = expenses_2022 nocenter nowindows nocompletecols
      style(report) = [foreground=black backgroundcolor=white]
      style(header) = [font_size=2 backgroundcolor=dark gray foreground=white]
      style(column) = [backgroundcolor=dark white];
   columns ('Employee' id) qtr, exp;
   define id / group ' ' format=id_to_name.;
   define qtr / across 'Quarter';
   define exp / analysis sum ' ';
run;
ods html close;
```

The report relies exclusively on the Expenses_2022 data set and defines columns for ID, quarter (Qtr), and expense (Exp). Note that Qtr is defined as an ACROSS variable, which instructs the REPORT procedure to include multiple data set observations within a single report row. Thus, despite Jim's expenses occurring across four observations, they appear in one row within the report. The HTML output for the report is shown in Figure 9.1.

Figure 9.1: Expense Report Baseline Functionality

Employee	Quarter			
	1	2	3	4
Jim Halpert	$1800.00	$2149.00	$2250.00	$1915.00
Kelly Kapoor	$200.00	$400.00	$600.00	$750.00
Stanley Hudson	$2300.00	$2290.00	$1980.00	$2510.00

Adding Getter Functionality to Support Dynamically Color-Coded Report

Consider the need, however, to evaluate for each employee whether that employee exceeded allowable expenses for each month. This analysis requires a comparison of the employee's maximum quarterly allowance, maintained in the Personnel data set and unavailable to the REPORT procedure, which relies on the Expenses_2022 data set. The typical solution in SAS requires that the two data sets be merged, that each employee's maximum allowable expenses be added to each observation in the Expenses_2022 data set, and that the calculation be performed either preceding the REPORT procedure or within a COMPUTE block of REPORT.

However, a straightforward *getter function*—introduced in Chapter 6—can retrieve each employee's maximum value from the Personnel data set when the employee's ID is passed as an argument. Thus, similar to how the ID_TO_NAME user-defined format maps employee ID to employee name, the GET_MAX_EXP user-defined function, demonstrated in Program 9.32, maps ID to that employee's maximum allowable expense, which is returned by the function.

Program 9.32: Defining a Function to Retrieve Employee Maximum Allowed Expense from ID

```
proc fcmp outlib = work.funcs.office;
   function get_max_exp(id);
      length max_expenses 8;
      declare hash h(dataset: 'personnel');
      rc = h.defineKey('id');
      rc = h.defineData('max_expenses');
      rc = h.defineDone();
      rc = h.find();
      return(max_expenses);
      endfunc;
quit;
```

The updated REPORT procedure in Program 9.33 adds a Dummy variable, which is declared in the DEFINE statement to be a COMPUTED variable, which in turn facilitates the addition of a COMPUTE block in which the report can be dynamically modified.

Program 9.33: Designing a Report That Flags Expense Excesses

```
ods html path="&loc";
title;
proc report data = expenses_2022 nocenter nowindows nocompletecols
      style(report) = [foreground=black backgroundcolor=white]
      style(header) = [font_size=2 backgroundcolor=dark gray foreground=white]
      style(column) = [backgroundcolor=dark white];
   columns ('Employee' id) qtr, exp dummy;
   define id / group ' ' format=id_to_name.;
   define qtr / across 'Quarter';
   define exp / analysis sum ' ';
   define dummy / computed noprint;
   compute dummy;
      do col = 2 to 5;
         col_num = '_c' || strip(put(col,8.)) || '_';
         if vvaluex(col_num) > get_max_exp(id) then
            call define(col_num, 'style', 'style = [backgroundcolor=very light red]');
         end;
      endcomp;
run;
ods html close;
```

User-defined functions and subroutines are permitted within COMPUTE blocks of the REPORT procedure, so the block bears further scrutiny. COMPUTE blocks must be defined using the COMPUTED keyword, after which the COMPUTE statement initiates the COMPUTE block. The NOPRINT option instructs SAS not to print the Dummy variable in the report; however, the column nevertheless must be counted when numbering columns from left to right:

```
define dummy / computed noprint;
compute dummy;
```

The DO loop iterates from columns two through five, which includes the four quarters:

```
do col = 2 to 5;
```

Because Qtr is defined as an ACROSS variable that spans multiple columns, the Qtr variable name cannot be used in subsequent computations. The _C#_ notation must be used instead to reference columns, where "#" represents the column number. Thus, on the first iteration of the DO loop, Col_num will be initialized to _C2_, which corresponds to the first Quarter—that is, the second column of the report:

```
col_num = '_c' || strip(put(col,8.)) || '_';
```

The VVALUEX built-in function extracts the value from the _C2_ variable, which is subsequently compared to the return value of the GET_MAX_EXP function. In other words, this logic evaluates whether the employee has spent too much money for a particular month, and if so, calls the DEFINE subroutine to modify the background color of that specific cell to "very light red":

```
if vvaluex(col_num) > get_max_exp(id) then
    call define(col_num, 'style', 'style = [backgroundcolor=very light red]');
```

At this point, the END statement terminates the loop after all four quarters have been evaluated, and the ENDCOMP statement terminates the COMPUTE block:

```
    end;
endcomp;
```

The output of the report is demonstrated in Figure 9.2, which now shows the quarters that Jim, Kelly, and Stanley exceeded their allowances in very light red.

Figure 9.2: Expense Report with Color-Coding to Identify Expense Excesses

	Quarter			
Employee	**1**	**2**	**3**	**4**
Jim Halpert	$1800.00	$2149.00	$2250.00	$1915.00
Kelly Kapoor	$200.00	$400.00	$600.00	$750.00
Stanley Hudson	$2300.00	$2290.00	$1980.00	$2510.00

The report is an improvement because it immediately identifies excessive spending. However, its functionality could be improved if color-coding more precisely identified the amount by which an employee's maximum was exceeded. A user-defined subroutine can calculate not only the amount of excess spending, but also the associated color that the amount's cell should be highlighted—based on business rules that delineate colors in some meaningful way.

Differentiating Report Color-Coding Based on Subroutine Business Rules

The QUANT_EXP subroutine in Program 9.34 again leverages a hash object to retrieve each employee's maximum allowable expenses, after which the excess (if any) is calculated. All nonzero excesses (in which an employee overspent) cause the Color variable to be initialized to some non-white value, with darker values indicating greater excesses. Note that the OUTARGS statement declares the Over and Color variables as call by reference so that their modified values will be available in the calling program (the COMPUTE block).

Program 9.34: Defining a Subroutine to Quantify and Color Code Excess Expenses
```
proc fcmp outlib = work.funcs.office;
   subroutine quant_exp(id, exp, over, color $);
      outargs over, color;
      length max_expenses 8;
      declare hash h(dataset: 'personnel');
      rc = h.defineKey('id');
      rc = h.defineData('max_expenses');
      rc = h.defineDone();
      rc = h.find();
      over = 0;
      if exp > max_expenses then do;
         over = exp-max_expenses;
         if over < 100 then color = 'very light yellow';
         else if over < 200 then color = 'orange';
         else if over < 300 then color = 'very light red';
         else color = 'red';
         end;
      put id= exp= over= color=;
      endsub;
quit;
```

In Program 9.35, the REPORT procedure is again updated to leverage QUANT_EXP to color code cells based on how much each employee exceeded the maximum allowable expense.

Program 9.35: Designing a Report That Color Codes Excess Expenses
```
ods html path = "&loc";
title;
proc report data = expenses_2022 nocenter nowindows nocompletecols
      style(report) = [foreground=black backgroundcolor=white]
```

```
         style(header) = [font_size=2 backgroundcolor=dark gray foreground=white]
         style(column) = [backgroundcolor=dark white];
    columns ('Employee' id) qtr, exp dummy;
    define id / group ' ' format=id_to_name.;
    define qtr / across 'Quarter';
    define exp / analysis sum ' ';
    define dummy / computed noprint;
    compute dummy;
        do col = 2 to 5;
            col_num = '_c' || strip(put(col,8.)) || '_';
            length this_exp 8 over 8 color $30;
            color = 'white';
            call missing(over);
            this_exp = vvaluex(col_num);
            call quant_exp(id, this_exp, over, color);
            call define(col_num, 'style', 'style = [backgroundcolor='
                || strip(color) || ']');
        end;
    endcomp;
run;
ods html close;
```

Now, Color is initialized to "white" within the COMPUTE block and will be modified by the QUANT_ EXP subroutine only if the quarter's expenses exceed an employee's maximum. If that occurs, the business rules within QUANT_EXP will return that amount of excess (Over), as well as the color the cell should be shaded (Color). The updated report is demonstrated in Figure 9.3 and shows the far greater degree to which Kelly overspent as compared to Jim and Stanley.

Figure 9.3: Color-Coded Expense Report (by Amount of Excess)

Employee	Quarter			
	1	2	3	4
Jim Halpert	$1800.00	$2149.00	$2250.00	$1915.00
Kelly Kapoor	$200.00	$400.00	$600.00	$750.00
Stanley Hudson	$2300.00	$2290.00	$1980.00	$2510.00

Adding More Getter Functionality to Query a Lookup Table

At this point, one final, updated report is desired, which will link employees to their associated employee profiles (via a URL) and display the amount of excess spending when a user hovers over a color-coded cell. A second getter function can be constructed, which retrieves an employee's personnel profile URL from the Personnel data set when the employee's ID is passed as an argument. Program 9.36 defines the GET_EMP_PROFILE function, which again leverages a hash object to perform the lookup operation.

Program 9.36: Defining a Function to Retrieve Employee URL from ID
```
proc fcmp outlib = work.funcs.office;
   function get_emp_profile(id) $100;
      length employee_profile $100;
      declare hash h(dataset: 'personnel');
      rc = h.defineKey('id');
      rc = h.defineData('employee_profile');
      rc = h.defineDone();
      rc = h.find();
      return(employee_profile);
      endfunc;
quit;
```

The final report is defined in Program 9.37. The GET_EMP_PROFILE function is called to retrieve the URL for each employee, after which the DEFINE subroutine uses the URL argument to associate this URL with the ID column. In other words, clicking a user's name will now link to that user's profile. The QUANT_EXP subroutine is again called, and the Over_text variable is initialized to a text statement that describes by how much money an employee exceeded the allowable amount. The Over_text variable is temporarily displayed (via the FLYOVER option) whenever a user hovers over a color-coded cell.

Program 9.37: Designing a Report That Prints Excess Amount and Links to Employee Profile
```
ods html path = "&loc" file = 'Excessing_Spending.html';
title;
proc report data = expenses_2022 nocenter nowindows nocompletecols
      style(report) = [foreground=black backgroundcolor=white]
      style(header) = [font_size=2 backgroundcolor=dark gray foreground=white]
      style(column) = [backgroundcolor=dark white];
   columns ('Employee' id) qtr, exp dummy;
   define id / group ' ' format=id_to_name.;
   define qtr / across 'Quarter';
   define exp / analysis sum ' ';
   define dummy / computed noprint;
   compute dummy;
      call define('id', 'URL', get_emp_profile(id));
      do col=2 to 5;
         col_num = '_c' || strip(put(col,8.)) || '_';
         length this_exp 8 over 8 color $30 over_text $40;
```

```
            color = 'white';
            call missing(over);
            this_exp = vvaluex(col_num);
            call quant_exp(id, this_exp, over, color);
            call define(col_num, 'style', 'style = [backgroundcolor=' || strip(color)
                || ']');
            if over > 0 then do;
                over_text = strip(put(over,dollar8.2)) || ' over budget!';
                call define(col_num, 'style/merge', 'style = [flyover="' || strip(over_text)
                    || '"]');
                end;
            end;
        endcomp;
run;
ods html close;
```

The results of the final report are displayed in Figure 9.4.

The final report achieves dynamic functionality facilitated through multiple user-defined functions. For example, the GET_EMP_PROFILE function extracts the URL for each employee from the Personnel data set—a separate data set from the one on which the report is based. The QUANT_EXP subroutine also queries the Personnel data set to retrieve each employee's maximum allowable expenses, after which this value is evaluated against actual expenses, and business rules within the subroutine return the applicable color-coding if the employee has overspent. Finally, hovering over any of the highlighted cells (not shown) will display a message that reveals by what amount the employee overspent for a specific quarter.

This level of dynamic functionality within the REPORT procedure could be conceived without the use of user-defined functions; however, it would require the prior joining of external data sets, and the addition of numerous variables to support calculations. Rather, by incorporating user-defined functions and subroutines within the COMPUTE block, a more direct solution is supported and software complexity is minimized.

Figure 9.4: Report Demonstrating Gradated Color-Coding, Flyover Text, and Hyperlinked Employee Names

Employee	Quarter			
	1	2	3	4
Jim Halpert	$1800.00	$2149.00	$2250.00	$1915.00
Kelly Kapoor	$200.00	$400.00	$600.00	$750.00
Stanley Hudson	$2300.00	$2290.00	$1980.00	$2510.00

Conclusion

The FORMAT procedure and the REPORT procedure provide two alternatives for invoking user-defined functions. The creation of user-defined formats that call user-defined functions is invaluable because it expands the ways in which functions can be applied—for example, inside MEANS, FREQ, PRINT, and other procedures that support the FORMAT statement. Similarly, this chapter demonstrated how the INPUT statement and INPUT function can validate and clean data by applying user-defined informats that call user-defined functions. Calling user-defined functions and subroutines inside the REPORT procedure COMPUTE block was also demonstrated, and can yield more flexible functionality that requires far less code. In sum, wherever and however user-defined functions and subroutines are leveraged, you will find the familiar trail of improved software quality—DATA steps, SAS macro language, and SAS procedures that are unmistakably more maintainable, modular, reusable, configurable, and readable due to the benefits of FCMP.

References

DiIorio, Frank C. 1997. SAS Applications Programming: A Gentle Introduction. Belmont, California: Duxbury Press.

Google. 2023. Client Libraries for Google Maps Web Services. https://developers.google.com/maps/web-services/client-library.

Google. 2023. Google Maps Platform Pricing. Google. https://developers.google.com/maps/billing-and-pricing/pricing.

Google. 2023. googlemaps. Google. https://github.com/googlemaps/google-maps-services-python.

Google. 2023. google-maps-services-python/googlemaps. Google. https://github.com/googlemaps/google-maps-services-python/blob/master/googlemaps/distance_matrix.py.

Google. 2023. Use API Keys. Google. https://developers.google.com/maps/documentation/javascript/get-api-key.

Guido van Rossum, Barry Warsaw, Nick Coghlan. 2013. PEP 8 - Style Guide for Python Code. https://www.python.org/dev/peps/pep-0008/.

IEEE. 2005. IEEE Std 1220™-2005. IEEE standard for the application and management of the systems engineering process. Geneva, Switzerland: IEEE.

International Organization for Standardization and International Electrotechnical Commission. 2012. ISO/IEC 19770:2012. Information technology--Software asset management--Part 1: Processes and tiered assessment of conformance. Geneva, Switzerland: International Organization for Standardization and International Electrotechnical Commission.

International Organization for Standardization and International Electrotechnical Commission. 2014. ISO/IEC 25000:2014 Systems and software Engineering – Systems and software product Quality Requirements and Evaluation (SQuaRE) – Guide to SQuaRE. Geneva, Switzerland: International Organization for Standardization and International Electrochemical Commission.

International Organization for Standardization and International Electrotechnical Commission. 2017. ISO/IEC/IEEE 24765:2017, Systems and software engineering--Vocabulary. Geneva, Switzerland: International Organization for Standarization and International Electrotechnical Commission.

Martin, Robert C. 2009. Clean Code: A Handbook of Agile Software Craftsmanship. Upper Saddle River, NJ: Pearson Education, Inc.

SAS Institute Inc. 1991. SAS® Technical Report P-222: Changes and Enhancements to Base SAS® Software. Cary, NC: SAS Institute Inc.

SAS Institute Inc. 2020. SAS® 9.4 Procedures Guide, Seventh Edition. Cary, NC: SAS Institute Inc. https://documentation.sas.com/api/docsets/proc/9.4/content/proc.pdf.

SAS Institute Inc. 2020. SAS® 9.4 Functions and CALL Routines: Reference, Fifth Edition. Cary, NC: SAS Institute Inc. https://documentation.sas.com/api/docsets/lefunctionsref/9.4/content/lefunctionsref.pdf.

SAS Institute Inc. 2020. SAS® 9.4 Functions and Call Routines: Reference, Fifth Edition: LOWCASE Function. Cary, NC: SAS Institute Inc. https://documentation.sas.com/?docsetId=lefunctionsref&docsetTarget=n0rrwqm16uiv4vn1t0jj0jvidgao.htm&docsetVersion=9.4&locale=en.

SAS Institute Inc. 2021. SAS® 9.4 Functions and CALL Routines: Reference, Fifth Edition: CATX Function. Cary, NC: SAS Institute Inc. https://documentation.sas.com/?cdcId=pgmsascdc&cdcVersion=9.4_3.5& docsetId=lefunctionsref&docsetTarget=n0p7wxtk0hvn83n1pveisbcp2ae9.htm&locale=en.

SAS Institute Inc. 2021. SAS® 9.4 Functions and CALL Routines: Reference, Fifth Edition: UPCASE Function. Cary, NC: SAS Institute Inc. https://documentation.sas. com/?cdcId=pgmsascdc&cdcVersion=9.4_3.5&docsetId= lefunctionsref&docsetTarget=p0ilulfezdl4ykn17295t8tnh4xc.htm&locale=en.

SAS Institute Inc. 2021. SAS® 9.4 DATA Step Statements: Reference: ARRAY Statement. Cary, NC: SAS Institute Inc. https://documentation.sas.com/?cdcId=pgmsascdc&cdcVersion=9.4_3.5&docsetId=lestmtsref& docsetTarget=p08do6szetrxe2n136ush727sbuo.htm&locale=en.

SAS Institute Inc. 2022. SAS® 9.4 Functions and CALL Routines: Reference, Fifth Edition. Cary, NC: SAS Institute Inc. https://documentation.sas.com/doc/en/pgmsascdc/9.4_3.2/lefunctionsref/titlepage.htm.

SAS Institute Inc. 2022. SAS® 9.4 and SAS® Viya® 3.5 Programming Documentation. Cary, NC: SAS Institute Inc. https://documentation.sas.com/doc/en/pgmsascdc/9.4_3.5/proc/p048tu5gixqaxin1ej7b7yuyhn86. htm#n18rmdt275t45rn13qn0jdskhq7i.

SAS Institute Inc. 2023. DATA Step DECLARE Statement: Hash and Hash Iterator Objects. Cary, NC: SAS Institute Inc. https://documentation.sas.com/doc/en/pgmsascdc/9.4_3.5/lecompobjref/ p00ilfw5pzcjvtn1nfya9863fozd.htm.

SAS Institute Inc. 2023. PROC FCMP and DATA Step Differences. Cary, NC: SAS Institute Inc. https:// documentation.sas.com/doc/en/pgmsascdc/9.4_3.5/proc/n1aozmc89vjkpzn1q6a54nleh56o.htm.

SAS Institute Inc. 2023. Configuring SAS to Run the Python Language. Cary, NC: SAS Institute Inc. https://go.documentation.sas.com/doc/en/bicdc/9.4/biasag/n1mquxnfmfu83en1if8icqmx8cdf.htm.

US National Park Service. 2023. *Death Valley: Weather.* https://www.nps.gov/deva/learn/nature/weather-and-climate.htm.

Index

%SYSCALL macro statement, 19, 123, 125
%SYSFUNC macro function, 18, 123-125, 172,
        227-229
AUTOMATIC, 49
ERROR, 304-307
4GL, 5

A
abstraction, 4
ADD method. *See* hash object, ADD method
ADDMATRIX subroutine, 108, 125
argument, 23-24, 44
array, 71-73, 81-134, 235-237
        constants, 67-68, 97-98
        defined, 45, 81
        dynamic, 102-103, 111, 116
        explicit, 82-85
        implicit, 83-85, 112-114
        multidimensional, 105-109
        parameter, 46, 56
        reverse, 118-120
ARRAY statement, 46, 82-87, 97, 106-107
        NOSYMBOLS option, 102-103, 107,
        110, 116
Art Carpenter, xviii, 169-170
ATTRC function, 25

B
Bart Jablonski, xvii, 82
binding, 44, 50
built-in function, 25-26
BYTE function, 3

C
call, 16, 20
        See invocation

call by reference, 41, 52-56, 100, 104-105
        binding, 44
        See OUTARGS statement
call by value, 41, 50-51, 63-65
        binding, 44
call method, 50-51
        defined, 50
        See call by reference
        See call by value
call routine. *See* subroutine
CALL statement, 18
callable module, 2, 8
        defined, 20
calling module, 2, 16
        defined, 20
CHAR function, 3
CHECK method. *See* hash object, CHECK method
CMPLIB system option, 35-36
CNTLIN option. *See* PROC FORMAT, CNTLIN option
COMPRESS function, 73-76, 94-95, 154, 159, 308
COMPUTE statement. *See* PROC REPORT, COMPUTE
        block
configurability, 7, 10-11, 123
        defined, 10
COUNTW function, 94

D
DECLARE HASH statement. *See* hash object,
        DECLARE HASH statement
DECLARE HITER statement. *See* hash iterator
        object, DECLARE HITER statement
DEFINEKEY method. *See* hash object, DEFINEKEY
        method
DEQUOTE function, 171-173
dictionary object, 247-251
dictionary parameter, 46

DIM function, 87, 161
DO loop, 65-66
DO OVER loop, 112-113
Don Henderson, xvii, 82
DOSUBL function. *See* RUN_MACRO function, vs.
        DOSUBL function
double coding, 37
dynamic performance. *See* software quality,
        external
DYNAMIC_ARRAY subroutine, 102-103, 107-108

E
encapsulation, 8, 99-100, 122, 143, 308
ENCRYPT option, 16, 197-200
        defined, 36-38
ENDFUNC statement, 40
        vs. ENDSUB statement, 79
ENDSUB statement, 40
exception, 304-305

F
FILE LOG statement, 68-71
FIND method. *See* hash object, FIND method
Frank Dilorio, xviii, 3, 17-18
function,
        call. *See* call
        compilation, 29
        declaration, 40
        defined, 2, 22-23
        definition. *See* implementation
        invocation. *See* invocation
        naming, 42-43
        nesting, 18-19
        package, 30, 32-34, 36
        specification. *See* specification
        vs. procedure, 21-22
        vs. subroutine, 2, 16-17, 22-23
FUNCTION statement, 40-41, 42, 56, 59
        VARARGS option, 46, 56-59
functional discretion, 12
        defined, 8
functional equivalence, 4-5, 9
        defined, 4
functionality. *See* software functionality

G
geocoding, 263-286
getter, 203, 206-208, 218-220, 313-316, 318-320

Gettysburg Address, 93-94, 152-153
global variable scope. *See* variable scope
Gordon Ramsay, 263, 269, 278

H
hardcoding, 9, 27, 137, 289
        defined, xi
hash object, 135-168, 243, 245-247, 300-301
        ADD method, 155, 157-158
        CHECK method, 140
        DATA step, 138-140
        DATA step vs. PROC FCMP, 141-142,
        197-199
        DECLARE HASH statement, 139,
        146, 151
        defined, 135
        DEFINEDATA method, 146-147, 151, 161,
        163, 167-168
        DEFINEKEY method, 139, 146, 151, 161,
        167-168
        FIND method, 146-147, 151, 155, 161,
        206
        ORDERED option, 158
        OUTPUT method, 210-211
        REPLACE method, 155, 157-158,
        209-210
hash iterator object, 156-158
        DECLARE HITER statement, 156-157,
        160-161
        FIRST method, 156
        LAST method, 156
        NEXT method, 156, 158, 161
        PREV method, 156
hash parameter, 46

I
implementation, 15-16, 28
        defined, 15
IN operator, 114-117
index, 200
integrity, 8, 12
interoperability, 6, 13, 62, 253
INV subroutine, 125
invocation, 34, 123-125
        defined, 16

K
key-value pair, 135, 137, 213-214

L

least privilege, 12
local variable scope. *See* variable scope
loose coupling, 169
    defined, 8
Lora Delwiche, xvii, 254
Louise Hadden, xvii, 36
LOWCASE function, 3, 13
    specification, 14

M

maintainability, 7, 11-12, 81-82, 89, 99
    defined, 11
masking, 187
master data, 136
matrix algebra, 125-134
    See ADDMATRIX subroutine
    See INV subroutine
    See MULT subroutine
    See ZEROMATRIX subroutine
MEAN function, 87-88
median, 95-96
memoization, 223, 239-251, 275-282
    defined, 239
MISSING subroutine, 41-42, 138, 140
MODIFY statement, 211-212, 214
modularity, 7-8, 11-12, 195, 311
    defined, 7
monolithic software, 7-8, 12
MULT subroutine, 126

N

NOSYMBOLS option. *See* ARRAY statement,
    NOSYMBOLS option

O

OF operator, 88, 90-91, 109-111, 117-119
OPEN function, 24-25
OTHERWISE statement, 155
OUTARGS statement, 22, 41, 44, 51-52, 56, 91,
    103-104, 147, 169
    See call by reference
OUTLIB option. *See* PROC FCMP statement, OUTLIB
    option

P

package. *See* function, package
parameter

array. *See* array parameter
    declaration, 44-45
    defined, 24, 44
    optional, 47-48, 73-76, 94-96
parameter-less function, 48-50
Paul Dorfman, xvii, 82
PDV, 86
performance. *See* software performance
PROC FCMP statement, 28, 162
    OUT option, 211
    OUTLIB option, 30-31
PROC FORMAT
    CNTLIN option, 137-138, 144-145, 289,
    305-307
    OTHER option, 289-291, 293-294
PROC REPORT
    COMPUTE block, 289-290, 311-320
PROC SORT, 21
PROC SQL, 17, 149-150, 189-190
procedure, 148-149
    defined, 21
program data vector. *See* PDV
PUT statement, 71-73
    See FILE LOG statement
Python component object, 253-287
    INFILE method, 257-259
    SUBMIT INTO statement, 260-262

Q

QUIT statement, 38-40

R

RANK function, 3
READ_ARRAY function, 126, 131-133
readability, 11, 97, 99, 114, 135, 143, 273
    defined, 9
recursion, 223, 229-239
    defined, 229
REPLACE method. *See* hash object, REPLACE
    method
requirements. *See* software requirements
return code, 52-54
    defined, 24
RETURN statement, 76-79, 100, 103
    defined, 24, 76-77
return value, 22, 59-62, 169
    defined, 24
    implications with RUN_MACRO, 174-176

reusability, xi, 1-2, 7, 26, 27-30, 57, 169, 230
    defined, 11
    vs. fly-by-night function, 29
Richann Watson, xvii, 36
Richard DeVenezia, xvii, 82
Rick Wicklin, xvii, 125
ROUND function, 48
RUN_MACRO function, 169-195, 197-201, 211-212
    defined, 170
    variable scope, 179-184
    vs. DOSUBL function, 191-195
RUN_SASFILE function, 169, 195-197, 201

S

SAS. *See* everywhere!
SAS macro language, 164-168, 205-206
SAS practitioner. *See* a mirror!
SAS Viya, 19
    See the future!
SAS/IML, 125, 129-130
scalability, 5, 87-88, 158-159, 161
scalar, 23, 44-45, 51, 63, 81, 103-104, 126, 250, 290
    defined, 45
SDLC, 13-14
SELECT statement, 155
setter, 203, 208-215, 217-218, 220-222
signature, 40-41, 56, 59
    defined, 40
software development life cycle. *See* SDLC
software functionality, 2-3, 13, 15, 62
software performance, 6, 241-242, 246-247, 296-301
software quality, 6-7
    external, 7, 82
    internal, 7, 82
    See configurability
    See integrity
    See interoperability
    See maintainability
    See modularity
    See readability

    See reusability
    See scalability
software requirements, 6, 13, 35, 101, 206
SORT function, 22
    vs. SORT subroutine, 22-23
SORTC subroutine, 109-111, 158-159
SORTN subroutine, 109, 158-159
specification, 13-15, 25-26, 48
    defined, 13
static performance. *See* software quality, internal
STATIC statement, 223-229, 234-235, 239-243
STREAMINIT subroutine, 22, 121, 240
subroutine, 2, 16-19, 22-23, 28, 30, 40-42, 50-51, 54-55, 59, 76, 79, 100, 123, 150
    defined, 22
SUBROUTINE statement, 40-41, 42, 56
SUBSTR function, 120-122
Susan Slaughter, xvii, 254
SYMPUTX subroutine, 179-181

T

tech specs. *See* specification

U

UPCASE function, 3
user-defined function, xi, 1-2, 26

V

VARARGS option. *See* FUNCTION statement, VARARGS option
variable scope, 24, 44, 51, 63, 68, 99, 103-105, 147
    See RUN_MACRO function, variable scope

W

WHEN statement, 155
WRITE_ARRAY function, 126, 133-134, 211

Z

ZEROMATRIX subroutine, 104, 108, 126

www.ingramcontent.com/pod-product-compliance
Lightning Source LLC
Chambersburg PA
CBHW081049220326
41598CB00038B/7037